INSIGHT GUIDE

RUSSIA
BELARUS & UKRAINE

PUBLICATIONS
Part of the Langenscheidt Publishing Group

ABOUT THIS BOOK

Editorial

Project Editor
Jane Hutchings
Managing Editor
Clare Griffiths
Editorial Director
Brian Bell

Distribution

UK & Ireland
GeoCenter International Ltd
The Viables Centre , Harrow Way
Basingstoke, Hants RG22 4BJ
Fax: (44) 1256-817988

United States
Langenscheidt Publishers, Inc.
46–35 54th Road, Maspeth, NY 11378
Fax: (718) 784-0640

Australia & New Zealand
Hema Maps Pty. Ltd.
24 Allgas Street, Slacks Creek 4127
Brisbane, Australia
Tel: (61) 7 3290 0322
Fax: (61) 7 3290 0478

Worldwide
APA Publications GmbH & Co.
Verlag KG (Singapore branch)
38 Joo Koon Road, Singapore 628990
Tel: (65) 865-1600
Fax: (65) 861-6438

Printing

Insight Print Services (Pte) Ltd
38 Joo Koon Road, Singapore 628990
Tel: (65) 865-1600
Fax: (65) 861-6438

©1999 APA Publications GmbH & Co.
Verlag KG (Singapore branch)
All Rights Reserved
First Edition 1990
Third Edition 1999

CONTACTING THE EDITORS
Although every effort is made to
provide accurate information in
this publication, we live in a
fast-changing world and would
appreciate it if readers would
call our attention to any errors or
outdated information that may
occur by writing to us at:
**Insight Guides, P.O. Box 7910,
London SE1 1WE, England.
Fax: (44 171) 403-0290.**
e-mail:
insight@apaguide.demon.co.uk

This guidebook combines the
interests and enthusiasms of
two of the world's best known
information providers: Insight
Guides, whose titles have set the
standard for visual travel guides
since 1970, and Discovery
Channel, the world's premier
source of nonfiction television
programming.

The editors of Insight Guides
provide both practical advice and
general understanding about a
destination's history, culture, institutions and people. Discovery
Channel and its popular web site,
www.discovery.com, help millions
of viewers to explore the world
from the comfort of their home
and also encourage them
to explore it first hand.

How to use this book

◆ The **Features** section,
with a yellow colour bar,
covers the area's history and culture in lively authoritative essays
written by specialists.
◆ The **Places** section, with a blue
bar, provides full details of all the
sights and areas worth seeing.
The chief places of interest are
coordinated by number with specially drawn maps.
◆ The **Travel Tips** listings section,
with an orange bar, at the back
of the book, gives information on
travel, accommodation, restaurants and other practical aspects.

The contributors

This new edition of *Insight Guide:
Russia, Belarus & Ukraine*, which
builds on the previous edition
edited by **Anna Benn**, was
edited by **Jane Hutchings**,
assisted by managing
editor **Clare Griffiths**.
Hutchings, a former
London *Sunday Times*

Magazine journalist and freelance editor, has worked on a number of Insight titles.

The book's main contributor, **Jonathan Bastable**, offered invaluable advice throughout the project and wrote the chapters on *Land and Climate*, *Windows on the West*, *The Emperors*, *The Rise and Fall of the Soviet Union* and picture stories on the Moscow Metro and the Trans-Siberian Railway. Bastable lived in Russia for many years and is writing a book on the Cathedral of Christ in Moscow.

Russian graduate **Esther Wolff** wrote the feature on *Life Today*, while *Insight on the Hermitage* was written by art historian **Catherine Phillips**, who also revised **Ivan Samarine**'s chapter on art. Phillips' chapter *The European North* was updated for this edition by writer and *St Petersburg*

Times journalist **John Varoli**. Varoli also worked on the chapters on St Petersburg and The Golden Ring, and wrote new pieces on the Russian media and film. The feature on *Women in Russia* is by **Olga Lipovskaya** while credit for the updating of music chapter goes to **Iosif Raiskin**. **Rowlinson Carter's** chapter on religion has been updated by Moscow-based **Robin Minney**. Business reporter **Kirill Koriukin** updated the chapter on his home town of Moscow, originally by **Anne Lavelle**, and also wrote the story on the mafia. **Iain Law**, who works for the British Council in Moscow, revised the chapter on food, updated those by **Natalia Kardashenko**, **Adam Tanner** and **Michael Hetzer** on the Volga, Urals and Siberia and wrote the colourful *Insight on Lake Baikal*. The chapter on the Southwest was written by **Charmaine Bickley**, while **Vladimir Brodetsky**'s work on the European South was updated by Moscow resident **Joanna Baskott**.

The feature essays on Belarus and Ukraine were written by **Tim Gould**, a political analyst and reporter living in Kiev. He also extensively revised the Belarus and Ukraine chapters by **Joanne Levine** and **Albert Lantuch** and wrote the Crimea picture story.

Like all Insight Guides, this book owes a lot to its striking photographs, many of which are by **Cathleen Naundorf**, **Jim Holmes** and **Tony Perrottet**. Picture research was by **Susannah Stone**. The book was proofread by **Liz Clasen** and the index compiled by **Penny Phenix**.

Map Legend

— ·· —	International Boundary
— · —	National Park/Reserve
— — —	Ferry Route
Ⓜ	Metro
✈ ✈	Airport: International/ Regional
🚌	Bus Station
Ⓟ	Parking
❶	Tourist Information
✉	Post Office
🕇 † ✝	Church/Ruins
†	Monastery
☾	Mosque
✡	Synagogue
🏰 🏯	Castle/Ruins
∴	Archaeological Site
∩	Cave
🗿	Statue/Monument
★	Place of Interest

The main places of interest in the Places section are coordinated by number with a full-colour map (e.g. ❶), and a symbol at the top of every right-hand page tells you where to find the map.

Insight Guide
RUSSIA
Belarus & Ukraine

CONTENTS

The magnificent exterior of The Catherine Palace, St Petersburg

Places

Travel Tips

THE RIDDLE OF RUSSIA

Everything about the country is monumental: its turbulent

history, its cultural achievements and, above all, its size

Russia cannot be understood
With the mind,
Nor can she be measured
By a common yardstick.
A special character she has:
In Russia one can only have faith.
—Fyodor Tyutchev, 19th-century poet

Such understanding has never come easily to outsiders. "Russia is impenetrable," wrote the American historian Henry Adams in 1895, "and any intelligent man will deal with her better, the less closely he knows her." Sir Winston Churchill, trying to predict Russia's behaviour in 1939, coined the masterly description: "a riddle wrapped in a mystery inside an enigma."

Such mystery always fascinates, of course, and since the raising of the Iron Curtain at the end of the 1980s, curious tourists have poured into Russia, many of them venturing beyond the cities of St Petersburg and Moscow to find out what provincial and rural Russia is like. Just as Russians are discovering that foreigners are not, in the words of the poet Yevgeny Yevtushenko, "all spies with cameras in their buttons, radio transmitters in the heels of their shoes, and pockets full of Colorado beetles", so Westerners are having their own preconceived ideas overturned. Siberia, for example, is shedding its *Gulag Archipelago* image and revealing itself as a stunningly beautiful and diverse land so vast that a pocket of the Old Believers sect stumbled upon in the 1980s was unaware of the fall of the tsar.

Meanwhile, Russia's pre-Revolution culture has emerged from cold storage. Religion has resumed its important role in society, and art, music and literature are rediscovering their pre- and immediate post-Revolutionary vigour. Added to these is the explosive energy of Russia's "New Culture", in which young Muscovites and St Petersburgers are experimenting with new modes of expression – and not all of them copied from the West. There is a darker side, too: the gap between rich and poor has widened alarmingly, while economic uncertainty and organised crime have had a destabilising effect.

While much of this book is dedicated to Russia, there are also sections on Belarus and Ukraine. Although these have become fully independent states, they are included because of their cultural and historical links with Russia. Minsk and Kiev, the capitals of Belarus and Ukraine respectively, remain alluring tourist destinations and the countryside of both states offers much of cultural and scenic interest, combined with the sunshine resorts of the Black Sea. ❑

PRECEDING PAGES: Kuzma Minin and Dmitry Pozharsky monument, Moscow; ceiling panel, Moscow Metro station; busking on Moscow's Arbat; caviar is good for you.
LEFT: Space Obelisk, Moscow.

A BOUNDLESS LAND

*To make sense of the immensity of Russia, its varied and dramatic scenery
and its diverse climates, one must begin with the land itself*

The vastness of the Russian land is hard for Westerners to grasp. The territories of the Eastern Slavonic peoples – the Russian Federation, the Ukraine and Belarus taken together – comprise around 18 million sq km (7 million sq miles). This is twice the size of the United States, and more than 73 times the size of Britain. Russia ranges across 11 time zones. When citizens in westerly Kaliningrad are getting up in the morning, their fellow countrymen on the Pacific seaboard are home from work and thinking about going to bed. Train journeys in this country are measured in days rather than hours.

Russia reaches well into the Arctic Circle. The world's largest polar city is Murmansk, built on the uppermost fringe of the Kola peninsula at the point where the warm Gulf Stream licks the coast. Because it takes advantage of this geographical accident, Murmansk is Russia's only ice-free seaport in the north. But in the south, Russian territory extends into the balmy climes of the Black Sea. Here, around the coast to the west, is the Crimea. Once the Soviet Riviera, this sun-washed peninsula is now the jewel of an independent Ukraine. In better times this was wine-making country. It is still fertile land, sheltered by the tall, sharp crags of the Caucasus.

White nights of June

Russia's landmass is the thicker end of a great wedge, which has its point in the west. (This geopolitical fact alone helps to explain 500 years of Russian foreign policy: the further west Russia's borders lie, the shorter is its frontier and so the easier to defend.) The Eurasian wedge extends to the north and east for 10,460 km (6,500 miles), so Moscow is roughly on the same latitude as Glasgow, and St Petersburg is on a level with the Shetland Islands. Consequently the days are long in summer and short in winter. Murmansk is in darkness round the

clock from November to March, while St Petersburg has made an annual festival of its "white nights", a week in June when the city is bathed in an eerie, nocturnal translucence, which makes it difficult to sleep.

The climate across Russia is continental: that is, short hot summers with long cold winters.

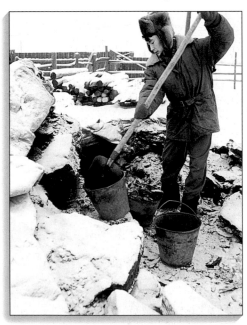

The Ukraine has briefer, milder winters due to its more southerly location. Temperatures of minus 20°C (minus 4°F) are not unusual in Moscow in January, and the winters in Siberia are cold beyond description. The coldest inhabited place on earth is Oimyakon, in the diamond-rich uplands of Yakutia, where daytime temperatures of minus 70°C (minus 94°F) have been recorded.

East-west divide

Only one geographical feature interrupts the great, level Eurasian plain between the Carpathians and the Far Eastern highlands. Like the spine of a book laid open on its face, the

LEFT: young worker in the fields of Siberia.
RIGHT: long, cold winters are a feature of the climate.

Urals run in a straight line for 1,930 km (1,200 miles) from the Barents Sea in the north almost to the Caspian Sea in the south. These low mountains are the official boundary between Europe and Asia, and between European Russia and Siberia. But they are not a formidable natural barrier, and no invader was ever stopped by the Urals.

To the west of the Urals lies the most populous part of Russia, and Belarus and Ukraine. Belarus is landlocked; its terrain is hilly in places, and about a third of it is forested, but the glacial soil is rich. The traditional crops are rye, buckwheat and potatoes, which are the sta-ples of the diet throughout the region. Peat is harvested in the flat marshes south of Minsk, and used in power stations; Belarus has no fossil fuels on its territory.

The Ukraine is richer. It has unexploited reserves of coal and it has another form of black gold, the *chernozem* or "black earth" which covers two-thirds of the land. It is this chocolate earth, together with the relatively mild climate, which made the Ukraine the traditional "bread-basket of Europe".

In the summer the Ukrainian countryside resembles its blue-and yellow national flag: all the eye can see is a thick ribbon of ripe yellow

TOXIC EARTH AND POISONED SEAS

For all its natural beauty, the former Soviet Union is a land of ecological nightmares. The Chernobyl disaster of 1985 is symbolic of the dangers, but even that catastrophe pales next to the environmental damage that was done in earlier Soviet times. The nuclear installation at Chelyabinsk-65 in Siberia is a kind of serial Chernobyl. It has had several massive accidents, the worst in 1957. It is still spewing nuclear waste into Lake Karachai, officially the most radioactive spot on Earth. An hour's exposure on the lake's shoreline can be fatal. Nuclear contamination is only part of the picture. Much of the pollution is the result of the Stalinist drive to industrialise at any cost. Lake Baikal, the largest body of fresh water on the planet, is in grave danger of irreversible poisoning from the paper-pulping plants on its shore. The acid rain which falls on the Kola peninsula, and has devastated thousands of hectares of forest, is the result of the gases released from nickel refineries. And in Dzerzhinsk, the centre of Russia's chlorine and pesticide industries, almost the entire population is ill, and the life expectancy for adults has dropped into the forties. These are just a few examples: there are hundreds of equally grave problems. And the future is bleak. According to one American study, by the year 2015 only 20 percent of Russian babies will be born healthy.

wheat under a blue band of sky. The same good land underlies much of the Russian south. Here the main crop is winter wheat, sown in the autumn and protected from the cold by a layer of snow. Further to the north, all kinds of farming are to be found in the cleared expanses between the ancient forests: dairy, pigs and poultry, oats, root crops, flax and potatoes.

Tundra, taiga, steppe and forest

A satellite's-eye view of the Russian plateau would show that, east of the Urals especially, it is divided east to west into four broad vegetational zones. Three of these zones are so dis-

of snow melts, the moss and lichen burst forth and the ground is carpeted with bright and hardy flowers. Later in the year migratory birds pass through, and regiments of furry animals – silver foxes, wolves, ermine, ferrets and lemmings – emerge from the southern forests. But as winter and darkness draw in again, the only animals which can survive the tundra are polar bears and seals.

The tundra gives way to the taiga, a gigantic and almost impenetrable belt which accounts for about a third of the world's forest. This zone is about 5,000 km (3,000 miles) long and 1,000 km (600 miles) wide. The insulating effect of

tinctive that they are known to geographers by their Russian names: the tundra, taiga and steppe. The fourth zone is the great swathe of mixed forest which has fed hunters and hindered farmers for generations.

The tundra is the northernmost belt. At its most extreme, in the Arctic, it is a cold, white, lifeless desert. A little further south a few stunted trees grow, but their roots are shallow because they cannot penetrate the eternal permafrost. In spring, when the uppermost layer

---

LEFT: steppe landscape in the Orenburg Region of the southern Urals.

ABOVE: a European beaver at the water's edge.

such a density of trees means that in its deepest corners the snow almost never melts and even the permafrost persists.

The result is a "drunken forest" where overtall spruce tilt at tipsy angles in the shallow top soil. The species of tree varies from region to region over this wooded ocean: there are pine, larch and, in the southern reaches of Siberia, the archetypal Russian birch. This dark kingdom is the habitat of the sable, prized for its fur above all other animals, as well as of the Russian bear, the lynx, and in Siberia the elk and the maral deer. In summer black swarms of bloodthirsty gnats and midges make the area of the taiga almost uninhabitable for humans.

The taiga shades gently into a variegated stripe of mixed forest, where the trees are deciduous, such as oak, ash and maple. In European areas the trees have been systematically cleared for agriculture, but chestnuts abound in the Ukraine, where they are considered a national tree, as the birch is for Russia. East of the Urals the mixed forest covers an area far beyond Russia's borders. There are few animal species unique to this zone, though the last European bison are to be found living in conservation areas.

South of the forest is a relatively narrow strip of open grassland running from Romania to

China. This area is known as the steppe. It is easily traversed, and as such has served as the main highway for nomadic peoples travelling from Asia to Europe. The soil here is prone to erosion by the freezing winds of winter and the thunderstorms of summer.

In the Siberian steppe there is a sense of emptiness and desolation which is increased by the fact that much of the native fauna – antelopes and wild horses – has been hunted by man to extinction. But in the air, the magnificent steppe eagle is still in evidence, and underfoot there is a variety of small and exotic rodents such as the bobak marmot, the five-toed jerboa and Chinese striped hamster.

Rivers and other riches

These four bands are criss-crossed by great, meandering rivers. In Siberia they flow from south to north (unlike the Volga, Europe's longest river, which flows north to south into the Caspian Sea). The longest of the Siberian waterways, at 5,700 km (3,360 miles), is the Ob, though the Yenisei and the Lena are both more than 3,200 km (2,000 miles) long.

In the Brezhnev era of the 1970s there was an ill-conceived plan to reverse the flow of the Siberian rivers to irrigate the cotton fields of Central Asia and save the Aral Sea. The plan was abandoned, and the Aral is now a desert of poisonous dust.

Before it was destroyed by overuse and chemical pollution it ranked as the second biggest inland lake in the USSR. The biggest in the world is the Caspian Sea, on Russia's southern flank. In Siberia, near the Mongolian border, is the world's deepest freshwater lake, Baikal. Drawn on a map the lake looks tiny, but it holds more water than the entire Baltic Sea, and is home to 960 species of animal found nowhere else in the world.

Untapped mineral wealth

Beneath all this variety is a buried treasure chest of mineral riches. Western Siberia has vast untapped deposits of coal, iron ore and natural gas. The Urals are studded with emeralds, rubies, malachite, jasper and gold. The diamond deposits in Yakutia are thought to be immense, enough to unbalance the world market if their mining and sale are not carefully controlled.

Beyond the highlands of Yakutia and the now abandoned Gulag zone of Kolyma is the eastern seaboard, where Russia is washed by the waters of the Pacific Ocean. Here is the Kamchatka peninsula, a strange proboscis on Russia's eastward-looking face which is dotted with active volcanoes.

Here, too, is the Chukotsky peninsula, on the tip of which is Cape Dezhnev. This is where Russia's territory runs out. It is the country's easternmost point. On a clear day you can stand on the shore of the Bering Strait and wave across to America. ❏

LEFT: In Siberia the summer months are warm enough for trekking and other outdoor activities.
RIGHT: a wild elk majestically surveys his territory.

Decisive Dates

THE FIRST RUSSIANS

The region around the Moskva and Volga rivers was settled from pre-historic times by Finno-Ugrians, Indo-Europeans and Germanic tribes who supported themselves by hunting and fishing. Scythians inhabited the steppes.

AD 400–600 Eastern Slavs migrate into what is now Ukraine and western Russia.

800–900 Swedish Varangians (Vikings) under Prince Rurik advance southwest along the rivers establishing strongholds at Novgorod and Kiev, "the mother of

Russian cities". Polotsk on the Dvina River forms the nucleus for Belarus.

900–1240 Kiev becomes the centre of the Russian empire; trade flourishes with Byzantium.

988 Christianity is introduced from Constantinople.

THE MONGOL YOKE

1200–1300 While Alexander Nevsky defends Russia's western borders from Swedish attack, Batu Khan, grandson of Genghis Khan, invades from the east, conquers Moscow (1238) and sacks Kiev (1240). For the next 250 years, Russian princes are forced to pay tribute to the Golden Horde (Mongols).

1300–1400 Poland captures Belarus and Ukraine.

1328 Ivan Kalita ("Moneybags") is designated Grand

Prince by the Khan. He moves from Vladimir to Moscow, where he builds his kremlin (fortress).

1380 Grand Prince Dmitry, grandson of "Moneybags", challenges the Mongols in the Battle of Kulikovo but cannot prevent them from sacking Moscow. The city recovers to become a symbol of Russian unity. The power of the Mongols begins to wane.

1462–1500 Ivan III, "Grand Prince of Moscow and All Russia", refuses to pay Moscow's tribute to the Mongols, whose domination comes to an end. Russia succeeds Byzantium as the "Third Rome".

THE RULE OF THE TSARS

1547–84 Ivan IV (the Terrible), is crowned Tsar of All Russia. He defeats the Tatars in Kazan (and builds St Basil's Cathedral in celebration) and Astrakhan, colonises Siberia, reduces the power of the wealthy boyars (nobles) and sows the seeds of serfdom.

1584–1613 Anarchy and civil war prevail; Boris Godunov presides over The Time of Troubles.

1613 Tsar Mikhail Romanov restores stability.

1648 Bogdan Khmelnitsky launches the Ukrainian offensive that drives out the Poles. The Pereyaslav agreement of 1654, which grants autonomy to Ukraine, is soon undermined: east Ukraine falls under Russian control following a Cossack revolt, 1667; west Ukraine and Belarus come under Polish rule.

A WINDOW ON THE WEST

1682–1725 The widely-travelled tsar, Peter the Great, son of Alexei Romanov, introduces Western ways, reforms the civil service and army, and builds a modern navy. He recaptures the Baltic coast from the Swedes and starts building his new city, St Petersburg, at the mouth of the River Neva. In 1724 St Petersburg becomes the official capital of Russia.

1725–62 Under Peter's heirs the court becomes Westernised and alienated from the people.

1763–96 Catherine II (the Great) ushers in a period of enlightenment. She reforms local government, liberalises the penal code, founds hospitals and invites leading architects to St Petersburg who give the city its classical look. Belarus and Ukraine are recaptured from Poland, Crimea is conquered and the mineral wealth of Siberia is exploited.

THE EMPERORS

1796–1825 Catherine's son, the military dictator Paul I, is assassinated in 1801. He is succeeded by the more liberal Alexander I.

1812 Napoleon invades and occupies Moscow. The inhabitants set fire to the city. Napoleon withdraws.

1825–55 Decembrist Rising in St Petersburg is

crushed by Nicholas I in 1825. He rules with obsessive attention to detail, but lacks initiative to deal with the big issues, such as food and clothing for the Russian army in the Crimean War (1853–56).

1855–81 Alexander II liberates the serfs, 1861. He is assassinated by revolutionaries, 1 March 1881.

1881–94 Rapid industrialisation under the repressive rule of Alexander III leads to a huge increase in the size of the urban working class.

ABDICATION AND REVOLUTION

1894–1917 The last tsar, Nicholas II, is unable to contain the groundswell of revolutionary activity.

1898 Social Democratic Party is formed under Vladimir Lenin.

1905 Bloody Sunday (9 January): 140,000 workers march to the Winter Palace.Troops open fire; 100 marchers are killed, hundreds wounded. The Tsar agrees to establish the Duma (State Assembly).

1914 Russia enters World War I against Germany.

1917 Russia is on the brink of economic and political catastrophe. Tsar Nicholas II abdicates. A provisional government is set up. On 25 October the Bolshevik Central Committee, under Lenin's leadership, seizes power in the Great Socialist Revolution. Lenin nationalises industries and introduces radical agricultural reforms.

1918 Treaty of Brest–Litovsk ends war with Germany. The Tsar and family are murdered. Civil war rages until 1922 when Lev Trotsky's Red Army declares victory.

COMMUNISTS TAKE CONTROL

1922 Lenin declares the Union of Soviet Socialist Republics (USSR); Moscow becomes the official capital. Lenin dies in 1924 and Petrograd is renamed Leningrad in his honour. Joseph Stalin wins power struggle and starts the first Five Year Plan of industrialisation and agricultural collectivisation backed up by a purge in which millions either die or are deported.

1941–45 Adolf Hitler invades the USSR; 25 million citizens die in the Great Patriotic War. Victory over Germany is declared on 9 May 1945.

1953 Stalin dies. Nikita Khrushchev emerges as leader. A cultural thaw ensues.

1955 Eastern Bloc countries sign the Warsaw Pact declaring a military alliance.

1964–82 Leonid Brezhnev reverses Khrushchev's reforms and imposes a regime of censorship. He

intervenes in Czechoslovakia (1968) in the name of protecting socialism, and invades Afghanistan (1979). The Cold War with the West and arms race with the USA continue until *détente* and the Strategic Arms Limitation Talks (SALT) of the late 1970s.

THE DAWN OF DEMOCRACY

1985 Mikhail Gorbachev introduces reforms based on the principles of *perestroika* (restructuring), *glasnost* (openness), democratisation, and a market economy. Satellite states agitate for independence.

1991 A failed coup d'état by hardline communists leads to the eclipse of Gorbachev, the collapse of communism and the disintegration of the USSR. A

fragile federation of the republics, the Commonwealth of Independent States, takes its place. Russia under Boris Yeltsin becomes successor state to USSR.

1993 In October the intense political struggle between president and the reactionary parliament turns violent. There are running battles on the streets of Moscow, and Yeltsin uses tanks to shell the parliament building. In the aftermath, the presidency is granted sweeping powers.

1996 Boris Yeltsin wins a second term as president.

1998 In the grip of economic crisis, the rouble is devalued. Yeltsin appoints Yevgeni Primakov as prime minister to restore stability. Yeltsin's failing health sees Primakov acting as president until the end of Yeltsin's term in 2000. ❑

PRECEDING PAGES: the Time of Troubles, Moscow.
LEFT: Catherine the Great.
RIGHT: Vladimir Lenin.

BEGINNINGS

Of all the migratory groups to cross Russia in the Dark Ages, the Slavs
and the Vikings were the most influential

The 9th-century Viking conquest of hitherto stateless Slavs scattered across modern Russia, Ukraine and Belarus was traditionally made to sound like an act of high-minded charity. "Our land is great and rich but there is no order in it," the Slavs are reputed to have cried. "Come and rule over us." Prince Rurik of South Jutland in Denmark was ready to oblige. He made himself master of Novgorod, the most northwesterly Slav settlement, and within three years of his death in 879 his successors, who came to be known as Varangians, had extended their rule to include Smolensk and Kiev.

The invitation – such as it was – fitted in perfectly with the Varangian desire to monopolise the lucrative trade route between the Baltic and the Black Sea, which happened to pass through the allegedly rich but disorderly land in question. The main artery of this largely river-borne trade was the Dnieper (Dnipro) River, and of the settlements which the Varangians deigned to rule over, Kiev was the most valuable strategically. It was accordingly declared "the Mother of Russian cities".

Kiev was only one, but by far the grandest, in a network of embryonic city-states which various Varangian princes established and fought over among themselves. The estate of Yuri Dolgoruky of Suzdal was the beginning of Moscow while Prince of Polotsk's settlement on the Dvina River was the nucleus of Belarus.

It was not until the Mongol invasions of the 13th century that the focus of Russia moved away from Kiev to the north. Viewed from the forests, the depopulated area around Kiev was seen as "Ukraine", meaning the borderland.

Ukraine was also referred to as "Black" land because of its dark rich soil, but it was common land on which the semi-nomadic population had the right to roam on payment of a kind of licence fee to the ruling prince, and "Black" became synonymous with these property rights.

LEFT: an ancient hero of Rus defends his kingdom.
RIGHT: Rurik, the legendary 9th-century Viking prince who was invited by the Slavs to rule over them.

"White Russia", on the other hand – the translation of "Belarus" – drew attention to the fact that the territory was not common land but subject to the feudal tenure which applied while it was, as we shall see, under Polish administration. The people living on it were tied serfs.

Three Russias therefore came about, even if

the dividing lines were historically and geographically fluid: Great Russia, born of Muscovy and these days simply called Russia; Ukraine, which picked up yet another name, Little Russia; and White Russia (Belarus).

Cultural melting pot

To begin with, there were no ethnic or cultural divisions. Migration across the northern plain from Central Asia into Europe had long been taking place before Rurik and his Vikings sailed south. The Slavs who supposedly invited the Vikings to come and rule over them were relatively recent arrivals, mostly 5th and 6th century, who spoke kindred Slavonic languages.

They followed in the wake of Finno-Ugrians who ended up in Finland and Estonia, Indo-Europeans who became Lithuanians and Latvians, and a host of Germanic tribes who, one way or another, became not only Germans but French and Anglo-Saxon English, which helps to explain why even into this century Russians were inclined to describe all non-Slavic Europeans as "Germans".

There was a high degree of fusion between the newly arrived Slavs and earlier inhabitants. The Lithuanians were spread across the plains and forests until, under pressure from the Slavs, they retreated to the marshy Baltic shores. The

high cheekbones, darkish complexion and broad nose typical of the Great Russian are attributed to the Finno-Ugrians, obviously a far cry from notions of fair-haired, blue-eyed Scandinavians, a different group altogether.

The Varangians did fit the Scandinavian model, but they were only a military elite and it was a case common throughout history of conquerors being assimilated by the numerically superior conquered. It is unrealistic to think of the Varangians as being anything other than bona fide Slavs quite soon after their conquest.

Cultural comparisons between modern Russians and the tribes who roamed the northern plain long before the Slavs are irresistible. Russians cheerfully admit to being a trifle xenophobic and, according to Herodotus, the ancient Greek historian, the Scythians, who inhabited the steppes in the 5th century BC, had "an extreme hatred of all foreign customs". Herodotus was sceptical about Scythian descriptions of people living even farther north. According to them, they had goats' feet, could turn themselves into wolves if the occasion arose, and slept for six months at a time like hibernating animals. He did not doubt, however, that the northern winters were so cold that the inhabitants could drive wagons across frozen rivers and lakes and if necessary make war on them. "The ground is frozen iron-hard, so that to turn earth into mud requires not water but fire."

The Empire moves east

The Scythians eventually had to make room for new migrants arriving from Central Asia, and it was the overflow of these northern tribes – notably Huns, Goths, Visigoths and Vandals – across the Danube that spelt the end of the Roman Empire in the West. With repeated sackings of Rome, the Empire was moved from west to east, specifically to the ancient Greek colony of Byzantium, nicely positioned at the narrow Bosphorus crossing to control what was becoming the greatest trade route in the world, the one between Europe and the East.

The Mediterranean provided the obvious connection between Byzantium and Western Europe, but it was plagued by pirates. In any case, Northern Europe had something special to offer the markets of Byzantium: amber from the Baltic shore, furs and honey from the Russian forests and fair-skinned slaves. It was this trade via the Dnieper and to some extent the Volga that attracted the Varangians.

By the time the Slavs had settled along the Dnieper, the transplanted Roman Empire had made Constantinople, the Christianised capital of the East, the richest and most glamourous city on earth, Greek in flavour rather than Roman. Rome was degenerating into a run-down dump on a dirty river.

The Slavs arrived at the tail-end of the transition from Rome to Constantinople. They drifted in different directions on reaching Europe and later assumed regional characteristics on either side of considerable natural boundaries like the Carpathian mountains, or because they were split by alien invaders such as the Finno-Ugrian Magyars, the founders of Hungary. The Slavs in the Balkans came to be recognised as Southern Slavs, or "Yugoslavs", while those in the West took on the national identities of Poles, Czechs and Slovaks. The future Great, Little and White Russians were lumped together as Eastern Slavs. The first split in the homogeneity of the Eastern Slavs was between those who elected to remain on the steppes, which were reminiscent of the grasslands they had left behind in Central Asia, and

SAILING TO BYZANTIUM

Every spring a flotilla would sail down the Dnieper to the great city of Constantinople with its cargo of furs, honey and luckless slaves, in order to return with gold, silk, wines and spices.

Vikings needed to trade with Constantinople.

In 957 Princess Olga of Kiev joined the Dnieper River traders to see the fabled sights of Constantinople and was so impressed that she defied powerful pagan traditions to be baptised as an Eastern Orthodox Christian. This was a most portentous development. The Christian world was then torn by a contest between the Eastern and Western Churches for converts among the heathen hordes of Europe, the forces of Rome being led by the German-

those who ventured into the northern forests. The plain-dwellers grew rye and barley and kept a few cattle on the side.

The main drawback to living on the plain was exposure to new and invariably hostile migrants arriving from Asia. The forests, on the other hand, were relatively safe. Furthermore, the natural products of the forest, notably furs, honey and wax, were so plentiful that the forest-dwellers generally had surpluses available for trade. It was their surplus wealth which the

LEFT: a Finno-Ugrian tribeswoman.
ABOVE: Prince Vladimir, who converted to Christianity in 988 and adopted Eastern Orthodoxy.

dominated Holy Roman Empire founded by Charlemagne in 800. The Western Church was then doing well, having won over the the kings of Poland and Norway among others. The most notable Orthodox success had been with the formidable Bulgarian Empire.

Princess Olga tried to persuade her son, Svyatoslav, to follow her example but he was more interested in a military campaign which in due course added the Volga region to Kievan Rus. The question of the religious allegiance of the Eastern Slavs was passed on to his successor, Prince Vladimir, and he was not to be rushed either. Vladimir wished to hear not only from advocates of Byzantium and Rome but also those of Islam and Judaism. They were invited to state their cases, the lead being given to the Jewish representatives. Both they and the Muslims who followed made a poor impression by mentioning circumcision and abstention from pork and alcohol.

The Pope's emissaries were able to guarantee flexibility on the issues of circumcision, pork and alcohol, but they were obliged to add that a certain amount of fasting was required. Vladimir's response to the prospect of fasting was unambiguous: "Depart hence!"

Forewarned, the Byzantine Greeks launched into a history of the world, saving until last a

painting which showed in terrifying detail just what an infidel could expect come the Day of Judgement. Vladimir was unsettled by this revelation, but reserved final judgement until emissaries could visit Constantinople and confirm that joining the Eastern Church would bring material benefits. They returned to say that the city was so magnificent they had wondered whether they were in heaven.

Vladimir's alignment with Byzantium was formalised by his baptism at Kherson in 990 and cemented by marriage to Anna, the Byzantine emperor's sister. This illustrious marriage brought up a point of principle which had so far been overlooked. Vladimir was already

married several times over and had a harem that he had no intention of giving up. The Orthodox authorities and his brother-in-law quietly conceded the point. Vladimir was truly, says the chronicle recounting these events, a *"fornicator immensus et crudelis"*.

The rise and fall of Kiev

Kiev acquired a cathedral, named after and modelled on St Sophia's in Constantinople, and numerous churches. It was more emphatically than ever the outstanding Russian city of the age, but not for long. The eastern Mediterranean, long closed to traders by pirates and the Arabs who had taken over the Levant, was reopened by the success of the early Crusades. The sea route to northern Europe through the Strait of Gibraltar was longer, but it could take ships of any size and eliminated porterage. The value of the Dnieper route dwindled and so did Kiev's profits from it.

The Varangian princes were inclined to move north. Prince Yuri Dolgoruky, founder of Moscow, also acquired Kiev only to be told the city had become virtually worthless. "Here, father, we have nothing," his son said, "let us depart to Suzdal while it is still warm." The same son inherited Suzdal, and in 1169 he proved his point by sacking Kiev and casually tossing the princedom to a younger brother.

In both trade and religion, Russia's orientation had been towards Constantinople, but in 1204 the Fourth Crusade abandoned its avowed purpose of fighting the infidel Turk in the Holy Land in order to ransack Constantinople and put a hostile "Latin Emperor" on the throne of Byzantium. Baldwin, the emperor in question, was not long in office, but the reprieve became meaningless in the light of what was developing unseen thousands of miles away.

While Alexander Nevsky ("of the Neva") defended Russia's western borders from Sweden, a different threat was gathering force in the east, where Temuchin Bagatur, the chief of a Mongol tribe, had conquered China in nine years, a victory which prompted him to assume the name of Genghis Khan, "Ruler of the World". He meant to make that boast good by finding out what lay west of the Ural mountains and conquering it as well. ❑

LEFT: Prince Yuri Dolgoruky, founder of Moscow.
RIGHT: Alexander Nevsky defeats the Swedes.

THE MONGOL YOKE

The Mongols – or Tatars – descended on Russia like a whirlwind,
and the reign of terror they imposed lasted for hundreds of years

The Tatar onslaught took the Russian people by complete surprise. It was a vicious, bloody bolt from the blue. Even now, the folk memory of the Tatars' bloody rule is an indelible scar on the national psyche. Russian mothers can still be heard invoking the name of a long-dead Tatar commander to frighten naughty children. "Eat up your greens," they say, "Or Mamai will get you."

The Russians' first encounter with these fearsome aliens on horseback came in 1223, when an army was smashed at the Kalka River by a Tatar detachment which then melted back into the steppe. News of this strange catastrophe rippled through to the cities of Russia, but no more was heard of the dangerous horsemen from the east, and Russia fell back into its usual complacency.

The Kalka outriders were no more than an advance guard, sent by the Mongol Emperor Genghis Khan to investigate the rich pickings to the west. The real invasion came in 1236, under the command of Genghis Khan's own grandson Batu Khan, and this time it was utterly devastating.

Tatar onslaught

The Tatars were the most awesome fighting force the world had seen, not excluding their contemporaries, the Crusader knights. They were undeterred by the Russian winter, and in fact preferred to campaign when the earth and the rivers were frozen. The frost and the ice provided a hard surface for their ponies, which were trained to dig through snow to find grass.

Every Mongol warrior kept two or three ponies in tow, and this gave them remarkable speed and endurance. They never went into battle without first erecting dressing stations. Soldiers wore an undershirt of raw silk next to their skin. This light vest sank in under the impact of an arrow, enabling the barbed head to be drawn

out without aggravating the wound. Their small bows had a range far longer than the English long-bows used at the Battle of Crécy (1346), and could be fired from the saddle at a gallop.

The Tatars' preferred method was to pick off enemy strongholds one at at a time and let the news of their victory travel ahead to weaken

the resolve of the next target. The city of Ryazan, a small vassal state of Suzdal, was one of the first to fall.

Grand Prince Yuri of Ryazan tried to buy off Batu Khan with gifts, but laughed at the Khan's suggestion that he hand over his own wife as part of the tribute. Khan was not joking; he put the Grand Prince to death on the spot.

The Khan then laid siege to the city, breaching its defences just before Christmas 1237. "The pagans entered the cathedral church of the Most Holy Mother of God," recount the chronicles, "And there they put Yuri's mother, Grand Princess Agrippina, and her daughters-in law and the other princesses to the sword.

LEFT: the Mongols acquired a bloodthirsty reputation.
RIGHT: Genghis Khan, the Mongol emperor, who sent an advance guard to survey all that lay to the west.

They consigned the bishops and the clergy to the flames and burned them in the holy church. They spilt much blood on the sacred altars. Not one man was left alive in the city. All lay dead together. And all this came to pass because of our sins."

Moscow and, to the northeast, Suzdal and Vladimir were subdued in similar fashion. Novgorod was the next prize on the Tatars' path, but the city was spared by an unseasonal thaw. Novgorod became an island in

DESTRUCTION OF KIEV

Following the sacking of Vladimir in 1240 the Mongols moved south to mount a devastating attack on Kiev, sparing only St Sophia's Cathedral and a few houses. A visitor to the scene five years later reported that skulls and bones still littered the streets.

already too late for Russia. The country was now condemned to the Tatar yoke, cut off from all the great advances of the Renaissance which were destined to take place in Western Europe over the next centuries. All of subsequent Russian history – the frantic westernising of Peter, the agonies of serfdom and emancipation, the wily wartime machinations of Stalin, the uncritical embrace of capitalism in today's Russia – can be read as an attempt by the Russian state to catch up with all that it missed out on during this period, to win recognition from the West for Russia having borne the Tatar yoke alone, for having absorbed the killer blow on behalf of all Europe.

But this is to run ahead. When Batu Khan rushed home in 1241, he left his Russian domains in the charge of a detachment whose base, Sarai (encampment), was near the site of the present-day city of Volgograd. This particular detachment was known as the Golden Horde, and in time their name became synonymous with the Tatar regime.

a vast sea of mud, and the Tatars chose to turn back rather than attempt to wade through it.

Under the yoke

By 1241, the Tatars had conquered most of Hungary, Romania and Poland, and it seemed that nothing could stop them. But just as Europe lay within his grasp, Batu Khan learned that his uncle, the Emperor Ogedei, had died in the Tatar capital of Karakorum. Batu Khan decided to go home and fight his corner in the domestic power struggle.

This timely death, and the snap decision it drew from Batu Khan, saved Western European civilisation from a second Dark Age. But it was

The rise of Moscow

That regime, once its dominion was established, revolved around the business of tax-collecting. The Tatars were not interested in imposing their culture, and while only too happy to burn down churches to encourage prompt payment of tribute, they did not interfere with the religion of their subject peoples. Consequently, the Russian church became a focus of Russian nationhood, and the local vassal princes of cities such as Moscow found that they could still wield a good deal of power, just so long as they made sure they paid their tribute to the Golden Horde at Sarai.

All this time, no one in the West had the smallest idea, or expressed any interest in, what had become of Russia. Only cities such as Novgorod and Pskov, which lay beyond the Mongol orbit, retained links with the Baltic cities and the world beyond.

Behind this medieval Iron Curtain the insignificant but strategically placed city of Moscow (which together with its lands is known to history as Muscovy) was growing strong. Successive grand princes of Muscovy had gained favour with their absentee landlords, the khans of the Golden Horde, and in 1328 a prince named Ivan was put in charge of collecting and delivering all taxes and tributes. This dubious honour earned him the nickname "Kalita" ("Moneybags").

Moreover, troops of the Muscovy principality were used to crush revolts against the Tatars instigated by lesser princes. In this way the Moscow state slowly took on both the political authority and the methods of the Golden Horde.

A PRICE TO PAY

Moscow's annual tribute to the coffers of the Golden Horde was 4,000 roubles compared with the more important city of Vladimir, which paid 85,000 roubles.

"Dmitry of the Don"). The Tatars came back and wreaked vengeful havoc on Moscow in 1382, but the story of the 100 years that followed is one of gradual decline for the Golden Horde.

The Tatar yoke ended in anticlimax in 1480. Ivan III, the incumbent Grand Prince of Muscovy, had been withholding tribute for 20 years. However, when it came to a Kulikovo-style showdown, neither side had much of a stomach for the fight.

The Mongols turned their backs and retreat-

Russian princes retaliate

Ivan Kalita's grandson, Grand Prince Dmitry, was the first Muscovite prince to feel strong enough to challenge the Tatars's demands in battle. In 1380 he met the Mongol host at the Field of Kulikovo on the River Don and, sensationally, he defeated them.

This battle was Russia's Agincourt, a pivotal moment in the country's history. Dmitry's victory shattered forever the myth of Tatar invincibility (he was afterwards dubbed "Donskoi",

LEFT: a 16th-century miniature depicting combat between Russians and Tatars in 1238.
ABOVE: 13th-century encampment of invading Tatars.

ed, and Ivan let them go. The Golden Horde decamped to the area south of the Don, and established a state of its own, the Khanate of Astrakhan, which survived until it was conquered by Ivan the Terrible.

The Tatars' legacy in Russia is immense. It is there in the language; it is there in the casual ease with which centuries of leaders have been prepared to spill blood; it is there in the very faces of the people. The high cheekbones and slightly Asiatic features characteristic of many Russians are a legacy of the Tatars: a Tatar provenance is clearly visible, for example, in the face (and indeed in the ruthless politics) of Vladimir Ilyich Lenin. ❑

THE FIRST OF THE TSARS

The new caesars ruled Russia with an iron hand,

persecuting treacherous nobles and laying the foundations of serfdom

A wandering German knight ventured into Muscovy some six years after Khan Ahmed had meekly brought 250 years of Mongol overlordship to an end. The report he made to the Holy Roman Emperor, Frederick III, was full of strange and fascinating things.

The title which anyone addressing the Grand Prince of Muscovy was required to know by heart was a measure of recent military successes. He was "Ivan, by the grace of God, Sovereign of all Rus, and grand prince of Vladimir and of Moscow and of Novgorod and of Pskov and of Tver and of Yugria and of Vyatka and of Perm and of Bolgary and of others".

Frederick was impressed and sent word that as Holy Roman Emperor he was prepared to bestow on Ivan the title of king. "We have been sovereign in our land from our earliest forefathers," came the reply, "and our sovereignty we hold from God." Ivan III, who had played an important role in consolidating the Muscovite state, was in fact using the title tsar, a derivation of caesar, because the Orthodox Church had proclaimed Moscow the third Rome after Byzantium. His son, Ivan IV, was crowned Tsar of all Russia in 1547.

Reports filtering through to the West of Italian architects and engineers engaged in strengthening Moscow's defences and building churches and cathedrals aroused enormous curiosity. In 1553 Sir Richard Chancellor, an English seaman, was looking for a northern sea route to China when storms forced him to land near Archangel in the White Sea. Local fishermen informed him that he had wandered into the realm of Ivan Vassilievich.

Chancellor travelled inland with a view to meeting this king, a journey which he described as colder and more uncomfortable than anything he had ever experienced at sea. It was only after "much ado" that he came to Moscow, "the chief city of the kingdom and the seat of

the king". The 12 days Chancellor spent waiting for an audience were an eye-opener. Moscow was larger than London, he thought, but "rude and without order". The nine churches in the Kremlin he considered "not altogether unhandsome" but he did not think the royal palace compared with "the beauty and elegance of the

houses of the kings of England". The king, Ivan IV, he learned, commanded an army of more than 200,000 mounted archers, and what he heard about the system of government sounded like tyranny.

Chancellor was dazzled by the splendour of the court when at last he got to see it. A hundred courtiers were dressed in gold down to their ankles. The king himself, Chancellor reported, was not only dressed in gold but had a gold crown on his head and a gold sceptre inlaid with precious stones. All the tableware at the state banquet he attended was gold. He dined on roast swan and other dishes accompanied by copious quantities of mead which had to be drained to the last drop. Ivan was clearly impressed by what Chancellor told him of England, so much so that he decided there and then that he wished to marry the English queen, the redoubtable Elizabeth I. Chancellor secured a favourable trade agreement for English merchants and said he would forward the proposal.

Ivan the Terrible

Chancellor's suspicions of tyranny at work were well-founded. Ivan IV (1530–84) came to be known in his own lifetime as "Ivan the

Terrible", although it should be noted that "Awe-inspiring" is a more apt translation of the Russian. Ivan IV succeeded to the throne when he was only three, and owed his early survival to the clever machinations of his mother and regent, the Polish Princess Elena Glinskaya. She was eventually poisoned by the lesser nobles (boyars). Instead of murdering the young tsar at the same time, it suited the boyars to let him be. Ivan continued to live in the palace, but the boyars used it as a kind of playground, helping themselves to anything that caught their fancy, Ivan's toys included.

These experiences fired in Ivan a desire for revenge, but to begin with he participated lustily in the unbridled licence of palace life. He is reputed to have rollicked in the company of several hundred women before his 16th birthday, when it was thought he ought to get married. He chose Anastasia for his wife, the daughter of a minor noble family named Romanov.

Ivan's foreign policy was to win the remaining fragments of the Mongol Empire. He conquered the Kazan khanate on the Upper Volga in 1552, a victory he celebrated by building St Basil's Cathedral in Moscow. The capture of Astrakhan four years later made him master of the Volga from Moscow to the Caspian. These victories opened the way to the conquest of Siberia, a task entrusted to the Stroganov family of merchant-adventurers protected by the Cossack hero Yermak and his men.

With the Stroganovs energetically at work, Ivan looked west towards the Baltic, especially as the Turkish conquest of Constantinople in 1453 had made the Varangian trade routes down the Dnieper and Volga redundant. Ivan's Baltic ambitions ran into stiff opposition. The Teutonic Order of Knights had dug themselves into Estonia and were in possession of Narva, the port which was Russia's most obvious Baltic outlet. Neither Denmark nor Sweden were inclined to sit back and let the Russians encroach, and farther south Poland and Lithuania had united to become a powerful force.

At home Ivan reformed the legal codes and introduced local self-government. He grew increasingly ruthless in his determination to reduce the powers of the boyars. He confiscated boyars' estates, and installed his own placemen, called *pomeshchiki*, to run them. He ensured that the *pomeshchiki* had the labour they needed by confining the peasants to the land, thus laying the cornerstone of Russian serfdom. Peasants who risked the death penalty by running away often headed south to the steppes where they joined the growing number of footloose adventurers and fugitive slaves who together constituted the Cossacks.

To enforce his repressive measures Ivan instituted the *oprichnina*, a kind of cross between a Spanish inquisition and a palace guard. They were the first incarnation of Russia's secret police, and they set a precedent for many of Ivan's successors up to and including Stalin. The *oprichnina* wore black, rode black horses and on their saddles they carried a broom and a severed dog's head to symbolise their role as purifiers of the state and their ferocious loyalty to the tsar.

The worst example of Ivan's terror resulted from his conviction that Novgorod was seething with treachery. In 1570 he sentenced the entire population to death and thousands of inhabitants were killed in the space of five weeks. As Russia braced itself for his next move, Ivan died.

> **CHECKMATE**
>
> Ivan the Terrible liked to play chess, but only according to his own rules. These eliminated the king from the board, so that the king could never be checked.

treason. In so doing he invoked the wrath of the boyars, and when a young man arrived with a Polish army swelled with Russians and Cossacks and claiming to be Dmitry, half-brother of Fyodor (who had died in mysterious circumstances in 1591), the nobles believed him. Following Godunov's death, the false Dmitry was installed as tsar.

The troubles finally came to an end with the advent of the Romanovs: Mikhail Romanov was elected tsar in 1613, mainly on the strength of his family's connec-

Time of Troubles

Ivan's heir was his second son, the simpleminded Fyodor (he had accidentally killed his eldest son in a fit of anger) and so began Russia's "Time of Troubles", a bleak period of anarchy, civil war and invasion. Fyodor's regent and successor as tsar was Boris Godunov (1551–1605). While Godunov reformed the justice system and encouraged trade with Western Europe, he, too, had a ruthless nature and was swift to persecute anyone suspected of

tion by marriage to Ivan the Terrible. He was followed by his son Alexei, who began to open Russia to Western influences and so lay the foundations for the momentous reign of his son, Peter the Great.

Meanwhile, restrictions on the free movement of serfs imposed in the mid-17th century led to a number of peasant rebellions. In 1670 Stepan (known as Stenka) Razin and his force of 7,000 Cossacks captured the Volga-Don region, including the towns of Tsaritsyn, Astra-khan and Saratov. Razin was finally defeated by the tsar's Western-trained army and was executed in Moscow's Red Square. He lives on as a folk hero, immortalised in songs and stories. ❏

LEFT: Ivan the Terrible, tyranny at large.
ABOVE: Tsar Boris Godunov in troubled times.
RIGHT: the False Dmitry, mysterious interloper.

WINDOWS ON THE WEST

Peter and Catherine both looked to the West for ideas that would transform Russia into a progressive nation

Peter was in every sense a giant of a man: not just in stature – though at 2 metres (6ft 7in) and with a Herculean physique, he towered above his fellow countrymen – but also in his titanic energy and appetites, in his vast breadth of interests, in his capacity for kingly generosity and bloodthirsty rages. But the biggest thing about Peter was the scale of his ambition and the size of his achievement. He set himself the task of hauling Russia out of the thick mud of medievalism and onto the paved highway of European civilisation. He wanted his Russia to be a modern state and a great power, and he did not care what it cost.

The child tsar

Peter was born in the Moscow Kremlin in 1672. His mother, Natalya Naryshkina, was Tsar Alexei's second wife. At the age of 10, in 1682, he was proclaimed tsar along with his sickly elder half-brother, Ivan. But his ambitious and wilful half-sister Sophia chose this moment to foment a revolt among the Streltsy, the palace guard, against the Naryshkin faction at court. The coup turned into a frenzied bloodbath.

The boy Peter was spared, but many of his relatives and courtiers were hacked to death before his eyes. It is hard to imagine the impression this made on the 10-year-old prince, but by all accounts Peter showed no emotion as he watched the butchery.

Sophia was installed as regent and Peter, still co-tsar, was sent into semi-exile to Preobrazhenskoye, a hunting lodge near Moscow. Here, in the country, Peter was left largely to his own devices. Guided by his own insatiable curiosity, he set up a "toy regiment" with his young playmates. This game of soldiers soon became deadly serious: Preobrazhenskoye was transformed into a barracks where Peter drilled and trained with a small army of teenage men-at-

arms, fully equipped with artillery, dark-green uniforms and tricorn hats. Out of Peter's adolescent experiments grew the Preobrazhensky regiment, for 200 years the proudest and most elite unit in the Russian army.

Preobrazhenskoye also happened to be near the "foreign suburb", the home of Western

merchants and specialists, many of whom had come to Russia in the reign of Peter's father. Peter spent days in this Little Europe, and saw that the foreigners had all sorts of knowledge that was new to him and to Russia. One of these foreigners, a Dutchman, taught Peter to sail a Western-style boat on the River Moskva. Peter, already an accomplished carpenter, resolved to learn the art of boat-building. Now the three passions of his life were in place: a fascination with the West; a gift for waging war; a desire to build a navy.

As soon as he was old enough to do so, Peter put an end to the regency. After a brief power struggle, Sophia was confined to Moscow's

LEFT: Peter the Great, mastermind behind the westernisation of Russia in the 18th century.
RIGHT: Catherine I, wife of Peter the Great.

Novodevichy monastery and Peter came back to the city. He continued to rule jointly with Ivan until the latter's death in 1696.

Peter's "year out"

As soon as he was sole and undisputed tsar, Peter did something so unprecedented, so radical, that it was perceived by many of his subjects as a downright blasphemy. He went abroad. No Russian tsar had ever left the country, but for more than a year Peter travelled round Western Europe. This was no ordinary diplomatic progress. Peter's aims were practical: he went to lectures on anatomy, made

tion in which Peter personally took part. Red Square ran with the blood of the mutineers, and their corpses hung on the Kremlin walls for months after. Peter's vengeance for the massacre of his mother's family was complete.

Peter had come back from the West inspired to build a modern navy. To achieve this he needed a port, and so he spent most of his reign in a protracted war with Sweden to win a stretch of Baltic coastline.

Building St Petersburg

Peter finally wrested the province of Karelia from Swedish control, and on this marshy

shoes, visited cannon foundries, but chiefly spent his days working as an apprentice in the shipyards of Holland and England under the transparent incognito of Peter Mikhailov. He felt that the way to learn any subject was to immerse oneself in the basics, and he applied this principle to his new civil service and remodelled army: everyone started at the lowest rank and worked their way up.

Peter's travels were cut short by the news that the Streltsy had once again risen against him. The revolt had been put down by the time Peter got back to Moscow, but he was determined to deal with the rebels once and for all. There was an orgy of torture and public execu-

desolate piece of land, at the mouth of the River Neva, he built his seaport. The human cost of the construction is incalculable – thousands died of disease or mishap – but Peter got what he wanted: a modern city, a "window on the West", and a shop window in which the West might admire his achievements. He equipped it with the trappings of a civilised society: Western style palaces and ministries, a university, a library, museums. To symbolise the break

---

ABOVE: *Peter the Great at Deptford Dock*, by Daniel Maclise.

RIGHT AND FAR RIGHT: two of Catherine the Great's lovers, Count Potemkin (left) and Alexis Orlov.

with the old Byzantine ways of Moscow, he designated the new city the capital of Russia and named it Petersburg (Peter's city).

Meanwhile Peter sent hundreds of young Russians west to learn the technologies and skills which Russia lacked. He also invited a range of Western specialists to Russia. More radically still, he insisted that Russians adopt Western dress and manners, hence the tax on beards, which was Peter's way of declaring that the Westernising reforms were not just a passing whim.

By the time Peter died in 1725, at the age of 53, Russia had indeed changed irreversibly. No lesser personality could have shaken Russia out of its age-old slumber. Peter's successors could not turn the clock back, and some, notably Catherine the Great, made it their business to carry on the work of this remarkable man.

Six monarchs reigned over the next 37 years: Peter's wife Catherine I, his grandson Peter II, then his niece Anna, followed by Ivan VI, Elizabeth and Peter III (ineffectual great-grandson of his namesake). During this period, some of Peter's achievements were eroded or corrupted. The court became Westernised to the extent that it was completely cut off from the world of the peasant masses, almost an alien ruling class;

THE LOVERS OF CATHERINE THE GREAT

Catherine was no great beauty, but she possessed an ability – part womanly instinct, part cold calculation – to inspire loyalty as well as passion in the men who wooed her. There were many such men in the course of her life, and for this her enemies dubbed her "the Messalina of the North". Among the first was Grigory Orlov, a leader of the coup that brought Catherine to power and the murderer of her demented husband. But before that, while Peter III was Emperor, she secretly had a son by Orlov. The infant was smuggled from the Winter Palace in the pelt of a beaver – *bobr* in Russian. In memory of this, the boy was named Alexei Bobritsky, and his descendants are still one of the proudest families in Russia. Before Orlov, there had been an assignation with Stanislaus Poniatowski, a Polish count. When Catherine tired of him she installed him as King of Poland, a typically Catherinesque conjunction of political and emotional convenience. But the great romance of her life came when she was 51. This was Grigory Potemkin, a shaggy, one-eyed giant of a man who conquered the Crimea for the love of his Empress. Catherine, for her part, was glad to surrender to so grand and untamed a personality. He was not her last love – she continued to take lovers into her sixties – but he was the one she always came back to, like a prodigal wife.

the nobility found ways round Peter's merito-cratic rules, and reasserted its ancient privi-leges; the God-fearing lower classes began to forget the impossibly tall Antichrist who made them shave their chins.

Catherine the Great

Peter III was deposed by his young German wife Catherine. In the coup that brought her to power Catherine showed the skills she was to exhibit throughout her life: a politician's instincts, a lack of sentimentality, an appetite for personal glory, and a habit of making her lovers her closest advisers and political allies.

Catherine's reign began in the spirit of the Enlightenment. As a Westerner herself, she was aware of the backwardness of her adopted land and, like Peter, she was determined to impose change for the better. She liberalised the penal code, introduced plans for primary education, reformed local government, founded hospitals and orphanages, expressed the view (in her cor-respondence with Voltaire as well as to her advisers) that rulers were called to serve the state. She invited the leading architects of the day to Russia, and it was during her reign that Petersburg first acquired its cool, classical char-acter. These are some of the achievements that merit her title "the Great". Catherine was also

possessed of an imperial acquisitiveness which would have made Peter proud. In her reign the Crimea was conquered, and Russia thus gained a port on the Black Sea at last. And at her behest, the vast riches of Siberia – the furs, the forests and the minerals – were exploited.

A turning-point in Catherine's reign was a peasant revolt of such scope and fury that it nearly tore the Russian state apart. The leader of the revolt was a Cossack, deserter Emelian Pugachev. In 1773 he appeared on the south-ern fringe of the Empire making the unlikely claim that he was Peter III, Catherine's mur-dered husband. Enough people chose to believe him – outlaws, disaffected Cossacks and Old Believers, Moslem Kalmuks and Tatars – for him to raise a ragbag army. Serfs flocked to him in their thousands: for what did they have to lose? Pugachev captured the city of Kazan and put it to the torch. The serfs of Nizhny Novgorod rose up and laid waste the entire region. As Pugachev's confidence grew, so did his ferocity. His shabby juggernaut rolled on, murdering and raping as it went.

A loyal army, hurriedly recalled from the war with the Turks, headed Pugachev off when he marched on Moscow. Pugachev turned south, and this retreat damaged his prestige. He was betrayed by his own lieutenants and handed over to Catherine's forces, who paraded him through the desolate provinces in a cage. He was put to a cruel death in Moscow.

After Pugachev, Catherine's rule slowly took on a darker hue. Her early intentions to abolish serfdom were abandoned, and in fact by the end of her reign the serfs were more numerous and more tightly bound than ever, the human prop-erty of the landowners.

Catherine's youthful plans and mature achievements were diminished still further after her death in 1796. Her son, the new Tsar Paul I, hated his mother, and set about undoing her legacy the moment he came to the throne. He introduced a Prussian-style military dictatorship, and heaped scorn on his mother's memory and accomplishments. But it did not last long. He was assassinated in 1801, strangled with his own nightshirt by supporters of his dreamy son Alexander. Russia's 19th century had begun as it was to continue: in bloodshed and turmoil. ❏

LEFT: Catherine the Great in her prime.
RIGHT: Catherine in later years at Tsarskoe Selo.

FIVE EMPERORS

The last five Russian autocrats were unable to control their wayward land.

For a century the country zigzagged between repression and reform

Russia began the 19th century in hopeful mood. Mad Paul was dead and the new tsar, his son Alexander, was a man of known liberal views. One of Alexander I's first acts as tsar was to abolish the secret police (they were soon reinstated).

These years were dominated for Russia, as for all Europe, by the problem of Napoleon. Alexander chose to make peace with the French Emperor at Tilsit in 1807. But as with Russia's dealings with another European dictator 130 years later, a treaty did not put an end to the aggressor's ambitions, it merely bought a little time: France invaded Russia in 1812.

The war with Napoleon was one of those occasions – again, the comparison with Hitler is inescapable – when Russia was roused from lethargy to awesome heights of righteous fury. Ancient class enmities were forgotten as the nation rallied to the flag. When the French took the old capital, Muscovites put the city to the torch and rendered it uninhabitable. Napoleon had no choice but to turn back. His army was harried all the way by partisans, regular troops – and by "General January and General February", the merciless Russian winter. Of the 450,000 French troops who crossed the Niemen into Russia, barely 100,000 completed the long march home.

After the defeat of Napoleon, Alexander became increasingly distracted. He had always been weak and indecisive (the writer Alexander Herzen famously described him as "Hamlet crowned") and now he indulged his growing interest in religious mysticism, leaving the country in the hands of the deeply reactionary minister Count Arakcheyev.

The Decembrist uprising

Alexander died unexpectedly in 1825, and his death provoked a constitutional crisis which set the tone of Russian history for a century to come. A group of officers had been planning a coup against the tsar. They were all acquainted with life in the West – many had fought the French all the way to Paris – and they were convinced that Russia could take her place in the European family of nations if the autocracy were abolished and replaced with a constitu-

tional republic. Alexander's death provided them with their opportunity. On the day the army was due to take its oath of allegiance to the new tsar, Alexander's brother Nicholas, they led their troops onto Senate Square in St Petersburg, and faced up to the ranks of loyal guardsmen ranged on the far side. It was a freezing December morning, and for most of the day the two sets of troops stood eyeing each other in the cold and confusion. Most of the soldiers under the command of the plotters had no idea that they were the pawns in a revolt.

While negotiators rode back and forth across the square, the builders who were then working on the new St Isaac's Cathedral threw a few

---

LEFT: the liberally inclined Tsar Alexander I.
RIGHT: Alexander I meets the French Emperor, Napoleon, at Tilsit in 1807 to discuss peace terms.

bricks from the scaffolding at the massed troops. As evening fell, there was a brief and bloody exchange of cannon fire, and then the revolt simply fizzled out.

All the plotters were arrested and some were interrogated by Nicholas personally. The ringleaders were executed and others were sent to Siberia. The incident became known as the Decembrist uprising after the month when it took place. It left Nicholas with a pathological dread of revolution which he passed on to his successors like a hereditary ill-

BLACK LOOKS

Nicholas I was renowned for his intolerance: he ordered imperial guardsmen to wear only black moustaches; other colours, he decreed, had to be painted black.

dress, decided which university students should be awarded prizes, designed the buttons for bandsmen's uniforms, suggested changes to Pushkin's poems. The inadequacy of Nicholas's regime was exposed by the Crimean war. It was ironic that an empire run on strict military lines could not win a war on its own soil. It was a matter of intense humiliation for Nicholas personally that the British and French troops, with supply lines running halfway round the world, were better armed and fed than the Russians fight-

ness. Nicholas's own treatment for the revolutionary disease was to put the patient on ice.

For the 30 years of his rule, Nicholas was the cold, cold leader of a frozen country. He inaugurated a government department called the Third Section, the function of which was to extinguish any spark of dissent, indeed any sign of original thought. This department was headed by Count Benckendorff, another of those ideological policemen that Russia so often produces. Nicholas himself functioned as a kind of supreme government inspector, taking a minute interest in the day-to-day running of his unhappy empire – especially in matters of discipline. He sacked civil servants for scruffy

ing in their own back yard. Nicholas died – one might almost say he died of shame – before the war was declared at an end.

Alexander II frees the serfs

His son Alexander II came to the throne convinced of the need for reform. The national disaster of the Crimea, he understood, was due to the backwardness of Russia, and in particular to the iniquitous institution of serfdom. Alexander signalled his good intentions by releasing

LEFT: Nicholas I lived in fear of revolution.
RIGHT: the 1905 Bloody Sunday massacre in which hundreds of workers died when guards opened fire.

the last surviving Decembrists from exile, and then set about the complex task of liberating his nation of peasant slaves. The emancipation of the serfs came in 1861, not without terrible problems and injustices, but nevertheless it came: no more would Russians sell their fellow Russians like cattle.

Despite the changes for the better, or more likely because of them, revolutionary groups were more active than ever during the reign of the Tsar Liberator. These men (and women) were a different breed from the well-intentioned aristocrats and reformers of the past. They were anarchists and extremists, firm believers in assassination as a political weapon. Their chief target was, naturally, the tsar himself: there were many attempts on his life: a bomb in his train, another in the Winter Palace, a lone gunman who chased the emperor down the street. Each attempt on his life led to a crackdown which in turn justified the next murderous attempt. And in the end they got him. On 1 March 1881, Alexander's legs were blown off by a suicide bomber as he rode in his carriage through St Petersburg. He bled to death in the Winter Palace. Later that day, he had been due to issue a promulgation granting Russia a limited constituent assembly. The announcement was cancelled.

Return to repression

And so, in the now familiar rhythm, the pendulum swung back towards repression. The first days of the reign of Alexander III were especially brutal, were marked by widespread semi-official pogroms against the Jews. In the years that followed national minorities were forcibly Russianised, censorship was tightened, and access to education was restricted for the working classes. At the same time, the working classes were swelling as a result of the policies of Alexander's chief minister, Sergei Witte, who instituted an astonishingly rapid process of industrialisation. Thousands of miles of railway were laid (the Trans-Siberian railway was begun in 1891), a vast coal industry was founded in the Don basin, and foreigners queued up to invest in this new Russia. The process continued under the last tsar and his prime minister Peter Stolypin. But the combination of political repression and a large urban

STOLYPIN – TSARISM'S LAST HOPE

After 1905, Peter Stolypin was Russia's last hope of avoiding the catastrophe of revolution. He said he needed 20 years of stability to rescue Russia – he got five years of chaos. He was made prime minister in 1906, at a time when government officials were being murdered by terrorists at a rate of more than 100 a month. Stolypin answered violence with violence. He set up courts-martial which tried and executed assassins so swiftly that they were often in their graves before their victims. Having crushed the revolution, Stolypin passed laws to liberate peasants from the rustic tyranny of the commune and from feudal practises such as strip farming. Peasants were invited to buy land, sow whatever crops they chose, and employ workers. (The able peasants who seized this opportunity were annihilated as kulaks, or exploiters, under Stalin.) Stolypin also presided over an industrial boom which made Russia an emergent economic superpower. He tried to work with the fractious Duma, but was hamstrung by the disapproval of the weak and stubborn tsar. Yet given more time and luck, Stolypin might just have steered the Russian state out of the path of disaster. His luck ran out in 1911: he was assassinated at the Kiev Opera in full view of his Imperial employer. His successors were well-meaning nonentities, and Russia blundered on into the abyss.

proletariat was dangerous: the revolutionary brew was beginning to bubble again.

In 1894 Alexander III died in his bed – by now no mean achievement for a tsar. He was succeeded by his son, Nicholas, a devoted family man of limited intelligence and imagination.

The last tsar

The accession of Nicholas II was marred by a dreadful accident which set the tone for his entire reign. A crowd of half a million gathered to celebrate

UNDER A SPELL

Rasputin's gaze, said the French ambassador to Russia, "was at once piercing and caressing, naive and cunning, far off and concentrated." In conversation, "his pupils radiated magnetism."

at Khodynka Field near Moscow, where they were plied with free beer from coronation mugs. At some point in the afternoon an urgent rumour circulated among the crowd that the beer was running out. There followed a drunken stampede for the booths, and thousands of people, mostly women and children, were crushed to death.

Khodynka was not the last pointless loss of life in Nicholas's reign. Far worse was to come. In January 1905, in the midst of war with Japan, a priest named Father Gapon led a demonstration of aggrieved workers to the Winter Palace. It was a huge but loyal gathering – many of the workers were carrying icons and portraits of the tsar. But when they reached Palace Square they were met by mounted guards, who panicked at the sight of so large a crowd and opened fire. The carnage was terrible, and it sparked a full-scale revolution. Within days the entire country was on strike. A new kind of workers' committee, dubbed a soviet, sprang up in the capital and other cities. The leader of the Petersburg soviet was a fiery young Jew named Lev Trotsky.

The 1905 revolution, which Lenin later referred to as the "dress rehearsal", was put down by a mixed policy of repression and concession. A kind of pale parliament, called the Duma, was set up to advise the tsar. But it was heavily weighted in favour of the land-owning gentry and deeply resented by Nicholas, who saw it as an affront to his God-given right to rule. It was, in any case, too late for parliamentary democracy.

By 1905 the autocracy was unreformable. The revolutionaries bided their time in foreign exile, and Nicholas gradually retired into the bosom of his beautiful family. The scandalous symptom of the rottenness of the regime was that Nicholas allowed a profoundly sinister peasant healer, Grigory Rasputin, to dominate his wife and dictate to his ministers.

Riot and revolution

The collapse of the autocracy, when it came, was an anti-climax. On a February day in 1917, hungry people queueing for bread began to riot. The troops who were routinely sent to disperse them were themselves peasant conscripts, and they joined the rioters. The rule of law simply evaporated in a moment.

Revolution spread through the land just as it had done in 1905, only this time nothing short of the tsar's abdication would placate the angry, tired masses. Nicholas gave in. With a weary flourish of his pen, he put an end to 304 years of rule by his family. Eighteen months later came the Romanov dynasty's mournful postscript: gunsmoke, blood and bayonets in a far-flung Siberian basement.   ❏

LEFT: the infamous Rasputin, whose domination of the tsarina led to his assassination by a group of nobles.
RIGHT: Nicholas II and his family at Peterhof, 1901.

THE RISE AND FALL OF THE SOVIET EMPIRE

Russia's communist experiment is a central fact of 20th-century history and its consequences will endure well into the 21st century

The fall of the Romanov dynasty in March 1917 was greeted with relief and jubilation, but it did not solve Russia's political crisis. The war with Germany raged on, and at home the many fragmented political factions – Mensheviks, Socialist Revolutionaries, Constitutional Democrats, Liberals, Bolsheviks, Monarchists – were at each other's throats. A provisional government was established, but in the cities food was scarce, and the chance of popular unrest high. In the midst of the chaos and the infighting Lenin, the exiled leader of the Bolshevik faction, arrived back in Petrograd (St Petersburg).

Vladimir Lenin (1870–1924) had been a professional revolutionary all his life. After the usual apprenticeship – expulsion from university followed by a string of terms in tsarist prisons – he had escaped to the West, where he spent his middle years organising congresses, publishing clandestine newspapers and writing theoretical pamphlets.

The October revolution

Lenin's grand theory, the core idea of Bolshevism, was that the coming revolution must be led by a small band of dedicated activists, otherwise it was bound to become watered down into mere social reform. Lenin expounded this view with all the power of his great intellect. He possessed self-discipline to an awesome degree, and he devoted every waking moment to the cause (his only personal pleasure was chess, at which he was unbeatable). Yet he never expected to get the chance to put his ideas into practice. The March revolution took him, as it did everybody, by surprise.

Now that the revolutionary opportunity was there, the single-minded Bolsheviks were best placed to make the most of it. They struck in

the autumn, seizing control of key institutions around Petrograd and arresting the provisional government in one night. It is this coup, not the popular uprising of the previous spring, which was for 74 years celebrated in Russia as the

pivotal event in modern history, the Great October Socialist Revolution.

In the months that followed the Bolshevik putsch, the Cheka, the new secret police, began the long work of rooting out "counter-revolutionaries". Meanwhile Lenin withdrew unilaterally from the war with Germany. But peace did not come to Russia, as the country was plunged into a civil war. For three years the Bolshevik regime tottered, but did not fall.

By 1921 the country was, once again, in a state of utter ruin. At this moment Lenin made a bold move: he announced a return to a market economy. Peasants were to be permitted to sell their produce for a profit; city-dwellers were to

LEFT: poster of Lenin directing the Revolution.
RIGHT: a commander of the Red Army wears his heart on his sleeve.

set up and own businesses. Moscow and Petrograd filled up with Art Deco restaurants where jazz-age Russian yuppies celebrated the fact that the good times were back.

Many Bolsheviks in Lenin's own government were horrified by this "New Economic Policy" (NEP). For them, any kind of trade was un-Marxist and bound to lead down a slippery slope to petty-bourgeois capitalism. But Lenin saw it as an essential tactical retreat. The old devil of the profit motive was the only thing which could get the economy moving again. When the time came, they would stuff the devil back in its sack. It is not clear how long Lenin

intended NEP to last. It was in full swing when he died in January 1924, having been incapacitated by a stroke more than a year before. The power struggle that followed was in the oldest Kremlin tradition. It lasted four years and was won by the rank outsider, Joseph Stalin.

Stalin's brutal regime

Stalin, unlike most of the top-ranking Bolsheviks, was not a middle-class intellectual. He was the son of a Georgian cobbler, and made his name in the revolutionary underground by leading "expropriations" – bank robberies – in the Caucasus. He played a very

THE REVOLUTION'S SPURNED GENIUS

Lev Trotsky (1879–1940) was the haughty ringmaster of the Russian Revolution. He was the only thinker in the movement who could argue on equal terms with Lenin, and he was a writer of such polemical brilliance that he was known as "the Pen". As Menshevik chairman of the St Petersburg soviet (workers' committee) he played a leading role in the 1905 uprising, and this practical experience of revolution gave him huge authority. In 1917 he defected to Lenin's Bolsheviks, consigning his former Menshevik allies to the "dustbin of history". He garnered yet more influence as architect of the victorious Red Army, and was seen as the natural successor to Lenin. But after Lenin's

death, his ancient feuds with the leader were disinterred and made to look like disloyalty. Moreover, his intellectual conceit did not make him a popular figure, and his long years as a Menshevik were held against him: the Bolsheviks were deeply snobbish about party pedigree. In 1927, Stalin expelled him from the party, then from the country. In exile, Trotsky railed eloquently but impotently against "the gravedigger of the revolution", while his own achievements – his very name – were expunged from Soviet history. Stalin had him murdered in Mexico City in 1940. Trotsky's books include *History of the Russian Revolution*, *Stalin* and *Diary in Exile*.

minor role in the October Revolution, but had since established himself as a good organiser. At the time of Lenin's death, he occupied the key post of general secretary, which meant that he controlled appointments within the party machine. It was through this office that he levered himself into power, out-manoeuvring factions led by high-profile leaders such as Trotsky.

Once swathed in Lenin's mantle, Stalin brought NEP to a halt and launched the first Five-Year Plan, a massive

DESERTING HIS POST

At the start of the war with Germany, Stalin locked himself away. It seems he had a nervous breakdown. Foreign minister Vyacheslav Molotov announced the news of war to the Russian people.

branded as *kulaks* (peasant exploiters) and herded into the burgeoning gulag; millions more died in artificially engineered famines, particularly in the Ukraine.

The Great Terror

These measures were backed up by a purge of indescribable horror. The secret police, now renamed the NKVD, swept through the country like the *oprichnina* of old, their task to arrest "enemies of the people". It was as if the vicious, pathological personality of Stalin had

programme of state-led industrialisation intended to transform the Soviet Union into a modern power.

The parallel collectivisation of agriculture aimed to harness the country's productivity and bring it under state control. But the mass of peasants refused to be herded into collective farms; many killed their cows and sheep rather than hand them over.

Stalin's response was brutal. He effectively declared war on the countryside. Millions were

LEFT: Trotsky as Commissar of Defence.
ABOVE: Khrushchev extolling the virtues of maize.
RIGHT: Leonid Brezhnev, guardian of the Cold War.

been magnified and unleashed against the entire nation. In blind terror, arrestees denounced everybody they could think of, thereby providing new crops of pseudo-enemies to be harvested. Others denounced neighbours and workmates out of sheer ideological zeal.

The Great Terror of the 1930s was a silent slaughter of millions upon millions of people; entire nationalities were deported. And through it all, in factories and schools, happy workers and happy workers' children sang the Stalinist anthem: "I know no other country where a man can breathe so free..."

After the Terror it was almost a relief when, in 1941, Hitler invaded the Soviet Union. Here, at least, was an enemy one could speak about openly and hit back at. The Soviet people threw themselves into the fray, and yet more millions died in what Russians have called the Great Patriotic War. There were countless acts of epic heroism, particularly in Leningrad (Petrograd had been renamed to commemorate Lenin in 1924), which was besieged for 1,000 days but did not surrender.

As with the Mongol invasion centuries before, Russians felt that they had taken the full force of barbaric onslaught upon themselves, thereby saving the West from submission. The defeat of Germany in 1945 left Russian troops

and it is a measure of his success that when he was subsequently deposed it was not thought necessary to liquidate him physically.

In the cultural thaw that accompanied "de-Stalinisation" Russians had a tiny intoxicating taste of freedom: to read, to speak, to criticise. It was not much – and as the tanks on the streets of Budapest in 1956 proved, it had very definite limits – but it was never forgotten.

Nikita Khrushchev is fondly remembered in Russia for other reasons too. He increased state pensions, was fanatical about planting maize (during the Khrushchev years, Soviet shops overflowed with cornflakes and pop-

in the heart of Europe. In a way, this was a fulfilment of Peter the Great's dream: a Russian state at the heart of Europe, respected and even feared by its Western neighbours.

Stalin's final years in office were a time of renewed mass paranoia. A grand purge was in the pipeline when he died in 1953. His successor, after the usual power struggle, was Nikita Khrushchev.

Cultural thaw

Khrushchev's great achievement, the act for which he will forever have the gratitude of the Russian people, was to denounce Stalin's Terror. He declared the nightmare to be over,

corn), and he launched a massive and much-needed housing programme: the five-storey apartment blocks which abound in the suburbs of most Soviet cities are known in his memory as *khrushchevki*.

But Khrushchev made some terrible blunders: he brought the world to the brink of nuclear war by provoking the Cuban missile crisis; he quarrelled with China and so divided the world communist movement; he clowned around on the world stage, thumping tables at the UN with the heal of his shoe. It was to put a stop to these alarming and embarrassing escapades that he was removed by a conspiracy of cautious, faceless Party men.

The grip tightens

One of these Communist careerists – Leonid Brezhnev – replaced him. Brezhnev's tenure represented a return to a mild form of Stalinism. A monstrously bloated cult of personality grew up around this unappealing man, who unblushingly awarded himself high honours, including even the Lenin Prize for Literature. On the international stage, Brezhnev was a monumental disaster for his country. In 1968, he crushed the Prague Spring, Czechoslovakia's experiment with liberal socialism; and in 1979 he sent Soviet forces into Afghanistan, committing his country to an unwinnable war.

Under Khrushchev and Brezhnev the USSR became deeply embroiled in the Cold War. The arms race against America was a huge drain on a Soviet economy crippled by the age-old sicknesses of indolence and absenteeism. Consumer goods were scarce, and became practically non-existent by the end of the 1970s.

> **TWO SIDES OF THE MAN**
>
> Khrushchev's tombstone in Novodevichy cemetery is a bust of his head, one side of which is black, the other white. This symbolises his personality and achievement: part good, part bad.

People would stand for hours in queues to buy a frozen chicken, or leave their work and rush to a shop where, it was rumoured, there had been a delivery of shoes. The black market became endemic, and was in fact the only efficient part of the economy.

All this decrepitude was covered in a thick blanket of lies. Brave individuals who spoke out were quickly silenced, or worse, they were declared insane as psychiatry became a weapon of the KGB (secret police). Christians were oppressed; Jews were persecuted, but refused permission to leave for Israel or the USA; the people were paralysed by cynicism.

The dawn of perestroika

This was the situation inherited by Mikhail Gorbachev in 1985. (Neither of Brezhnev's two successors – Yuri Andropov and Konstantin Chernenko – had survived much more than a year in office.) Gorbachev believed passionately in the communist ideal, but saw that the whole system was in need of a drastic overhaul; this project was given the slogan *perestroika*, restructuring (or "retuning", as of a sound but neglected piano). He knew he needed

FAR LEFT: Gorbachev wins popularity on the streets.
LEFT: Boris Yeltsin, following a Congress meeting.
ABOVE: the Baltic States call for independence.

the genuine support of the people, and decided that the way to win it was to be honest about the country's problems. This part of the plan was called *glasnost*, usually rendered "openness", though a more accurate translation would be "frankness", because the Russian word implies owning up to what is already clear.

Perestroika was not intended to make the USSR more Western, still less to dismantle the communist system. It was all done under the banner of a "return to Leninist principles". At

OUT WITH THE OLD

Gorbachev has said that he has not seen Yeltsin since Christmas Day 1991. On that day Gorbachev went to his Kremlin office only to find Yeltsin was already there, feet on the desk, drinking whisky.

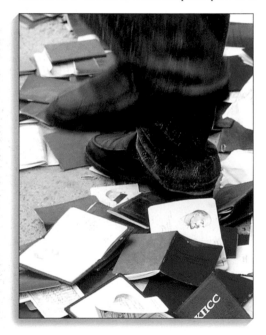

the same time, Gorbachev was careful to endear himself to the West: he put an end to some of the grossest human rights abuses of his predecessors (for example, he released the dissident physicist Andrei Sakharov from internal exile); he allowed the satellite states to pursue *glasnost* locally; he talked seriously about disarmament, and he cleverly made this look as though he was merely doing the world a favour; and all the while he used his vast personal charm to win dollar support for his reforms.

But Gorbachev had sown the seeds of his own downfall. The spotlight he turned on the Soviet system only revealed that it was rotten beyond repair. The limited debate under *glasnost* soon broadened into a discussion of the legitimacy of the entire regime. The peoples of East Europe, who had always viewed communism as the oppressors' tool, turned on their Communist leaders. In 1989, the Soviet sphere in Europe fell apart in a series of popular revolts from Berlin to Bucharest. Gorbachev, to his credit, just let it happen.

The USSR tottered on for two years. An attempted coup against Gorbachev in the summer of 1991 was the regime's pathetic death rattle. Gorbachev was sidelined: he was president of a geopolitical entity that was about to disappear. Power now devolved to the new President of the Russian republic, Boris Yeltsin.

Capitalism arrives

The new man in the Kremlin was master of a much-reduced domain. Russia was suddenly a smaller state than it had been at any time since Catherine the Great. But it was at least free of the responsibilities of Empire and of ideological constraints of communism. Yeltsin threw open the doors and invited capitalism in. Within a year Russia had all the trappings of a free market economy, both good and bad: a stock market, hyperinflation, robber millionaires, homelessness, food in the shops, mafia cartels.

The market economy was never given the chance to put down roots and stabilise. Yeltsin constantly changed tack, throwing out the government and its policies by presidential decree, and bullying opponents into submission.

When the reactionary parliament opposed him he sent tanks into Moscow and shelled their stronghold; he used similar strong-arm tactics, on a much bloodier scale, against the separatist republic of Chechnya. In his second term, as his democratic credentials wore thin, he looked less like a Westernising reformer in the tradition of Peter the Great (which is how he saw himself), more like a sad repeat of Leonid Brezhnev: unaware, drunk and helpless.

At the dawn of a new century, no-one could see where Russia's path was leading: the road ahead was as dark and twisted as at any time in the nation's long history. ❑

LEFT: destroying Communist Party membership cards.
RIGHT: a mural shows the way to a bright new future.

LIFE TODAY

Capitalism has brought with it unexpected hardships,

yet the Russian people remain remarkably resourceful in their ability to survive

French intellectual and writer Joseph de Maistre (1753–1821) summed up the Russian character thus: "Scratch the Russian and you will find the Tatar." Situated at the crossroads between Europe and Asia, Russia is a country of incredible ethnic diversity. Apart from the dominant Slavic group, which makes up some 82 percent of the population of the Russian Federation, there are an estimated 85 native peoples, groups of vastly varying number, culture and origin. From the Tofalars in Central Asia to the Chukchi in the far north, each of these peoples has its own language, none of which is related to Russian. Many of these languages and cultures are now threatened, mainly as a result of Soviet policies which intruded on traditional ways of life.

Soviet influence

The Soviet era left its imprint on the Russian majority, too, both materially and culturally. More than a decade after Communism began to crumble, it is still visible not only in the country's general state of decay but in people's mentalities. Just as physical remnants of the old regime linger – Lenin's Mausoleum, certain place-names, the occasional statue – so the effect of seven decades of stifling dictatorship is only slowly wearing off.

Communism taught people not to take the initiative in case they were blamed for mistakes. Factory workers grew lazy because they knew they would be paid regardless of the rate of production. A complex culture of subordination coupled with defiance has developed, and the capitalist reforms are having to fight the established tradition of deceiving Big Brother and looking after your own.

As a result, Russia is developing its own extreme breed of capitalism. Businesses are springing up all over the place, but the service

is still appalling; the idea of free trade has taken off, but that of paying taxes has not yet caught on. Trying to do business in Russia today is a colossal undertaking: even sending a fax seems to take a whole day.

Endless delays are caused by government departments, which can take months to issue

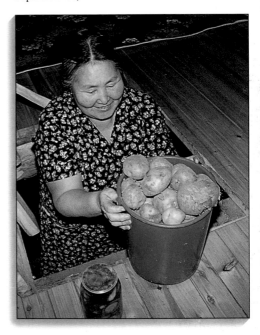

any kind of permit; indeed, many of the committees in charge of reviewing cases have not even been set up yet. Many offices close, without warning, for "cleaning days" once a month or so; an application can be faulted on virtually any grounds, such as the whim of the clerk processing it.

Split personalities

The Russian is famous for having "two faces": that of the man or woman on the street, and that of the man or woman at home.

It is striking that Russians are relentlessly rude and unpleasant when you meet them in any formal public situation, yet delightfully

---

PRECEDING PAGES: keeping in touch in Moscow; girls at the Catherine Palace, Pushkin.
LEFT: a young Russian.
RIGHT: storing potatoes for winter.

warm and generous in personal relationships. Clerks at the railway station will shout at you if you queue at the wrong desk – or even at the right one. Shop assistants will sit sulkily filing their nails or reading a book as you try to catch their attention; when you finally succeed, you are greeted with a surly "What?"

But in private life, these same clerks and shop assistants are transformed into big-hearted individuals for whom friends and family – not to mention friends of friends and family – are everything. The "Russian spirit" is a great stereotype, but it is certainly true that Russians are very emotional and loyal towards those they

The dichotomy between public and private life is difficult for outsiders to understand. There is probably no single explanation, but it is likely that years of Communist corruption have taught Russians not to trust anyone they don't know. As the proverb goes, "You don't really know a man until you've eaten a sack of salt with him". Above all, Russians' unyielding bluntness may well find its roots in their country's long history of being a peasant nation.

Peasant roots

It should not be forgotten that until the middle of the 20th century Russia was inhabited almost

love. Another celebrated feature of the Russians is their hospitality. An invitation to dinner will entail not only elaborate and abundant *zakuski* (starters), a large main course and a sugary dessert, but also numerous toasts with the best vodka, to "friendship", "reunions" and "health".

SAY IT WITH FLOWERS

Russians love flowers, especially roses. In winter, street-sellers display them in glass boxes warmed with candles to protect the petals from frost. When bringing a bunch to your hostess, be sure to present an odd number: even numbers are for funerals.

entirely by peasants. During the 1930s the country was transformed, within a single generation, from a nation of illiterate agricultural workers to an educated proletariat, thanks to Stalin's massive industrialisation drive which was radical on many fronts: politically, economically and socially.

This incredibly rapid change has meant that people's peasant roots are still fairly strong, and are reflected in their clan-like tendencies: firm loyalty and boundless generosity towards those they know, severe mistrust and hostility towards those they don't.

A manifestation of this mentality is found in Russians' fierce patriotism, which applies not only to Russia but to the whole of the former Soviet Union. A Soviet census conducted in 1989 found that nearly 25 million Russians lived outside Russia, while according to one survey, almost as many considered themselves to be Soviet as to be Russian.

Russians' attachment to their country reminds one of a child's relationship with its parent: the parent can be stern, severe, even harsh, but is still adored by the child. A Russian will refer to Russia as "our" country, in the collective, conjuring up a real

THINKING TIME

Before setting out on a journey, Russians traditionally assemble their suitcases in the hallway and sit on them together for a moment to collect their thoughts.

tremendous resilience has served them well, under Tsarism and serfdom, revolution, civil war, Stalin's purges, and the whirlwind of capitalism with its accompanying hardships.

Yet it is questionable whether this capacity to withstand harsh and lengthy ordeals is not itself part of the problem. The Communist tradition of building for the future, of suffering today so that the next generation can enjoy tomorrow, has instilled an almost boundless patience in the Russian people. They await change, they

sense of a united people, history and culture; equally, they will refer to peoples of the former USSR as "our".

Nowhere is this patriotism expressed more starkly than in Russians' defence of the "motherland", time and time again. The degree to which Russians have suffered for their country is remarkable, and perhaps unsurpassed by any other nation – you need only to reflect that the period of the "Great Patriotic War" of 1941–45 saw the deaths of some 27 million people. Their

LEFT: newly-weds pay homage to Russia's past at the Tomb of the Unknown Soldier.
RIGHT: an evening at home in St Petersburg.

do not demand it. Only in 1998, after months without pay and years on or below the poverty line, did miners on the far eastern island of Sakhalin begin to register their dissatisfaction with the Yeltsin administration through strikes. Ominously, a survey conducted in August 1998 found that some 65 percent of respondents believe the government "can no longer count on people's patience".

Attitudes to change

Psychological adjustment to the break-up of the USSR has been very difficult for Russians, many of whom considered its entire expanse to be their homeland. Despite the fact that Russia is still the world's largest country, and although it was widely recognised that the Soviet Union could not have survived unchanged indefinitely, the Russian people feel impoverished by the loss of their empire, an enormous, and enormously powerful union of which they were extremely proud.

By the same token, Russians have mixed feelings towards the period that has followed the union's collapse. The majority supported President Yeltsin in his reform movement, reasoning that the gains of free speech, information, politics and religion have compensated for the loss of stability and material security. Yet a significant minority – as represented by the strength of the Communist Party in the Duma (the Russian parliament) – maintains that "*ranshe bylo luche*" ("things were better before"). This view is not difficult to understand, especially when one considers that it is held largely by the poor and the old, who have lost most through all the turmoil and upheaval.

What is of concern to democrats, though, is that latterly this opinion seems to be gathering favour among those who formerly supported change. The increasing clout of the Communist Party (witness the bullying tactics used against President Yeltsin following his sacking

THE DARK SIDE OF REFORM

Ironically, the freedom of information brought by Yeltsin's reforms may yet bring about their downfall. Russians are now more aware of social problems which, although long-standing, were hidden by the dark secrecy of the Communist culture. Today's Communist Party has also profited from the fact that the past is almost inevitably seen through rose-tinted glasses, particularly by pensioners remembering their youth. However, the backlash against the reform movement also stems from real worries, such as rising crime, unemployment and poverty. During the 1990s, 37 percent of the population was living below the officially defined poverty line.

of Prime Minister Kiriyenko in August 1998) indicates that disillusionment with the capitalist reforms has finally set in.

The initial heady thrill of consumerism, of new freedoms and opportunities, is beginning to wear off; the drunken festivities have given way to thumping hangovers. To be sure, food, clothes and foreign travel can all now be bought – but at a price few can afford.

The old Communist hierarchy based on position has not, after all, disappeared, it has merely been replaced by one based on money. Furthermore, the new elite strongly resembles the old, composed largely of former Party bosses and their hangers-on. As before, those who get on do so through contacts rather than merit. The corruption found in Russia's government is a prime example of the old system masquerading as the new.

Yeltsin himself, along with most of his colleagues, is a former Communist politician. More oligarchic than democratic, the government is in cahoots with Russia's seven wealthiest tycoons, the best known of whom is the mathematician-turned-billionaire Boris Berezovsky. The former Prime Minister Victor Chernomyrdin has his fingers in many pies, including Russia's largest natural gas company, Gazprom, whose privatisation he over-

professionals such as doctors, scientists and academics, despite the fact that these careers have never been well-rewarded financially: Russians have been taught to labour for the joy of intellectual satisfaction alone.

The Russian education system relies heavily on rote learning and can be criticised for its rigidity. Certainly there is little room for independent thought, but it does leave its children with a thorough knowledge of their town or region's history, of literature, music and ballet.

What is more, the range of opportunities on offer – with specialised dancing, music, sports and foreign-language schools – is astounding. It

saw. Profits from Russia's biggest industries are siphoned off by the country's mafia and government officials.

Education, training and leisure

As a rule, Russians are highly trained and the nation's biggest asset at the moment is its human capital. It is in danger of losing this, however, if people cannot afford to study (although, interestingly, student numbers are currently on the rise). The country has a high proportion of

LEFT: demonstrators in search of stability and order demand a return Communism.
ABOVE: vodka, salad and conviviality at the *banya*.

RUSSIAN BANYAS

A *banya* is the Russian equivalent of the Finnish sauna, the main difference being that the heat is wet rather than dry. Every town has its *banya* and the cities have several. During the long winter nothing gets the circulation going better than exposing the body to steaming heat followed by the shock of the icy plunge pool (or, if you're visiting a *banya* in the countryside, a quick roll in the snow). More invigorating still is the tradition of first covering the body in honey to smooth the skin, then beating it with a *venik*, a bunch of birch twigs. It is inadvisable to eat during a *banya*, but Russians quench their thirst with beer (never vodka), as it is believed to prevent dehydration.

is not uncommon for chess, karate and skating as part of the everyday school curriculum.

The pursuit of these interests was encouraged by the Communist policy of making theatre, ballet and classical music affordable for all. Every large city had its own companies, and an evening at the opera was as commonplace as a trip to the cinema. Books, too, were extremely cheap to buy.

As prices rise, however, live entertainment is gradually being usurped by television, showing tacky South American soap operas which have Russian audiences gripped. In the cities, nightclubs and bars have mushroomed, and

cater for all tastes in music from garage to jazz. Many attract a trendy clientele. Most young Russians are fashion-conscious and women especially are always smartly turned-out and carefully made-up.

Outdoor recreation is widely enjoyed, as Russians love nothing better than an excursion to their *dacha* (country cottage) to pick wild berries or mushrooms. *Babushki* (grannies) returning to the cities with loaded baskets are a common sight, as *dachas* and their vegetable plots have become a vital source of subsistence for many. Winter sports include sledging and cross-country skiing, at which most Russians

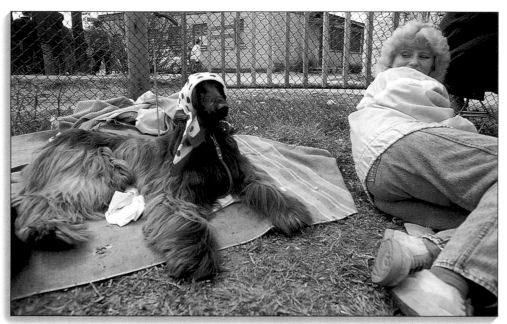

FESTIVAL HIGHLIGHTS

New Year is the high point of Russia's annual festivals; 10 days later, the "old New Year" celebrations begin, in accordance with the Julian calendar. Victory Day comes a close second (9 May), followed by International Women's Day (8 March). There are days for each of the professions, such as "policemen's day", when everyone is cruel to policemen. Revolution Day is still celebrated on 7 November. In the religious calendar, the Orthodox Easter overshadows Christmas, which is barely acknowledged. Churches throng with believers exchanging the greeting *"Christos voskres!"* ("Christ is risen!"). The reply is *"Vo istinye voskres!"* ("He is risen indeed!").

are quite accomplished. Those who are brave enough (nicknamed "walruses") even swim, cutting holes in the ice for a quick winter dip.

Russians adore animals and transport their dogs out to the *dacha* for some exercise at weekends. It is prohibited to take them on the Metro, however, so they hide them in zip-up bags or blanket-covered baskets. Cats tend to be left at home, but their owners will often bring back some twigs from the country as a present to their housebound pets.

High-rise homes

The vast majority of city-dwellers the length and breadth of Russia live in tiny flats in enormous high-rise blocks. Indeed, in some parts of the country, entire cities are made up of row upon row of these bleak dispiriting buildings.

While Westerners may associate such structures with crime, poverty and misery, in Russia they do not carry the same connotations. In true Communist spirit, they are inhabited by representatives from every social stratum. By any standards, Russian living conditions are extremely cramped: many flats have only one

"new Russians" who convert them into generously-sized "Euro-standard" apartments.

LIVING SPACE

The average living area for each person in Russia is 16.4 sq metres (20 sq yards) as opposed to 60 sq metres (71 sq yards) in the United States; 5.5 million people live in *komunalki* (communal flats).

The cost of living

The phenomenon of the extended family, largely eroded in the West, is one of Russia's most valuable resources: rent is cheaper if the flat is registered in a pensioner's name, and grandparents provide free childcare for working parents. The young and the old have a special place in Russian society (not least inasmuch as they are both

room besides the kitchen and bathroom, and larger flats invariably house a substantial extended family.

A fair number of *komunalki* (communal flats) still exist, too. Made famous by the novelist, Fyodor Dostoyevsky, these are reserved for the very poorest. Whole families live in a single room, sharing the kitchen and bathroom with their fellow tenants. Admittedly, however, things are starting to change. Increasingly, *komunalki* are being bought up by the affluent

LEFT: a pampered pet, evidence that the Russians are great animal-lovers.
ABOVE: high-rise apartments in St Petersburg.

given priority for seats in the Metro). Children are adored and utterly spoilt, while pensioners and war veterans, are treated with great respect.

One of the most attractive aspects of Russian society is its supportive and generous social networks, which go a long way to explain how millions of Russians today are managing to get by on what appear to be impossibly small sums of money.

Whereas prices of food and clothing are starting to parallel those in the West, wages and state benefits remain at a staggeringly low level. It is almost impossible to conceive that the average teacher's salary, for example, is approximately one-fortieth of that of his or her counterpart in the West, while a Russian doctor earns less in a month than most doctors in the West earn in a day. Similarly, the ordinary pension is at least 20 times lower, while the student grant is disappearing altogether. Add to this the fact that many workers in the public sector have not been paid for months, or else are paid in tins of fish or bags of wheat, and it seems miraculous that Russians survive at all. The cost of rent, heating, electricity, water and telephone calls is still heavily

> ## NAME GAME
>
> All Russian names have a diminutive form (Aleksandr – Sasha; Maria – Masha; Viktor – Vitya). Many have several: Irina, for example, can become Irisha, Irishka, Irishenka and Irinuchka.

these adjustments are very hard indeed. Unsurprisingly, the tradition of dependency on the state combined with the instability of the financial markets means that Russians have a rather different attitude to money from Westerners. The concepts of saving and investment have not really caught on, mainly because most people can't afford to save money anyway.

The capitalist system has undoubtedly been set back still further by the events of 1998, whereby those who put their faith in it saw their life savings wiped out overnight by the devaluation of the rouble.

New Russians

As a result of this uncertainty, many people spend what they have when they have it, because who knows what it will all be worth tomorrow? Those who can summon the cash splash out on trips abroad (Cyprus is a popular holiday destination) and other luxuries, or even "invest" it by stocking up on cabbages or cucumbers to pickle, in anticipation of a hike in prices during the long winter. The visible wealth on the streets of the big cities – in the form of fast cars, furs, mobile phones – belongs to the emerging class of so-called "New Russians": young, rich and flashy *biznesmeny* with money to burn.

"New Russians" are different from the Russia's mafia (*see page 78*), although there is some overlap. While the latter are associated with guns and violence, the former are akin to wheeler-dealers with sharp minds and a nose for business. Both break the law inasmuch as they dodge their taxes, but that is hardly surprising, given that any law-abiding businessmen would find themselves giving away 90 percent of their income to the state. Indeed, the absurdly complicated taxation system makes it difficult for even the most upright citizens to work out what they owe.

subsidised by the state, yet it takes a substantial chunk out of their meagre wages.

From the point of view of economic efficiency, the withdrawal of subsidies can only be a good thing, when it is considered that under Communism people would happily leave lights on and taps running as they chatted on the telephone for hours, while the local power station would burn up its full quota of fuel whether the winter was harsh or not, for fear of having its ration cut the following year.

Yet for Russians already bewildered by the roller-coaster of rocketing prices, revaluation and, most recently, devaluation that has characterised the post-Communist period so far,

One of the most pressing issues for the Russian government today must surely be to unravel this tangle, as it cannot hope to fuel its reforms as long as the payment and collection of taxes remains unworkable.   ❑

LEFT: counting the roubles – ice-cream is popular whatever the weather.

Freedom of Speech

O ne of the most important and far-reaching changes in Russian society since 1988 has been the dismantling of the Communist Party's total control over the Russian media. This newly gained freedom, however, has come under pressure from Russia's feuding elite, the "oligarchs". Since the mid-1990s, they have bought up the most influential media in order to promote their platform and strike at their opponents.

Paradoxically, this has made the Russian media one of the most pluralistic in the world. As feuding interests attempt to compromise their opponents with exposures and revelations, the public is given a great deal of insight into how the country is ruled.

Most of Russia's national media is controlled by six entities – ranging from the federal government to the country's leading businessmen. TV is by far the most important medium in Russia. Newspaper reading has declined dramatically from its peak during the *perestroika* era, when people avidly read every issue because it brought forth material on some hitherto taboo subject. Nevertheless, freedom of the press has lead to an explosion in the publications available: Russian *Cosmopolitan* has become one of the most successful *Cosmopolitan* magazines in the world, with a circulation of 500,000. English-language newspapers, such as the *Moscow Times* and *St Petersburg Times*, are also available.

Officially, the federal government still controls the single largest media arsenal – three TV stations, three radio stations, three news agencies, and three newspapers. The government has a 51 percent stake in the country's most watched TV station, ORT (Public Russian Television). But ORT is not entirely in the government's pocket. Boris Berezovsky, widely considered to be Russia's most powerful oligarch, has taken control of ORT by putting his allies on the board of directors. Berezovsky, who has made his money in cars and oil, also owns two of Russia's influential daily newspapers, *Novaya Izvestya* and *Nezavisimaya gazetta*.

Vladimir Gusinsky, perhaps Russia's most powerful media mogul, owns NTV (Independent Television). It is Russia's second most influential station, catering to the educated and wealthy elite. Its news shows are the most popular in Russia. Gusinsky

RIGHT: competing financial and political interests have resulted in a lively press.

has also expanded into film production, cable TV, and radio with Radio Echo Moscow.

But if control of TV is necessary to capture the hearts and minds of most average Russians, newspapers are still important. Gusinsky's "7 Days" owns the influential daily *Segondya*, and the popular weekly magazine, *Itogi*, which is produced together with the USA's *Newsweek* magazine.

Alexander Smolensky's Kommersant publishing house produces some of Russia's most authoritative publications, such as *Kommersant Daily*, Russia's equivalent of Britain's *Financial Times*.

Vladimir Potanin, head of the powerful Unexim group, which has stakes in precious metals mining,

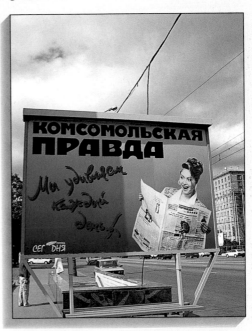

oil, and defence industries, controls the most popular daily tabloid, *Komsomolskaya Pravda*.

Russia's oil and gas magnates have also gobbled up chunks of the media. Since 1997 the media war front has shifted to regional centres such as St Petersburg and Yekaterinburg, where stakes in TV stations and newspapers are being snapped up by the most powerful interests.

While many observers see the oligarchs, or the swallowing up of the media by the oligarchs as a pernicious development, freedom of the press is, in fact, worse off in the regions where the oligarchs have not arrived. In such areas, local governors have carved out fiefdoms for themselves and have an almost total monopoly over the local media. ❑

THE WOMEN OF RUSSIA

The concept of motherhood has always been central to Russian culture,
yet women still have some way to go to achieve an equal status in society

The name "Russia" has a feminine gender in the Russian language and according to Russian tradition the country itself has a feminine soul. The myth of "mother Russia", deriving from the divinity of "mother earth" is central to the history of Russian culture from pre-Christian times to the present day. This is reflected in Russian fairytales, folklore, art and social structures.

Until the 13th century many Russian women had a certain status, power and even equality in some spheres of life, including military affairs. The situation changed when the central government moved from Kiev to Moscow. With the introduction and growing influence of Byzantine religion and the militarisation of Muscovite society, particularly during the Tatar invasion, the status of women diminished and the Christian doctrine of "female impurity" spread to Russia. Women from the upper classes were confined to the realm of domestic life and their status there was the lowest.

In rural areas, in peasant communities, women continued to have some freedom and power. They worked in the fields with the men, and often ruled the roost at home, particularly if their husbands were serving in the army. They could even become *starosta*, the head of a rural community.

Female achievers

Russian history is full of outstanding women who played key roles in the political, cultural and social life of the country.

Catherine the Great, who ruled Russia from 1762 to 1796, extended the territories of the country, introduced new liberal laws and improved educational institutions. Her foreign policy made Russia one of the greatest European countries. Her friend and companion Catherine Dashkov (born Vorontsova) was the first woman in the world to become the head

LEFT: images of womanhood – *Traktoristka* (the Tractor Driver), by Georgy Gurianov.
RIGHT: "Emancipated Women Build Socialism".

of an Academy of Sciences, an institution which she herself founded, together with the Russian Academy of Arts.

Other outstanding figures include Vassilisa Kozhina, who led the peasant army during the Napoleonic War, and Sofia Kovalevskaya, a mathematician, astronomer, physicist and

writer. The first female astronaut, Valentina Tereshkova, was also Russian.

In the 19th century, Russian women were more prominent as instigators of social and political change than women anywhere else in Europe. They campaigned for equal education of the sexes, organised charity fairs for women from a lower social background and worked as nurses in the Crimean War. They fought for social justice and equality on the barricades of the Paris Commune and in the underground terrorist groups in St Petersburg.

Many of them were educated in Europe. Thousands of women belonging to *Narodniki* (Going to the People) walked down muddy country tracks to take literacy and social consciousness to the peasants. Equality of the sexes was a popular concept, particularly among the urban intelligentsia. The women who supported the cause were known as *Ravnopravki* (women for equal rights). They organised small ventures, providing jobs for other women, and published newsletters and journals.

Opportunities open

In 1917 feminist ideas were swallowed up by socialist ideology. However, a decade later, Russian women again achieved a certain equality and social status. Besides the right to vote

of mother, Soviet women were also expected to work in factories and collective farms, as well as in professional spheres.

During World War II women fought alongside men on the battlefields, serving as doctors, surgeons and nurses. There were women pilots and women snipers in both the artillery and among the marine troops. Women formed the overall majority of the workforce in the plants and factories producing arms and military equipment, and constituted the bulk of labour in the collective farms.

During the Soviet period Russian women enjoyed increased success in professional

which was guaranteed by the new Soviet Constitution, the state provided a child daycare system, free abortion and a new marital law which made husbands provide child support in cases of divorce. Marriage and divorce became very easy and the ideas of free love were expressed and supported by a prominent Bolshevik and feminist leader, Alexandra Kollontai.

Stalinist industrialisation and militarisation of the Soviet state put a new demand on women to produce more soldiers and workers for the Motherland. A special tax for childless families was introduced and abortion became illegal in 1936. Divorce procedure in court became far more complicated. As well as fulfilling the role

spheres. In 1988, 52 per cent of the labour force were women, and the same percentage applied to those who possessed higher education, such as university teachers, doctors and lawyers. But since the family tradition was and still is very patriarchal, women were also supposed to carry the double burden of domestic chores and childcare. Equality was harder to achieve in reality than on paper.

The Soviet period, marked by the declining economy of the state, was especially hard on Russian women. Poor household equipment (lack of washing machines, vacuum cleaners and the nonexistence of dishwashers), a poor (though cheap) system of childcare, and a deteriorating medical service, made Soviet women resent the achievements of "emancipation".

Perestroika ushered in new aspirations for social and political change. However, it didn't improve the position of women. If anything, their situation has become worse than before. In the preceding period women were guaranteed 33–34 per cent of parliamentary seats. The first election in the democratic period left women with 5–6 per cent of seats in the Russian parliament and in all local governing bodies.

WOMEN IN FOLKLORE

Among the fairytale images of feminine strength are *Rusalki*, the virgin mermaids with powers of witchcraft; *Baba Yaga*, a witch with a wooden leg, and *Vassilisa Premudraya* (Vassilisa the Wisest), a woman who is far wiser and cleverer than any of the men.

Growing unemployment has hit women particularly badly. Statistics for Moscow and St Petersburg estimated that up to 75 or 80 per cent of the unemployed are women, most of them professionals with higher education.

The return of the sex-object

Today, the social and cultural climate is even more conservative than before. The growing power of the Orthodox Church, overwhelmingly dominated by men, and a popular obsession with the mythological past have produced a new concept of womanhood in Russian society. The idea of equality is illogically associated with the rejected ideas of Communism, and therefore considered misguided and wrong. The former concept of woman-comrade, and woman-friend, is being replaced by woman-wife and woman-mother. A new phenomenon, prompted by the Westernisation of Russian society through advertisements and films, is the image of woman as a sex-object.

Women's response to this development is not simple. Some believe that their place is in the home as wives, mothers and caretakers. Others are struggling for the economic survival of their children and themselves in a difficult economic reality. Those who are active socially and politically are operating in a changed society.

The experience of building a civil society is new to Russia, but women are actively bringing it about. They have formed various political, social, environmental and cultural groups, associations of women in business, single mothers

and widows. There are professional unions of women writers, women journalists and university-educated women. Freedom of the press has produced many new women's journals and newspapers.

Despite their differences in content and purpose, these publications indicate a growing desire of women to express themselves. Like their 19th-century predecessors, they are striving to maintain and improve their social and political status and are reluctant to give

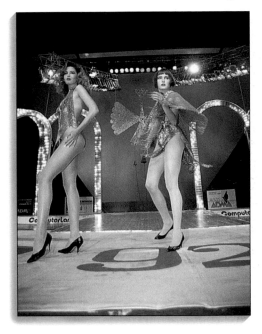

in to conservatism. Despite the hardship of everyday life, Russian women still form the majority among the producers and consumers of cultural values. In museums and theatres, in libraries and exhibitions you will see far more women than men.

In cities and villages it is the women who do the shopping and take care of the children, it is the women who help the poor, and it is the women who perform the duties of social workers. The battle to achieve real equality and status for women in Russian society might be long, but the evidence of Russian history, the strength and great abilities of the women themselves, are proof that it will be won. ❑

LEFT: women labourers on site.
RIGHT: the proliferation of Western culture has brought with it a demand for glamour.

RUSSIA'S MAFIA

The mafia is assiduously at work in Russia, but it is the activities
of the street thugs that could catch the visitor unawares

The Moroccan track and field star Hicham El Guerrouj was among some 50 athletes who, in late 1998, balked at coming to the Grand Prix Final in Moscow, asking for a "more serene venue". He changed his mind at the last moment, and, before going home with a chunk of a US$1 million jackpot, said, "I was

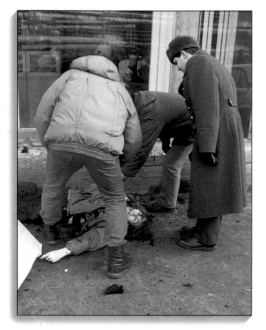

told Russia is a criminal country, but after I came here, I could see it's a nice and beautiful country and Russian people were very kind to me." Guerrouj had no way of knowing that while he was racing his way to victory a police task force was storming a private mansion in Odessa, Ukraine, where top mafia ringleaders from all over the former Soviet Union were gathered to discuss a grave financial problem. They had made the blunder of investing much of their "mutual benefit fund" in state securities, on which the government had defaulted the month before.

In fact, the mafia having problems on such a scale is the reason why a foreign athlete, tourist or exchange student will never be threatened by it or even feel its presence. It's of minor league thugs that foreign visitors must beware.

Russia is indeed a criminal country. To get an idea of the extent to which Russia's powers that be are laced together with the mafia, one only has to look at Boris Berezovsky, the most notorious of the country's "oligarchs" who are believed to manipulate the government for personal gain. Admittedly, the entrepreneur raised funds for and organised Boris Yeltsin's successful 1996 re-election campaign. However, many observers believe he was behind two subsequent government reshuffles in 1998. He is now Executive Secretary of the CIS, the union of former Soviet republics.

Berezovsky, who controls ORT, Russia's biggest television channel, and several newspapers, also has stakes in other industries including Russia's main airline company, Aeroflot, and Sibneft, a major oil company. Aeroflot director general Valery Okulov is married to Yeltsin's daughter Elena. Her sister and top presidential aide, Tatyana, is also said to be Berezovsky's confidante.

In 1996, *Forbes Magazine* linked Berezovsky to the assassinations of several men who stood in the way of his conquest of Russia and branded him "the Godfather of the Kremlin". Berezovsky denied the allegations, took *Forbes* to court in the UK and lost.

The most high profile murder the Russian state was trying to pin on him was that of Vladislav Listyev, a popular television host and head of ORT who attempted to break up an advertising monopoly at the channel run by an associate of Berezovsky. Listyev was gunned down at his apartment door in 1995, and Berezovsky was one of the first people to be interrogated in the case, which remains unsolved.

Guns for hire

The visitor to Russia, however, doesn't need to worry about Berezovsky and his ilk. If you were to meet them, you would probably find them refined and amiable men. Consider instead Dmitry Kashnitsky, a 23-year-old unemployed St Petersburg resident who recently placed an advertisement in a local publication that read: "Seeking any kind of one-time-only, dangerous work." He soon found a client. A man who tried to get a St Petersburg residence permit through an arranged marriage hired Kashnitsky for US$6,000 to get rid of his wife and her mother after they discovered his real motives.

"Life here has reached the point where people look for killers in the newspapers," an investigator in the case told a local newspaper. One St Petersburg reporter said this was the 13th case of a contract killer found through a newspaper advertisement in the past few years.

In the first five months of 1998, 356 murders were on the books in St Petersburg, of which 12 were said by the police to be contract killings.

Spot the gangsters

You will easily spot the generic mafia specimen in a casino or a night club – or driving his Mercedes 600 or Jeep Grand Cherokee down Moscow's Tverskaya. These are known as "New Russians". Whoever coined the term in the early *perestroika* years meant the fledgling Russian middle class. However, it soon became a byword for thieves.

People also refer to mobsters as "Robin Jackets". They indeed used to sport robin jackets, as well as Adidas sweat pants a few years ago. Most have long since donned Pierre Cardin suits, but you can't miss the thick gold bracelets and chains with crosses around their necks. The gangsters' cars often have a blue flashing light on top to amplify the don't-mess-with-me message. (By law, only top officials are allowed flashing lights.)

At the bottom of the mafia food chain are small-time bosses who control drug and prostitution rackets as well as street confidence tricksters. Their operations enjoy a steady supply of cheap labour from the provinces; they also have full co-operation from the local police. The venality of law-enforcement officers at all levels is a scourge. The small-time

mafiosi rightfully consider foreigners easy game and often target tourists. They will approach visitors on the street offering the most lucrative dollar exchange rates, but the temptation should be avoided. Count on these guys to vanish in the middle of the negotiation with both your dollars and their roubles. Even Muscovites fall victim of the "exchangers", and can tell you about their experience of being cheated out of dollars on the street.

The mafiosi peddle Bolshoi tickets outside

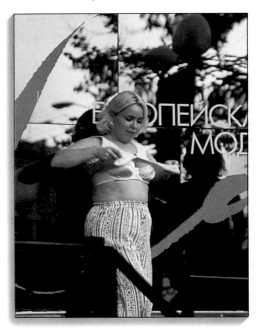

the theatre for twice the booking-office price and sell fake icons. They will send a prostitute to a tourist's hotel room door armed with barbiturates with which to lace the client's drink so that she can clean out his room while he sleeps peacefully.

Even gypsies begging for money in central Moscow are controlled by local gangs. Beware of gypsies hanging round railway stations and the Kremlin – while little children stretch out their hands begging for a piece of bread, older ones will steal the unsuspecting visitor's wallet and camera. In other words, be on your guard and you'll find the cities of Moscow and St Petersburg are generally safe places. ❑

LEFT: meeting a violent end on the streets.
RIGHT: prostitutes are often linked to mafia gangs and may drug their clients before robbing them.

A TASTE OF RUSSIA

Traditional cuisine is making a comeback as Russian
restaurants compete for custom alongside multinational chains

The popular belief that Russians survive on a diet of potatoes and beetroot alone, with a healthy portion of *ogurtsi* (small cucumbers) and vodka to aid the digestion is not actually that far from the truth. These are indeed national favourites. However, with a little less prejudice and a desire to discover the truth,

your stay in Russia can be enriched and your palate educated by the wealth of cuisines on offer. From the Ukrainsky *borshch*, that infamous but delicious beetroot soup, normally served in a *gorshok* (deep clay pot) with *petrushka* and *smetana* (fresh parsley and sour cream), to the frozen *sibirskie pelmeny*, a small boiled pastry parcel of meat, mushrooms or potatoes, the national cookbook is as comprehensive as the country is big.

The years since *perestroika* have seen a renewal of the European influence in every walk of Russian life, including the kitchen. The sunny summer streets of towns buzz with café-life, and with trendy bars below street level. In

addition to the foreign fads, there is a noticeable revival of traditional Russian restaurants catering for every pocket from the modest student stipend to the extravagant, no-holds-barred, *novy-Russky* (new-Russian) cash-filled handbags for men.

In the 19th century, Russia was in thrall to all things French, and borrowed from Paris not only its food, but also its theatre, poetry, architecture and fashion in hats. The French influence is felt in the penchant for thick sauces for meat, in the love of complicated salads, and in the huge variety of cream-filled tortes to be eaten at the end of the meal with *chai* (tea). One such cake is the *ptiche moloko* (bird's milk), so called because it is supposed to be so fine that it cannot possibly be created by humans.

Tempted by *zakuski*

The glory of Russian cuisine is the genuine desire of the host to see his or her guests fed and watered to capacity – a desire that springs from the quintessence of the Russian soul: generosity and pride. It is the tradition to load the dinner table in advance with a vast variety of *zakuski* (hors d'oeuvres).

The *zakuska* plays an important role in the process of dining in Russia, and can save the inexperienced from certain disaster when drinking with the locals. Russians may have a big heart, but their capacity to consume alcohol is tremendous. As a guest in a private home you will be treated in style to the best your host has to offer. However, don't expect any leniency when it comes to drinking, you will have to imbibe your share. Toasting is as important, and here, too, you won't be let off the hook with a moderate "cheers". Toasts can last for minutes and are a science of their own. The formula to remember is your host, the women present and the spread in front of you.

In fact, the *zakuski* are the main event of the meal, and it is an experience as daunting as it is appetising to look on a table laden with red and black caviar, a selection of cold meats, garlic sausage, smoked sturgeon, salmon, the array of potato salads, mushrooms in sour cream, pickled cabbage, beetroot vinaigrette, goat's cheese, as well as the usual liquid ensemble of deep-chilled vodka, *shampanskoye*, and syrupy Georgian wines.

Every hostess will confide in you her secret recipes and claim that nobody beats hers. Popular favourites include *seledka pod shuboi*, literally, "salted herring in a fur coat", which is a delicious combination of fish, beetroot, boiled (and grated) egg and mayonnaise, and *domashni*

MOSCOW TAKEAWAY

In competition with McDonalds, Mayor Luzhkov initiated a chain of Russian cafés in Moscow known as Russkoye Bistro, serving local fast food: *piroshki* (pies), sweet and savoury, with *kvas* and *chai* to wash them down.

tan – which make liberal use of typical Asian ingredients such as coriander leaf, fruit and meat together, walnuts, vine leaves, chillies, beans and flavoured breads – can be found in the Russian home as well as on the menu in restaurants. Meat in these Asian countries will more often than not be boiled – with the tasty exception of *shashlik*, which is normally made from sheep and grilled over hot charcoal. This favoured dish is known throughout the CIS, and the chef, nor-

piroshki (homemade pies), which can be stuffed with cabbage, meat, mushrooms or apricots. By the time the second course arrives, most diners are already too replete to lift a fork.

Asian specialities

Russians can also call on the spicy southern, almost Mediterranean traditions in food. The cuisines of Armenia, Georgia and Azerbaijan, as well as Uzbekistan, Kazakhstan and Kygizs-

PRECEDING PAGES: seafood restaurant window.
LEFT: *solianka* (stew) and *borshch*.
ABOVE: celebratory pie.
RIGHT: barbecue time.

mally the man of the house, will be passionate about the preparation and cooking of what some may simply call a barbecue.

The *pelmeny* puts in an appearance wherever you are in the CIS: you'll find it smaller than usual in Siberia – but made in vast quantities for the winter; it comes large, flat, fried and known as *cheburek* throughout Central Asia and the Transcaucasus, or *manti* in Kazakhstan; the more wholesome version in Georgia is known as the *khinkali*.

All of these are found on the *zakuski* section of the menu, and the most expensive restaurants will have them waiting on the table when clients arrive. Other *zakuski* include *zhulien* (julienne), slices of smoked and non-smoked red and white sturgeon and *kolbasa* (salami-like sausages). *Salat* (salad) is often simply tomatoes and cucumbers, but green salads comprise *travky* (literally, "grasses") which in reality can be a refreshing plate of fresh basil, dill and other green herbs.

Traditional dishes

The Russian cookbook may now be as cosmopolitan as any other, but the traditional meals as eaten during the reign of the tsars would have been very different. *Kisel* (blancmange), made from oatmeal, was the basis of most

meals and was eaten with savoury and sweet foods alike. *Shchi*, a soup made from *kislaya kapusta* (sauerkraut) and meat or fish, would probably feature in every main meal of the day.

The fruits of Russia's abundant forests have long been harvested. Berries such as *brusnika*, *chernika*, *klyukva*, *zemlinika*, *golubika*, *malina*, and *yeshevika* (foxberry, bilberry, cranberry, wild strawberry, blueberry, raspberry and black-berry) were gathered and used to make preserves, jams, desserts and drinks – as indeed they are still today. Vegetables such as *brukva*, (swede) *redka*, (radish) *markov* (carrot) and *chesnok* (garlic) were staple foods, too.

What remains traditional today is the *blin* (pancake), which is eaten both as a savoury and sweet dish. *Bliny* with lots of honey, *smetana* and red caviar are natural choices of filling for hungry Russians.

Bliny are eaten at *Maslinitsa*, the week leading up to the *veliki post* (great fast of seven weeks) before Easter, which in turn is celebrated at the end with a *kulich*, a light, Easter cake similar to the Italian Christmas *panettone*. A delicious sweet dish, *paskha*, synonymous with the celebration of Easter is prepared from *tvorog* (curds) with dried fruits and sugar.

The upper echelons of society would have known a different menu, one which shocked many visiting dignitaries with its richness and quality. Carp in *smetana*, baked *osyotr* (sturgeon) and *okorok* of ham (baked leg of ham in pastry with fruit and spices) were some of the dishes served to important visitors and the ruling class. Great pies of fish and meat, *zapikanky* (bakes) of rice, *smetana*, eggs and sugar and *kulebyaki* (more pies) with fillings of cabbage,

VODKA IS NOT THE ONLY DRINK

Russians are great *chai* (tea) drinkers and make as much fuss over their *chai* as the British. Before the onslaught of imported flavoured teas, Russians would eagerly add mint, cherry and currant leaves to their brew. Piping hot green tea is a favourite on a summer's day to cool the brow. Other *napitki* (drinks) include *kvas*, made from rye bread, currants and spices, and *medovuka*, a mixture of honey, spices and water; both are experiencing a comeback, thanks in part to Moscow's Mayor Luzhkov's challenge to McDonald's and Coca-Cola. *Sbiten* – *medovuka* with alcohol – is one of the many *nastoiki* and *nalivki* that are considered national drinks. *Nastoika* tends to be bitter and made from berries and herbs and, on occasion, chilli peppers; *nalivka* is sweet and aromatic. The common element is vodka – no less than 40 percent! Armenian cognac should be taken chilled with slices of lemon to complement the rich, smooth flavour. *Kindzmariuli* and *Khvachkara* are Georgian sweet red wines not to be missed, while *Mukuzani* and *Saperavi* are red and dry. Stalin was reputed to prefer the young, dry and white Tsinindali and *Yereti* wines. *Shamanskoye* (champagne) should be *polusukhoye* or *polsladkoye* (semi-dry or semi-sweet). Try *Sovietskoye*, *Nadezhda* or *Novi Svet*. *Pivo* (beer) has improved dramatically and varieties of Baltica can be found in European Russia, and even abroad.

mushrooms and meat, or fish, were common for those that could afford it. *Khren* (horseradish sauce) was often the only addition to the natural juices that the dish was cooked in. *Kholodets*, or aspic is another favourite method of preparing meat and fish.

Welcome treats

Possibly the greatest sign of respect that can be shown to a guest is the giving of *karavai*, an intricately decorated bread shaped like a cake, which is presented, normally at the border of a village or as the guest

> ### CAVIAR ON THE MENU
>
> *Beluga, osetrina* and *sevruga* are translated as one, "sturgeon", and produce black caviar. Red caviar comes from salmon.

The *gribok* (mushroom) is at the heart of a national pastime: whole families spend their weekends together in the country gathering mushrooms to preserve for the rest of the year in various concoctions of vinegar, spices and herbs. The culture of mushroom-gathering is one instilled from an early, age and most Russians will be able to recite a lengthy list of edible, and deadly, sorts.

The marinading of *griby* and *ogurtsi* (mushrooms and cucumbers) is another passion of the Russians, and one of the few occasions when

enters the house, and is accompanied by a small pot of salt. This ritual symbolises the wealth of the village, or host. One is expected to break off a corner, dip it in the salt and taste it before advancing. As bread was eaten with every meal and was what people survived on during the harder times, it was seen as dear to life and therefore a sign of readiness to welcome newcomers. It is a tradition often observed at weddings, when the two newly related mothers prepare the *karavai* for the newly-weds' return.

Russian men will glady role up their sleeves and help out in the kitchen.

A real treat when visiting Russia is tasting the *ikra* (caviar) which comes in *chornaya* and *krasnaya* (black and red) and is sold by the kilo to the rich and in little tins to the tourists. Be sure to check the date stamped on the packaging before making your purchase.

Red caviar is best eaten on white bread spread with a generous layer of butter, and black from little egg-baskets (made from the white of hard-boiled eggs, carefully cut into a basket form). Despite being significantly cheaper than at home, black caviar in a restaurant can still push up your bill dramatically. ❏

LEFT: vodka is available in both plain and flavoured varieties, including lemon and pepper.
ABOVE: Caucasians enjoy the local produce.

THE RELIGIOUS REVIVAL

The relationship between Church and State has not been an easy one

and even today the renaissance in open worship has its opponents

The gradual rehabilitation of churches since the late 1980s, together with the congregations they attract and the growing number of novices entering the priesthood, constitutes something of a religious revival in Russia. Some see it as a triumphant repudiation of the propaganda drummed into Russians over four generations by State organs such as the Society of the Militant Godless. Others draw comparisons with the rise of Islamic fundamentalism in the Asian republics of the former Soviet Union, a manifestation of confused societies dredging through their past for some kind of cultural anchor.

Religion in Russia should not be equated with, say, Roman Catholicism in Poland, itself undergoing a renaissance. The latter is a more political and intellectual force at loggerheads with everything atheistic Communism represented. Russian Orthodoxy, on the other hand, was never intellectualised as Christianity in the West was by the likes of Thomas Aquinas in the 13th century. The Russian faith was and is rooted in worship, not scholastic theology, and it is not inconceivable that it could have contrived a *modus vivendi* with Communism as it did with tsarist absolutism.

Who goes to church

Visitors to a Russian Orthodox service will be struck by the highly orchestrated ritual. There are no books in evidence, but almost everyone seems to know the procedure. Even those who don't, can cross themselves and bow at almost any time. The air is thick with incense, the richly coloured icons hold pride of place, and there is close interaction between clergy and congregation, communicating with one another through the medium of splendidly sonorous chant. Anyone familiar with the Greek Orthodox liturgy can see their common Byzantine source.

Anyone who visited Russia in Communist times will be struck not only by the large number

of churches open, especially in Moscow and St Petersburg, but also by the age range of the worshippers. One or two Moscow churches even provide a carpet and toys for tiny children. Even in less accommodating churches, people feel free to come and go. Closer acquaintance will reveal that nearly all middle-

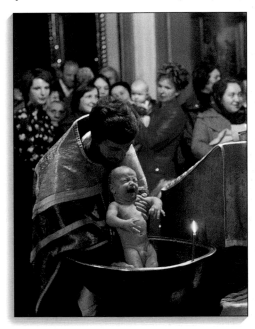

aged and younger Christians, at least in the cities, are well-educated, while poorer, working-class people are to be found only in the few churches that undertake serious social involvement, such as prison visiting and distribution of food and clothing. In addition, there are the sometimes bossy *babushkas* (grandmothers) and other elderly people who have been faithful through the decades of persecution.

Of course, the enthusiasm for getting baptised, a craze which started in the late 1980s, has produced many nominal Christians who no longer go to church; some of these, in particular, are inclined to look back to times before Bolshevism, with a view to reliving past glories

---

PRECEDING PAGES: Orthodox iconostasis.
LEFT: Church of the Resurrection, St Petersburg.
RIGHT: a baby is baptised.

of the Russian Empire. Russian culture is closely interwoven with Christian values and symbols, and even Communism could not conceal this. But nostalgic fantasy can lead to alarming ideas. One of these is a desire to restore an absolutist monarchy. A small minority of Orthodox church-goers are monarchists.

The role of Church and State

The Russian Church had a peculiar role in society, because it never went through the process which eventually separated Church and State to varying degrees in the West. Ivan the Terrible directed arbitrary horrors against the church

GREGORIAN CALENDAR

The Russian Orthodox Church observes the Gregorian Calendar, known as "old style". This means that church festivals are 13 days later than in the West – so, for example, Christmas Day is on 7 January rather than 25 December. The Church Council of 1918–19 decided to follow the State and adopt the Julian calendar ("new style"). Obviously every diocese must lose the 13 days simultaneously, but State persecution and the arrest of bishops prevented it from being announced. Recent suggestions for change have met strong resistance from the mass of church-goers, but there can be no doubt that it will happen within a few decades.

in the 16th century (for which he undertook exaggerated penances), but the Church was not finally subjugated until the early 18th century, as part of the westernising reforms of Peter the Great. Peter abolished the office of patriarch, and made the synod an organ of State, presided over by a government official – not necessarily a Christian – who had power to appoint and move bishops, and parish priests were even required to report to the police some of the things heard in private confessions. When their time came, the Russian Communists regarded themselves as the ultimate spiritual authority, in exactly the same way as they assumed command of the armed forces.

The messianic manner in which the Bolsheviks presumed to convert the whole world to Communism was uncannily reminiscent of the phenomenon of Moscow as "the Third Rome". (Constantinople became "the Second Rome" after Rome was overrun by barbarians in the early 5th century.) Although the Russian Church had progressively distanced itself from its Greek origins by adopting Old Slavonic for liturgical purposes (the Cyrillic alphabet was invented specifically to facilitate the translation of Byzantine Greek texts into Slavonic languages) and replacing its Greek bishops with native Russians, the bonds remained close, if only to counter the hostility of Western Christianity to the Eastern rites as a whole.

The fall of Constantinople to the Turks in 1453, just as Russia had emerged from the Mongol yoke, was therefore a devastating blow to the Russian Church, and Ivan III decided it was Moscow's sacred duty to become "the Third Rome", the beacon of the True Faith. This mission ultimately led to what were in large part religious wars with Roman Catholic Poland in which the latter was no less determined to win Russia for the Pope and Rome.

Old Believers

In the mid-17th century Russia was plunged into a religious dispute, which, unlike the Reformation, was about ritual rather than doctrine. Nikon, a peasant monk who was a close friend of the Romanov Tsar Alexei Mikhailovich, became patriarch in 1652. He decided to bring Church ritual into conformity with contemporary Byzantine practice. In effect this meant people crossing themselves with three fingers rather than two and a few changes in verbal formulas. These proposals were opposed by conservatives within the Russian Church who came to be known as "Old Believers".

Nikon was an authoritarian and uncompromising character, and persecution was fierce and even cruel in some places. It continued into the reign of Peter the Great when the Old Believers refused to surrender their beards in the interest of bringing Russian society into line with Western Europe, where men were in the habit of shaving. Old Believers fled to remote areas rather than shave.

Colonies of Old Believers exist to this day, and have at least two active churches in Moscow. When official persecution ceased, many Old Believers chose to remain in their remote colonies. They became famous for their hospitality, although if the visitors were not Old Believers any plates or glasses they used had to be smashed afterwards. Guests were expected to leave money for replacements.

Monasticism

Russian monks could claim much of the credit for opening up vast tracts of the Russian interior. Taking after the desert fathers of Syria and Egypt, they went deep into virgin forests to find sites for secluded monasteries. The forest was their desert. The tireless energy with which they made these remote areas habitable was their undoing because they were trailed by peasants pleased to exchange their labour for the right to settle on the monastic lands as tenants. These arrangements were preferable to serfdom, and led to the monasteries becoming the biggest and richest landowners in Russia. Many monks were content to capitalise on their enterprise and become landlords, but others preferred to push the frontiers ever outwards and start all over again. The cycle repeated itself until monasteries ringed the White Sea and encroached on the fringes of Siberia.

St Sergius of Radonezh (Sergei Radonezhskiy, 14th century) is the best known and most popular of the monks who simultaneously Christianised and colonised Russia. His tomb is revered at Sergeyev Posad monastery, 50km (30 miles) outside Moscow, probably the holiest shrine in the country. It resembles a walled

LEFT: women sit in quiet contemplation at Moscow's Victory Park Church.
RIGHT: a monk reads from an ancient text.

fortress and contains no fewer than seven churches and one of the Orthodox Church's theological seminaries. There is also provision for visitors, with a museum and shops.

The Church under Communism

The Tsar's abdication in February 1917 was welcomed by the Church which saw its opportunity to break free from State control and to restore the office of patriarch after a gap of two centuries. Patriarch Tikhon, who had been metropolitan archbishop in North America, was elected. Some people welcomed the Bolshevik revolution and Lenin's decree of 23 January

1918 which separated Church from State and schools from Church. This separation turned out to be rather one-sided, as the State took over all Church property, and placed obstacles in the way of free association and travel.

This was before serious persecution began. The famine of 1921–23 persuaded Patriarch Tikhon to hand over much of the Church's gold and silver plate, stipulating only that sacred vessels be melted down by Church authorities and handed over in the form of bullion. This was done, raising enormous sums, but accounts show that all the money went into Party funds, and none, apparently, to the famine victims. The Party, or often just local officials, wanted to take everything. Tikhon issued an appeal to resist the theft of Church property, and the result was 1,500 "bloody conflicts", followed by exile to Siberia or execution for the culprits. Tikhon was also arrested and ecclesiastical Communist sympathisers usurped his position. They declared the patriarchate void and called on "every faithful churchman…to fight with all his might together with the Soviet authority for the realisation of the Kingdom of God upon earth…and to use all means to realise in life that grand principle of the October Revolution."

The faithful proved to be unmoved by the call and stayed loyal to the patriarchate rather

than the alternative "Living Church" offered to them. The Living Church derived from sincere moves for reforms within the Church dating back to the 1880s. There was a general desire for change, but little agreement on detail. Various groups amalgamated and the Communists saw this as an opportunity to split the Church. They favoured the Living Church with privileges, including free travel, while restricting everyone else. Gradually, believers saw through this trap and deserted the group, unfortunately leaving to this day the suspicion that moves for change are tainted with Bolshevism.

Tikhon was arrested and urged to repent in order to resume his duties. "I was filled with

hostility against the Soviet authorities," he said on his release in 1923. "I repent of all my actions directed against the government." Tikhon's confession reaffirmed the traditional solidarity of Church and State.

The Church moves underground

More serious was the statement made by Tikhon's successor, Patriarch Sergei in 1927, although the content was very similar to that of Tikhon, his predecessor. Assuming that both these confessions had been made under duress, elements of the Church went underground. Taking their cue from the Communist cell system, they used passwords to make themselves known to one another. Priests in plain clothes would pop up unannounced in villages, administer to the faithful, and as suddenly disappear.

In 1927, the year in which the first Five-Year Plan commenced, intellectuals and Christians were denounced as enemies of the revolution. Tax collectors swooped on churches and, if the sum demanded was not met, they were boarded up. Teaching religion to children under 18 was forbidden except in private houses and to groups of no more than three children at a time.

Stalin relaxed the ban on Church activities during World War II in an attempt to lift morale. Everyone could see that the Germans were allowing churches to open in the territories they occupied, and after they withdrew the churches remained open by popular demand. When the war was over, however, controls were reimposed in the form of intense anti-religion propaganda in schools and general intimidation of anyone who aired religious convictions.

Under Khrushchev and Brezhnev, many believers served terms in prison for holding prayer meetings or conducting baptisms – not because they were crimes as such, but because they constituted anti-Soviet agitation. The few officially registered places of worship were infested with KGB informers. Bibles and other religious texts were unavailable except on the black market. Persecution intensified in the early 1960s, and more churches were closed under Khrushchev than had been under Stalin.

The Communist state went to great lengths to discourage religious observance. For example, at Easter, the high point of the Orthodox calendar, state television would schedule a rare night of rock music. Those who went to midnight mass would encounter police and volunteer militia whose job was to stop anyone under 40 from entering the church. They were not actually forbidden to enter, but it was made clear that names of those attending "cult events" would be noted by the authorities.

When Gorbachev introduced *perestroika* in the 1980s, Christians of all denominations sensed freedom, and took every opportunity to come into the open. The millennium celebration of Russian Christianity, held in 1988, was a big international event. The present Russian members of the Orthodox Church. Roman Catholics were totally suppressed. Islam had a marginally easier time because most Russian Muslims live in communities which are ethnically not Russian, and less easy to control from Moscow. There are Buddhists too, and a well-established Buddhist temple can be visited in St Petersburg .

Today, there are Pentecostal churches in many parts of Russia, missions from Mormons, and other sects, mostly from Korea and North America. The

20TH-CENTURY SAINT

A statue was unveiled in London's Westminster Abbey in 1998 to commemorate St Elizabeth Feodorovna, one of Russia's most famous martyrs of the Communist era of religious persecution.

constitution makes a fairer separation between Church and State, but today's politicians like to appear in public from time to time with an archbishop somewhere in the background.

Other faiths and denominations

All religions suffered repression and persecution under Communism. The Baptists, an active (though not so numerous) union of Protestants who trace their origins in Russia to 1870, were in turn tolerated and persecuted like the

LEFT: a nun pictured in 1908.
ABOVE: religious freedom allows an Orthodox ceremony to take place outdoors.

scale of this theological invasion has latterly begun to alarm both Orthodox churchmen and some politicians. Under pressure from right-wing nationalists, and with some support from the patriarchate, Boris Yeltsin passed laws which curb the religious activity not only of sinister sects such as Aum Shinrikyo (which allegedly gassed the Tokyo metro in 1995). However, fears that the laws would damage established denominations such as the Roman Catholics and the Baptists have so far been unfounded. It seems, though, that the pendulum is swinging back again towards intolerance and persecution. Perhaps the struggle for religious freedom in Russia is not yet over.   ❑

ART AND INSPIRATION

*Early Russian icon painting was to have a profound influence
on the avant-garde work of the 20th century*

Russia's art and culture was for 700 years – from the official adoption of the Orthodox faith in 988 until the time of Peter the Great – largely derived from Byzantium. After the Roman Emperor Constantine, the first Christian emperor, moved the capital from Rome to Constantinople, now Istanbul, in 323, civilisation and Christianity prospered in this new Byzantine Empire for a millennium.

Soon after the Turks captured Constantinople in 1453, Moscow became "the Third Rome", the legitimate heir to Rome and Byzantium. All art produced in Russia served the one ideal of a Christian, theocentric view of the universe. Byzantine art – and hence Russian art – was subject to strict rules regarding what could be depicted and how, in keeping with the dogma of the Orthodox religion. We should not seek to apply Western humanistic criticism to icon painting: in doing so we are seeing things that were not necessarily intended and not seeing other things that were. The austere spiritual power that radiates from icons is a reflection of a universe with God at its centre. Their painterly language and use of colour and line are powerfully expressive; so much so that icon painting was to exert profound influence the avant-garde at the beginning of the 20th century, and in turn have a vital effect on 20th-century painting worldwide.

Pre-15th century

Both wall paintings and icons survive from before the 15th century, but most painters at this time were either Greek masters invited to Russia, or their Russian pupils working faithfully in the Byzantine tradition. The most famous, and probably one of the last of these Greek painters to make his career in Russia, was Theofan, called "the Greek", who arrived in Novgorod around 1380. Few works have

survived which can be positively attributed to him. A panel showing the Transfiguration in the Tretyakov Gallery in Moscow is probably by him or a pupil.

In 1240 the fire-worshipping Tatars reached and took Kiev, and there followed a period of occupation which lasted until the Muscovite

victory at the battle of Kulikovo in 1380. Only the far north of Russia, including the merchant city state of Novgorod, remained unaffected by the Tatars. Cut off from Constantinople until the late 14th century, the icon painting of Novgorod and the northern monasteries, to which learned Slavs from much of occupied Russia fled, was for a time forced to fall back on its own resources. These icons are markedly provincial yet highly expressive, with their vivid colours and unsubtle, folkloric designs. They are best seen in Novgorod's Museum of Architecture and Ancient Monuments.

One superb example is the mid-15th-century *Battle of the Novgorodians with the Suzdalians,* an unusual work in that it is not based on a biblical event, but commemorates a battle that took place in 1169. The subject matter and its treatment reveal much about its Novgorodian creators; this town of merchants, a member of the international Hanseatic League, was a place of very down-to-earth people, interested in concrete facts and simple story-telling set out in a decorative and easily comprehensible manner. Although the painterly language derives from Byzantium, there is nothing particularly spiritual about the bold and rhythmic use of reds and whites in the work. And the Novgorodians were not "helped" by this icon; Moscow

defeated Novgorod in 1471, and a century later the city fell completely under the dominance of Moscow.

Theofan, Rublyov and Dionisius

After the defeat of the Tatars at Kulikovo in 1380, Moscow began to re-emerge as the heir to Byzantium, not only in its imperial aspirations but also in its painting style. Theofan, who moved from Novgorod to Moscow some time before 1400, worked on the iconostasis of the Annunciation Cathedral in the Kremlin together with a young Russian monk, Andrei Rublyov. We know the latter's name from references in contemporary documents, but it was not until 1904, when his famous *Holy Trinity* (now in the Tretyakov Gallery, Moscow) was cleaned for the first time, that scholars were able to get an idea of his style.

The panel was painted for the Trinity-St Sergius monastery outside Moscow, in memory of its founder, St Sergius of Radonez (*circa* 1314/9–92). Rublyov, who had entered the monastery as a monk before leaving to pursue his career as a painter, was asked to return in 1422 in order to decorate the new stone church, and it was during this time that he painted the *Holy Trinity*.

It is difficult to imagine a greater contrast in styles than that between the nervous, expressionistic Theofan and Rublyov. But it was Rublyov who had the greater influence over the next half-century. A late 15th-century *Entombment* (in the Tretyakov Gallery) by an anonymous master uses a combination of mathematics, music and rhythm to achieve a devastating harmony. The theme of the icon is grief,

AN ICON WITH MIRACULOUS POWERS

The Mother of God of Vladimir is the greatest miracle-working icon of Russia. According to Orthodox tradition, it is one of three likenesses of the Virgin Mary that were painted by St Luke during her lifetime. Legend states that in the 5th century the icon was taken to Constantinople, where it remained until the middle of the 12th century (in fact, research suggests it was painted in Constantinople in the early 12th century). It arrived in Kiev in the 1130s and was placed in a convent in Vyshgorod. In 1155 Prince Andrei Bogolyubsky took the icon north on a campaign. As he crossed the River Klyazma, the horses carrying the icon were unable to go forward. Taking this as a sign, the prince

built a church there, in the village of Bogolyubovo (loved by God). The icon was later placed in the prince's new church at Vladimir and it went on to play an important role in Russian history: tsars were crowned in its presence; it accompanied Prince Andrei Bogolyubsky to victory against the Volga Bulgars (it supposedly sent out fiery rays to protect the prince's soldiers); and it is credited with saving Moscow from the Tatars on two occasions, and from the Poles on another. The fame of the icon was such that it was copied all over Russia and all icons of this type are known as *The Mother of God of Vladimir*. It now occupies a slightly forlorn position in the Tretyakov Gallery in Moscow.

but whereas a European painter would have expressed the grief through facial expressions, the Orthodox painter does not concern himself with private feeling. The grief in this icon is that of the loss of Christ, the son of God, and even the mountains grieve. Christ's body, bound in white, is laid out, a horizontal, long note, against which a small rhythm of hands and faces is constructed, slowly fading as it moves towards His feet; behind is a rhythm of colour and rhetorical gesture, reaching a high point with the scarlet-robed Mary Magdalene's outstretched arms. Even nature submits itself and inclines towards the dead Christ.

The last major figure in classical icon painting is Dionisius (1450–1508). Again, little can be firmly attributed to him, and the main basis for an evaluation of his style is a cycle of frescoes in the Ferapontov Monastery, 570 km (350 miles) north of Moscow. He deployed a delicate colour scheme, applying pale, translucent washes of paint over fine, precise drawing, to achieve an elegant solemnity. In the Tretyakov Gallery, one can see biographical icons of the sainted metropolitans of Moscow, Peter and Alexei, which exude a dignified mysticism.

Opening up to the West

When Ivan the Terrible killed his son in 1598, he put an end to the dynasty that had ruled Muscovy since its beginnings. The early 17th century brought military defeat and, for the first time, ideological confrontation with the Catholics to the west. The Poles overran Moscow in 1605 and 1610, and despite the coronation of Mikhail Romanov in 1613, Polish influence and Catholic claims in Russia continued well into the century.

Russia could no longer live behind closed borders, protected from the pervasive culture of the Germano-Latin West. Forced to seek help first from Sweden, and then from England and Holland in order to overcome the military threat posed by Poland, Russia opened herself up to Western trade; it was not long before Dutch engravings, and Piscator's Bible in particular, found their way to Russia, and this inevitably had an effect on icon painting. The best icons were now produced in the tsar's workshops in the Armoury Palace of the Moscow Kremlin.

The 17th century was a period of transition; as so often happens when a culture begins to lose its way, ornament and decoration preoccupied the new generation of painters. Elaborate, jewel-encrusted silver covers that obscured the image, miniature paintings to rival those of Persia, fine gold decoration; and, to the horror of those who upheld tradition, naturalism.

According to Avvakum (circa 1620–82), champion of the Old Believers, Christ was portrayed in the new icons "with a plump face, red lips, curly hair, fat arms and muscles… which altogether make him look like a German, big

bellied and fat." Theological arguments aside, the golden age of icon painting was dead.

Secular themes

Peter the Great began an enforced Westernisation of an unwilling population. He moved the capital to St Petersburg, a new city without the history and religious baggage of Moscow, inviting foreign artists and craftsmen to come and work and to teach Russians. St Petersburg was to be the cradle of the new secular art, while Moscow remained a Holy city, a city of icons and incense. By the end of the 18th century there were a number of good portrait painters (Levitsky, Rokotov, Borivikovsky) who largely

---

LEFT: *The Virgin of Tikhvin*, 17th century.
RIGHT: *Harvesting: Summer* by Alexei Venetsianov, an early 19th-century representation of rural Russia.

imitated French and German painters, and an embryonic school of history painting. The Romantic Orest Kiprensky (1782–1826) spent most of his unhappy life in Italy, and is remembered for his classic portrait of Pushkin in the Tretyakov Gallery.

Painting recaptured its Russian voice again at the beginning of the 19th century, with Alexei Venetsianov (1780–1847). While the fashion, in Russia and elsewhere, was for neoclassicism, Venetsianov turned his attention away from Ancient Greece and Rome and focused on

Russian peasant life. *Harvest Time: Summer* in the Tretyakov Gallery shows a peasant girl in the traditional, colourful costume, breast-feeding her child while work continues. It is a simplified, rather than an idealised, vision of peasant life, for the idealisation is only in the deliberate beauty of the scene, and the bright, calm colours of the Russian countryside.

The second quarter of the 19th century was dominated by Karl Bryullov (1799–1852) and Alexander Ivanov (1806–58). Each is well known for one monumental work (Bryullov's *Last Day of Pompeii* and Ivanov's *Christ's Appearance before the People*, both in the Russian Museum, St Petersburg), and they were both instrumental in raising the social standing of the artists, who had hitherto served, but not been part of, society. Bryullov, who is alleged to have refused to paint Nicholas I's portrait because the latter turned up late for the first sitting, lived in Italy for many years, and it was there that he painted his masterpiece. Its allegorical allusion to the collapse of antiquity and, by extension, the old regime, has perhaps been overplayed by Soviet critics, but the canvas, for its sheer size and drama, made Bryullov famous all over Europe.

Spotlight on the bourgeoisie

Nicholas I was a man of his time, conservative and of bourgeois tastes, and his reign marked a departure from neoclassicism and romanticism, towards genre painting and realism. During the 1840s and early 1850s, Pavel Fedotov (1815–52) painted canvases depicting the bourgeois: the gestures and expressions are often so exaggerated as to be funny, and social criticism is never far from the surface. During the next decade Vasily Perov (1834–82) produced more serious works; humour was now more bitter, and during the Soviet period, anyone who idealised the pre-Revolutionary past was shown Perov's paintings: drunkenness, poverty, peasant backwardness and the corruption of the Church were among his favourite themes.

By the 1870s, painting and campaigning for social reform had become so intertwined that the Society for Travelling Art Exhibitions, known as the Wanderers, was formed. They took it upon themselves to tour the Empire with their exhibitions, which were intended to educate the population and press for social reform.

The Wanderers are best represented by Russia's greatest realist, Ilya Repin (1844–1930). Repin lived a long, productive life, but his reputation was made with large-scale canvases such as *The Volga Bargehaulers* and *The Zaporozhie Cossacks Writing a Mocking Letter to the Turkish Sultan* (both in the Russian Museum). These monumental paintings have a photographic quality that makes a direct appeal to the viewer. They greatly impressed the simple people who had never come into contact with painting before. The historical paintings of Vasily Surikov (1848–1916), Vasily Vereshchagin (1842–1904) and Viktor Vasnetsov

(1848–1926), also executed on a huge scale, were similarly didactic. Landscape painting also enjoyed a revival in the second half of the 19th century. Ivan Aivazovsky (1817–1900), an extremely prolific painter of seascapes, achieved enormous fame in Russia and abroad for his dramatic canvases. Among the best is *The Wave* (Russian Museum). There is a museum devoted to him in Feodosia, his birthplace in the Crimea.

The years between 1885 and 1925, saw the most extraordinary explosion of cultural life in Russia, during which Russian art – not only painting, but also music and literature – was

not fit comfortably in any movement, came to the colony in 1890; he became obsessed with visions of demons, which he painted in great quantity, and died in an asylum. He was perhaps the first to break the mould of the Wanderers' legacy, and to return to painting as an end in itself, rather than as a vehicle for social comment. His genius lay in the twin powers of draughtsmanship and imagination.

Vrubel's break with tradition encouraged others to follow his example. One who did so was Valentin Serov (1865–1911). Again, Serov's outstanding characteristic is his sure draughtsmanship; he had the ability to render a face, a

among the most exciting in the world. Instrumental in this was the railway tycoon Savva Mamontov, who gathered young talent about him at his Abramtsevo Estate, near Moscow. Many of the most gifted artists spent time there, and the estate became a hothouse of activity in many media – sculpture, ceramics, architecture and art history – with a particular inclination for the study and revival of Russian folk art.

Mikhail Vrubel (1856–1910), a painter whose genius was so extraordinary that he does

figure or an expression in just a few fluid lines. His portrait of the dancer *Ida Rubinstein* (Russian Museum) is outstanding.

Art for art's sake

The year 1898 saw the founding in St Petersburg of the *World of Art* magazine by a group of intellectuals who shared an idealisation of the past and an interest in "art for art's sake". Their worldly outlook now seems both decadent and prophetic. This was the pictorial accompaniment to Alexander Blok and the "Silver Age" of Russian poetry. Leon Bakst (1866–1924), one of the founders of the group, became famous in the West as a costume designer for

LEFT: *The Last Day of Pompeii* by Karl Bryullov.
ABOVE: *The Zaporozhie Cossacks Writing a Mocking Letter to the Turkish Sultan* by Ilya Repin.

Diaghilev's Ballets Russes in the 1910s, but he is second only to Serov in his abilities as a portraitist. Another member, Nikolay Roerich (1874–1947), explored the theme of ancient Rus in his brightly coloured work. Konstantin Somov (1869–1939), the most "decadent" of all, was fascinated by harlequins, fireworks and ladies in 18th-century costume, which he meticulously rendered on canvas. Boris Kustodiev (1878–1927) joined the group late, in 1911; his work, which sometimes bor-

OPEN HOUSE

Two influential, early 20th-century collectors of Impressionist paintings, Sergey Shchukin and Ivan Morozov, opened their doors once a week to allow Muscovites to view these important works.

Mikhail Larionov (1881–1964) and his wife, Natalia Goncharova (1881–1962).

Together with Pavel Kuznetsov (1878–1968), they formed the Blue Rose Group in 1906. Kuznetsov's main preoccupation was with colour, and from Symbolist beginnings, influenced by Puvis de Chavannes, he reached his artistic peak in the 1910s and 1920s, when he painted a series of mystical landscapes of the Caucasian steppes. Goncharova drew her inspiration from Russian folk art and icon painting, and her best work, with its strong linear rhythms and striking colour scheme, reworks Byzantine draughtsmanship.

Larionov delighted in the unexpected and the shocking. Close in spirit to his contemporaries, the Futurist poets, he was the first Russian neo-primitivist, and produced a series of paintings of soldiers in which anatomy is deliberately distorted; in 1913 he turned to semi-abstract painting, having devised a system known as Rayism, by which he painted not objects but the rays emanating from objects, which by their intersection could define space.

ders on caricature, celebrates the larger-than-life world of the provincial Russian merchant class; enormous ladies at tables straining under the weight of *samovars*, pots of jam, and pies stuffed with sturgeon, buckwheat, boiled eggs and rice. It is a world familiar to readers of Gogol, and one that was shortly to disappear, liquidated in Stalin's camps. Among his best paintings are pictures of fairs, but he was also a fine portraitist, and enjoys the distinction of having painted a portrait of the singer *Chaliapin* (Chaliapin Museum, St Petersburg).

The years 1906–11 witnessed the formation of dozens of groups, splinter groups and exhibitions. Two of the most active figures were

Moscow's avant-garde

In 1910, Larionov helped to organise the first exhibition of the Knave of Diamonds group, which included works by foreign artists, and four compositions by Wassily Kandinsky (1866–1944). It was an important event in the history of the avant-garde, for it generated an independent Moscow-based group.

Kandinsky, who spent much of his career in Munich, can be considered the first true abstract painter; his brand of expressionism was concerned primarily with spirituality, and to achieve it he used explosions of colour and line, often including traces of figurative elements. Kazimir Malevich (1878–1935), meanwhile, began his career with Symbolist paintings, moved on to neoprimitivist works inspired by Larionov, but towards 1912 was beginning to develop a style of his own, which he called Suprematism. This was an attempt to break from representation of the visible world, to concentrate on space and through painting to forge a link with absolutes of everything and nothing. The supreme symbol of this period is his painting *Black Square* (*circa* 1914), which is everything its name suggests.

A similarly uncompromising attitude towards art and the public is found in Vladimir Tatlin's work (1885–1953). His legacy is Constructivism; a type of semi-abstraction by which he sought, often with the help of relief, to penetrate the essence of objects, and then of material itself. Among his greatest works, however, is a self-portrait of 1911 in the Russian Museum. Painted in tempera, it recalls icon painting in its use of curved lines and highlights.

The dream like world of Marc Chagall (1887–1985) is represented by early paintings in the Tretyakov and Russian Museums. He was the youngest of the avant-garde painters,

painting, to be illuminated from within. The Russian Museum contains several outstanding examples of his work, including *The Bathing of the Red Horse* (1912).

This frenzy of artistic activity took place against a background of political intrigue, World War I, the Revolution and finally the Civil War. Many avant-garde artists greeted the new society with open arms, applying their talents to propaganda and public information art. The works of the photographer Alexander Rodchenko (1891–1956) and the poet-artist Vladimir Mayakovsky (1893–1930) were to define international poster and book design

spent most of his life abroad, and other than a penchant for neoprimitivism had little in common with his contemporaries.

Kuzma Petrov-Vodkin (1878–1939) also sought to use the language of icon painting: his large canvases are built of areas of strongly contrasting colours, usually including a brilliant, almost luminous red. He deliberately manipulated space to give an impression of flatness, and played with shadow and highlight in such a way that his figures seem, as in icon

LEFT: *Portrait of Chaliapin* by Boris Kustodiev.
ABOVE: *The Bathing of the Red Horse* painted by Kuzma Petrov-Vodkin in the early 20th century.

effectively until the 1980s. But disillusionment set in, and while some artists chose exile, those who remained and sought to practise their art were finally brought down by an official decree of 1932, which established Socialist Realism as the only acceptable form of art.

Now began a strange period during which many talented artists applied some of the more acceptable discoveries of the avant-garde to utopian paintings on Soviet subjects. Some confined themselves to the new heroes of proletarian society – the workers and peasants, sportsmen and women, students at the new literacy colleges – but others went still further, producing vast works showing Lenin and

Stalin, Party Congresses and political meetings.

This was a time for huge public commissions, for works of art to fill skyscrapers, for paintings, mosaics, for metro stations, creating palaces for the people. Many of these Stalinist buildings and their interiors survive, a symbol of the utopian euphoria which reigned, and which is often disregarded in Cold War assessments of the Soviet past.

But there was no "underground" at this time: the under-

OFFICIAL ART

The Soviet era was a time of opportunity for the willing artist. Painters such as Samokhvalov and Deineka represent the best official art of the period, although there were many second-rate artists who came to the fore due to their willingness to compromise with political demands.

painters such as Andrey Mylnikov and Boris Ugarov produced bland, non-controversial pictures of Pushkin, of power stations, of Moscow as the symbol of a contented Soviet Union – but without the inspirational mood of the 1930s – the underground came into its own. Sots Art and Moscow Conceptualism – which produced artists such as Erik Bulatov, Ilya Kabakov and Komar and Melamid, artists who used the Soviet clichés to make a statement of opposition, or who held up the everyday non-political realities of Soviet society for scrutiny – were just the tip of the iceberg. St Petersburg, meanwhile, retained its emphasis on formal qualities, on line and colour. Artists became more radical, and in 1974 they showed their works publicly – which resulted in the bulldozing of a whole exhibition in Moscow in that year.

Searching for direction

But with the 1980s and *perestroika*, the relaxation of controls, and the massive explosion in exhibitions – public exhibitions, not cramped in small apartments – Russian art found itself facing a crisis. Despite the massive popularity of Russian art abroad, the lesser artists of the underground had made their reputations on opposition, on the expression of dissent. Once the point of opposition was removed, Russian art had to learn to see itself not as a political statement, but as an expression of intellectual and artistic aims.

Moscow and St Petersburg, which still dominate the art scene, have emerged from the crisis, but remain divided as ever. St Petersburg remains a city of painting, sculpture and creativity. Timur Novikov's New Academy of Arts propagandises a return to the values of pre-Revolutionary art, to beauty, to neoclassicism. Meanwhile Moscow's artists continue to place emphasis on conceptualism and per-formance, with Alexander Brener spraying a dollar sign on a Malevich, and Oleg Kulik taking on the persona of a dog, biting visitors to the gallery. ❑

ground was a post-war, post-Stalin phenomenon. Artists such as Pavel Filonov (1883–1941) and Vladimir Sterligov (1904–1973) continued to work throughout the 1930s and 1940s, but were not allowed to exhibit. They designed book covers and scenery, taking one or two students, to whom they passed on the knowledge they alone possessed.

With the "thaw" of the 1950s and 1960s, a flood of artists who propounded "formalist" – non-Socialist Realist – theories emerged, exhibiting in apartments and studios, tolerated but not accepted by the authorities. The true divide between official and unoffical became clear at the end of the 1960s. While "acceptable"

ABOVE: *Improvisation* by Wassily Kandinsky, 1911.
RIGHT: *Colour Dynamic Composition* by Aleksandra Alexandovna Ekster (1884–1949).

LITERATURE

Russia's literary heritage is one of the greatest in the world. At every step it reflects the tragic, comic, glorious history of the country

Russian literature is rooted in an ancient oral tradition which lives on in the national passion for jokes, elaborate toasts, proverbs, fairytales and aphorisms. The literary tradition began with the *byliny*, folk tales told by minstrels in the courts of Kiev over 1,000 years ago, and continued with *The Lay of Igor's Host*, a kind of 12th-century Russian *Beowulf*. The opening words of this long saga are known to every educated Russian, and even in pale translation can send a shiver up the spine: "Is it not fitting, o my brothers, to begin with the old songs, the hard tales of Igor, son of Svyatoslav, and his battles..."

Literary genius

But the man held to be the founder of modern Russian literature is Alexander Pushkin. He was born in 1799, in an age when French was still considered the only language suitable for literary expression, and Russian was held to be the argot of the kitchen and the farmyard.

Pushkin's work took Russian to new and undreamed-of heights. His instinctive feel for the cadences of the Russian tongue, acquired at the knee of his peasant nanny, was transmuted by his genius into deathless lyric poetry, prose, verse novels and plays. It is present, too, in the long poem, *The Bronze Horseman*, and the verse novel *Evgene Onegin*.

Pushkin's place in Russian literature cannot be overstated; he is not just its source, he is the landscape against which its story unfolds. He set the pattern for Russian men of letters in other ways, too: he was harassed by the authorities (Tsar Nicholas I acted as his own personal censor), and he met a tragic end, killed in a foolish duel at the age of 37.

Pushkin's immediate heir was Mikhail Lermontov. He circulated a bitter poem immediately after Pushkin's death blaming the philistine court of Nicholas I for the loss of Russia's

great poet. The authorities paid Lermontov the compliment of exiling him to the Caucasus, and, not for the last time, official punishment boosted a young writer's reputation. In the dramatic mountains of the south, Lermontov wrote poetry which developed the existential idea of the "superfluous man", the view that in Nicholas's Russia, indeed in the world at large, there is no outlet for the energies of men of talent and feeling, so life consists of frittering away time on meaningless diversions such as love and war, and in taking what solace there is in nature. This philosophy is expressed with deep eloquence in his novel, *A Hero Of Our Time*. Lermontov lived by the idea, breaking hearts and picking fights until he, too, was killed in a duel. He was 26.

A very different light was cast on Russia by Nikolai Gogol, the third great literary talent of Russia's first flowering. Gogol's gift was for the grotesque. His hilarious short stories (*The Two Ivans*, *The Nose*, *The Overcoat*) are

PRECEDING PAGES: Yevgeny Yevtushenko at work.
LEFT: Leo Tolstoy on his estate at Yasnaya Polyana.
ABOVE: Alexander Pushkin, Russia's literary hero.

populated with pompous provincials, uppity civil servants, and all sorts of shallow, greedy gargoyles. But beneath the surface runs a dark seam of fear: perhaps his clownish world is not a burlesque, perhaps humanity really is that ugly. Gogol himself certainly came to believe so. One senses it in his farce, *The Government Inspector*, and in the novel *Dead Souls*, written as he descended into a private hell of religious mysticism and inexplicable guilt.

Great storytellers

The next generation comprises the three giants of Russian letters: Ivan Turgenev, Fyodor

portraying the oppressed: his first book was *Hunter's Sketches*, short stories about the lives of serfs, and many readers think it is his best.

Turgenev was a Western writer: moderate, restrained and economical. Dostoyevsky was the opposite: his books are full of madly excitable people given to passionate ideas and dizzying swings of emotion, people who are buffeted by sin and repentance, who are, in a word, Russian. Dostoyevsky used this gallery of tortured souls to explore the biggest questions: good and evil, freedom and responsibility, salvation and damnation. His mature novels – *The Brothers Karamazov, Crime and Punish-*

Dostoyevsky and Leo Tolstoy. All three dealt with the burning issues of their day – serfdom, Russia's Asiatic and European heritage, the revolutionary movement. But what makes all three of them great is that their works rise above the issues that inspire them. They are all marvellous storytellers. For example, Turgenev's Bazarov, the hero of *Fathers and Sons*, was interpreted by contemporaries to be a vicious caricature of a revolutionary idealist; but modern readers see a well-meaning man whose rational world is thrown into turmoil when he falls in love with a beautiful widow. Turgenev's portrayal of women is one of his strengths; he is also masterful and compassionate when

ment, *The Devils* – are strong meat, and profoundly absorbing works of art.

While Dostoyevsky's doleful gaze was fixed on the dark vortices of the Russian soul, Leo Tolstoy could not tear his eyes from the great, gaudy pageant of Russian society. Tolstoy the Preacher wanted to condemn its frivolity, but Tolstoy the Artist could not resist glorying in it all. This tension is at the heart of both *War and Peace* and *Anna Karenina*, either of which might justifiably be named the greatest novel ever written. *War and Peace*, a vast panorama of the Napoleonic era, is the more ambitious work. Its scope is as deep as it is broad. The focus zooms in and out, alighting at one moment on the daydreams of a teenage girl, at another on great armies in battle. To read the book is like climbing a mountain: it takes stamina and dedication to get there, but the view from the summit is magnificent.

Tolstoy was a nobleman by birth, as had nearly all Russian writers been since Pushkin. At the turn of the 20th century, the voice of the bourgeoisie made itself heard in the stories and plays of Anton Chekhov. The boredom and sense of failure that hangs around his heroes can be seen as a reflection of the

> ## WINNING WORDS
>
> Five Russian writers have won the Nobel prize for literature. They are Ivan Bunin, Mikhail Sholokhov, Boris Paternak (who was forced to refuse it), Alexander Solzhenitsyn and Joseph Brodsky.

writer, and later became a kind of godfather of Soviet letters. To his credit, he used this position of authority to protect young writers from the excesses of the Stalinism regime.

Immediately before the Revolution Russian poetry re-asserted itself. Never before had so many gifted and varied poets arisen at one time. There were the Symbolists who elevated poetry to a kind of mystical religion of which they were the high priests; there were the Futurists, bold experimenters who refused "to cling to

political impotence and shallow roots of the middle classes, soon to be uprooted and borne away on a tidal wave of revolution.

Poets and proletarians

The future belonged to the working masses, whose authentic coarse tones resound in the vibrant, colourful works of Maxim Gorky (his play *The Lower Depths* and his autobiographical sketches *Childhood, Apprenticeship and My Universities*). He was the first truly proletarian

---

LEFT: Maxim Gorky and his literary circle.
ABOVE: Anton Chekhov.
ABOVE RIGHT: Fyodor Dostoyevsky.

Pushkin's coat-tails", as Vladimir Mayakovsky put it, and who wanted to remake the language as the Revolution would remake the country; there was the rowdy peasant Sergei Yesenin whose life and poetry are a long lament for the doomed Russian countryside; there were the Acmeists, exquisite craftsmen who saw poetry as a refined verbal architecture; and there were poets who either stood apart from these movements or transcended them: Alexander Blok, Boris Pasternak, Anna Akhmatova.

Prose came back into fashion in the 1920s, and dramatic accounts of the revolutionary upheaval vied for attention with joyful comic writing, much of it hailing from Russia's sunny south: Babel's *Odessa Tales* and *Red Cavalry*, Sholokhov's *And Quiet Flows the Don*, the anecdotal short stories of Zoshchenko and Zamyatin, Ilf and Petrov's *Twelve Chairs*.

Promoting the cause

In the 1930s Stalin's grip on the arts tightened. Henceforth literature was to be harnessed for the socialist cause. It was still a high calling because writers are, said Stalin, "engineers of the human soul", and as such a vital element of the production line which turns out right-minded Soviet citizens. This mandate was, of course, a death sentence on real literature.

Indeed it led directly to the death of many writers: Yesenin and Mayakovsky had already committed suicide in despair; Osip Mandelshtam, Nikolai Gumilev and Isaak Babel were swallowed up by the Terror. Of the first rank of writers only Pasternak and Akhmatova survived. Akhmatova's poetic account of those years, *Requiem*, is a monument of world literature and a testament to her imperishable dignity.

The novelist Mikhail Bulgakov once remarked that "manuscripts don't burn", meaning that the impulse to create and consume literature is made stronger when it is attacked, that this impulse is in fact indestructible. Stalin failed in his attempt to amputate the human spirit, and the Soviet people's hunger for books was made all the sharper. This is why it was common in the USSR to see queues of people waiting to buy some slim volume of civic verse or collection of short stories.

Bulgakov was himself one of the writers who satisfied Russians' spiritual hunger. *The Master and Margarita*, his tale of how the devil visits Moscow and wreaks havoc, is one of the most profound (and funny) novels of the century. Russians are always amazed to learn that it is not revered in the West as it is at home.

A brief thaw

The Master and Margarita was published only in 1965, 25 years after Bulgakov's death. This was the time of the Thaw, the heady period under Khrushchev when many banned works saw the light of day. The key event of the Thaw was the publication of *One Day in the Life of Ivan Denisovich*. This short story, a pitilessly truthful snapshot of gulag life, was the debut

VOICES OF DISSENSION

Russia has had dissidents for almost as long as it has had books. One of the first was Alexander Radishchev, whose account of serfdom under Catherine the Great, earned him long years in Siberia. A more sinister precedent was set when the 19th-century philosopher Peter Chaadayev was declared insane for criticising the tsarist regime. But dissidence is now associated with the Soviet era, especially its last years when the system was oppressive enough to punish free thinkers, but not so despotic as to murder them. The leading anti-Soviet writer of this time was Alexander Solzhenitsyn. His novels *Cancer Ward* and *First Circle*, and his history of the camps, *The Gulag Archipelago*,

were all published abroad. He was exiled in 1970, but returned home to see his work printed in his native land. Solzhenitsyn was the godfather of dissidence, but there was never a unified movement. Indeed, dissidents often objected to each other as much as they did to the state. *Inakomysliye* (thinking otherwise) covered all kinds of writing and opinions: Marxist historian Roy Medvedev, religious poet Irina Ratushinskaya, human rights activist Andrei Sakharov, Nobel laureate Joseph Brodsky, *samizdat* heroes Sinyavsky and Daniil, and comic novelist Vladimir Voinovich. All are worth reading for their own sake, as well as for what they have to say about the repressive regime.

work of Alexander Solzhenitsyn. It made him famous overnight and led to a flood of camp memoirs as "rehabilitated" writers unburdened themselves of their terrible experiences.

Poets also benefited from the Thaw. There appeared in the 1960s a group of young poets – Yevgeny Yevtushenko, Andrei Voznesensky and others – who chose to declaim their verse to an audience. Some of them set their poems to music. These singer-poets are known as bards, and the best – Bulat Okoujava, Vladimir Vysotsky, Alexander Galich – were hugely popular because their subjects and images were so often taken from humdrum Soviet reality: trolley-

Aldous Huxley, Joseph Brodsky – were all read in the 1970s, but secretly by torchlight.

In search of a modern Tolstoy

By the time *glasnost* brought a sunnier dawn, officially approved literature had grown stagnant, and the best writing of the Soviet period was banned or bowdlerised by the censor. Even the politically harmless classics were unavailable. In this absurd situation, all Gorbachev had to do to win sympathy from the intelligentsia was to let them read whatever they wanted. He did just that, and for a couple of years there was a reading frenzy, as eager *intelligenty* devoured

buses, communal flats, the lives of geologists, hockey players, army conscripts.

As the Brezhnevian winter set in many freethinking writers found themselves out of favour with the censors. Popular works passed from hand to hand in typewritten copies, a homemade method of publication which became known as *samizdat* ("self-publishing", a pun on the state publishing organisation, Gosizdat). Works by banned Westerners and Russian emigrés – George Orwell, Vladimir Nabokov,

LEFT: *Anna Akhamatova* by Natan Altmann, 1914.
ABOVE: Vladimir Mayakovsky.
ABOVE RIGHT: Alexander Solzhenitsyn.

the poetry of Marina Tsvetaeva, the satires of Aksyonov and Zinoviev, and (at long last) the novel *Doctor Zhivago*. There was a simultaneous boom in new works, of which the best was *Children of the Arbat*, Anatoly Rybakov's memoir of a Moscow childhood.

The post-Communist era, by contrast, has been marked by a descent into pulp. Pushkin and Dostoyevsky have been forced off the shelves by novelisations of Hollywood movies. This is a sad but no doubt temporary decline in the written word. The fall of Communism is surely a great theme in the epic Russian tradition; when it finds its Tolstoy or its Pasternak, that will be a book worth queueing for. ❏

THE MUSIC MAKERS

*Influenced by their early folk and ecclesiastical traditions, the country's musicians
have created, to worldwide acclaim, an authentic Russian sound*

Russian music is often said by those outside the country to have dated from the 1830s and 1840s, when Mikhail Glinka became the first Russian composer to obtain European recognition. In fact, the country has a rich musical tradition that originated in the folk songs of the eastern Slavs who settled in the

region about 1,300 years ago. This folk music, which celebrated all events of life from working in the fields to weddings and festivals, served as the foundation for the great Russian classical musical tradition that burst forth in the mid-19th century.

The first professional musicians (*skomoroki*) appeared in the 11th and 12th centuries in the courts of the Russian princes in Kiev and Novgorod. *Skomoroki* were travelling troupes of actors who played a variety of instruments unique to Russia, such as the *guslee* (stringed instrument), *rozhok* (wind instrument) and *volinka* (wind instrument akin to the bagpipes). The Orthodox Church also played a strong role

in the development of Russian music from the 10th century when it became the religion of the state. Its liturgical monotone and style of singing had a powerful impact on the Russian composers of the 19th and 20th centuries.

But the Church had a negative effect, too, causing Russia to become isolated from the musical trends in Europe. Orthodox liturgy dictated that only the human voice could be used in divine worship, and for a long time secular performers were regarded by the Church as "messengers of the devil who turn people's minds from God with songs and trumpets and games". The only instrument permitted by the Church were bells, and the Russians developed bell-ringing to a sophisticated level. Today, after 70 years of silence under Communism, the art of bell-ringing is enjoying a revival; the resonant pealing can be heard on Saturday evenings and Sundays before services.

Despite the dominance of the Church, Tsar Ivan III created a secular court choir in the 15th century. Towards the end of the 16th century, as contact with the West increased (Elizabeth I, for example, sent an organ and virginals to Ivan the Terrible), even church music began to move with the times. By the 17th century, five-line notation, polyphony and major and minor keys were gradually introduced to the liturgy, allowing it to obtain a richer sound and effect.

With the foundation of a court theatre during the reign of the enlightened Alexis Mikhailovich (1645–76), a secular musical tradition grew from the seeds sown by Ivan III, but it was during the reign of Peter I that the greatest innovations occurred. By moving the capital from Moscow to his new city of St Petersburg in 1703, Peter transformed conservative, pious Muscovy into the modern state of Russia at a stroke. Along with all the architects and craftsmen imported to modernise his backward country came foreign musicians to play in the new military bands and sing in the new state choir. Music soon became an integral part of everyday court life. Yet Peter was not very musical himself, so music-making remained entirely foreign in origin. For the vast majority of the population, hearing music meant either going to church or listening to folk songs.

By the mid-18th century the Russian court had its own orchestra, and a special theatre was built for the performance of opera, which soon became the rage among the aristocracy, thanks largely to the patronage of the imperial family. Indeed, opera became so popular in the 18th century that wealthy landowners such as Count Sheremetev (whose enchanting minia-

originally a serf musician) and their successors Alexander Alyabev and Alexei Verstovsky should not be overlooked, even if their Italian training meant that their music did not sound very Russian. They were the first Russian musicians to compete with foreign counterparts on their own level, and they did much to raise musical standards.

Peter the Great's relentless westernising encouraged the nobility to regard Russian culture with contempt, but the upsurge of patriotism which

ture theatre can be visited at Ostankino) were soon setting up their own companies and orchestras on their estates, using serfs as well as foreign artists as performers.

Glinka marks a turning point

It is customary to view Mikhail Glinka (1804–57) as the first genuinely Russian composer. But the achievements of 18th-century composers such as Dmitri Bortnyansky, Maksim Berezovsky and Yevstignei Fomin (who was

PRECEDING PAGES: Mstislav Rostropovich, cellist.
LEFT: travelling musicians.
ABOVE: Mikhail Glinka, 19th-century opera composer.

followed Napoleon's defeat in 1812 swelled hearts with national pride. A new generation of artists, musicians and writers appeared on the scene who were anxious to create a genuinely Russian culture.

Among them was Glinka, whose two operas marked a turning point in the history of Russian music. Both *A Life for the Tsar* (1836) and *Ruslan and Lyudmila* (1842) combined Western techniques of composition with music that was clearly inspired by native folk sources. They were unashamedly Russian works.

Glinka's operas are traditionally considered to be the cornerstone of classical Russian music. His musical plays laid the foundation for the Russian symphonic school, and his vocal compositions are the first examples of the Russian romance. Alexander Dargomizhsky (1813–69) continued the search, begun by Glinka, for a national Russian musical style.

Since opera was government-controlled in tsarist Russia, the conservative tastes of the St Petersburg aristocracy for foreign music in particular continued to determine what works were performed. Public concerts, which were held on a regular basis from the end of the 18th century, were

allowed only during the five-week period of Lent, when the Imperial theatres were closed. There was still no professional training available for budding Russian musicians.

A distinctly Russian sound

Anton Rubinstein (1829–94), the virtuoso pianist and composer who did the most to change this situation during the liberal years of Alexander II, was more concerned with raising general standards of musicianship than with promoting specifically Russian music. He founded the Russian Musical Society in 1859 (the first organisation that was allowed to hold concerts throughout the winter season) and the

St Petersburg Conservatoire in 1862. Similar institutions were founded in Moscow by Rubinstein's brother Nikolai. Not all Russian musicians favoured Rubinstein's reforms.

In particular, the group of Slavophile composers which gathered around Mily Balakirev in the 1860s vigorously opposed the professionalism of the Conservatoire training and its classical Western orientation. In an attempt to keep Russian music free from foreign contamination and preserve its independent status, Balakirev (1837–1910) started a rival Free School of Music.

Together with Alexander Borodin (1833–87), who earned a living as a well-respected chemist, Nikolai Rimsky-Korsakov (1844–1908), who forged a successful career in the navy, Modest Musorgsky (1839–81) and César Cui (1835–1918), Balakirev set about promoting a native Russian musical tradition, believing that art belonged to the people and should be realistic in style.

It is to these composers that Russian music owes much of its distinctive sound. Drawing on the melodies of native folk song and Eastern music, they sought inspiration in the legends of Russian history and literature. Borodin based his opera *Prince Igor* (1874) on a 12th-century epic poem, Musorgsky turned to Pushkin for his masterpiece *Boris Godunov* (1874), and Rimsky-Korsakov created magical operas that had their source in Russian fairytales.

A contemporary of the "Five" was Pyotr Tchaikovsky (1840–93), one of the first students at the St Petersburg Conservatoire. Despite his tuition by foreign professors, the Russian element in his music is unmistakable. Besides the six major symphonies, the piano concertos and the ever popular ballets, Tchaikovsky is also best remembered for his operas, which drew on the works of Pushkin and Gogol. *Evgene Onegin* and *The Queen of Spades* are perhaps his greatest works in this genre.

By the end of the 19th century, Russian music was being performed regularly, and the conservatoires of St Petersburg and Moscow were producing composers, conductors and performers of great talent. With the exception of the Imperial theatres, the government had little control over musical life.

POOR RELATION

Under Nicholas I thousands of roubles were spent on the resident Italian opera troupe, while the Russian Opera had to struggle to make ends meet.

The brightest stars at the turn of the century were the singer Fyodor Chaliapin and the composers Sergei Rachmaninov (1873–1943) and Alexander Scriabin (1872–1915), the most famous graduates of the Moscow Conservatoire where they studied with Sergei Tanyeyev (1856–1915), a composer, pianist and musical theorist who had been Tchaikovsky's student.

Rachmaninov, best known for his major contributions to the piano repertoire (but also a composer of some magnificent symphonic works), was himself a highly accomplished pianist, and was able to earn a good living on the concert platform during his long years of

Sergei Prokofiev (1891–1953) and Dmitri Shostakovich (1906–75).

Composers of the 20th century

Igor Stravinsky (1882–1971) and Sergei Prokofiev became the real innovators in the field of composition. Stravinsky, one of the great musical giants of the 20th century, came to world prominence when Diaghilev staged his ballets, *The Firebird* (1910) and *Petrushka* (1911), in Europe as part of his famous "Ballets Russes" seasons. His *Rite of Spring* (1913) was considered so modern when it was first performed that it caused an uproar all over Europe.

exile after the Revolution. Scriabin, in whose works the influence of Wagner, Liszt and Chopin can be clearly heard, formed close links with the mystical Russian Symbolists who emerged in the early years of the 20th century.

Nikolai Rimsky-Korsakov shaped the musical life of St Petersburg at this time. It was his students, including the music professors Anatoli Lyadov (1855–1914) and Alexander Glazunov (1865–1936), who in turn influenced two of the leading Russian composers of the 20th century –

LEFT: Pyotr Tchaikovsky, composer.
ABOVE: Dmitry Shostakovich working on his Seventh Symphony in besieged Leningrad, 1941.

Stravinsky continued to blaze new paths in music for the rest of his long career, his eclectic works transcending narrow national boundaries. Like Rachmaninov, he lived in exile after 1917, visiting his homeland only in 1962.

Prokofiev completed his studies, as Stravinsky had, at the St Petersburg Conservatoire with Rimsky-Korsakov, but he, too, left the country in the aftermath of the Revolution, leaving Russia bereft of its greatest talents.

The Soviet muse

While the 1917 Revolution had a cataclysmic effect on musical life in Russia, with theatres closing and concert series abandoned, it also injected it with energy. The years just after the Revolution were a time of experimentation. People attended the opera for the first time and vast musical and dramatic spectacles were organised to commemorate the events of 1917.

Music became an important weapon for propaganda purposes. But until new composers appeared who could write morally uplifting Socialist music, the Bolsheviks were content for the old repertoire to be performed. Innocuous opera titles were often changed for ones that were more politically charged.

The greatest period of artistic tolerance came during the 1920s. Two rival musical organisa-

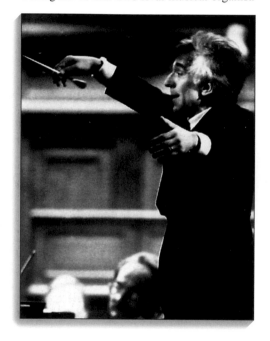

tions formed in 1923: the avant-garde and modernist Association of Contemporary Music, which favoured experimentation, and the Russian Association of Proletarian Musicians, which was the more militant of the two, dismissing all past music as bourgeois and alien.

The period from the 1920s to the 1940s was the heyday of the composer and music teacher Nikolai Myaskovsky (1881–1950), who wrote 27 symphonies, among other works. Other talented composers to appear during the 1920s were Nikolai Roslavets (1881–1944), later a victim of the purges, whose major contribution to the development of atonal music is now beginning to be recognised, and Alexander

Mossolov (1900–71), whose famous orchestral work full of mechanical sound effects, *The Iron Foundry* (1926), is a testament to the early years of Soviet industrialisation.

By far the most gifted composer to emerge during the early years of Soviet power was Dmitry Shostakovich (1906–75), whose *First Symphony* was first performed in 1926 when he was just 20 years old, and followed by another masterpiece, his opera *The Nose* (1928), based on Gogol's short story.

For a time, Leningrad (as St Petersburg became known) vied with Berlin to be the centre of musical experimentation, but towards the end of the 1920s, as ideology came to play a bigger role in artistic life, the freedoms enjoyed by Soviet artists gradually disappeared.

Music for the masses

In 1932, the Union of Soviet Composers was formed and music was placed under direct government control. Composers were told that they had to write music according to the doctrine of Socialist Realism. In other words, music had to be understandable to the masses and nationalistic in character. It was to depict "reality in its revolutionary development".

It was not until 1936, however, that composers really came under pressure to conform. Shostakovich's great operatic masterpiece *Lady Macbeth of Mtsensk* was first performed to great acclaim in 1934, but things started to go wrong following a Moscow performance in January 1936 attended by Stalin. The next day an editorial entitled "Chaos Instead of Music" appeared in *Pravda*. Shostakovich's opera, and avant-garde music in general, was subjected to a merciless attack. He responded with his *Fifth Symphony*, a darkly ambiguous work subtitled "A Soviet Artist's Reply to Just Criticism". His relationship with the authorities was ever after to be tortuous and complicated. It determined the content of the music he was to write over the next four decades. But while Shostakovich paid lip service to the ideology of the Soviet regime, beginning with his *Fourth Symphony*, he carried out subtle resistance to the established order, as did most composers.

Accusations of decadence

The attack on Shostakovich in 1936 signalled the beginning of a systematic destruction of the Soviet musical intelligentsia. After the temporary hiatus caused by World War II, the purges intensified. During the first Congress of Composers held in 1948, Shostakovich, together with Prokofiev, Aram Khachaturian, Myaskovsky, and a number of others, was found guilty of "formalism". By refusing to write music filled with bright, optimistic melodies, these composers were accused of following the "cult of atonality, dissonance and disharmony", which reflected the "decay of bourgeois culture".

Khrushchev's accession to power heralded

MUSICAL HERESY

In the 1940s and 1950s Western music was banned from the concert platform and in the classroom was denounced as "decadent" and "reactionary".

hear the music of Schoenberg and Webern for the first time. It was a brief thaw. Another bleak period of isolation and repression followed Khrushchev's removal from power in 1964. In the musical sphere it was spearheaded by Tikhon Khrennikov, who presided as head of the Union of Composers from 1948 until its collapse in the aftermath of the 1991 coup.

The Soviet conservatoires, however, produced an array of outstanding talents, among them the pianist Svyatoslav Richter, the con-

the thaw in cultural life, symbolised by the great success of Shostakovich's *Tenth Symphony* in 1953. Restrictions began to be slowly relaxed and contacts with the West were cautiously resumed.

Stravinsky was allowed to return to Russia in 1962 and visits made by Western musicians such as Leonard Bernstein, Glenn Gould and Aaron Copland made a huge impact on the new generation music students. It came as something of a shock for these young Russians to

LEFT: the pianist and conductor Vladimir Ashkenazy's heralded return to Russia in 1989.
ABOVE: Moscow Music Academy.

ductor Gennady Rozhdestvensky and the violinists David and Igor Oistrakh. Young Soviet musicians and conductors took gold medals in international competitions.

The opera and ballet troupes of the Bolshoi Theatre, the symphonic orchestra under Mravinsky and Svetlanov, as well as many other talented musicians successfully made tours to the West to great acclaim. And in Moscow, the International Tchaikovsky Competition has enjoyed great prestige since its inception in 1958.

Despite all these glittering successes, many greatly gifted artists, including the cellist Mstislav Rostropovich, the violinist Gidon

Kremer and the pianist Vladimir Ashkenazy, were forced either to emigrate abroad or defect. Meanwhile, "official" composers continued to churn out leaden operas and orchestral works, and were rewarded for their efforts with trips abroad and privileged lifestyles, while avant-garde composers such as Alfred Schnittke (1934–98), Sofia Gubaidulina, Nikolai Karetnikov (1930–93) and Edison Denisov (1929–96) made a living in the best way they could, knowing that their works could never be performed to the public.

Their music, which represented a defiant and triumphant statement of the values they steadfastly continued to believe in, also faithfully reflected the troubled times in which they lived.

Together with a growing interest in the musical avante-garde, one of the leading figures of this era was Giorgi Sviridova (1915–98) who embodied the national musical traditions. From the 1960s to the 1980s, Sviridov's creative talents were especially prevalent in choir and vocal-symphonic genres.

A new flowering

All this changed when Mikhail Gorbachev came to power in 1985. With *glasnost* came an explosion of Soviet cultural life, as artists and writers were allowed to travel abroad freely, and previously forbidden works were published and performed.

Rostropovich and Ashkenazy both made much-publicised return visits to Russia, concert repertoires widened and Russian music started to become popular in the West.

Today, the St Petersburg school of music is best represented by Galina Ustvolskaya, Lucian Prigozhin (1926–94), Sergei Slonimsky, Boris Tishchenko, Yuri Falik, Alexander Knaifel, and their younger colleagues. Notable musicians from the Moscow school include Boris Tchaikovsky (1925–96), Vyacheslav Artemova, Eduard Artemov, Vladimir Martinov, and the husband-and-wife team of Dmitry Smirnov and Elena Firsova.

Amid the general economic crisis in Russia, which has left musicians, orchestras and musical institutions struggling to survive financially, musical life continues to thrive and is even enjoying a period of revival. The number of symphonic and chamber orchestras has been growing in recent years, and music festivals and competitions have become an inherent part of the music scene. Traditional concert venues are being supplemented by churches, whose warm acoustics and rich decor contribute to the ambiance.

Opera and ballet companies such as the Mariinsky (formerly Kirov) Theatre tour abroad and Russian conductors and musicians are much sought after internationally. All this goes to show that Russia has retained its status as a music superpower. ❑

THE POP-ROCK SCENE

Russian pop music is alive and well despite a preference among the young for Western bands. Improved finance in the music industry and better sound and recording equipment in the 1990s has led to the emergence of a number of world-class acts including Tequilajazz, a hard-rocking trio from St Petersburg. Russian rock legends such as Yuri Shevchuk's DDT, Boris Grebenshikov, Kolibri, and Auktsion perform at home and abroad while Linda, an angst-ridden female singer, tackles social issues ranging from war to drugs. Perhaps the most successful Russian rock group of recent years has been the innovative band, Mummi Troll, from Vladivostok.

LEFT: Mummi Troll, a ground-breaking rock band from Vladivostok.

The Film Makers

Film, said Lenin, was one of the most important tools in forging a socialist society. Indeed, the Soviet Union built up a powerful film industry that was useful in forming the mentality of the new socialist man, as well as providing entertainment in a drab world. Cinemas were built in every town. Cheap tickets and a limited choice of other forms of entertainment meant that large crowds were always assured.

Since the collapse of the Soviet Union, Russian film has struggled to find its bearing amid the new reality. The economic crisis of the 1990s, the drastic decline in state film subsidies, the onslaught of Hollywood, video piracy, and dirty, poorly-maintained cinemas, have resulted in dark days for the Russian film industry and a decline in audiences.

American films are all the rage. Most Russians, while complaining about the pernicious moral influence of Hollywood films, will dismiss new Russian films as "too depressing".

Contemporary directors such as Nikita Mikhalkov, Alexander Sakurov and Alexander Rogozhkin, have adjusted successfully and produced some of the finest works in the history of Russian cinema. Rogozhkin's *Peculiarities of the National Hunt* (1995), a comedy about Russian hunters and the national character, is a rare example of a financial blockbuster.

Mikhalkov's *Burnt by the Sun*, a chilling film about Stalin's purges, won the 1995 Academy Award for Best Foreign Film. Sergei Bodrov's *Prisoner of the Mountains* and Pavel Chukrai's *The Thief* were also nominated in 1996 and 1998 respectively. The former is about Russia's brutal war in Chechnya, while the latter tells the tale of a boy growing up in Russia, in the care of a thief, amid the destruction wrought by World War II.

Despite the economic problems, gaining the freedom to create has indeed been a significant development. Some directors have broken away from the state-owned, former monopoly film studios to create their own, such as the STV Film Studio in St Petersburg and NTV-Profit in Moscow.

Since 1896, when the first film in Russia was shown in St Petersburg's Aquarium Theatre (now a Chinese restaurant) Russian film has been a tale of two cities – Moscow and St Petersburg. The state-owned Lenfilm, founded in 1918, is known for "high cinema" – intellectual and artistic classics, as well as experimental work, in the vein of Alexander Sakurov's acclaimed film *Mother and Son* (1997).

St Petersburg's film industry, however, is in a poor shape compared to its Moscow counterpart. Mosfilm has always produced light-hearted or politicised films, such as the popular comedies of Leonid Gaidai, *Diamond Arm* and *A Woman in Captivity in the Caucasus*. In 1998 it received a boost when the mayor of Moscow, Yuri Luzhkov, donated US$15 million towards film making and another US$5 million for new equipment. St

Petersburg has so far gone without such a sponsor.

The Moscow-based Gorky Film Studio began to make a name for itself at the end of the 1990s with its production of low-budget intellectual movies aimed at young people. St Petersburg's private STV studio has also done much to help young directors. It produced Alexei Balabanov's 1997 hit, *Brother*, a brutal and realistic film about growing up in Russia's criminal world.

Despite the hardships many directors are learning to adjust to Russia's new capitalist reality. "The Soviet film age is over, and a new generation of creative talent has matured," said the late film critic, Sergei Dobrotvorsky, in August 1997. "Money is the key. No money. No film." ❑

RIGHT: the award-winning Russian film *Burnt by the Sun*, directed by Nikita Mikhailkov.

RIDING THE SLOW TRAIN TO VLADIVOSTOK

The Trans-Siberian Railway is one of the epic journeys. It takes over a week to travel its length, and the route lies through Russia's dark heart

A trip across Russia on the Trans-Siberian Railway is more like an ocean voyage than a train ride. The cities of Siberia are strung along the route like islands, and each one is like a new port of call. Half the fun of getting to them lies in the empty stretches between landfall, when you get to know your fellow-travellers.

The Trans-Siberian is also the best way to *feel* the immensity of the Russian hinterland, as for day after day the train ploughs its chugging furrow through dense, dark forest. The journey is perhaps more spectacular in winter, when the snow fields extend to the horizon and the glare from this great unruffled white blanket is blinding. In summer, Siberia is hot and dusty, though the longer days mean there are more hours in which to soak up the view, fewer to spend in your compartment with a pack of cards and a bottle of vodka.

The classic Trans-Siberian route will take you to Vladivostok – "Conqueror of the East" – on Russia's Pacific seaboard. From there it is a short hop in a plane to Japan. But another option is to dip south along the Trans-Mongolian, skirt the shining banks of Lake Baikal, and strike out across the Gobi Desert to China. Either way, at the end of a week you will be a seasoned train-dweller: for days after you will continue to feel the rhythmic hammering of the wheels beneath your feet.

▷ **ALL ABOARD**
Stops are a chance to stretch your legs. But do not stray too far from the train: they do not always stick to the timetable, and have been known to leave early.

▽ **MOVABLE FEAST**
The restaurant cars are of unpredictable quality. Be sure to take plenty of dry and canned food with you, to be on the safe side.

▷ **COACH MAKER**
It is worth making friends with the conductress, who will then keep you supplied with tea and gossip.

MOCKBA

◁ ON TO THE GOBI
This train is branching south through the Gobi Desert to Ulan Baatar. Some trains go through Mongolia and all the way to Beijing.

△ PASSING TRADE
One can often buy food en route. But in hard times shops close when the train arrives, so that travellers do not clean them out.

△ SWING A CAT
Compartments for two are small but cosy. They are neatly designed to convert daily from bedroom to sitting room and back.

▽ END OF THE LINE
Vladivostok is the last stop. Once a closed city, it is now a boom town doing more business with Tokyo than with Moscow.

THE IRON ROAD TO THE EAST

The Trans-Siberian Railway was one of the great engineering projects undertaken during the period of rapid industrialisation under the last two tsars. It was begun in 1890, and its primary purpose was to link European Russia with the new city of Vladivostok, which had been founded only 30 years before, but had grown rapidly into a major port. Like the great railroads of the American West, the Trans-Siberian also had the effect of opening up the land for urban adventurers. All the old towns on its route – Yaroslavl, Yekaterinburg, Krasnoyarsk, Irkutsk, Khabarovsk – grew bigger when they became staging posts along the iron road. The railway was finished in 1905, just in time to serve as a supply line in the Russo-Japanese war. In 1918 it carried the tsar and his family on their last journey to Yekaterinburg. The railway played a military role once again in 1941, when thousands of factories in European Russia were rapidly dismantled and shipped wholesale down the line to Siberia, where they churned out tanks and guns beyond the reach of the advancing Germans.

PLACES

*A detailed guide to the entire country, with principal sites
clearly cross-referenced by number to the maps*

Travel to Russia becomes more exciting each year because of
the greater freedom to explore. Even now that so many of the
former republics such as the Baltics (Estonia, Lithuania and
Latvia) and Asian states have gained their independence, Russia
remains a vast, enigmatic and diverse territory.

The European North, which stretches into the Arctic Circle, is one
of Russia's wildest and most beautiful regions. One of the main
attractions of St Petersburg and the palaces which surround it is the
splendour, principally reflected in the architecture, of the imperial
past. A tour to St Petersburg often takes in the country's capital,
Moscow, as well. The question as to which city is superior has been
hotly debated for more than two centuries and continues to this day
among both Russians and foreigners.

Even though two-thirds of Moscow was burnt by Napoleon in
1812, the city gives us a feel for the age and history of the country
and, with its myriad onion-domed churches, for holy Russia, too.
Equally, with some of its many monuments to Communism intact,
we are made aware of the more recent Soviet past. The city's Rus-
sianness attracts some people as much as St Petersburg's European-
ness attracts others.

The theme of holy Russia continues as one explores the Golden
Ring of churches, kremlins and medieval towns which surrounds
Moscow, and a boat trip on the Volga takes in rural Russia as well as
such towns and cities as Astrakhan along its banks. The mountainous
southern region of the Caucasus, with its spa towns and hot springs,
attracts walkers and climbers alike.

The Ural Mountains mark the boundary between Europe and Asia,
with the forests, lakes and rivers of Siberia extending to the shores
of the Pacific and Arctic oceans. Cutting through Russia, from
Moscow in the west to Vladivostok in the east, is the famous Trans-
Siberian railway.

Belarus and Ukraine are included in this book, because both geographically and culturally they are closely linked with Russia and
they share a common history – Kiev, capital of Ukraine, is where
the traveller will discover the origins of "Rus". Crimea, with its hot
climate and beaches, is still one of the most popular holiday areas for
many Russians, though it is now part of Ukraine.

The dramatic differences between the lands that make up Russia,
Belarus and Ukraine add to their great appeal. You can tailor a visit
to suit your own interests and at last wander freely without an accompanying guide. ❑

PRECEDING PAGES: the Trans-Siberian railway; an effective way to travel in the
northeast; driving across Lake Baikal in winter.
LEFT: Catherine Palace, Pushkin, a present from Peter the Great to his wife.

Russia

0   500 km
0   500 miles

N

Arctic Circle

UNITED KINGDOM

NORTH SEA

Amsterdam
NETHERLANDS

GERMANY
Berlin

DENMARK
København

Praha
POLAND
Warszawa

NORWEGIAN SEA

NORWAY
Oslo
Glittertinden ▲2469

SWEDEN

Stockholm

BALTIC SEA

FINLAND
Helsinki

Nordkapp

Bjørnøya (Norway)

Svalbard (Norway) ▲1712

A R

Zemlya Frantsa-Iosifa

BARENTS SEA

Murmansk

Kolsky poluostrov

Novaya Zemlya

▲1547

KARSKOYE MOR

Tallinn
ESTONIA
Riga
LITHUANIA
Vilnius
Minsk
BELARUS
Smolensk

Sankt Peterburg
Ladozhskoye oz.
Novgorod
Onezhskoye oz.

Solovetskiye ostrova
BELOYE MORE

o. Kolguyev

Arkhangelsk

Severnaya Dvina

o. Vaygach
poluostrov Yamal

Dikson

Gydansky poluostrov

Nori

Vorkuta

G O R Y

Zapadno-

Novy Urengoy

Pura
Taz

Yenisey

2665
Carpathian Mts.

Kyiv
MOLDOVA
Chişinău
Odesa
UKRAINE
Kharkiv

Moskva
Yaroslavl
Volga
Vologda
Nizhny Novgorod
Voronezh
Don
Ulyanovsk
Saratov

Kirov

Kazan
Perm
Kama
Samara
Ufa
g. Yamantau ▲1640

Vostochno-

Yevropeyskaya

ravnina

Syktyvkar

g. Narodnaya ▲1895

Pechora

Nyagan

Yekaterinburg

Ob

Surgut

Sibirskaya

RUSSIA

ravnina

Tomsk

Krymsky pivostriv
Rostov-na-Donu
Krasnodar
BLACK SEA
Sochi

g. Elbrus ▲5642
GEORGIA
Tbilisi
TURKEY
Yerevan
ARMENIA
Büyük Ağrı dağı ▲51
AZERBAIJAN
Baky

SYRIA
Al-Mawşil
Tabrīz
IRAQ
Baghdād
Tehrān

Volgograd
Don
Ural'sk
Orenburg
Astrakhan
Aktyubinsk

Tyumen
Chelyabinsk
Kustanay

Omsk

Novosibirsk

Kemero

Novokuznet

Ishim
Irtysh

Barnaul

Altay

g. Belukha ▲4506

Ch

CASPIAN SEA

plato Ustyurt

ARAL SEA

KAZAKHSTAN

Astana

Karaganda

Semipalatinsk
Aksoran ▲1565

Balkash

Syrdarya

Turkmenbashi
Nukus
Kyzylkum
TURKMENISTAN
Karakumy
Ashgabat
5604
Qolleh-ye Demāvand
3117
Mashhad

Kzyl-Orda
Amudarya
UZBEKISTAN
Samarkand
Dushanbe
TAJIKISTAN
g.Garmo ▲7495
Kashi

Chu
Ile
Bishkek
Tashkent
KYRGYZSTAN
pik Pobedy ▲7439
PAMIR
7708

Almaty
Ystyk-köl

TIEN SHAN

Ürümqi

Lop n

SYRIA
IRAN
Al-Mawşil
IRAQ
Baghdād
Al-Başrah
KUWAIT
Al-Kuwayt

Kühhā-ye Zagros
4548
Esfahān
Yazd
Shīrāz

Tigris / Al-Furāt
Dijlah

Kühhā-ye
Elburz
IRAN
AFGHANISTAN
Herat
HINDU KUSH

Takla Makan

6161

IC OCEAN

CHUKCHI
SEA

USA

mys Dezhneva
Bering Strait

**Chukotsky
poluostrov**

o. Vrangelya

St Lawrence

VOSTOCHNO-
SIBIRSKOYE
MORE

Pevek

Anadyrsky
zaliv

BERING

Anadyr

SEA

1785

Severnaya
Zemlya

Novosibirskiye
ostrova

MORE
LAPTEVYKH

mys Chelyuskin

1146

Koryakskoye nagore

2562

Kolymskoye nagore

Indigirka

Kolyma

Anadyr

o. Karaginsky

Komandorskiye
ostrova

Sredinny khrebet

oluostrov
Taymyr
Taymyr

Tiksi

Verkhoyansky

Khatanga

Yana

g. Pobeda
▲ 3003

khrebet Cherskogo

zaliv
Shelikhova

4688
Vlk. Klyuchevskaya
Sopka

Verkhoyansk

2389

Lena

khrebet

Magadan

S r e d n e -

g. Kamen
▲ 1664

Aldan

Vilyuy

Amga

**poluostrov
Kamchatka**

Petropavlovsk-
Kamchatsky

Yakutsk

s i b i r s k o y e

Mirny

Aldan

o. Iony

m. Lopatka

SEA OF OKHOTSK

loskogore

nnaya Tunguska

kamennaya Tunguska

Lena

Vitim

2255

Stanovoy khrebet

Shantarskiye
ostrova

Kurilskiye ostrova

Angara

3072

S t a n o v o y e

Tynda

n a g o r e

Zeya

Komsomolsk-
na-Amure

o. Sakhalin

1609

Amur

Bratsk

Shilka

Da Hinggan ling

Amur

2090

Tatarsky proliv

Yuzhno-
Sakhalinsk

Krasnoyarsk

Chita

Khabarovsk

oz. Baykal

Blagoveshchensk

Argun

Sikhote-Alin

Irkutsk

Ulan-Ude

Hailar

Yichun

g. Munku-Sardyk
3491

Selenga

Qiqihar

Songhua jiang

Ussuri

2290

Hokkaidō

isey

y a n

Kerulen

oz. Khanka

Nakhodka

Sapporo

2800

Harbin

Vladivostok

Ulaan Baatar

Changchun

2750

Paektu-san

SEA OF JAPAN

Sendai

Changajn Nuruu

ajn Nuruu

2034 ▲

Shenyang

NORTH
KOREA

JAPAN

Honshū

Fuji-san
3776

Tōkyō

M O N G O L I A

P'yongyang

Nagoya

G O B I

Baotou

Sŏul

Osaka

CHINA

Beijing

Lüda

SOUTH
KOREA

6305 ▲

Tianjin

Pusan

Shikoku

Kitakyūshū

Yinchuan

Shijiazhuang

Huang he

Jinan

Qingdao

YELLOW
SEA

Kyūshū

Moscow

0 _____ 500 m
0 _____ 500 yds

MOSCOW

*Russia's capital invites exploration. Domed cathedrals,
baroque palaces and soaring Soviet edifices compete for attention
amid the bustle of modern European city life*

Map on page 142

Moscow's first mention in historic chronicles is a brief note in an annal written in 1147 indicating that there was a small settlement surrounded by small hills on the banks of the Moskva River. Such limited mention is not surprising: Moscow lay on the extreme borders of the Suzdal Knyazhestvo (principality), the centre of which was far to the southwest in Kiev. When Prince Yuri Dolgoruky arrived in 1156, Moscow must have been no more than a cluster of wooden huts. However, he saw its potential as an outpost against the Tatar Golden Horde and ordered a kremlin (fortification) to be built.

Historians believe the name Moskva derives from an old Slavonic word meaning "wet", probably an allusion to the marshy countryside that surrounded the site. The broad Moskva River winds through the city and used to be swelled by a number of smaller streams and rivers, so the site was ideal for a fortress. However, the Tatars still torched it at regular intervals, even after Grand Prince Ivan Kalita ("Moneybags") built stone walls around the settlement in the early 14th century. The walls were white-washed and earned Moscow the name "belokamennaya" (literally white-stone).

As Ivan Kalita's power and prestige grew, so did Moscow. But his real coup was managing to persuade the Russian Metropolitan to move the Holy See from Kiev to Moscow. As chief centre of both religious and secular power, Moscow was on the map. The city blossomed during the reign of Ivan III (the Great), in the mid-15th century. Ivan dealt with the Tatars effectively and was the first prince to take the title "tsar", the Russianised form of Caesar. To match his new status, he imported Italian architects to create a new kremlin. Many of the cathedrals and the walls they built still stand.

PRECEDING PAGES: Moskva River and the Kremlin. **LEFT:** St Basil's Cathedral. **BELOW:** monument to the worker and the woman collective farmer.

The Kremlin

When the Italian architects Fioravanti, Ruffo and Solari had finished their job in 1495, praise was effusive and another "eighth wonder of the world" was added to that already lengthy list. But the accolade was not entirely undeserved. The imposing red-brick walls running around the **Kremlin** ❶ are 2,230 metres (7,316 ft) long, 20 metres (65 ft) high and 6 metres (20 ft) wide in some places. It has four gates and 19 towers. Inside, the Italians created three stone cathedrals to replace the humble wooden structures that had existed. These came to symbolise tsarist power: the Uspensky was used for coronations, the Blagoveshchensky for baptisms and weddings, and the Arkhangelsky for funerals.

The main entrance for visitors (open 10am–5pm) is the **Troitskaya Bashnya** (Trinity Tower) ❷ that

Central Moscow

0   500 m

0   500 yds

crosses Alexandrovsky Gardens and the Neglinka River (which was channelled into a large stone underground pipe on the orders of Catherine II in the 18th century). In pre-Revolutionary times this gate was used for regal entrances. Napoleon, in 1812, obviously didn't know this – although his army entered the Kremlin this way, he used the **Spasskaya Vorota** (Spassky Gate) ❸. He is supposed to have lost his famous tricorn hat in the process, making it unlucky, according to popular lore, to pass through the Spassky Tower wearing a hat.

At one time the Kremlin was considered almost impregnable. Its southeastern side is protected by the Moskva, and a deep moat, which once linked the Moskva and Neglinka rivers, takes care of the remaining walls. The **Arsenalnaya Bashnya** (Arsenal Tower) had its own well which fed a secret reservoir and an underground passage to the Neglinka River. During long sieges, the garrison could thus come and go as they pleased.

Although the Russian tricolour now flutters above the Kremlin, the symbols of Soviet power are still apparent in the red stars topping five of the towers. These have been there so long (since 1937) that most Muscovites don't feel strongly about their removal. But there is one Soviet eyesore that still makes Muscovite blood boil – the steel and glass **Dvorets Syezdov** (Palace of Congresses) ❹ that was planted in the middle of the Kremlin in 1961. (The architect, Mikhail Posokhin, is also responsible for the soulless Novy Arbat, formerly Kalininsky Prospect.)

Several ancient monasteries inside the Kremlin walls were demolished in Soviet times, but the complex retains its ancient beauty. The former **Arsenal** ❺ buildings were constructed by Peter the Great between 1701 and 1736 and its facades are hung with Napoleonic military trophies. The **Oruzheinaya Palata**

Trams, buses and trolleybuses operate from 6am to 11.30pm. You'll need a talon (ticket), obtainable in strips from street kiosks.

BELOW: the Kremlin Cathedral.

The Cap of Kazan, made for Ivan the Terrible in the 16th century to mark his victory over the Tatars in Kazan, features in the Armoury Museum collection.

BÈLOW: Kremlin's Gate Tower.

(State Armoury) **❻** at the foot of the **Borovitsky Bashnya** (Tower) houses the oldest Kremlin museum. It has armour, but pride of place goes to the valuables accumulated by the Russian aristocracy, in particular diamonds and jewellery.

The three original cathedrals still dominate the heart of the Kremlin, with the grandiose **Uspensky Sobor** (Cathedral of the Assumption) **❼**, built by Fioravanti, as centrepiece. This is a prime example of European Renaissance building combined with Byzantine traditions. Inside is a remarkable collection of frescoes devoted mainly to the Virgin, in addition to the famous 14th-century Trinity icon. It is here that the city's bishops and patriarchs were interred.

To the south is the contemporary **Blagoveshchensky Sobor** (Cathedral of the Annunciation) **❽**, which was built as a private church for Moscow's Grand Princes. The cathedral started life as a three-domed, galleried building in the Pskov style (Ivan III had opted for Russian rather than foreign stonemasons for this particular project). As this was essentially a private church, the builders set it on a very high foundation so that its entrance would be accessible from the second floor of the royal palace. Ivan the Terrible thought the cathedral should be more imposing, so he ordered the addition of four small chapels surmounted by a cross and cupola. The result matched Ivan's nickname, so two more domes were added to restore the building's balance.

The Annunciation is generally regarded as superior to the other early cathedrals. Built on the site of a wooden structure of the same name, it inherited the original church's iconostasis, painted by two of the greatest names in Russian iconography: Feofan the Greek and Andrei Rublyov. Its floor is tiled with agate and jasper, a gift from the Shah of Persia. Portraits of the Grand Princes hang alongside biblical fathers and Greek and Roman luminaries such as Aristotle, Plutarch and Virgil: doubtless an attempt by the princes to portray themselves as enlightened rulers.

Next to the Annunciation is the **Arkhangelsky Sobor** (Archangel Cathedral) **❾**, built in the early years of 16th century by Venetian architect Alevisio, nicknamed Novy (the new), because an Italian of the same name had worked in Moscow before him. It was here that the princes and tsars were buried until Peter the Great built his new capital in 1712. Portraits of dead aristocrats watch over the bronze sarcophagi containing their remains.

The Kremlin's focal point is the **Kolokolnya Ivana Velikogo** (Bell Tower of Ivan the Great) **❿**. Started by Ivan, it was augmented by Boris Godunov. Some said he undertook the building work as a penance for murdering Prince Dmitry, the legitimate heir to the throne. Although Boris had been elected tsar, many people saw him as an upstart: they must have been delighted to see the bell tower grow shakier the taller it rose – like the tsar's hold on power. But it survived and is still the tallest structure in the Kremlin. It carries the inscription: "By the grace of the Holy Trinity and by order of the Tsar and Grand Prince Boris Fyodorovich, Autocrat of all Russia, this temple was finished and gilded in the second year of their reign."

Ivan III was a prolific builder. The **Granovitaya Palata** (Palace of the Facets) **⓫** is perhaps the most fabulous of the secular buildings he initiated. Unlike any other structure in Moscow, the palace is a pure example of Italian Renaissance architecture, designed by Ruffo and Solari. It was here that the tsars received foreign ambassadors and other dignitaries and the whole place was decorated as a showpiece. The frescoes are painted on backgrounds of gold, and you'll even find a portrait of Ivan the Terrible in the guise of the "Just Knight" in the Hall of Facets.

These are the oldest buildings in the Kremlin, but over the centuries myriad others have been erected between them. Until the modern Palace of Congresses was built, the most recent was the **Bolshoi Kremlyovsky Dvorets** (Great Kremlin Palace) ⑫ built by Konstantin Thon, architect of the Cathedral of Christ the Saviour. Just in front is the spectacular **Teremnoy Dvorets** (Terem or Belvedere Palace) ⑬ now only accessible through the Great Kremlin Palace. Built along the lines of traditional wooden houses, it was first occupied by Mikhail Romanov's family.

The first of his line, Mikhail (1613–45), and later his son Alexis, used this palace to conduct state affairs. It was meant to convey the power and unity of the Russian state so the interiors are lavish to say the least. Before becoming tsars of Russia, the Romanovs were just one of many noble families. Young Mikhail was elected tsar by a council of all Russia following a long period of popular unrest and occupation by the Poles. The Poles were finally driven out in 1612 by a patriotic army that rallied to Russia's banner at the religious settlement founded by St Sergius just outside Moscow. Led by Prince Pozharsky and organised by a patriotic merchant called Minin from Nizhny Novgorod, the national army advanced on the capital and forced the Poles and the pretender they had put on the throne to flee. Pozharsky and Minin were immortalised in bronze in 1818; their statue stands outside the entrance to St Basil's Cathedral on Red Square.

Tucked between the Uspensky and Palace of the Facets is the tiny **Tserkov Rizopolozheniya** (Church of the Deposition of the Robe) ⑭, commissioned by Patriarch Geronty in 1480 to commemorate an argument with Ivan III about whether a church procession should follow the course of the sun or vice versa. The religious leader threatened to resign if Ivan didn't admit he was wrong. The Grand Prince finally gave in and the church was built by masons from Pskov (Geronty wasn't having any of the new-fangled Italian-style architecture in vogue in Moscow at that time). Initially, the church served as a private chapel for the Russian patriarchs, but it was requisitioned by the Romanovs for their own use in 1653.

The eastern side of the Kremlin is reserved for government buildings. The main structure is late 18th-century and was designed by Matvei Kazakov for the Moscow Department of the Senate, which was then located in St Petersburg. After the Revolution, Moscow became the capital and the top floor of the **Senatskaya** ⑮ was used by Lenin as an apartment building from 1918 to 1923.

Although the buildings inside the Kremlin are the main attractions, some of the 20 towers that line the walls are worth mentioning. The oldest, **Taynitskaya Bashnya** (Tower of Secrets) ⑯ in the southern wall,

Map on page 142

TIP

The best time to visit Moscow is during the summer months of May to August when the temperature is around 18°C (62°F) and can rise to 30°C (86°F). In the snowy winter the temperature can fall as low as −30°C (−22°F)

BELOW: Tsar Bell on display outside the Bell Tower of Ivan the Great.

An eternal flame burns on the Tomb of the Unknown Soldier in the Alexandrovsky Gardens along the west wall of the Kremlin.

BELOW: two of the city's war heroes.

has fascinated scholars for centuries. It has an underground passage to the river, but it is also thought to have been the site of Ivan the Terrible's famous library. The collection was started by his grandmother, Sofia Paleologue, who brought a wealth of manuscripts to Moscow as part of her dowry. Some believe the library is still hidden beneath the Kremlin walls, probably under the Arsenal Tower overlooking the Alexandrovsky Gardens. A Russian scholar thought he had found it in 1934 but Stalin ordered him to stop searching.

Another of the towers that shouldn't be missed is the **Spasskaya Bashnya** (Spassky Tower) located by the Spasskaya Vorota. Built in 1625, its Gothic and Renaissance splendour served as a fitting background for the state entrances of the tsars. In the 20th century, the guard of honour for Lenin's mausoleum passed through here on the choreographed march to the revolutionary's tomb.

Red Square

Touching the wall as you leave the Kremlin is supposed to bring you luck and ensure your return. **Krasnaya Ploshchad** (Red Square) **17** adjoins the eastern side of the Kremlin, but to get there you'll have to leave the Kremlin through the Trinity Gate and walk round as only top brass are allowed to use the Saviour's Gate on the square itself. Walk through **Alexandrovsky Gardens**, with its old lime trees and remarkable 19th-century grotto in the Kremlin's wall, past the **Mogila Neizvestnogo Soldata** (Tomb of the Unknown Soldier) **18** – still a popular spot for wedding pictures – and turn right. The ketchup-coloured building on your left is the city's **Gosudarstvenny Istorichesky Muzei** (Historical Museum) **19**, which houses a rare collection of artefacts and traces Russian history right up to the present day (open 11am–5pm; closed Sun, Mon).

Red Square started life as the eastern moat protecting the Kremlin, but this was eventually filled in and the resulting square was cobbled in the 15th century. For much of its history the square was crammed to bursting point with wooden galleries of market stalls where merchants from all over the world set up shop. The whole place formed a major fire hazard and the Great Fire of Moscow that destroyed much of the old city in 1737 started here.

The **Mavzolei Lenina** (Lenin Mausoleum) ❷⓪, which partially obscures the red Kremlin wall, still houses the great man's embalmed body, but people no longer queue for hours to see the waxen features. The building itself was designed by Shchusev in 1930 and replaced a wooden structure built just after Lenin's death.

The area of the Kremlin wall between the Nikolskaya and Senatskaya Towers is the burial place of top Soviet statesmen, public figures and military leaders. Here lie such names as Maxim Gorky, Lenin's wife, Nadezhda Krupskaya, spaceman Yuri Gagarin, nuclear physicist Igor Kurchatov, and John Reed, the American journalist whose book on the birth and early years of the Russian Revolution, *Ten Days That Shook the World*, was a revelation to subsequent generations of Marxists throughout the Western world. It describes Western governments' attempts to undermine and destroy the Revolution, and until the 1960s seemed to explain and even justify the burgeoning paranoia and suspicion of the young Soviet state.

Sobor Vasiliya Blazhennogo (St Basil's Cathedral) ❷① is to Moscow what the Eiffel Tower is to Paris, or Big Ben is to London. It is essentially Muscovite. There is a story that Ivan the Terrible had the architects blinded so they could not build anything like it again. Ivan shaped Red Square and much of old

Map on page 142

BELOW: Historical Museum from Maneznaya Square.

The 40-ton bronze Tsar Cannon was cast in a Moscow foundry in 1586. The biggest cannon in the world, it was once positioned in Red Square to repel enemy attacks, but never fired a shot.

Moscow. He built St Basil's, more properly known as the Pokrovsky Sobor (Cathedral of the Veil), to commemorate major victories over the Tatars. Every victory (nine in all) added a new chapel to the structure, each one dedicated to the saint on whose day the victory was won. The whole golden-domed complex became known as St Basil's when one of the chapels was dedicated to Basil the Blessed, a holy man who predicted that Ivan would murder his first-born.

In the 17th century Red Square became a centre of political debate and was the venue for many popular uprisings. The **Lobnoye Mesto** (a raised circular platform in front of the cathedral) was used for religious services and for reading tsarist decrees. The square served also as a place of execution (it is said that as a child Ivan the Terrible had a small wooden tower built on top of the Spasskaya Tower so he could watch beheadings in private). Later the leader of the 1671 peasant revolt, Stenka Razin, was executed here and in 1648 the Streltsy mutineers and supporters of Tsarina Sofia, Peter the Great's half-sister, also met their deaths on Red Square.

It's hard to judge just how the wooden city of Moscow looked because Muscovites put it to the torch in order to frustrate the imminent arrival of Napoleon and his troops in 1812. By the time Napoleon arrived he found the buildings in flames and anybody who was anybody, and a lot who weren't, gone.

In retrospect, you could say Moscow should be grateful to Napoleon. The reconstruction transformed the city from a medieval warren of small alleys and streets into an elegant capital whose main streets and quarters were dominated by stylish mansions and buildings. In charge of the massive project was an architect called Osip Bovet. He restored the kremlin wall and rebuilt the shopping galleries that lined the eastern side of Red Square. These were later replaced

BELOW: wedding party visits the Tomb of the Unknown Soldier at the Kremlin.

by the still magnificent **GUM** building, with its pastel interiors and ornate fountain. GUM opened in 1893, was nationalised in 1921 and celebrated its centenary by returning to the private sector following an auction of the retail units that make up what was once the most up-market shopping mall in Russia.

In the late 19th century another red-brick building was added to the northern end of Red Square, just opposite the Historical Museum. It housed the city's Duma or council until the Revolution. After Lenin's death it became a museum devoted to the father of the country and housed the city legislature, both of which have now moved to other locations.

On Manezhnaya Sqaure, just off to the right of Red Square, is the newly restored **Voskresenskiye Vorota** (Resurrection Gate) with a tiny chapel. The gate was pulled down by Stalin to make way for tanks that used to roll across Red Square on revolutionary holidays. Next to the gate is the **statue of Marshal Georgy Zhukov**, who led the Soviet Army to victory over Germany in 1945.

A street by any other name

The Kremlin and Red Square may have been the heart of the original city, but its arteries were the old quarters that clustered around them. The city was built in rings, with main roads to important towns, such as Smolensk, Tver and Kaluga, radiating in a wagon-wheel pattern that still exists today. Not surprisingly, these roads became major thoroughfares and until the Revolution were simply named after the places they led to. Since 1917 they have had different names – Kalininsky Prospekt (now Novy Arbat), Ulitsa Gorkogo (now Tverskaya) and Leninsky Prospekt respectively. In day-to-day speech and on street signs most of them have reverted back to their original names. Other street

Map on page 142

The name "Red" Square was a happy coincidence when the Bolsheviks came to power in 1917. In old Russian the word "red" also means beautiful and this is the source of the square's name.

BELOW: GUM, Moscow's famous shopping mall.

names are clues to the trades and businesses once conducted there, e.g. Meshchanskaya (petty bourgeois street), Zhivoderka (abattoir road) or are derived from a monastery or church.

The Kremlin formed the central ring, followed by the former **Kitai-Gorod wall** which bordered the Kremlin to the northeast. The wall was 2.5 km (4 miles) long and had 12 towers and several gates. Built in the mid-16th century around the original market-place, its name derives from the Mongolian word for "middle", i.e. middle fortress. It is thought that Ivan the Terrible's mother, Elena Glinskaya, first coined the name – she came from a place called Kitai-Gorod in Poland. These walls have not survived, but remains can be seen on Teatralnaya Ploshchad, close to the Metropol Hotel, and on Kitaisky Prospekt in Zaryadye.

The third ring accounts for Moscow's reputation as the "white city". These walls ran 9 km (5 miles) along what is now the **Bulvarnoye Koltso** (Boulevard Ring), had 10 gates and 17 blind towers, and were built of white stone. They were constructed in the early 16th century and served as a sturdy defence for the outskirts of Moscow until they were demolished in the late 18th century.

The final ring, **Zemlyanoi Val** (Earthern Wall), was constructed at the end of the 16th century and was really a rampart. Two hundred years later it was replaced by gardens which gave their name to a whole area: the **Sadovoye Koltso** (Garden Ring) follows the course of the original ramparts.

Merchants of Moscow

Many of the old streets of Kitai-Gorod lost a lot of their original charm at the same time. This was one of Moscow's liveliest quarters and runs due east from the north end of Red Square. **Nikolskaya** (formerly October 25 St) was known

BELOW: fashionable dressing.

SUBTERRANEAN MOSCOW

Moscow has a secret which, *glasnost* notwithstanding, the Kremlin says nothing about: an underground city with one section beneath the suburb of Ramenki about 6 km (4 miles) southwest of Red Square. It is designed to accommodate 30,000 party élite and their families for as long as 30 years in the event of a nuclear war. Ivan the Terrible laid the foundations of subterranean Moscow to give his *oprichniki* militia secret access from his palace to various parts of the city. The KGB, successor to the *oprichniki*, built a tunnel to ferry prisoners from prison to their headquarters.

But these efforts were nothing compared to the refinements of Leonid Brezhnev in the 1960s and 1970s. The Ramenki complex was built on several levels over 200 hectares (500 acres) with streets wide enough to take cars. It has its own metro linking it to central Moscow and Vnukovo airport. There are cinemas and swimming pools, and warehouses filled with food. As for the old jest about Moscow's "wedding-cake" ministry buildings being perilously close to the breaking strain of the earth's crust, it seems that they are almost as deep underground as they are tall, and each has its own stop on the private "Metro 2" and other concealed links with the underground warren.

as the "street of enlightenment" as the city's first higher education facility, the Slavonic-Greek-Latin Academy, was located at Nos 7–9. Further up the street on the same side is a magnificent Russian Gothic building with a sundial adorning its facade. Built in 1814 as the Orthodox Synod's printing house, it printed the first books in Russian. Today, it is the History and Archives Institute.

Turning right into **Bogoyavlensky Pereulok** you'll see the magnificent **Bogoyavlensky Sobor** (the Church of the Manifestation) ❷❸ on your right, parts of which are 13th-century, but whose main facade is a typical example of 17th-century Moscow baroque. It was founded in 1290 by Prince Daniel Nevsky, the same man who built a string of fortified monasteries, including the Danilov, around the city. Ilyinka used to be the Moscow equivalent of Wall Street, but during the Soviet era the bank buildings and the Mercantile Exchange (at No. 6) were confiscated and turned into public offices – the Exchange became the Soviet Chamber of Commerce and Industry. Contemporary photographs show a lively commercial street cluttered with bright advertisements. Today it's all rather grey.

If you go right into **Ilyinka** (formerly Kuibyshevskiy) Ulitsa and left into **Khrustalny Pereulok** (Crystal Alley) at the exchange corner you'll see the **Gostiny Dvor** (Old Merchant Arcade) ❷❹, another of the city's famous shopping arcades. When it was completed in 1805 by the Italian architect Quarenghi it was considered a major accomplishment. Its elegant, white Corinthian pillars still retain their original magic. The building, which was warehouse space for decades, is now being restored to its original glamour. Some stores have already opened on the side facing Ilyinka, and if you can gain entrance, check out the magnificent open arcade on the opposite side and imagine how it must have

Map
on page
142

Moscow has several colourful food markets (rynky). Tsentralny Rynok (Central Market) is on Tsvetnoy Bulvar.

BELOW: the White House, Russia's government building.

The Mayakovsky Museum, Myasnit-skaya Ulitsa 3–6, is devoted to the life of the poet Vladimir Mayakovsky, who worked here before his suicide in 1930 (open Mon–Thur noon–8pm; Tues, Fri–Sun, 10am–6pm; closed Mon).

BELOW: checking out the pet market.

looked when it was home to the most exclusive and chic boutiques in town.

At the south end of Khrustalny turn into **Varvarka** (formerly Razin Street). Ironically, the revolutionary name given to this once exclusive street of nobles and wealthy merchants' homes was that of the Cossack rebel Stenka Razin. Little remains of the old street. Around 20 tiny churches and a number of houses were demolished to make way for the staggering **Rossiya Hotel ㉕** complex, reputed to be the biggest in the world with more than 5,000 rooms. But a stretch of the old Kitai-Gorod wall is still extant, along with the small **Tserkov Zachatiya Anny** (Church of the Conception of St Anne) ㉖, which was built at the time of Columbus's voyage to America.

To the right you'll see the Vasilievsky Slope running down to the **Bolshoy Moskvoretsky Most** (Bridge), which German teenager Matthias Rust used as a landing strip on his extraordinary flight to Moscow in the mid-1980s. The world held its breath when it was revealed that a teenager in a light plane had managed to dodge Soviet radar. As detente was well established and the Cold War beginning to thaw, most people thought Rust would be sent home with a slapped wrist. In the event, the Soviets imprisoned him for a short period before quietly letting him go home – on a scheduled flight, of course.

The humble-looking white-stone, wooden-roofed building (No. 8) was once the English embassy. It was presented to English merchants by Ivan the Terrible in the mid-16th century when the tsar was considering marriage to Queen Elizabeth I of England. The building was restored in the 1970s. Next door is the **Znamensky Monastyr** (Monastery of the Sign), with its five domes. Started in 1684, the belfry was added in 1789 and today the second floor is used as a venue for classical and religious music concerts. The building beside it (No. 10)

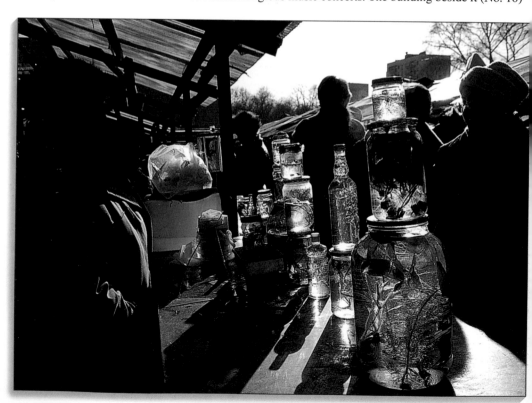

was the home of Mikhail Romanov, the first tsar of the dynasty which ruled Russia for more than three centuries. The house had fallen into disrepair, but in the late 19th century it was restored; only the ground floor is original. Now a museum, the **Muzei Palaty v Zaryadie** ㉗ (open 10am–5pm; closed Tues), it shows how the Russian nobility lived. The interiors are stunning .

Slavyanskaya Ploshchad runs northwest and if you cross it at its southern end you turn right onto **Ulitsa Solyanka** (Salt Street). For centuries, this eastern quarter was the centre of the artisans' guilds and it became notorious in the 19th century for prostitutes, brothels and criminals. The central marketplace at the top of **Podkolokolny Pereulok** was known as the Khitrovo and the pickpockets who thrived there were said to be so clever that they once stole a bronze cannon from the grounds of the Kremlin. To escape public disgrace, the Governor-General of Moscow ordered his men to find the cannon at all costs. As usual, the local police set up a meeting with the criminal bosses and the cannon was back in its place next day. But there's a twist to the tale. It was discovered that the returned cannon had itself been stolen from the opposite side of the Kremlin wall; the first cannon was never recovered.

You can easily spend a couple of hours in this picturesque quarter which is bordered by the Yauza River whose embankment makes a pleasant walk up to the **Yauza Boulevard**, the starting point of the Boulevard Ring. Solyanka and the main thoroughfares in the vicinity were popular residential streets for the nobility. Most of their mansion homes have either disappeared or have been turned into institutes or academies. The former home of the Naryshkin family at 14a is now the Obstetrics Institute. Peter the Great's mother was a Naryshkin and the family liked to remind everyone of its royal connections, so the palace

Map on page 142

BELOW: painting eggs for Easter.

they built (all gone now) had more than its share of pomp and circumstance. The Court of Wards erected in the 1820s and the 18th-century Foundling Hospital at Nos 14 and 16 are now the buildings of the Academy of Medical Science. Solyanka runs into Yauzskaya and ends up in **Taganskaya** (formerly Internatsionalnaya Ulitsa). Worth seeing is the former **Batashova Dvorets** (Palace) ㉘ at No. 1, another aristocratic legacy. Now the 23rd City Hospital, the palatial building set back off the street in its own landscaped gardens is a real jewel.

On Slavyanskaya Ploshchad, you could opt to walk up Lubyansky Proyezd and turn right onto **Ulitsa Maroseika** (formerly Bogdan Khmelnitsky Street). To your left in the central garden you'll see the **monument to the Grenadiers** killed at the battle of Plevna during the Russo-Turkish War in 1887. At the top of the square is the **Politekhnichesky Muzei** (Polytechnic Museum) ㉙, which was built between 1874 and 1907. It houses more than 40,000 exhibits tracing the development of Russian technology and science (open 10am–5pm; closed Mon and last Thurs in month).

On **Novaya Ploshchad** to the left of the museum is a former Baptist church (No. 12) which is now the **Muzei Istorii i Rekonstruktsii Moskvy** (Museum of the History and Reconstruction of Moscow) ㉚ (open 10am–5.30pm; Wed, Fri, noon–7.30pm; closed Mon and last day of month). The museum charts the changes in the city since 1812.

The old embassy quarter

A walk along Ulitsa Maroseika, which runs into Pokrovka (formerly Chernishevsky), takes you into the old embassy quarter. A lot of embassies can still be found here and in the area around **Chistiye Prudy** (Clean Ponds). Like most old cities, certain quarters of Moscow came to be associated with particular nationalities. In Ivan the Terrible's day, much of the land behind the Clean Ponds was owned by German merchants. To the northwest, the French set up shops in the streets around Markhlevskogo and Malaya Lubyanka; the English and Poles gravitated to Myasnitskaya (Kirov) Street between Markhlevskogo and Chistiye Prudy. By the end of the 17th century, Moscow's wealthy boyars had bought up much of the land and built superb palaces.

A cluster of noble dynasties dominated the area – the Dolgoruky family lived on Kolpachny Pereulok 1, the Lopukhins at Starosadsky 5, and the Botkins at Petroverigsky Pereulok 4 – all to the southwest of Chistiye Prudy. Their grand palaces are overshadowed by the splendid **Tserkov Arkhangela Gavriila** (Church of the Archangel Gabriel) ㉛ on Telegrafny Lane. Grand Prince Menshikov had the church built in the early 18th century and the tower still bears his name. Menshikov's aim was to top the Kremlin Bell Tower. It was the tallest building in Moscow and an old tsarist decree prevented the erection of anything higher. The Grand Prince was something of a favourite with Peter the Great, but when the tower was struck by lightning in 1722 no one lifted a finger to put out the ensuing fire which consumed the giant bronze statue of Gabriel mounted on top. The disaster

BELOW: a quiet moment at the church of the Archangel Gabriel.

on top. The disaster was seen as a sign of God's displeasure with the tsar's favourite. Muscovites had good reason to be angry with the tsar – he had moved the capital to St Petersburg some years earlier, relegating Moscow to provincial status. Another church worth seeing is **Tserkov Svyatovo Lyudovika** (St Ludovic's) **32** (Lubyanka Malaya 12). It's a working Catholic church founded by the French in the early 19th century.

Map on page 142

Myasnitskaya to Lubyanka

The corner of Myasnitskaya (formerly Kirov) Ulitsa and the newly named Chistiye Prudy (formerly Kirov) Ploshchad is dominated by what remains of the grand **Yushkov Dvorets** (Palace) **33**, built in the late 18th century by architect Vasily Bazhenov, when most of the boyars had become interested in philanthropy and art collections. The Yushkov family were famous for their balls. It is said that one Yushkov scion held a soirée that lasted three days – it ended only when the whole district had become disrupted by the crowds that had come to gape at the fireworks, music and the gorgeously dressed guests. From 1844 until recently the Yushkov Palace housed the Academy of Art and Sculpture.

The imposing Polytechnic Museum is devoted to technological advances in such fields as mining, electronics and space travel.

Next door is an amazing looking building that was constructed in the late 19th century for the tea-merchant Perlov. He was hoping to entertain the Chinese emperor's ambassador during Nicholas II's coronation celebrations so the classical three-storey house-cum-tea-shop was topped by a Chinese pagoda. The envoy never turned up, but the pagoda still graces the roof. Today, the shop sells tea from Georgia among a variety of brands.

A statue of Felix Dzerzhinsky, Lenin's closest associate and founder of the KGB, once cast a stony stare over Moscow's citizens in Lubyanskaya Ploshchad.

BELOW: Moscow's majestic Metro.

It was one of the first to go following the unsuccessful coup against Mikhail Gorbachev and his reformers in 1991. The busy square now has its old name back, although it also has some creepy connotations. **Lubyanka Prison ③** in the notorious KGB headquarters on the northeast side of the square can still send shivers up spines. It seems an odd location for the city's biggest children's store, but **Detsky Mir ③** is almost next door. It was built on the site of the Moscow foundry which in the 1580s produced the bronze Tsar Cannon now on display in the Kremlin.

The city's shopping centre

If you walk westwards down Ulitsa Okhotny Ryad (formerly Marx Prospekt) you'll come to **Neglinnaya Ulitsa**, the first street of the city's main shopping centre. Neglinnaya takes its name from the river which used to flow down to the Moskva on this site but has long since been channelled deep underground. The area became a mecca for shoppers in the last century when it was noted for its French fashion stores. Russia's first department store (now **TsUM**) was built in the late 19th century on **Ulitsa Petrovka** behind the Maly Teatr.

Nearby, on 1st Neglinny Pereulok, are the **Sandunovskie Bani**, the oldest public baths in the city. Built for a wealthy boyar's courtesans, they are elaborate. Taking a bath in Russia is a social event (although they don't go in for mixed bathing) and traditionally you would drink *kvas*, a home-brewed non-alcoholic drink resembling root beer, while steaming yourself clean.

At Trubnaya Ploshchad (Pipe Square), Neglinnaya crosses the Boulevard Ring and runs into **Tsvetnoi** (Flower) **Boulevard**, now famous for its excellent, though expensive, **Tsentralny Farmers' Market ③**. In the old days, its park

BELOW: a bouquet from the flower-seller.
RIGHT: the Bolshoi Theatre.

Map on page 142

TIP

When in the vicinity of TsUM, check out Petrovka 38, an imposing classical building that has housed the Moscow police department since the Revolution.

was best known as a shelter for the homeless. At Trubnaya, you may opt to turn right and walk a block to the busy Ulitsa Sretenka, running northeast.

Sretenka terminates at **Sukharevskaya Ploshchad** which was named after the tower that stood here until the 1930s. Sukharev was the only officer who remained loyal to Peter the Great during the Streltsy rebellion and the grateful tsar erected the tower in Sukharev's honour. Later on the square's associations were less lofty: it hosted an officially recognised weekly market for stolen goods. Permission for the market was granted by Governor Rostopchin following the great fire of 1812. When the wealthy Muscovites returned home, they found their homes stripped bare and scoured the market in the hope of retrieving their valuables.

This is also the location of the **Doctor Sklifasovsky Hospital** which was founded by the noble Sheremetyev family. Sheremetyevo, Moscow's international airport, is built on what was once one of their country estates. Turn left at Trubnaya, and walk along Petrovsky and Strastnoi Boulevards to **Tverskaya** (formerly Gorky) Ulitsa, the city's main drag. Tverskaya leads to the Kremlin, with Teatralnaya Ploshchad on the left.

Teatralnaya Ploshchad

Two main thoroughfares come together on Teatralnaya – Neglinnaya and Petrovka (named after the Vysoko-Petrovsky monastery built by Prince Ivan Kalita). The world-famous **Bolshoi Teatr** (Bolshoi, meaning "big", Theatre) ❸❼ dominates the northern side of the square. Formerly known as the Grand Imperial Theatre, it was built in 1825 and restored and remodelled following a fire some years later. Although internationally acclaimed as perhaps the world's greatest ballet company, nowadays the Bolshoi is feeling the pinch. Founded by the tsars, it became a Soviet flagship and as such enjoyed hefty state subsidies. Decades of neglect of the building's structure and rifts between performers and management have left the Bolshoi in a shaky state.

However, efforts have been made to rekindle the theatre's glory, and the government has released funds to revamp the Bolshoi as a part of an ensemble incorporating several buildings surrounding the square.

The Bolshoi's near neighbours are the **Maly Teatr** (Maly, "little", Theatre) ❸❽, the oldest drama hall in the city, and to its left, the **Detsky Teatr** (Central Children's Theatre). The Detsky opened in 1921 and Moscow's first professional theatre for children.

Famous hotels and mansions

The eastern side of Teatralnaya Ploshchad is home to the glamorous fin-de-siècle **Metropol Hotel** ❸❾, designed by a Scottish-Russian team, William Walcott and Leo Kekushev. Restored to its original glory, it is once again the best and most exclusive hotel in town. It's worth having a coffee in one of the ornate lounges if the room prices are beyond your reach. Opposite is the **Moskva Hotel**, one of the grotesque Stalinist edifices that now dot the city's skyline. The story goes that Stalin insisted on approving every construction plan made in the city. Two architects worked

BELOW: a new look for Maneznaya Square.

Gorky Park is a favourite place of relaxation for Muscovites, with its amusement park and Disney-style rides. It lies southwest across the Moskva River from the Kremlin.

BELOW: Moscow's State University.

on designs for the new hotel to house Soviet dignitaries and both were presented to Stalin. He initialled both, so both were built – after a fashion. Check the west facade and you'll see two very different towers at either end. The north side of the hotel is on Ulitsa Okhotny Ryad (Hunter's Row) which was known as Marx Prospekt during the Soviet era. It runs from Neglinnaya to Tverskaya (formerly Gorky) Ulitsa.

Okhotny Ryad was once a big covered market place where hunters would trade game, rabbits and such. Small stalls selling meat, fish, fruit and vegetables made it one of the dirtiest places in Moscow. The booths were dismantled after the Revolution, but following the 1991 coup people remembered the tradition and set up their own stalls. The city authorities had to designate special areas in the suburbs as flea markets so people could practise "market economy".

On the corner of Okhotny Ryad and Ulitsa Bolshaya Dmitrovka is a green-painted, white-colonnaded former mansion. Once the Nobles' Club, it is currently the **Dom Soyuzov** (House of Trade Unions) ❹. The mansion originally belonged to Prince Vasily Dolgorukov, the city's military commander in the early 1780s. In 1783 it was sold to the newly-established Assembly of the Nobles, who started a very exclusive club in the building. Said to be the most beautiful house in Moscow, the interior is stunning, but the building is only open to the public when the white and gold **Kolonny Zal** (Hall of the Columns) is used as a concert venue. Keep your eyes open for these concerts, because in the old days the hall saw the likes of Pushkin, Lermontov and even Leo Tolstoy tripping the light fantastic under the crystal chandeliers.

Moscow had a number of clubs for different social classes. The Tradesmen's Club was located in what is now the Stanislavsky Theatre on the street of the same name. The English Club has become the **Muzei Revolyutsii** (Museum of the Revolution), Tverskaya Ulitsa 21 (open 10am–6pm; closed Mon), while the Central House of Artists now occupies the site of the former German or Schuster Club.

Walk west down Okhotny Ryad and turn right into Tverskaya. On the opposite corner is the **National Hotel** ❹. Next door on Tverskaya is the first US embassy to the USSR – the Americans have moved twice since they left this building in 1954 and are now located on the Moskva River at the west end of the Novyi Arbat. Their former embassy on Tverskaya is now the Intourist office.

Okhotny Ryad runs down to the river and if you follow its route, you'll pass **Moscow University's** ❹ oldest building. Set slightly back from the street and fronted by a small garden, the classical yellow mansion was constructed between 1776 and 1793 by Matvei Kazakov and restored after the 1812 fire by Domenico Gilardi.

Just opposite on your left across the four-lane highway is the **Manege**, whose construction commemorated Russia's victory over Napoleon in the 1812 Patriotic War. The spacious hall was used for equine displays, military parades and exhibitions. There are no horses today, but exhibitions are still held here.

If you follow Okhotny Ryad down to the river, past the white marble **Russkaya Gosudarstvennaya**

Biblioteka (Russian State Library, formerly the Lenin Library) on your right, you'll see an astounding palace, **Dom Pashkova** ❸.

Built in the time of Peter the Great by the son of one of his administrators, Peter Pashkov, it was designed to vie with the Kremlin in magnificence and style. The money to build this gloriously baroque mansion had come from Pashkov's father Igor, who had made a fortune by investigating the book-keeping of the governor of Siberia, Prince Matvei Gagarin. Pashkov claimed the prince was lining his own pockets on the proceeds of lucrative diamond and grain deals. Although well-liked by the Siberians, Matvei was hanged and a great deal of his wealth and estates along with a few thousand serfs passed to the punctilious Pashkov and his family.

The last of the Pashkovs presented the palace to Moscow University which, in its turn, gave it to Count Rumyantsev to house his collection of art and manuscripts. After the Revolution, the art works were removed to the Pushkin, but the books remained and the mansion is now part of the state library.

The Russian State Library (Lenin Library) holds 30 million books in 247 languages.

Tverskaya Ulitsa

Moscow's best-known street is **Tverskaya Ulitsa**, the main thoroughfare since the early 19th century when wealthy nobles began building new palaces and imposing mansions in Moscow.

Tverskaya was the main road to St Petersburg, so members of the tsar's entourage were constantly shuttling between the two cities along this thoroughfare. It had two triumphal arches in Pushkinskaya (formerly Tver Gate) Ploshchad and at Belorussky Station. When Pushkinskaya Square was extended in the 1930s, the arch was dismantled brick by brick and relocated in

BELOW: peddling icons in the park.

The famous Filippov Bakery on Tverskaya is renowned for its raisin pie, said to have originated from before the Revolution when a police chief found a cockroach in a bun he was sold. Filippov ate the cockroach, saying, "But this is a raisin!" Then he bought a pound of raisins and created his raisin pie.

Kutuzovsky Prospekt across the river. The most incredible things were done to Tverskaya in the 1930s as part of Stalin's master plan to create a Communist capital of awe-inspiring proportions. It was straightened and widened. Several major buildings were moved deeper into the existing blocks of houses, including the former Governor General's residence which housed the Moscow Council of Deputies after the Revolution and is now the Mayor's Office; it also gained two storeys in the process.

The **Pushkin Monument** 🏛, about a third of the way up the street, was moved from one side of the boulevard to the other, into the small square in front of the grubby-looking Rossiya Cinema; the majestic Strastnoi Monastery was knocked down to accommodate the movie theatre. The building at No. 14 Tverskaya housed one of Moscow's biggest food stores. It was bought in 1898 by an entrepreneur called Yeliseyev who owned a chain of grocers. The "supermarket", **Yeliseyevsky Gastronom** 🏛, on the ground floor amazed even sophisticated Muscovites. The shop, which lay three-quarters empty in the hungry late 1980s and early 1990s, is now filled with imported Western groceries and luxury items.

About half-way up Tverskaya, is **Triumfalnaya Ploshchad** (formerly Mayakovskogo). The **Kontsertny zal imeni Chaykovskogo** (Tchaikovsky Concert Hall) 🏛 was built in 1940 to mark the centenary of the composer's birth. It has a giant 20-tonne pipe organ with 7,800 pipes and is a venue for the International Tchaikovsky Competition (tel: 299 3681). Across the square is the old **Pekin Hotel**. It has been done up and serves Chinese food. At the end of Tverskaya is **Belorussky Vokzal** (Station) 🏛, the terminus for trains from Western Europe and the start of the road to Sheremetyevo international airport.

BELOW: statue of Tchaikovsky.

Nikitskaya

Parallel to Tverskaya is **Bolshaya Nikitskaya Ulitsa** (formerly Gertsena). In the 16th century, this was the old road to Tver (known as Kalinin in the Soviet period). Ivan the Terrible stationed a garrison on this stretch of the road and it was later a coveted site for boyar mansions.

The **Orlov Dvorets** (Palace), at No. 5, is typical of 18th-century classical architecture. At No. 11, the former home of the Kolychev boyars is now the voice department of the Moscow Conservatory and was recently returned to the splendour of its original elegance.

The **Ekaterina Romanovna Vorontsovoi Dvorets** (Palace) is at No. 12. Ekaterina (1744–1810) was one of the first patrons of the arts in Russia. A great friend of Catherine the Great, Voltaire and Diderot, she developed into a true philanthropist and spent her fortune on sponsoring students, lectures and literary publications. She was head of the Russian Academy of Sciences from 1783 until 1796. After her death, the palace was bought for the Moscow Conservatory of Music, **Konservatoriya imeni Chaykovskogo** ㊽. Tchaikovsky, Glier and Neuhaus taught Rachmaninov and Scriabin here and the Great Hall is a venue for the International Tchaikovsky Competition held every four years. The Lesser Hall presents chamber music and recitals.

Not all the best palaces are on the left of the street. The **Menshikov Dvorets** (Palace), for example, is a classic piece of Moscow Empire style, incorporating six Corinthian columns in its facade. Unfortunately it is partly obscured by a hospital, so you have to reach it from Gazetny Pereulok (formerly Ogaryova).

Theatre buffs should head for the **Dom-muzei Stanislavskogo** (Stanislavsky Museum) ㊾ (open 11am–6pm; Wed, Fri, 2–9pm; closed Mon, Tues), just up the

Maps on pages 138 & 142

BELOW: winter games on Patriarchs' Ponds.

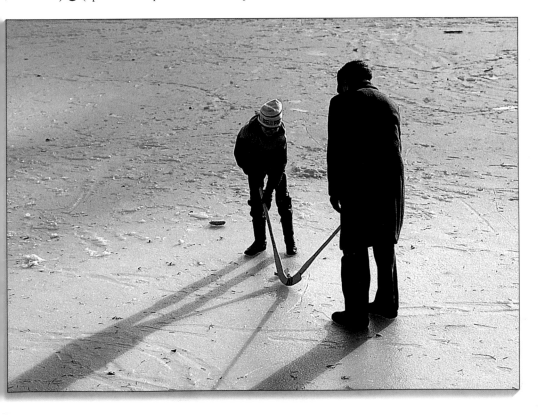

Moscow has seven railway stations and five airports. It has 132 metro stations on its 213-km (132-mile) underground network. Its two river ports are accessible from the sea by the Volga River and the Moscow Canal.

street and round the corner to the right at No.7. Stanislavsky transformed theatrical practice, and in particular the business of rehearsal. He made his actors literally live their part: they stayed in costume and in character day and night in order to achieve an understanding of the role. The desired result was a theatre which was convincing because it was realistic, rather than moving because it was mannered and rhetorical. The Stanislavsky approach has had a lasting influence on Hollywood, where his ideas were developed by Lee Strasberg of the Actors' Guild, and practised by followers of his such as James Dean, Marlon Brando and Robert De Niro.

At the same corner, Nikitskaya is crossed by Nikitsky (formerly Suvorovsky) Boulevard – the building on your right belongs to the TASS news agency. If you cross Nikitsky here, Nikitskaya continues on the opposite side of the boulevard but twists off to the left, turning into Malaya Nikitskaya. The church on your left is the **Tserkov Bolshogo Voznesenia** (Great Ascension) **50**. Besides having the best choir in the city, it is also a centre of monarchist activity.

Turn right onto Spiridonovka (formerly Ulitsa Alekseya Tolstogo) to find the side entrance to the fabulous art nouveau **Dom-muzei Gorkogo** (Gorky Museum) **51** (open Thurs, Sat, Sun 10am–5pm; Wed, Fri noon–7pm; closed Mon, Tues, last Thurs in month), which fronts Malaya Nikitskaya.

The house was commissioned at the turn of the 20th century by the merchant Stenka Ryabushinsky. Its architect, Fyodor Shekhtel, was the most exciting of the day and he finished the lyrically imposing building in 1902. It is one of the finest examples of an art nouveau interior in Russia – or indeed anywhere in Europe. Be sure to go inside, and don't miss the ceilings. When Gorky returned to the young Soviet Union in the early 1930s, he was presented with the house

BELOW: an artist on the Arbat.

TRETYAKOV GALLERY

On the south bank of the Moskva, opposite the Kremlin, is one of the greatest collections of Russian art in the country. The renovated **Tretyakovskaya Galereya** (Tretyakov Gallery; open: 10am–8pm; closed Mon), Lavrushinsky Pereulok 10, spans 1,000 years of Russian art, from early icons to 20th-century works.

The building itself is in the Russian style – an urban interpretation of a boyar's mansion built in 1900 to house the collection accumulated by the brothers Pavel and Sergei Tretyakov in the late 19th century. The two men, who had made their fortunes in textiles, later donated their collection and palace to the state. On the gallery's ground floor, the remarkable icon collection includes the Byzantine *Mother of God of Vladimir* and Andrei Rublyov's 15th-century *The Trinity*. You'll find 17th- and 18th-century portraits upstairs. The work of the 19th-century Wanderers such as Ilya Repin, and 20th-century paintings by Kandinsky, among others, feature alongside sculptures and engravings.

A short walk to the west brings you to the **Novaya Tretyakovskaya Galereya** (New Tretyakov Gallery; open 10am–7pm; closed Mon), Krymsky Val 10, housing Soviet and post-Soviet art. Communist statues pulled down after the 1991 coup have found refuge in its garden.

Map on pages 138–9

although he liked neither it or its architect. Follow Spiridonovka to the next corner on the right and turn down Spiridonievsky Pereulok. This will bring you to Malaya Bronnaya. Turn left and the street leads to **Patriarshiye Prudy** (Patriarchs' Ponds) ⑳, where Mikhail Bulgakov set the opening scene of his famous play *Master and Margarita*. On the corner is Margarita, a great restaurant. In the 19th century, this was Moscow's student quarter.

South across the river

The area opposite the Kremlin on the south side of the Moskva River, between the bridges of Kamenny and Moskvoretsky around the **Tretyakovskaya Galereya** ⑬ (Tretyakov Gallery; *see box on page 161*), comes as something of a surprise after the appalling 20th-century urban planning generally apparent in the old heart of the city. **Zamoskvorechye** (literally "beyond the Moskva River") was the artisan centre in the 17th century, hence street names such as Kadashevskaya (barrel-maker) and Novokuznetskaya (blacksmith). The nobility moved in during the 19th century and built palaces and mansions. Today, it is embassy country and the classical 19th-century buildings, with their chantilly stucco, give an idea of what Moscow must have been like before the Revolution.

Donskoy Monastery is named after the miracle-working "Mother God of the Don" icon.

The **Muzei V Tropinina** (Tropinin Museum; open Mon, Thur, Fri noon–6pm; Sat, Sun 10am–4.30pm; closed Tues, Wed) ⑭, Shchetininsky Lane 10, of 18th- and 19th-century portraiture is near the Tretyakov and shouldn't be missed.

When Prince Daniel Nevsky built his string of fortified monasteries in the 13th century, he dedicated the best and most beautiful to his patron saint. The **Svyato-Danilovsky Monastyr** (Danilov Monastery) ⑮ still stands today, enclosed by its white walls, due south from Moskvoretsky Most (Bridge) at the end of Ulitsa Bolshaya Ordynka. Recently, it was restored to its former gold-domed splendour and returned to the Orthodox Church. The patriarch now has his residence here.

BELOW: the new Cathedral of Christ the Saviour.

While south of the river, don't miss **Park Gorkovo** (Gorky Park) ⑯. It surrounds the landscaped Neskuchny Garden (literally "never dull") created by the millionaire industrialist Demidov on the south bank of the Moskva in the mid-18th century, the name of which derives from the fantastic collection of plants that lined the pathways. Today, Demidov's mansion is home to the Academy of Sciences. Leninsky Prospekt, along the south side of the park, is known as the Avenue of Soviet Science because more than 30 research centres are located here.

West to Old Arbat

Walking westwards up Ulitsa Vozdvizhenka from the Manege on Okhotny Ryad, you can't miss the broad eyesore of Ulitsa **Novy Arbat** (formerly Kalininsky Prospekt) starting at Arbatskaya Ploshchad and ending at the **Dom Pravitelstva** (Russian Government building) ⑰ overlooking the Moskva River. In the 18th century, the Romanov, Naryshkin and Sheremetyev families all had houses on this part of the street.

Novy Arbat is dissected by Nikitsky Boulevard at Arbatskaya Ploshchad and to your left is the beginning of the **Old Arbat**. The name derives from the

Arabic word for suburb, *rabat*. More than five centuries old, Arbat was the starting point of the road to Smolensk.

In the 18th century Arbat was popular with the aristocracy, who held soirées and literary salons in their homes. The Russian writer and revolutionary Alexander Herzen called it Moscow's St Germain, and true to its reputation the Arbat again became a mecca for artists when *glasnost* began. Satirical and political cartoonists, painters and sculptors, who couldn't get access to official art galleries, began exhibiting their work on the pedestrianised street. It has subsequently become a tourist trap, but in spite of that, the cafés, buskers and souvenir sellers make it lively and fun.

One building you shouldn't miss is the **Dom Melnikov** (Melnikov house) 🔞, tucked down a side-street off the Arbat in Krivoarbatsky Pereulok, about halfway along the pedestrian street on the left-hand side. It doesn't look particularly promising, which is why people rarely find the constructivist jewel built by one of the most innovative and creative architects.

Konstantin Melnikov was a founder member of the avant-garde arts movement that flourished in the first decade after the Revolution. Along with artists such as Kandinsky and El Lissitsky, he formulated a new and iconoclastic approach to the arts. But the movement which influenced the Bauhaus and De Stijl schools was short-lived in Russia. Only a few of the buildings remain. Melnikov's house is one of them. When Stalin decided that the proletariat should have neoclassical facades on their apartment blocks, Melnikov built himself a family home, a white cylindrical structure with lozenge-shaped windows.

The Arbat ends on Smolenskaya Ploshchad (Square), an enormous intersection which is dwarfed by the **Ministerstvo Inostrannykh Del** (Foreign

BELOW:
an ice house in
Gorky Park.

Ministry) **⑤**. There are seven of these Stalinist "wedding cakes" in the city: all were built in the late 1940s and 1950s. You either love them or hate them, but they are part of Moscow's heritage and have added their own specific contribution to the city's skyline.

Map on pages 138–9

On the arts trail

Following Peter the Great's lead, the nobles of the 18th century began taking the kind of Grand Tour that created the fabulous aristocratic art collections of Europe. The great Russian collectors, the Rumyantsevs, Golenishchevs, Shchukins and Morozovs, were both catholic and discerning in taste. Their collections were nationalised by Lenin in the early 1920s and brought together in the **Muzei Izobrazitelnikh Iskusstv imeni Pushkina** (Pushkin Fine Arts Museum) **⑥**, Ulitsa Volkhonka 12, two blocks southwest of the Kremlin.

The museum was founded at the end of the 19th century as a school of art and incorporated copies of all major sculptural works from around the world (the notion being that Russian artists could study the greats without leaving home). The reproductions are still there, but the Pushkin also has a wealth of original works, from ancient Egyptian art to a collection of Impressionists and Post-Impressionists, including Cézanne, Gauguin, Matisse and Van Gogh. It is housed in a purpose-built, (open 10am–7pm; closed Mon, last Tues in month) turn-of-the-century neoclassical style building .

Opposite the museum is the newly rebuilt **Khram Khrista Spasitelya** (Cathedral of Christ the Saviour) **❻**. The new church is a constructed copy of the original, which was built between the 1830s and 1880s. It soon became the outstanding symbol of the city. It was not just a church; it was also a monument

BELOW: Zurab Tsereteli's giant sculpture of Peter the Great.

SCULPTURE IN THE CITY

Walking around Moscow, you cannot escape the sight of a curious structure in the middle of the Moskva River between the new Cathedral of Christ the Saviour on the north bank and the New Tretyakov Gallery on the south. The giant sculpture of a figure on a sailing boat is Peter the Great. It is one of the many creations of Zurab Tsereteli, Moscow's most controversial sculptor. Tsar Peter I, founder of St Petersburg, is known to have detested Moscow, and it is a bizarre twist of fate that this sculpture has found a home here. According to Tsereteli's critics, it was originally intended to represent Christopher Columbus and had been commissioned by the United States for the 500th anniversary celebrations of the discovery of North America. The US is said to have rejected it on first sight.

The 60-metre (200-ft) bronze body had to be disposed off somehow and Tsereteli subsequently won a commission from Moscow's mayor, Yuri Luzhkov. The reincarnated statue raised an outcry in Moscow, but has so far survived a massive public campaign for its removal as well as a demolition attempt. You can sample other works by Tsereteli studded around Moscow, including interiors of the Cathedral of Christ the Saviour and his animalistic forms in the Okhotny Ryad shopping mall.

Map
on pages
138–9

*The Novodevichy
Monastyr (Convent)
is Moscow's second
most important
religious centre.*

BELOW: window of
Novodevichy
Convent.
RIGHT:
the International
Friendship Fountain.

to the Russian victory over Napoleon, a symbol of the idea that, with God's help, Russia could overcome any catastrophe. But to the new Soviet regime it was no more than an ugly reminder of the autocratic regime.

In 1931, to the horror of Muscovites, Stalin had the cathedral dynamited. In its place he planned to erect a gigantic skyscraper which, in turn, would also be the largest in the world. It was called the Palace of Soviets, and it was in effect a temple of communism. It was to be crowned with a statue of Lenin so colossal that its upper half would have been permanently lost in the clouds. But the plan was never realised. The skyscraper could not be made to stand up, and the gaping hole of the foundations was turned into the Moscow open-air swimming pool.

The demolished cathedral became a forbidden topic in the USSR, a non-building. It was as if the Cathedral of Christ the Saviour had never existed. But when communism collapsed, the resurrection of the church became a *cause célèbre*. The energetic mayor of Moscow, Yuri Luzhkov, took up the baton. To many Muscovites it is a tawdry piece of copycat architecture said to bear a price tag of US$500 million, a lion's share of which came out of the city budget. It was built in the astonishingly short space of three years in order to be ready for Moscow's 850th anniversary celebrations, and stands as much a monument to Luzhkov's tenure of office as a place of divine worship.

New Maiden Convent

The tsars had a love-hate relationship with the Orthodox Church. Some tsars used the Church for their own purposes, installing relatives as patriarchs, but others were suspicious of its power over the people. In the Soviet era, most of the Church's wealth and real estate were confiscated by the new authorities. But the Church and its members struggled on and when liberalisation took place it made a comeback.

In the meantime, Muscovites who wanted to be baptised sneaked off to Sergyev Posad (formerly Zagorsk), one of the few surviving Orthodox enclaves, 65 km (40 miles) north of Moscow. You only have to look around Moscow to see just how powerful the Church was, and could become again. Some of the city's major landmarks are religious, in spite of Stalin's efforts to redefine the skyline.

Perhaps one of the most beautiful religious complexes is the **Novodevichy Monastyr** (New Convent of the Maiden; open 10am–5.30pm; closed Tues) ❷. To the southwest of the Kremlin, strategically placed on a bend in the river, the convent was founded by Vasily III in 1524. From a distance the white walls topped by red roofs and 16 golden domes look picturesque, but the convent's history is chequered. The strong walls and fortified towers were used as a prison for trouble-making female nobles. A string of well-born women ended up here, including Peter the Great's half-sister Sofia and his first wife Evdokia. Check out the cemeteries: Chekhov and Scriabin lie buried in the old one, while Khrushchev and other Soviet big-wigs can be found in the new cemetery (open Wed–Sat 11am–4pm; closed Sun–Tues). ❑

PALACES BENEATH THE STREETS

Muscovites are extremely proud of their metro system, and they have every right to be. It is clean fast, efficient, cheap – and spectacular to look at

In most cities the metro is a dull way to get around: there is not much for a visitor to look at 20 metres (65 ft) under the ground. In Moscow, on the other hand, the metro is a primary tourist attraction. The stations are justly famed for their sumptuous and unique decoration. Where else in the world is the rumbling approach of the train heralded by a delicate tinkle of chandeliers?

The metro is a good way to travel for practical reasons, too. In a Russian winter, it makes sense to do one's waiting in the damp warmth of the underground rather than at a freezing bus stop. Throughout the cold months armies of *babushkas* (grandmothers) are employed to mop up the slush which passengers carry into the station vestibules on their winter boots.

The metro has its own very definite etiquette. When it comes to boarding a train it is every man or woman for themselves, and in rush hour it is a scrum between the people getting on and those getting off. But once on the train, invalids and pensioners have an indisputable right to seats.

This right is in the *Rules For The Use of the Metro*, a Soviet-era document which is displayed in every train. The first rule of the metro states, in true bureaucratic fashion, that passengers must obey the rules.

◁ **NEW SOVIET MAN**
The figures at Revolution Square portray the strata of an idealised Soviet society: workers, peasants and (left) serious-minded members of the new intelligentsia.

△ **POLISHED VAULTS**
Mayakovskaya, with its elegant arches, is true Art Deco chic. This shiny interior would not look out of place inside New York's Chrysler building.

▽ **UNDERGROUND ART**
Now that socialist realist statuary is out of fashion, Ploshchad Revolutsii (Revolution Square) is one of the few places you can see monumental Soviet art.

△ LIGHT FANTASTIC
Komsomolskaya is one of the busiest stations because it serves three railway terminals. It is also one of the most ornate, with its giant chandeliers and a terrace round the platforms.

DIGGING TUNNELS FOR SOCIALISM

The building of the metro was the centrepiece of the first Five-Year Plan. Like many of the industrial undertakings of the 1930s it was a symbolic project, intended to show that socialism could achieve anything capitalism could. The first line to be built was the red one, which runs to the southwest of Moscow. The stretch from Palace of Soviets station (now Kropotkinskaya) to Frunzenskaya was opened with much pomp in 1935. Kropotkinskaya itself is one of the most beautiful and restrained stations. It is lined with marble taken from the façade of the demolished Cathedral of Christ (now reconstructed nearby). It was only later, in the 1940s and 1950s, that it became fashionable to build in a style that one might call Soviet baroque. Newer stations are mostly utilitarian. In the suburbs, metro stations are lined with blank, easy-to-clean tiles. To enjoy the gaudy architecture of the metro, stay inside the Circle Line.

△ NEXT STOP...
The names of stations are not always obvious, so visitors should listen for the recorded announcements: "Doors closing, next stop..."

▷ GOING DOWN
Moscow has some very deep stations. This is because many were built in the war years and were first used as air raid shelters.

THE GOLDEN RING

*The princely towns of the Golden Ring reached their
zenith even before Moscow's inception. Here, beneath gilded onion
domes, is the historic centre of Muscovy*

Map
on page
174

A tour of the Golden Ring, heartland of ancient Muscovy, is one of the most popular excursions for foreigners and Russians alike. The region comprises a dozen or so medieval towns around Moscow – some entire museums in themselves – and is certainly solid gold as far as history and culture are concerned. The route starts and ends in Moscow, passing north through Sergiyev Posad, Pereyaslavl-Zalessky, Rostov Veliky, Yaroslavl, Kostroma, and turning south to Suzdal and Vladimir.

Sergiyev Posad

Sergiyev Posad ❶, lying 70 km (44 miles) to the north of Moscow along the Yaroslavl Highway, is the most convenient place to start the tour. Known in Soviet times as Zagorsk in honour of a communist party official who had never even visited the town, the name of Sergiyev Posad was reinstated in 1991 following pressure from the public and the Orthodox Church.

Sergiyev Posad (Sergei's town), bears witness to its founder, St Sergei of Radonezh, one of Russia's most revered holy men whose contribution to the nation's development was both spiritual and political. According to Dmitry Likhachev, Russia's contemporary leading moral and intellectual authority, St Sergei was admired as "the spiritual leader of the Russian people". He founded the **Troitse-Sergiyevsky Lavra** (Trinity Monastery of St Sergei) here in the mid-14th century. He also blessed Prince Dmitry Donskoi on the eve of the battle at Kulikovo (1380), Russia's first major victory over the Mongols after 150 years of subjugation.

The incomparable and splendid architecture of the monastery, one of the oldest seats of the Orthodox church, and the vast collections of ancient Russian painting and precious-metal artefacts are breathtaking. In 1930, the *lavra* (an honourary title meaning, in Greek, "main monastery") lost two of its greatest treasures: *The Trinity* icon, painted by Andrei Rublyov, Russia's acclaimed icon painter of the Middle Ages, was transferred to Moscow's Tretyakov Art Gallery; and the bells from the Trinity Belfry, which were the world's largest, were destroyed.

Today the monastery is a place of pilgrimage for members of the Orthodox Church, who flock to it in their thousands. They come to the white stone **Troitsky Sobor** (Trinity Cathedral) to honour the remains of the venerable St Sergei. The monastery was a formidable fortress in its time – during the Polish-Lithuanian invasion in the early 1600s it was under siege for 16 months. It also played an important cultural role. The Trinity School of book writing and

PRECEDING PAGES:
Trinity Monastery of
St Sergei.
LEFT: frescoes
decorate an
Orthodox cathedral.
BELOW: domes of
the Trinity Monastery
of St Sergei.

St Sergei of Radonezh, founder of the Trinity Monastery at Sergiyev Posad.

BELOW: a farmer fetches water.

colour miniatures dates from the 15th century and is a museum of national importance. The monastery itself has a clerical school (seminary) reputed to be a bastion of conservatism in the Orthodox Church compared to the more liberal seminary in St Petersburg. Since the late 1980s, young men have flocked to Orthodox seminaries and there is stiff competition for places.

The architectural highlights of the monastery include the dome and roof of the Trinity Cathedral and, inside, a beautiful iconostasis adorned by the works of Andrei Rublyov. The five-domed **Uspensky Sobor** (Assumption Cathedral), formerly the main church in the monastery, is the architectural centre of the ensemble. It was founded by Ivan the Terrible in 1559 and contains a vaulted ceiling that has no internal supports – a testimony to the technical accomplishments of Russian builders. The simple rectangular tomb near the northwestern corner of the cathedral contains the remains of Tsar Boris Godunov.

Along the south wall of the fortress is the 17th-century **Trapeznaya Tserkov St Sergei** (Refectory Church of St Sergei). Until recently the handsome Metropolitan's Quarters next door housed the residence of the patriarch of the Orthodox Church.

The jewel of the architectural ensemble is the five-tiered belltower, considered by many people to be the most beautiful in Russia. It was built by Dmitry Ukhtomsky in the middle of the 18th century. Today it attracts visitors from around the world and is often used by film-makers from home and abroad as a set location. Its remarkable silhouette is visible from some distance. (Monastery grounds open 10am–6pm. Museums 10am–5pm; closed Mon; monthly closing days: Treasury, first Tues and last Fri; Art Museum and History and Architecture Museum, last Wed. Tours are available.)

The Golden Ring

Pereyaslavl-Zalessky

Pereyaslavl-Zalessky ❷, the "town-on-the-waters," is even older than Sergiyev Posad. It is an hour's drive to the northeast, on the banks of Lake Plescheyevo. Founded together with Moscow by Prince Yuri Dolgoruky in the 12th century, Pereyaslavl claims to be the birthplace of the Russian navy. It was here that Peter the Great built his mock flotilla at the end of the 1600s, thus laying the foundations of Russian shipbuilding and seafaring. The episode is commemorated in the **Muzei Botika** ("Little Boat" Museum), at the southern end of the lake (open 10am–5pm, closed Mon). Pereyaslavl-Zalessky is also the birthplace of Prince Alexander Nevsky, who defeated an army of German knights on Lake Chudskoye in 1242.

A good place to start a tour of the town is at the heart of Pereyaslavl's **Kremlin**, where the white stone **Spasopreobrazhensky Sobor** (Cathedral of the Transfiguration of the Saviour), 1152–57, is the oldest in northeastern Russia. To the south of the cathedral stands the **Tserkov Petra Mitropolita** (Church of Peter the Metropolitan), 1585, with its faceted, hipped roof.

The pride of Pereyaslavl, the **Goritsky Monastyr** (Monastery), was founded between 1337 and 1340 during the reign of Muscovite Great Prince Ivan Kalita. The gate of the Goritsky Monastery is voluptuously decorated with a whimsical ornamentation. The monastery has a small museum (open 10am–5pm; closed Tues and last Mon in month).

The road leads on to **Rostov Veliky** (Rostov the Great) ❸, an hour's drive to the north. Admirers have dubbed the town "a symphony in stone" and "Russia's Eternal City". Standing behind Lake Nero and backed by the mid-Russia landscape, it has an undeniable fairy-tale quality. Rostov, like its ancient rival,

Map on page 174

BELOW: winter sunset at Suzdal.

A simple axe and chisel were the only tools used to construct some of the traditional buildings preserved in Suzdal's Museum of Wooden Architecture and Peasant Life (open 9.30am–3.30pm; closed Tues).

BELOW: typical wooden house at Abramtsevo.

Novgorod, has been called "the Great" for centuries. At the end of the first millennium it was one of the wealthiest and most populous centres in Russia. Today it is famous for its 18th-century **Kremlin**, the former residence of the metropolitan, resplendent with gold and silver towers, cupolas, and lace crosses. The treasures of the Kremlin include the 16th-century **Uspensky Sobor** (Assumption Cathedral), the 17th-century **Tserkov Spas-na-Senyakh** (Church of the Saviour over the Galleries) and **Tserkov Odigitrii** (Church of the Icon of the Hodigitria), as well as collections of icons, portraits, china and Rostov enamels.

Yaroslavl

Yaroslavl ❹, 57 km (35 miles) north of Rostov Veliky, is one of Russia's largest regional centres (pop. 600,000). In 1010 Yaroslav the Wise founded a fort on the banks of the Volga. Ancient legend has it that the prince came upon a bear which he killed with an axe. The bear became the local emblem and was included in the region's coat of arms. Today, the mascot greets visitors entering the town.

The abundance of frescoes and ceramic ornaments in its churches earned Yaroslavl the title "Florence of Russia". Most of the churches were built with money donated by local merchants. A breathtaking vista of white (the walls and towers of the Spassky Monastery) and gold (the domes of its 16th-century cathedral) welcomes the traveller arriving from Moscow. It is hard to take your gaze away from the tall **Tserkov Bogoyavlenia** (Church of the Incarnation; open 10am–1pm, 2–5pm; closed Tues), whose ceramic-tiled walls give it the appearance of being studded with jewels. In Sovietskaya Ploshchad, there is one of the masterpieces of local architecture, **Tserkov Ilyi Proroka** (Church of

ABRAMTSEVO ARTISTS' COLONY

The Abramtsevo country estate, 60 km (36 miles) northeast of Moscow, occupies a special place in Russian culture. Early in the 19th century it was owned by the novelist Sergei Aksakov and frequented by writers such as Nikolai Gogol and Ivan Turgenev. In the 1870s it was purchased by the railroad and industrial tycoon, Savva Mamontov, who put it at the disposal of some of the country's leading artists for the specific purpose of preserving the national heritage. It became the cradle of the neo-Russian style, the Russian variation of the Romantic and nationalist movements sweeping Europe in the 19th century, and strove to preserve Russian folk-art traditions and skills. It even had its own furniture and ceramics workshop. Abramtsevo was frequented by a wide range of painters, including Ilya Repin, Mikhail Vrubel, Isaak Levitan, Valentin Serov, Viktor Vasnetsov and Vassily Polenov. Russia's great singer, Fyodor Chaliapin, made his debut in Abramtsevo's theatre.

The heyday of Abramtsevo as an artists' colony came to an abrupt end when Mamontov's business empire went bankrupt in 1899. Today the estate's traditional timber buildings house a museum of literature and art (open 11am–5pm, closed Mon, Tues, and on the 30th of the month).

Map on page 174

Elijah the Prophet), which was built by the town's merchants in 1647. Its walls and vaults contain a vast museum of Russian paintings (open May–Sept: 10am–1pm, 2–6pm; closed Wed).

It was Yaroslal that preserved for Russia its greatest literary treasure, *Slovo o polku Igoreve* (The Lay of Igor's Host), a kind of Russian *Beowulf* written in the 12th century. The only surviving copy of the work was found here in the **Spaso-Preobrazhensky Monastyr** (Monastery) at the end of the 18th century. It is worth climbing the monastery's belltower for a fine view of the city (grounds open 10am–5pm). Yaroslavl is also the birthplace of the Russian national theatre. Fyodor Volkov, father of the Russian theatre, began his career in the town in the 18th century; the local Teatr Volkhova, in Ploshchad Volkhova, bears his name to this day.

Kostroma ❺, 70 km (43 miles) east of Yaroslavl, is closely linked with the Godunov and Romanov families. Tsar Boris Godunov's ancestors built the original **Ipatevsky Monastyr** (Monastery) in 1332 (open May–Oct: 9am–4.30pm; Nov–Apr: 10am–4.30pm; closed Fri). Godunov himself exiled the rival Romanovs to Kostroma during his reign and it was here in 1613 that Mikhail Romanov heard of his election to become tsar. **Ivanovo ❻**, 95 km (59 miles) south of Kostroma, is an important textile centre on the road to **Palekh ❼**, 65 km (40 miles) to its east, which is noted for its museum of icons and lacquer boxes (closed Mon and last Fri in month).

Suzdal

Travelling a further 60 km (37 miles) south of Ivanovo, **Suzdal ❽**, capital of Yuri Dolgoruky's Rostov-Suzdal principality in the 12th century, comes into

TIP

Suzdal is one of the better places to stay. It is well served by hotels, including the traditionally furnished wooden *izby* (peasant cottages) around Pokrovsky Monastery.

BELOW: cottages in old Suzdal.

Map on page 174

Suzdal has a good choice of restaurants serving traditional dishes such as mushroom soup, meat as the merchants cooked it, and medovuka, a Russian drink made from honey.

BELOW: Church of the Intercession, Vladimir.
RIGHT: *Mother of God* icon from Yaroslavl.

view. First impressions are of jagged cornices, hipped roofs and cupolas. Throughout the centuries the town suffered many destructive assaults, yet rose from the ashes every time. Wood and stone houses were built and several monasteries founded.

In the 19th century, when a railway was constructed between Moscow and Nizhny Novgorod, it passed Suzdal by. Shunned by progress, the town avoided becoming an industrial centre and kept its original image intact. There are more than 100 architectural monuments from the 13th to 19th centuries crowded into a small area of only 9 sq km (3 sq miles). Take a rest on the steep bank of the Kamenka River, and submit to the spell of its quiet beauty.

The town's most memorable sights include the orange-red walls of the - **SpasoYefimiyevsky Monastyr** (Monastery of the Lament of Christ), founded in 1352, the foam-white walls of the **Pokrovsky Monastyr** (Intercession Convent), the lacework of the gates leading to the **Rizopolozhensky Monastyr** (Monastery of the Deposition of the Virgin's Robe), the architectural finesse of the churches, and the indented silhouettes of the belfries. The townspeople built their churches outside the city walls; among the most important is the white stone **Rozhdestvensky Sobor** (Cathedral of the Nativity of the Virgin), 1225, with its dark-blue, gold-spotted cupolas.

Vladimir

The final town on the Golden Ring is **Vladimir ❾**, 35 km (22 miles) south of Suzdal and 190 km (113 miles) northeast of Moscow. Together with Novgorod the Great, Vladimir is often considered to be the birthplace of the Russian lands. As Kiev's splendour faded in the 12th century, Vladimir became the new capital of medieval Russia. But that status ended with the Mongol invasion in the middle of the 13th century and the rise of Moscow.

This pearl of ancient Russian culture was founded on the banks of the Klyazma River by Prince Vladimir Monomakh in 1108, although it was first mentioned in chronicles at the end of the 10th century.

The foremost sight in Vladimir is the 12th-century **Uspensky Sobor** (Assumption Cathedral), with its striking decor, perfect architectural forms, and frescoes by Andrei Rublyov and Daniil Chorny. But the most beautiful church in the city is the **Dmitrievsky Sobor** (Cathedral of St Dmitry), 1193–97, featuring splendid carvings of plants, birds, animals and hunting scenes on its facade. The third architectural marvel, the **Zolotiye Vorota** (Golden Gate), is a rare example of military architecture. It was built as a replica of the Golden Gate in Kiev and is a symbolic blend of impregnability and hospitality.

Another place well worth visiting is the Uspensky Sobor (Assumption Cathedral) in the 16th-century **Knyaginin Monastyr** (Princess Convent), located in the northwestern part of the city. Frescoes by 17th-century painters are the pride of the cathedral. It is these masterpieces of ancient Russian architecture that are the image of Vladimir. The historical centre of the city has more than 700 less valuable buildings dating from the 19th and the early 20th centuries. ❑

VYBORGSKAYA
STORONA

Finlandsky
Vokzal
M **1**
Ploshchad
Lenina

Liteiny
Most

4 KGB

Tavrichesky
Dvorets

TAVRICHESKY SAD

M CHERNYSHEVSKAYA

Kikiny
Palati

Smolny
Sobor
44

Smolny
Institut

Bolshoi
Okhtinsky Most

MALOOKHTINSKOYE
KLADBISHCHE

Fontanny Dom
Dvorets
41 Sheremetyevykh

Anichkov
Most

Dvorets
Beloselskikh-Belozerskikh
40

MAYAKOVSKAYA
M

PL.VOSSTANIYA
M
Ploshchad
Vosstaniya

NOVOCHERKASSKAYA **M**

DOSTOYEVSKAYA
M

Vladimirsky
Sobor
VLADIMIRSKAYA **M**

Moskovsky
Vokzal

Muzei
42 F.M.Dostoyevskovo

Hotel Moscow
PL.ALEXANDER
NEVSKOGO
Ploshchad
Alexander
Nevskogo

Alexander
Nevskova Most

Neva

LIGOVSKY PR.
M

NIKOLSKOE
KLADBISHCHE

Alexander
Nevsky
Lavra **43**
Troitsky
Sobor

Shlisselburgsky
Most

ZANEVSKY
SAD

Finlandsky
Zheleznodorozhny Most

St Petersburg

0   500 m

0   500 yds

ST PETERSBURG

St Petersburg is Russia's cultural capital, a stately city of islands, bridges and classical 18th-century palaces on the northern shores of the Baltic

Map on page 182–3

St Petersburg

Moscow

ankt Pitersburkh, Sankt Peterburg, Petrograd, Leningrad, Saint Petersburg – just as the city's name has changed over the centuries, so has its fortune. The history of St Petersburg has been one of continued struggle, destruction, and rebirth. Perhaps it is this constant tumult that has made it a living inspiration to some of the world's greatest cultural figures.

St Petersburg rose out of a swampy backwater on the Neva river delta at the beginning of the 18th century when Peter the Great realised his dream to build a new capital, a "Window on the West", that would open the way to European enlightenment and raise Russia out of its medieval past.

Peter named his new capital in honour of his patron saint using the Dutch pronunciation, Sankt Pitersburkh. He was enthralled with all things Dutch as he considered its civilisation to be the most advanced. Bringing "civilisation" to Russia, however, came at a medieval price. Historians estimate that at least 100,000 serfs and labourers died of exposure and disease while building the new capital. But by the end of the 19th century, when the city was called "Piter" by its inhabitants, it had indeed become great as the tsar-founder had envisaged and was a leading European cultural and scientific centre.

PRECEDING PAGES: Peter and Paul Fortress. **LEFT:** Alexander Column. **BELOW:** window in the Bolshevik headquarters, 1917.

Two changes of name

When World War I began in 1914, anti-German sentiment convinced Tsar Nicholas II, a cousin of the German Kaiser Wilhelm, to change the capital's name to the more Russian sounding Petrograd. Then in March 1918, the Bolsheviks, who had seized power the previous October, moved the capital back to Moscow while the Germans advanced on the "cradle of the Revolution".

As the Communist order established itself, it, too, wished to honour its heroes. In 1924, Petrograd's name was changed to commemorate the recently deceased founding father of the new Russian state. The city of Peter became the city of Lenin, Leningrad.

By 1924, a decade of war, civil war, famine, class strife, and the forces of nature – the city was hit by a devastating flood in that year – had left the former imperial capital in ruins. The magnificent buildings remained, but gone was the soul of a great civilisation as the cream of its society was either dead or had left the country in exile. Then with the onset of World War II the city experienced yet more suffering and destruction.

Undaunted, the people of Leningrad worked once again to rebuild their city into an important cultural, industrial and scientific centre. With the collapse of the Soviet Union in 1991, many of these accomplishments were swept away by the winds of change. Nevertheless, the new freedom has allowed the city to

The winter climate in St Petersburg is harsh, with strong winds and snow between November and late March. In summer, from the end of May to early July, there is an air of festivity due to the extraordinary White Nights, when the sun doesn't set.

win back its historical name and memory. As St Petersburg prepares to celebrate its 300th anniversary in 2003, the city is once again moving forward.

A beautiful misfit

From the beginning, St Petersburg has been something of an anomaly, a beautiful misfit, and a showpiece city. Peter the Great's vision of building a capital to rival the great cities of Europe seemed foolhardy to many, but in the end the great and stern tsar had the last laugh.

Peter gave his European designers – mostly second-rate, unemployed Italian, German and French architects – a huge amount of space to play with. Hence the city's layout of massive perspectives and ensembles of boldly symmetrical lines. The streets and buildings, although low, dwarf pedestrians. To appreciate the exterior of a building fully you have to view it from a distance, preferably from another island. This is particularly true when looking at the Hermitage.

As your eyes move along the city's embankment, the perfectly rectangular buildings disappear from sight into the vast flat Russian expanse and one architectural defect becomes obvious: with the exception of St Isaac's Cathedral, the Admiralty and Peter and Paul Cathedral, the buildings lack towers and turrets to accentuate their presence.

Tsarist tastes

Obviously, Peter the Great is not directly responsible for the St Petersburg that we see today, and few examples of the buildings of his era remain. His taste was simple and sparse. The preferences of his daughter, the Empress Elizabeth (1741–61) were much more fanciful. Her favourite architect, Bartolomeo

BELOW: aerial view of St Petersburg.

Rastrelli, liked colours and tended to decorate buildings as one would a cake for a great occasion, with piping and swirls. Catherine the Great (1762–96) was less frivolous in her tastes, but buildings were nevertheless grand in scope, and became even more so in the reign of Alexander I (1801–25) when they were designed to reflect the glory of Russia's victory over Napoleon and increasing foreign expansion.

Commerce and industrialisation before the Revolution brought the first railways which linked Moscow and St Petersburg in 1851, not to mention some fine examples of art nouveau at the turn of the century. Following the Revolution, the architecture of Stalin in the 1930s and 1950s was kept to the outskirts.

One outstanding feature of Stalin's time was the construction of the Leningrad metro, which started running in 1955. Besides the metro decorations (particularly impressive on the Kirov-Vyborg line) there is little art of the Soviet period in the centre of the city. However, 101 statues and busts to Lenin still stand. Some are in public places, but most are at factories and institutes. You will find a huge statue of Lenin outside **Finlandsky Vokzal** (Finland Station) ❶.

St Petersburg trams and buses run from 5.30am until midnight.

Despite extensive damage to older buildings during World War II, most of them have been rebuilt and faithfully restored to their original state. Today, lack of funding has left the city with a shabby look and buildings that have been restored stand out in marked contrast to their faded neighbours.

Literary connections

Architecture tells us much about a city, but equally revealing, particularly in St Petersburg, are the impressions of its famous writers whose works have immortalised many of its sights. Alexander Pushkin (1799–1837), Russia's equivalent

BELOW:
chess players in a city square.

Peter the Great is usually represented as a young man (as here), but in the grounds of Peter and Paul Fortress there is a sculpture by Michael Chemyakin portraying him seated in later life.

of Shakespeare, depicted St Petersburg's forbidding aspect in his poem *The Bronze Horseman*. The statue of Peter the Great, located on the river side in front of Isaakiyevsky Sobor (St Isaac's Cathedral), is known as the Bronze Horseman. In Pushkin's poem it comes to life and bears down on an enfeebled and terrified clerk called Evgeny. Pushkin also describes St Petersburg high-life in his poem *Evgeny Onegin*. The hero, one of literature's great dandies, becomes bored and disillusioned by an endless round of balls, restaurants and women.

Tolstoy takes up the same theme in his novels *War and Peace* and *Anna Karenina*, contrasting the spontaneity and simplicity of Moscow life with that of St Petersburg, which he saw as false, artificial and corrupt. Dostoyevsky, in marked contrast, wrote of low life and the poor.

In the poem *The Twelve*, Alexander Blok found in the 1917 Revolution a vision of the city's rebirth and the Second Coming of Christ. But he quickly became disenchanted with the barbarity of the Bolshevik regime, and died an untimely death in 1921.

Evgeny Zamyatin, in his short story *The Cavemen*, compared post-Revolutionary St Petersburg to a society of cave-dwellers, whose civilised values are subverted when the protagonist is forced to beg and then steal firewood in order to exist for just one more day.

A city under siege

Records of the city's suffering are not found only in literature, they also exist in living memory. The older generation remembers the Siege of Leningrad during World War II when the city was completely cut off from the outside world for almost 900 days. The Germans invaded Russia in July 1941 and reached

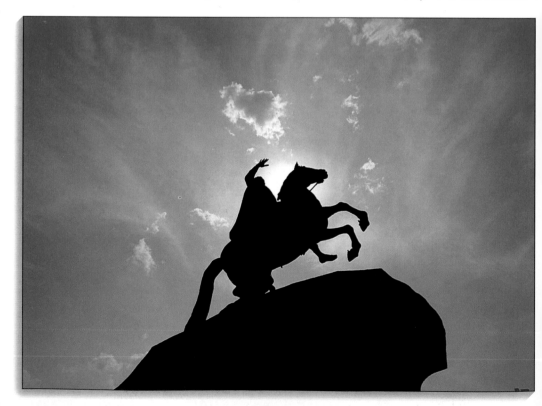

Leningrad in August of that year. The town was encircled and cut off from September, when mass bombing began.

Soviet troops finally broke through the blockade in January 1943 and provisions reached the city through Finland Station, but the siege did not end until January 1944 when the German armies were beaten back. Victory left nearly one million dead, most from starvation. Some 470,000 victims of the blockade are buried at the **Piskarovskoye Memorial Cemetery** situated on the northern outskirts of the city. The sheer size of this cemetery, with the dead buried in mass graves, gives a more chilling impression of the loss of life than any statistic.

Touring the sights

The most appropriate place to begin a tour of St Petersburg is **Petropavlovskaya Krepost** (Peter and Paul Fortress) ❷ (open 11am–6pm), built during the time of the Great Northern War, 1700–21. The first stone was laid on 16 May 1703 Old Style (unlike Europe and America who by this date had switched to the new Gregorian Calendar, Russia still used the calendar of Julius Caesar, which was 13 days behind the Gregorian).

The fortress, built on **Zayachy Ostrov** (Hare Island) according to plans drawn by Peter himself, was designed to stave off the enemy, occupying as it did a strategic position at the dividing point of the Neva into the Malaya (Small) and Bolshaya (Big) Neva. It became a notorious prisons – the Bastille of tsarist Russia. In 1917 the **Kommandantsky Dom** (Commandant's House) ❸ was one of the Bolshevik command posts for the storming of the Winter Palace. But today such an infamous place has become a favourite place of relaxation, and many city-dwellers flock to the beach in front of the fortress on pleasant sum-

Map on pages 182–3

TIP

Many streets have reverted to their pre-Revolutionary names causing confusion even among local residents. It often helps to know the old name, especially when taking a taxi.

BELOW: soaring spire of Peter and Paul Fortress.

CITY OF ISLANDS

St Petersburg is Russia's largest seaport and second largest city with an official population of just under 5 million. It lies 60°N, on the same latitude as Alaska, Hudson Bay, the southern tip of Greenland and Oslo. While the city originally straddled 101 islands at the mouth of the River Neva, which sweeps majestically through its centre, many have since disappeared as the rivers, streams and canals have been filled in. Today, the "Venice of the North" is situated on 42 islands linked by 432 pedestrian, car and rail bridges. Twenty of these are drawbridges, some of which rise each night between 2am and 5am, from the months of April to the end of November, to allow the passage of sea-going ships. The Neva flows westerly from Lake Ladoga, 74 km (46 miles) to the east, into the Gulf of Finland. Here, where it branches into three arms, separating the Petrograd Side and Vasilievsky Island from the mainland, the main channel is 400 metres (437 yards) wide.

Today, granite embankments contain the 68 rivers, canals, channels and streams which separate the islands. These waterways, Lake Ladoga and the sea freeze over in winter and icebreakers have to be used to keep the port open throughout the year.

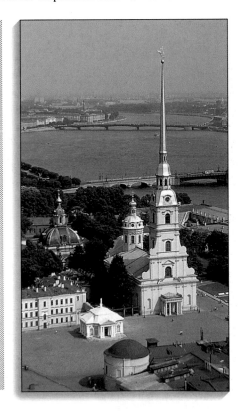

*During the White
Nights of June,
crowds gather at
2am on both sides of
the River Neva, near
the Hermitage, to
watch the raising of
the drawbridges to
allow sea-going
vessels to pass.*

mer as well as winter days. Though it is forbidden to swim there, many do, even in winter. There are various buildings for the visitor to see within the fortress, as well as temporary exhibitions. The major features are **Petrovskiye Vorota** (Peter Gate), built by Domenico Trezzini, who also designed the cathedral. The gate, originally built in wood and later in stone (1717–18), has hardly changed since it was built. The bas-relief above the tsarist emblem of the double-headed eagle depicts the Apostle Peter overthrowing Simon the Magus, an allegory of Russia's victory over the Swedes.

Petropavlovsky Sobor (Peter and Paul Cathedral) is rectangular in layout and quite unlike a traditional Russian place of worship. It bears a tall spire standing at 122 metres (400 ft), that was the tallest building in the city until the city's Television Tower (316 metres/1,036 ft) was built. On the top is an angel carrying a cross. In 1830, Pyotr Telushkin, a roofer, climbed to the very top, with the aid of just a rope, to repair the cross which had been struck by lightning.

Inside the church are the white marble tombs of most of the Romanov emperors and empresses, as well as some grand dukes. Peter the Great's tomb lies in the far right-hand corner. The remains of the last Russian tsar, Nicholas II, his wife, three of their children, and their four servants were buried here in 1998 having been transported from Yekaterinburg in the Urals where they were murdered in 1918. Their grave is situated in the **Yekaterinsky Pridel** (St Catherine Chapel), which is to the right as you enter through the main cathedral entrance. The last ruling Romanovs have been consigned to this private chapel for two reasons: Nicholas II renounced the throne; and commoners are buried with the royal family. The tombs of Alexander II, the tsar liberator who freed the serfs but was none the less blown up by leftist terrorists, and his wife are in great con-

BELOW: the cruiser *Aurora* outside the Nakhimov Naval Academy.

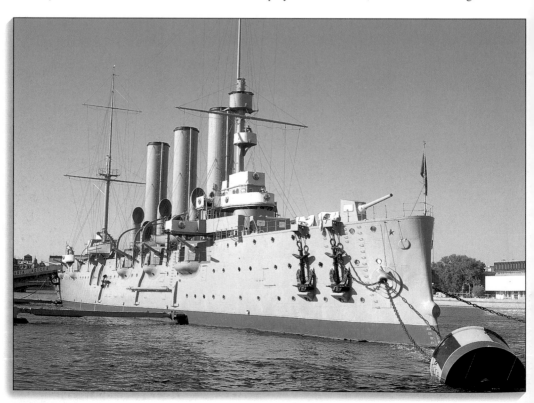

trast to the others. Theirs are the only ones not made of marble, but made instead from Altai jasper and Urals rhodonite.

In 1717 the fortress became a prison for political prisoners and the cells are now open as a museum in the **Trubetskoy Bastion**. One of its first prisoners, who was later beaten to death, was Peter the Great's son Alexei, who was falsely accused of plotting against his father.

Other distinguished inmates were Fyodor Dostoyevsky; Alexander Radishchev, author of *A Journey from St Petersburg to Moscow*, in which he criticised autocracy and serfdom; Nikolai Chernyshevsky, a Revolutionary democrat and author of *What is to be Done?*; Lenin's elder brother, Alexander Ulyanov, who was executed for taking part in the plot to murder Alexander III, and the socially-oriented writer Maxim Gorky, who wrote a Revolutionary proclamation calling for the overthrow of the monarchy.

In the Soviet period, political prisoners were taken to KGB **headquarters** ❹ (now FSB) on Liteiny Prospekt in a building nicknamed the "Big House", and not without reason. It is the tallest, biggest building in the city centre.

Peter and Paul Fortress has six bastions, one named Gosudarev (Ruler's) in honour of Peter the Great, and the rest named after his closest companions who supervised the construction of the fortress. A cannon shot is fired every day at noon from the **Naryshkinsky Bastion**.

The **Kommandantsky Pristan** (Commandant's Pier) offers one of the best views over the Neva. On the river banks near the fortress stands **Domik Petra Velikogo** (Peter the Great's Wooden Cabin) ❺, which is now a museum (open 10am–6pm; closed Tues). Although protected by stone on the outside, inside there is a perfectly preserved, two-roomed hut. It was made out of rough pine

Map on page 182–3

BELOW: view from the Grand Palace at Peterhof, west of St Petersburg.

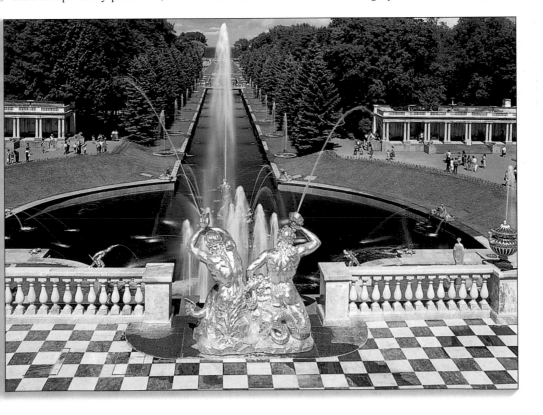

over a period of three days in 1703. Peter lived here for six years while overseeing the building of the city.

Moored in front of the blue **Nakhimovskoye Uchilishche** (Nakhimov Naval Academy) **6** on Petrogradskaya Embankment – designed in the style of Petrine baroque and completed in 1912 – is the cruiser *Kreyser Avrora* (*Aurora*) **7** (open for tours 10.30am–4.30pm; closed Fri), famous for its part in the 1917 Revolution. At 9.45pm on 25 October 1917, the *Aurora* fired a blank round, the signal for the Bolshevik forces to storm the Winter Palace, the seat of the provisional government. Prior to this, between 1904 and 1905, it served the tsarist government at the Battle of Tsu-Shima against Japan. Today, the cruiser once again flies the tsarist-era naval Flag of St Andrew whose blue diagonal cross on a white background is common in St Petersburg, home of the Russian fleet.

On the opposite side of the river is the tsar's modest **Letny Dvorets** (Summer Palace) **8** (open May–Oct, 11am–6pm; closed Tues) built by Domenico Trezzini in 1710. It has retained most of its original features, occupying two floors of identical layout, one for the tsar and one for the tsarina. Its simple exterior was later decorated by terracotta panels depicting scenes from mythology – including allegorical portrayals of the Northern War.

Letny Sad (the Summer Garden) in which the palace stands is the oldest garden in the city. Much of the work was done by the architect Jean Baptiste LeBlond. It was originally a formal garden with many rare plants and trees, an aviary and a grotto, but its appearance has changed over the years as Venetian statues were commissioned and buildings such as the **Chainy Domik** (Tea House) and a statue of Ivan Krylov (1768–1844), the author of children's fables, have been added but it is still one of the city's most peaceful and shady places.

The Metchet (Mosque), Troitskaya Ploshchad, is the only mosque in the city. It was built in 1912.

BELOW: Hermitage Museum.

Map on page 182–3

The path through the centre of the gardens leads as far as the Fontanka Canal and the red **Inzhenerny Zamok** (Engineer's Castle, also known as St Michael Castle) ❾. The castle was built by Catherine the Great's son, Tsar Paul I, with strong walls and a moat to prevent any attempt at assassination, the fate of which had befallen his father, Tsar Peter III, at Catherine's hands. But such efforts proved in vain: military officers bribed the guards and murdered Paul just 40 days after he had taken up residence. Paul's son, Alexander I, was complicit to the murder which put him on the throne. So much for 18th-century Russian family cohesion. The castle acquired its current name when it became a school for engineers in 1819. Its most famous student was Dostoyevsky.

St Petersburg is a federal city, with the official status of a "subject of the Federation". It is one of Russia's 89 regions, and the head of the city is called "governor" not "mayor".

The Hermitage Museum

The **Muzei Ermitazh** (Hermitage Museum) ❿ (open Mon–Wed, Fri, Sat 10.30am–6pm; Thur noon–8pm; closed Mon) is made up of four buildings, **Zimny Dvorets** (the Winter Palace), the Small Hermitage, the New Hermitage and the Old Hermitage. The Winter Palace was designed by the architect Bartolomeo Rastrelli, who started work on it in 1754, during Empress Elizabeth's reign. He built it, to use his own words, "solely for the glory of all Russia". It was the home of the imperial family, with the exception of Paul I, until 1917, when it became the seat of the provisional government.

The **State Collection** was originally the private collection of Catherine the Great (1729–96). She started collecting later than other European monarchs, but she did so in earnest, instructing her ambassadors in Europe to buy not just individual pictures, but entire collections. She housed them in her retreat ("Hermitage") and only a select few people were permitted to see them. The museum was not open to the public until 1852. During the siege in the 1940s, most of the artworks were successfully evacuated. Although renowned for its collections of Western European art, including early 13th-century Italian works, French Impressionists and modern art, the Hermitage has other important departments, notably those of pre-historic cultures, oriental and classical antiquities, as well as an exhibition of gold treasures that are among the finest in the world.

Of equal interest is the architecture of the interior: the Jordan Staircase, Great Hall, Large Throne Room and Gallery of the 1812 War, to name a few (see Insight On the Hermitage, page 206).

BELOW: the ornate Ambassador's Staircase at the Hermitage Museum.

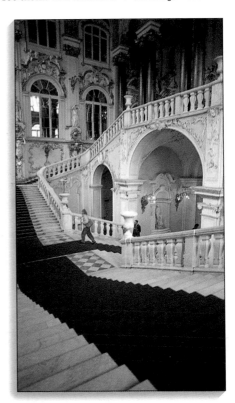

Palace Square

Behind the Hermitage is the impressive **Dvortsovaya Ploshchad** (Palace Square) ⓫, with its towering **Alexandrovskaya Kolonna** (Alexander Column) erected to the design of August de Montferrand to commemorate the victory of Russian armies in the Napoleonic War during the reign of Alexander I. It is made from a granite monolith transported from the northern shore of the Gulf of Finland. This 47.5-metre (156-ft) high column is held together entirely by its own weight.

On evenings, both summer and winter when there's no snow, the square is a favourite meeting place for teenagers on roller blades. On the south side of the

Dvortsovaya Ploshchad (Palace Square) is a popular venue for rock concerts during June's White Nights Festival.

BELOW: Alexander Column in Palace Square with the General Staff Building behind.

square is the curved, sprawling, neoclassical **Generalny Shtab** (General Staff Building), designed by Carlo Rossi (1775–1849). Its arch is decorated with a chariot of victory and statues of warriors,

Rossi designed many buildings in St Petersburg, most of which are painted pale yellow as opposed to the pale greens and blues preferred by Rastrelli. Before the Revolution many of the government buildings – with the exception of the Admiralty – were painted dark red (for example, the General Staff Building, the Winter Palace and the Senate and Synod).

At the corner of Palace Square is Millionnaya Ulitsa (Million Street), which runs behind the Hermitage to the Field of Mars. At the beginning of Millionnaya Ulitsa the porch of the New Hermitage building is supported by figures of Atlas, designed by a German architect, Leo von Klenze (1784–1864).

At the end of the street is the **Mramorny Dvorets** (Marble Palace) ⑫. It is faced with marble, which is a rarity in this city of plaster facades. The palace was commissioned by Catherine the Great for one of her favourites, Grigory Orlov, and the task of designing it went to the Italian architect Antonio Rinaldi (1709–94). Before the Revolution the palace was the home of various grand dukes, but in 1937 it became the city's Lenin Museum. Now it belongs to the Russian Museum and houses the National Portrait Gallery (open 10.30am–6pm, closed Wed).

The tsar used to review his troops in **Marsovoye Pole** (Field of Mars) ⑬. It was redesigned after the 1917 Revolution by the architect Lev Vladimirorich Rudnyev (who later built the famous skyscraper of Moscow University.) Some Communists who fought and died in the Revolution and Civil War are buried here where an eternal flame burns in the centre. But since the fall of communism

Map on page 182–3

few Russians pay their respects to the dead, and many wish they had not even bothered to make that ultimate sacrifice.

Decembrists Square

Along the embankment from the Hermitage is the city's most famous statue: **Medny Vsadnik** (The Bronze Horseman) ⓮, depicting Peter the Great on a rearing horse. It was cast from the model of the French sculptor Etienne Falconet and completed in 1782. The head of Peter the Great was designed by Falconet's pupil, Marie Collot, who never earned the recognition she deserved for this particular work.

The square in which the statue stands, **Ploshchad Dekabristov** (Decembrists Square) is where, on 14 December 1825, tsarist troops fired on 3,000 revolting soldiers and spectators, many of whom were innocently driven into action by revolutionary-minded young officers who wanted to turn Russia into a republic. The yellow buildings of **Senat i Sinod** (The Senate and the Synod) ⓯ were designed by Carlo Rossi between 1829 and 1832.

Nearby stands the golden spire of the **Admiralteistvo** (Admiralty) ⓰. This was one of the first buildings of the city, built in 1705, then replaced between 1806 and 1823 by the present neoclassical structure designed by Andrei Zakharov. It was used as a naval headquarters and as a shipyard. At the top of the spire is a weather-vane in the form of a ship, the emblem of the city. From the Admiralty the main streets of Nevsky, Gorokhovaya and Vosnesensky stretch out like an open fan. The fountains in front of the Admiralty are surrounded by statues of Russia's cultural heroes, including the writers Nikolai Gogol and Mikhail Lermontov, the composer Mikhail Glinka and the poet Vasily Zhukovsky.

BELOW: winter in the Field of Mars.

St Petersburg is the home of the Russian navy, which celebrated its 300th anniversary in 1996. Its headquarters are in the Admiralty.

BELOW: the golden spire of the Admiralty building.

St Isaac's Square

Isaakiyevsky Sobor (St Isaac's Cathedral) ⓱ stands in the square behind. It was built over a period of 40 years in the first half of the 19th century by the French architect Auguste de Montferrand. The dome is covered with 100 kg (220 lb) of pure gold. Forty-three types of stone and marble were used to decorate the lavish interior, including the lapis lazuli and malachite columns of the iconostasis. Among the general surfeit of visual splendour is a statue of the architect carrying a model of the cathedral in his hand. Montferrand very much wanted to be buried here, but his wish was denied by the tsar because of the Frenchman's Catholicism.

In the middle of St Isaac's Square stands a statue of Nicholas I on a prancing horse, by Pyotr Klodt. According to a Russian saying commenting on the obvious parallel with The Bronze Horseman: "The fool [Nicholas I] chases the wise man [Peter I] but St Isaac's stands in between."

Mariinsky Dvorets (Mariinsky Palace) ⓲, on the south side of the square, is now home to the city's Legislative Assembly. It was built between 1839 and 1844 by Andrei Stakenschneider. The palace was a present from Nicholas I to his daughter Maria. The bridge in front crossing the River Moyka is **Siny Most** (Blue Bridge) and is the widest in the city. Further along the Moyka in the direction of **Novaya Gollandia** (New Holland) is **Yusupovsky Dvorets** (Yusupov Palace) ⓳ (open for tours noon–8pm; closed Sun) at number 94, home of Rasputin's chief assassin. Rasputin was murdered here in 1916. The rooms have been restored to evoke the eerie atmosphere of the night of the murder; there is even a creepy wax figure of Rasputin . Behind the red brickwork of Novaya Gollandia, Peter the Great stored his ship-building timber.

Theatre Square

The Moika turns a bend along the Kryukova Kanal, bordering **Teatralnaya Ploshchad** (Theatre Square), home of the Mariinsky (formerly Kirov) Theatre and, opposite, the **Rimsky-Korsakov Conservatory**.

The **Mariinsky Teatr** ⓴, founded in 1730, is where some of the first Russian operas and ballets were performed, including Mussorgsky's *Boris Godunov* (1874) and Tchaikovsky's *Sleeping Beauty* (1890). Dancers such as Kschessinska, Pavlova and Nijinsky made their debut here. Today, the main theatre company is often on tour, but the second and third companies stage superb productions.

Maria, from whom the theatre took its name, was the wife of Alexander II. Kirov was the Secretary of the Leningrad Communist Party from 1926 until 1934. His murder at Smolny, then Communist Party headquarters and now the seat of the city governor, triggered Stalin's purges of the 1930s.

Beside Kryukova Kanal in **Nikolskaya Ploshchad** (St Nicholas Square) is the blue and gold **Nikolsky Morskoy Sobor** (Cathedral of St Nicholas) ㉑, otherwise know as the "Sailor's Church", built between 1753 and 1762 by Savva Chevakinsky. This working cathedral is often compared with Rastrelli's Smolny Cathedral. It is considered to be one of the finest examples of Russian baroque.

Vasilievsky Island

On the other side of the River Neva, facing The Bronze Horseman, is one of the oldest parts of the city, **Vasilievsky Ostrov** (Basil's Island). One of its more "modern" buildings overlooking the river is the **Akademiya Khudozhestv** (Academy of Arts) ❷, built by Catherine the Great in 1757 as a training ground for professional painters, architects, sculptors and engravers. In front of it, on a granite pier, stand two **sphinxes** which date from the 13th century BC. They were brought to St Petersburg from Egypt in 1832.

The **obelisk** standing next to the academy on its eastern side commemorates Russia's victory over the Turks under Field-Marshal Rumyantsev in the 18th century. The next building is the **Menshikovsky Dvorets** (Menshikov Palace) ❷, now a branch of the Hermitage Museum. Alexander Menshikov was a friend, enemy and rival of Peter the Great. As Menshikov's palace was finished before Peter's, it was used for large-scale entertainment. Peter staged an extraordinary event for his niece here: a wedding feast attended by dwarfs.

Walking east along the embankment, the terracotta-coloured building is called **12 Kollegi** (Twelve Colleges) ❷. Peter housed his *kollegia* (ministries) here; it is now part of St Petersburg University. The building's construction, in which a number of architects, including Rastrelli, participated, was set as a competition – Russia's first. Construction took 19 years and was completed in1741.

To its east, the **Akademiya Nauk (Academy of Sciences)** ❷ was built to house the expanding collection of the **Kunstkamera** (Chamber of Curiosities; open 11am–5pm; closed Fri), a museum of anthropology and ethnography next door. Inside, beneath the dome, is a collection of genetic freaks, embryos and human organs, all of which held a particular fascination for Peter the Great.

TIP

Mariinsky Theatre tickets can be more expensive for foreigners. In 1998 the Supreme Court ruled that price discrimination on the basis of nationality is illegal, so visitors should demand the cheaper rate.

BELOW: interior, St Isaac's Cathedral.

Siberian mammoth, one of the exhibits at the Zoological Museum of the Academy of Sciences (open 11am–5pm, closed Fri).

Vasilievsky Island's easterly "spit" offers one of the best views of the city. Many newly-weds come here to be photographed. The magnificent building which dominates the spit is now the **Voyenno-Morskoi Muzei** (Central Naval Museum **26**) (open Wed–Sun 10.30am–5pm). Before the Revolution it was the Stock Exchange. Until the 1880s this point of Vasilievsky Island was the city's port. The red columns were the lighthouses. They are decorated with the prows of boats representing four Russian rivers: the Volga, Dnieper, Neva and Volkhov.

Nevsky Prospekt

The 4.5-km (2.8-mile) **Nevsky Prospekt**, which runs southeast from the Admiralty to the Alexander Nevskova Most (bridge), is the most famous street in St Petersburg. Apart from the splendid architecture of Nevsky Prospekt, there is plenty of activity at street level. People might not walk gracefully or pose as in days gone by, and the street is not as clean as in Nikolai Gogol's time ("how spotlessly clean are its pavements swept and, good gracious, how many feet leave their marks on them!"), but Nevsky Prospekt remains a good place to take the city's pulse.

Starting from **Admiralteisky Prospekt**, the first important street which crosses the Nevsky is **Malaya Morskaya**. Gogol lived at No. 17. Here he wrote the first chapters of *Dead Souls*. Pyotr Tchaikovsky died at No. 8. The next street is the once fashionable **Bolshaya Morskaya**, home of the famous Fabergé shop (No. 24). It is still a jeweller, but has lost its former glory. The Nevsky crosses the River Moika where, on the right-hand side stands the green and white **Stroganovsky Dvorets** (Stroganov Palace) **27**, home of one of Russia's leading families. It was designed by Rastrelli, architect of the Winter Palace. The

BELOW:
Stroganov Palace.

next street on the left, **Ulitsa Bolshaya Konushennaya**, leads to the former stables. The residents of No. 13 Bolshaya Konushennaya, included the Russian writer Ivan Turgenev and, later, the ballet dancer Nijinsky. The musician Rimsky-Korsakov lived at No. 11.

A short distance along Nevsky Prospekt, on the right, stands the majestic **Kazansky Sobor** (Kazan Cathedral) ❷❽ with its 90-metre (295-ft) high dome and 96 columns, designed by the architect Andrei Voronikhin in the first decade of the 19th century.

In the square in front are statues of the heroes of the 1812 war, M.I. Kutuzov (who is also buried here) and M.B. Barklay de Tolly. From the 1930s, the cathedral was a Museum of the History of Religion and Atheism. Now it is just the **Muzei Istoriya Religii** (Museum of the History of Religion). Religious services have been restored and its cross has been replaced.

Opposite, at No. 28 Nevsky Prospekt, is the art nouveau **Dom Knigi** (House of Books) ❷❾ in what was the pre-1917 Russia head office of the Singer Sewing Machine Company. You can't miss the huge globe on the roof.

As you cross the **Griboyedov Kanal**, the multi-coloured domes of **Khram Spasa na Krovi** (Church of the Resurrection) ❸❶, also known as Saviour on the Blood, are visible. It was built on the site of Alexander II's assassination. This church has been extensively restored and is now open to the public.

Two interesting bridges by the same architect, W. Traitteur (1825–26), cross the Griboyedov as it flows away from Nevsky Prospekt to the right. The first is **Bankovsky Most** (Bankers' Bridge) on which stand guard two golden-winged griffins. The bridge is so named because the large building in front, housing the Institute of Finance and Economics, used to be the Russian Central Bank in tsarist times. Most of the country's gold supply was stored here. In ancient mythology, griffins stood guard over gold. Beyond is **Lvinny Most** (Lion Bridge) where two lions hold the suspension cables of the bridge in their mouths.

Continuing eastwards along the Nevsky, on the left-hand side in Ulitsa Mikhailovskovo is the luxurious **Grand Hotel Europe** ❸❶. The street on which it stands leads into **Ploshchad Iskusstv** (Square of the Arts), home of the Russian Museum.

The yellow classical building of the **Russky Muzei** (Russian Museum) ❸❷ (open 10am–6pm; closed Tues) was built by Rossi between 1819 and 1825 for Grand Duke Mikhail, Alexander I and Nicholas I's younger brother. Unlike the Hermitage it houses only Russian art and is a smaller, more manageable museum. The exhibits span almost 1,000 years of the history of Russian art, from a magnificent icon collection through works by avant-garde artists such as Malevich and Kandinsky to contemporary work.

Also in Ploshchad Iskusstv stands the **Sankt Peterburzhskaya Filarmoniya** (St Petersburg Philharmonia) ❸❸ and the **Maly Teatr imeni Musorgskogo** (the Small Musorgsky Theatre of Opera and Ballet) ❸❹. In the middle of the square is a statue of Pushkin by one of the city's leading sculptors, Mikhail Anikushin. Back on the Nevsky Prospekt, with Ploshchad Iskusstv behind you, notice

Map on page 182–3

The Taleon Club on Naberezhnaya Reki Moiki, off Nevsky Prospect, is one of the city's most elite venues, frequented by politicians and businessmen. Luxury cars draw up at the entrance under the watchful eyes of burly guards.

BELOW: shopping in a city arcade.

TIP

Alexander Pushkin,
"Russia's
Shakespeare", is a
cult figure in the city.
A visit to the Pushkin
Flat-Museum at 12
Moyka Embankment,
could be followed by a
concert at No. 20, the
Kapella Music Hall.

BELOW:
Beloselsky Palace.

the long yellow and white facade of **Gostiny Dvor** ❸ on the right-hand side. This is one of St Petersburg's largest department stores. Two blocks along the Nevsky on the left-hand side, at No. 58, is a food shop with an extravagant art nouveau interior, built for the rich merchant **Yeliseyev** ❸ and once the grandest delicatessen in St Petersburg.

Sadovaya Ulitsa runs beside Gostiny Dvor to **Sennaya Ploshchad** (Hay Square), a traditionally seedy area. Raskolnikov, in Dostoyevsky's *Crime and Punishment*, wandered here, where "types so various were to be seen that no figure, however queer, would have caused surprise".

To the right just after the junction of Sadovaya Ulitsa and Nevsky is **Ploshchad Ostrovskogo**, a huge square with a statue of Catherine the Great surrounded by her most prominent court officials, some of whom were her lovers.

This square is named after the playwright Alexander Ostrovsky. Its buildings include the **Russkaya Natsionalnaya Biblioteka** (Russian National Library; (not open to the public) ❸ and the **Alexandriinsky Dramatichesky Teatr** (Alexander Theatre of Drama) ❸, with its white Corinthian columns.

Behind the theatre, leading away from the right-hand corner of the square, is **Ulitsa Zodchego Rossi** (Street of the Architect Rossi). This street has perfect proportions with the width of the street equalling the height of the buildings. Among its buildings is the **Vaganova Ballet School** ❸, the training ground for some of the greatest names in ballet, including Pavlova, Nijinsky, Nureyev, Makarova and Baryshnikov.

Back on the Nevsky Prospekt, the next canal is the **Fontanka** with its impressive **Anichkov Most** (Anichkov Bridge). The horses which decorate the bridge are the work of the sculptor Pyotr Klodt. During World War II they were buried underground in the nearby gardens of the **Dvorets Yunikh Pionerov** (Palace of Young Pioneers), as were many of the cities' famous statues.

Behind the Anichkov Bridge stands the dark-red **Dvorets Beloselskikh-Belozerskikh** (Beloselsky-Belozersky Palace) **⓵**, built by Stakenschneider in 1847–48 for Prince Beloselsky-Belozersky.

To the left, on the banks of the Fontanka, is the yellow **Dvorets Shereme-tyevykh** (Sheremetyev Palace) **⓸** built by Chevakinsky between 1750 and 1755. One of its outbuildings, the **Fontanny Dom**, houses the **Muzei Anni Akhmatovoi**, the literary museum of Anna Akhmatova, one of Russia's greatest poets (open 11am–6pm; closed Mon and last Thurs in month).

At the next junction, Liteiny Prospekt, is the famous second-hand bookstore, **Bukinist** (No. 59). To the right, **Vladimirsky Prospekt** leads to a side street, Kuznechny Pereulok, where the **Muzei F.M. Dostyevskovo** (Dostoyevsky Museum) **⓶** is located. Here, the writer lived and died, and it now operates as a museum (open 11am–6pm; closed Mon). Nearby is the 18th-century, five-domed **Vladimirsky Sobor** (St Vladimir church).

At the very end of the Nevsky Prospekt is **Ploshchad Alexander Nevskogo**, where the **Hotel Moscow** stands. Here is the **Alexander Nevsky Lavra ⓷**, the oldest and most beautiful monastery complex in the city. Alexander Nevsky crushed two separate invading Swedish and German armies in the mid-13th century and was later canonised. His remains are buried inside the Lavra.

There are several cemeteries inside the complex, where some of Russia's most famous citizens are buried. In the **Lazarus Cemetery**, where Peter the Great's sister, Natalya Alexeyevna, lies, you will find the graves of famous architects, including Rossi and Voronikhin. The composers Mikhail Glinka,

Map on page 182–3

The twice-weekly St Petersburg Times *is the city's only English language newspaper. Covering politics, business and culture, it is one of the few independent voices – more than half of its readers are Russian.*

BELOW: the study in which Dostoyevsky wrote *The Brothers Karamazov.*

Pyotr Tchaikovsky, Modest Musorgsky and Nikolai Rimsky-Korsakov are buried in the **Tikvin Cemetery** opposite, together with Fyodor Dostoyevsky. Today, most famous people from the arts world are buried in the **Volkhov Cemetery**, a short drive from the Lavra.

Smolny Cathedral and Institute

Another religious building not to be missed is **Smolny Sobor** (Smolny Cathedral) **44**, situated in the area northeast of Nevsky Prospekt. Designed by Rastrelli, this pale blue and white building in the shape of a Greek cross seems to float rather than stand on the horizon. Smolny means "tar" and the site of the cathedral was used as a tar yard until 1723. Although construction began in the mid-18th century, the cathedral was not completely finished until the end of the 19th century.

In 1764 Catherine the Great created an institute next to the cathedral "for the education of well-born young ladies", the first of its kind in Russia. The **Smolny Institut** was housed in the yellow, neoclassical building designed by Giacomo Quarenghi between 1806 and 1808. In August 1917 this building became the headquarters of the Bolshevik Central Committee, and it was from here that Lenin led the uprising in October of that year.

Opposite the cathedral, two blocks along **Shpalernaya Ulitsa**, are the **Kikiny Palati** (Kikin Palace) and **Tavrichesky Dvorets** (Tauride Palace). Kikin was an associate of Peter the Great and although the palace has been rebuilt the basic structure dates from 1714. The Tauride Palace was built between 1783 and 1789 for Grigory Potemkin. Potemkin was one of Catherine the Great's favourites, arguably no less than co-regent in view of his influence over her. He is remembered for annexing the Crimea in 1783.

Crowds stood and cheered on Anichkovsky Most (Anichkov Bridge) when the horses were restored after World War II.

BELOW: Monplaisir at Petrodvorets.

Out-of-town palaces

A visit to St Petersburg is not complete without a trip to one or more of the five palaces now open to the public. Petrodvorets, the Catherine Palace at Pushkin (Tsarskoye Selo), and Pavlovsk attract the most visitors. They have been fully restored following the devastation of German occupation in World War II. The palaces at Oranienbaum and Gatchina are undergoing major restoration work.

Petrodvorets (open 9am–10pm; Grand Palace closed Mon and last Tues of month; Hermitage, Monplaisir closed Wed and last Thur; Marly closed Tues and last Wed) Peter's summer palace, is situated on the Gulf of Finland, 29 km (18 miles) west of the city. One of its most striking features is its fountains (which are turned off in the winter). The original palace was built by Peter the Great in 1720 to the design of Jean-Baptiste LeBlond. It was much simpler than the version that now stands, which was embellished and enlarged by Empress Elizabeth. But traces of Peter the Great and LeBlond show through the baroque glitz. They chose the magnificent site on a natural slope – a Versailles by the sea – and were responsible for the intricate fountains, a major feat on land consisting of marshy clay. Looking at pictures of Petrodvorets after the ravages of World War II, one wonders it was ever rebuilt. Some, but by no means all of its treasures were smuggled out in time to escape bomb damage. The Grand Cascade is the focal point of the water gardens in front of the **Grand Palace**, with the famous statue of Samson rending apart the jaws of a lion.

The gardens contain three pavilions. The first, the **Hermitage**, was where Peter entertained, helped by a "dumb waiter" device – a section of the round table was lowered below ground to be cleared and replenished. The **Marly** is built in a simple Dutch style and **Monplaisir**, at the water's edge, became Peter's favourite retreat; he could see the sea from his bed.

Inside, his taste is reflected in the beautiful oak staircase, oak study and the elaborate throne room, where his original throne sits. Catherine the Great later introduced such rooms as the Portrait Gallery, with its portraits of 368 women in different costumes.

About 12 km (7 miles) along the coast is **Oranienbaum** (open 11am–5pm; closed Tues; Chinese Palace closed Oct–May), built by Alexander Menshikov. It was the construction of Oranienbaum that inspired Peter the Great to build Petrodvorets. In the summer the **Chinese Palace**, built by Catherine, is open to the public, along with the **Coasting Pavilion**, though its roller coaster with wooden toboggans no longer stands.

Pushkin (formerly Tsarskoye Selo, the Tsar's Village) can be reached by train from St Petersburg's Vitebsk Station. This station is well worth seeing for its splendid Russian art nouveau interior. It was the first Russian station and the line between here and Tsarskoe Selo was the first Russian railway (1837).

Peter the Great's wife, Catherine I, chose the site for a stone country house, intended as a surprise for her husband while he was away in Poland. It seems to be the fate of each royal palace to be altered by successive monarchs and

Map on page 182-3

Frequent pilgrimages are made to the grave of St Ksenya Blazhennaya (the Blessed), in Smolenskoye cemetery. The 18th-century saint was endowed with gifts of healing and prophecy, and to this day many claim miracles from her.

BELOW: Catherine Palace, Pushkin.

THE AMBER ROOM MYSTERY

Of all the works of art that disappeared from St Petersburg's palaces during World War II, few have captured the imagination of historians and treasure hunters as much as the Amber Room. This priceless 18th-century masterpiece was made by German craftsmen in the early 1700s for the Prussian King Friedrich I's palace in Charlottenburg, Berlin. His son gave it to Peter the Great who fell in love with it on a visit to Berlin. In 1754 the Amber Room was mounted in the Catherine Palace at Pushkin. It comprised six large oak wall panels, covering more than 100 sq metres (120 sq yards), inlaid with six tons of amber, wall mirrors, and Italian mosaics containing precious stones. The room dazzled in sunlight, prompting one 18th-century British ambassador to call it the Eighth Wonder of the World. In September 1941 the Nazis removed it to the German city of Königsberg (now Russian Kaliningrad) on the Baltic coast where it was last seen in 1945. Its current whereabouts is unknown.

Over the past 20 years Russian craftsmen working at the Catherine Palace have been trying to recreate the room. About 40 percent of the restoration is complete and it has been opened to the public. But no progress has been made since 1996 because of a lack of funds.

Map
on page
182–3

The summer resort of Pushkin (Tsarskoye Selo) is said to have had the first electric street lighting in Europe. It was renamed on account of the poet having studied at the Lycée.

BELOW: flute-player at Catherine Palace.
RIGHT: the gilded domes of the Church of the Resurrection of Christ.

Peter's daughter, the Empress Elizabeth, decided to build a new and more opulent palace here in 1741. She asked Rastrelli to model it on Versailles.

It was enlarged by subsequent rulers, particularly by Catherine the Great, whose architect, the Scotsman Charles Cameron, gave the palace a more stately feel, but above all it is Elizabeth's own creation. The extravagant, baroque design is symbolic of the mood which dominated during her reign. In 1941 Tsarskoye Selo was occupied by the German army, which left the town and palace in ruins.

The interior of the restored **Bolshoi Yekaterinsky Dvorets** (Catherine Palace; open 10am–5pm; closed Tues and last Mon in month), like its exterior, is a mixture of styles by different architects: for example, the baroque of Rastrelli and the classicism of Cameron. The Great Hall, with its massive mirrors, wood carvings and glistening gold is perhaps the most sumptuous of all.

There is a great deal to see in the park, including the Upper and Lower Baths, the Hermitage, the great pond, the fountain of the milkmaid with the broken pitcher, inspired by one of La Fontaine's fables, and the Caprice. When visiting a palace that has been so highly restored, it is important to see the ruins, so a visit to the **Chinese Palace** is also recommended. In the grounds stand the **Alexander Park and Palace**. This smaller, more classical palace, which is not open to the public, was presented to Alexander I by his grandmother, Catherine the Great, on the occasion of his marriage.

The Halls of War and Peace

The next stop on the Electric Railway, some 4 km (2 miles) further, is **Pavlovsk**. The palace at Pavlovsk, much smaller than the others, was built by Catherine the Great for her son Paul and his wife Maria Fyodorovna. The architect, who was also commissioned to redesign the palace gardens in accordance with the then fashionable English style, was again Charles Cameron. Later, an Italian architect, Vincenzo Brenna, was brought in. The land was originally chosen for the royal hunt, on account of the abundant elk and wild fowl.

The rooms inside the palace reflect the personalities of Paul and his wife. Paul's militaristic interests can be seen in the Hall of War, Throne Room and Hall of the Maltese Knights of St John. His wife's Hall of Peace forms a pleasant and intended contrast.

The tapestries in the Carpet Room represent motifs from Cervantes' *Don Quixote*. There is a lot of French furniture on display, embroidered French curtains in the Greek Hall, and in the Hall of Peace a tripod-vase of crystal and red-gold produced in the St Petersburg glass factory in 1811. In Maria Fyodorovna's boudoir stands a piano imported from London. There is also a large collection of Sèvres porcelain pieces and a clock in Paul's study presented to him by Pope Pius VI.

The most important features of the large gardens are the Temple of Friendship (the friendship between Maria and her mother-in-law), the Centaur Bridge, the Cold Baths, the Apollo Colonnade and the Pavilion of the Three Graces. In time Paul transferred his affections to the palace at **Gatchina**, 45km (28 miles) south of St Petersburg. This stone-built palace changes colour with the movement of the sun. ❑

THE HERMITAGE: ART AS POWER

The Hermitage collection of Old Masters, sculptures, antiquities and archaeology remains a powerful symbol for St Petersburg and Russia

Art has always been political in Russia. Catherine II bought her first collection of 225 paintings in 1764 to get one up on Frederick of Prussia, who could not afford them. She went on to purchase vast national collections one after another – the Campana collection in Italy, the Crozat collection in France and the Walpole collection in England – until she had more than 4,000 paintings and 10,000 drawings. The sale of these works of art to Russia aroused storms of disapproval and political censure but, in each case, it also proved Catherine's wealth, power and cunning in the international arena.

The 19th century added rich archaeological collections – archaeology being a patriotic and political science important in proving the glory of the Russian land – and more paintings and applied art. All this came to the Hermitage, heir to the imperial collections, along with thousands of confiscated works including, after 1917, those of the Impressionists. During the Soviet era the Hermitage collection was a symbol of Soviet learning and magnificence, and today, with its 3 million pieces, it remains a great source of pride to Russians everywhere.

▷ **RICH COLLECTION**
The Benois Madonna by Leonardo da Vinci (above) and this 19th-century Russian silverware indicate the breadth of the Hermitage collections.

△ **THE WINTER PALACE**
Rastrelli's baroque palace (1754–62) dominates the central body of the Neva and the immense Palace Square. It is most beautiful at night, when richly lit.

▽ **LADIES OF ARLES**
The stunning display of Impressionist and Post-Impressionist canvasses includes this painting by Van Gogh, as well as work by Monet, Sisley and Pissaro.

AN IMPERIAL RETREAT

Catherine the Great inherited Rastrelli's new Winter Palace when she came to the throne in 1762. She wanted a more intimate space, however, and added a small pavilion to be a "Hermitage", with room for her art and tables for private dinners. She then added a second pavilion and galleries, forming the Small Hermitage (1764–67), and a Large Hermitage along the waterfront (1771–87). Here she hung her fast-growing collection, played billiards, and, after the addition of the theatre (1783–87), allowed guests to wander around after performances. In the 1830s Nicholas I decided to open the museum to the public. The New Hermitage opened in 1852. The Winter Palace was added to the museum after 1917, although for some years it was a Palace of Culture, showing films and lectures to the masses.

◁ **THE JORDAN STAIRCASE**
Once ambassadors ascended this staircase to be received at court. Today visitors can admire the stunning white marble and gold interior.

▷ **SASKIA AS FLORA**
Masterpieces by Rembrandt such as *The Sacrifice of Isaac*, *Return of the Prodigal Son*, *The Holy Family* and *Descent from the Cross* fill almost a whole room.

◁ **THE RED ROOM**
Space is flattened and tilted in Matisse's seminal picture of 1908. The fabric shown remained in the artist's studio to his death; he used it in many works.

▷ **SCYTHIAN STAG**
Visit the magnificent collection of gold, from 7th-century BC Scythian and Ancient Greek items to Oriental daggers and jewellery.

THE EUROPEAN NORTH

The North of Russia is a land of great beauty, of harsh winters and summer "white nights", where the life, traditions and architecture of old Russia can still be experienced

Map on page 212

Russians often say that the medieval city of Vologda, 500 km (310 miles) east of St Petersburg, is the gateway to the North, an area stretching from Finland in the west to the Urals in the east, and North to the Beloye More (White Sea) and Barents Sea.

The importance of the North dates from medieval times. When Kiev came under the Mongol yoke, many Russians fled north, taking their skills with them. Monks settled the region and founded monasteries which grew into important cultural centres. By the end of the 15th century, with the formation of a single Russian state under Muscovite rule, the northern border needed defending. A series of fortresses was constructed, often in the form of monasteries and with the active help of the monks such as at Solovetsky.

A rich heritage

In 1553 Richard Chancellor, an Englishman, opened up the northern waterways and foreign merchants sailed along the rivers Sukhona and Severnaya Dvina (Northern Dvina) en route to Moscow. Arkhangelsk (Archangel) was founded as a trading port and flourished, along with other towns such as Veliky Ustyug. Huge fairs attracted goods and traders from both East and West, from England, Holland, Greece, Armenia, China and Persia. There was a large community of English merchants in Arkhangelsk and an English wharf in the port. Local crafts – nielloed metalwork from Ustyug, carved ivory from Kholmogory – were valued all over Russia.

The North is rich in wooden churches, reflecting the wealth of the area between the 16th and 18th centuries, when the church was the centre of social and administrative life in a community. Indeed, the social significance of churches was so great that the *galilee* (covered "porch") was often larger than the church itself – in the case of the church of St Nicholas in the monastery of Muyezero, four times its size.

Peter the Great was in part responsible for the decline of the area when he ruled that the Gulf of Finland would be Russia's "Window on the West" and not Arkhangelsk as was previously. With the foundation of St Petersburg in 1703, the glorious days of the Russian North were suddenly over. Peter westernised his country by looking south rather than north. For 150 years the region was isolated from the mainstream of Russian life and the fairs and markets died for lack of goods. Towns and villages dependent on trade declined to provincial status.

What may have seemed to be a tragedy was, in ethnographical terms, the area's salvation. When the North was rediscovered in the late 19th century by ethnographers, then by artists, they found a society

PRECEDING PAGES: an admiring crew. **LEFT:** cubs at play. **BELOW:** an elderly inhabitant.

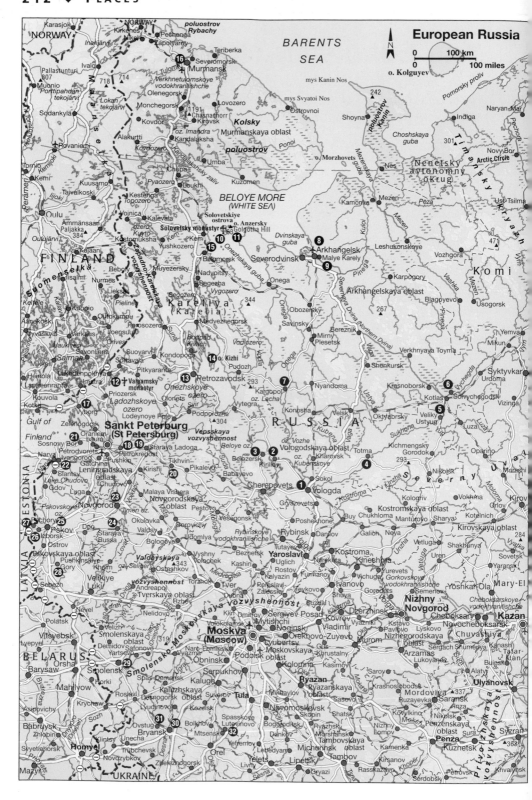

European Russia

which was living in the past. Not only were there hundreds of stone churches and monasteries set in magnificent landscapes, but there was a wealth of wooden buildings, religious and secular. What's more, the population had maintained age-old traditions, preserving fairytales, folk songs and customs which had already disappeared from much of Russia.

Artists flocked to the region. Nationalist composers such as Balakirev and Rimsky-Korsakov collected folk songs, incorporating the melodies in numerous compositions. Their art and music opened up the North to the world. For today's traveller who wants to get close to traditional Russian life and architecture, to understand how people lived in the past, this is the only place to go.

Map on page 212

Gateway to the North

Ivan the Terrible fortified **Vologda** ❶, building a **Kremlin** (fortress) to strengthen control over the North which became an important trade route with Europe during his reign. He received Chancellor here on his memorable voyage, and from here a Russian envoy was sent to England. The chronicles record how Ivan personally oversaw the building of **Sofiysky Sobor** (Cathedral of St Sophia), 1568–70, though, according to legend, when a red tile fell on his head as he walked round his new church the irate tsar set off for Moscow leaving the cathedral unconsecrated for 17 years.

The cathedral stands on the high bank of the River Vologda, in the centre of what was once the Kremlin. Its late 17th-century frescoes combine medieval monumentality and the contemporary decorative manner. The archbishop's residence, an attractive huddle of buildings by the cathedral, includes the baroque **Palati Iosifa Zolotovo** (Palace of Joseph the Golden), 1764–69.

Vologda itself is a charming city best seen from the river with its 18th-century churches and secular buildings running along the embankment. Of particular note are the **Tserkov Svyatikh Konstantin i Yel~Xena** (Church of SS Constantine and Helen), 1690, with its typical tent-shaped, free-standing belfry and, among the secular buildings, the **Dom Admirala Barsha** (Barsh Mansion), the neoclassical **Skuliabinskaya Bogadelnaya** (Skuliabin Almshouse) and the wooden **Dom Levashova** (Levashov House), as well as the enchanting wooden **Dom Zasetskikh** (Zasetsky House), 1790–95.

BELOW: the Vologda Tower and Moscow Gate of the Kirillov-Belozersky, Monastyr, Vologda

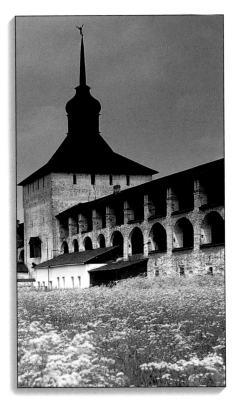

Monasteries of the North

On the northern edge of Vologda, on the road to **Beloye Ozero**, is the **Spaso-Prilutsky Monastyr** (Monastery of the Saviour on the Bend). To get the best view climb the steep wooden staircase under the roof of the Water Tower. From here you can see the oldest and most typical northern building in the complex: the stone **Spassky Sobor** (Cathedral of the Saviour), 1542, the jumble of buildings around it and, over the walls, the Sofiysky Sobor. During Napoleon's invasion of Russia, treasures from the Kremlin and many Moscow monasteries were stored here.

Rather than go by road, take a boat from Vologda to the **Kirillov-Belozersky Monastyr** (Kirillov-Belozersky Monastery), which stands on the edge of

The Monastery of Ferapontov contains remarkable 16th-century frescoes by the artist Dionisius.

Siverskoye Ozero (Lake Siverskoye), 120 km (72 miles) to the north. The boat winds past wooden windmills and churches before arriving at **Kirillov** ❷, where the monastery emerges from behind the trees, its white stone buildings and domes reflected in the water. The monastery was founded in 1397 and by the 17th century was one of the richest foundations in Russia, largely due to the sale of salt. Vasily III, tsar of Russia in the early 1500s, came here to pray for a child by his apparently barren wife, Elena, and the following year they were blessed with a son, who became Ivan the Terrible.

There are a number of 15th- and 16th-century churches, but the star is the **Uspenskaya Sobor** (Cathedral of the Assumption) with its superb frescoes and 17th-century iconostasis. Twenty kilometres (12 miles) northeast from the Kirillov-Belozersky Monastery is the **Ferapontovsky Monastyr** (Monastery of St Therapont) on the banks of **Borodavskoye Ozero** (Lake Borodava). Its main claim to fame lies in the frescoes in the **Rozhdestvensky Sobor** (Cathedral of the Nativity of the Virgin), painted in the first few years of the 16th century by Dionisius and his sons. The superb cycle, devoted to the life of the Virgin, is regarded as Dionisius's swan song. A romantic local legend attributes his appearance this far north to the death of his beloved wife and his subsequent desire to find peace in the monastery.

The town of **Belozersk** ❸, 40 km (25 miles) north of Kirillov, retains much of its wooden 19th-century appearance, plus the symbols of its wealthy past: the massive **Uspensky Sobor** (Cathedral of the Assumption), 1553, devoid of ornament; the heavy **Preobrazhensky Sobor** (Cathedral of the Transfiguration), 1670s, and the jolly **Vsemilostivogo Spasa** (Church of the Most Merciful Saviour), 1723. Most impressive of all are the remains of the ancient fortress, the high earthen ramparts which run around the old town.

Totma ❹, 200 km (124 miles) east of Vologda, is an attractive small town with superb 18th-century churches displaying fine monumental brickwork. Lunacharsky, the first Soviet Commissar for Enlightenment and friend of numerous avant-garde artists, was exiled here by the tsar between 1902 and 1904.

Veliky Ustyug ❺, 250 km (155 miles) north of Totma, is now a sleepy provincial centre. Once it was one of the great market towns of the North – hence "Veliky" (Great) – and its tiered churches, monasteries and mansions are strung out along the river. The 17th-century **Uspensky Sobor** (Cathedral of the Assumption) is the eighth building on the site. Of particular note are the **Tserkov Zhawn-Mironosets** (Church of the Holy Women), 1714–22, the baroque **Tserkov Simeona Stolpnika** (Church of Simeon the Stylite), 1725–65, and the **Mikhailo-Arkhangelsky Monastyr** (Monastery of the Archangel Michael), not to mention the wealth of 18th- and 19th-century mansions such as the **Dom Shilova** (Shilov House) on the embankment. It is an easy walk across the old town.

The Stroganov Masters

One of the richest periods in the history of Russian art is linked with the so-called Stroganov Masters, artists employed by the wealthy Stroganov family, who made their fortune from the salt mines along the

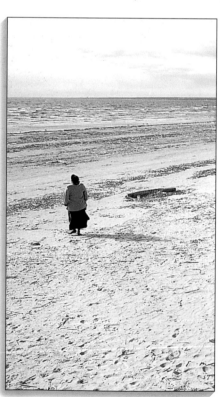

Severnaya Dvina River. The Stroganovs settled in **Solvychegodsk** ❻, 80 km (48 miles) north of Veliky Ustyug, and founded many fine churches, such as the fortress-like **Blagoveshchensky Sobor** (Annunciation Cathedral), 1560–79, which was the Stroganovs' own church, treasury and citadel, standing adjacent to their grounds. The cathedral is still rich in icons and frescoes.

They also founded the **Yavleniya Bogorodtsi Monastyr** (Monastery of the Presentation of the Virgin), 1689–93, its carved white stone details set off against the red brick and coloured tiles. The local museum contains many more icons and pieces of applied art linked with the Stroganovs and the town still has plenty of picturesque wooden buildings. Solvychegodsk is a well-known health resort, with salt and mud baths, particularly good for the relief of rheumatism.

Arkhangelsk region

In the region bordering the White Sea is the small town of **Kargopol** ❼, 427 km (257 miles) south of Arkhangelsk, yet another point on the important trading waterways of the north. Its key position on the River Onega led to a boom between the 16th and 17th centuries, manifested in the highly decorative white stone **Blagoveshchensky Tserkov** (Church of the Annunciation). The opening up of the northern trade route created the need for a port near the mouth of the Severnaya Dvina on the White Sea. In 1584 the town of Novye Kholmogory was founded; it later became know as **Arkhangelsk** (Archangel) ❽. By the beginning of the 18th century this was the centre of Russian shipbuilding. Now it is a big timber-logging and fishing area, known to the West through centuries of foreign trading links and the area's occupation by anti-Soviet Allied European and American troops immediately after the Revolution (1918–19). The great

Map on page 212

Arkhangelsk's nearby satellite town of Severodvinsk was one of the most top-secret cities in the Soviet era. It was, and still is, the centre of nuclear submarine production for the Russian navy.

BELOW: Vologda with the Cathedral of St Sophia.

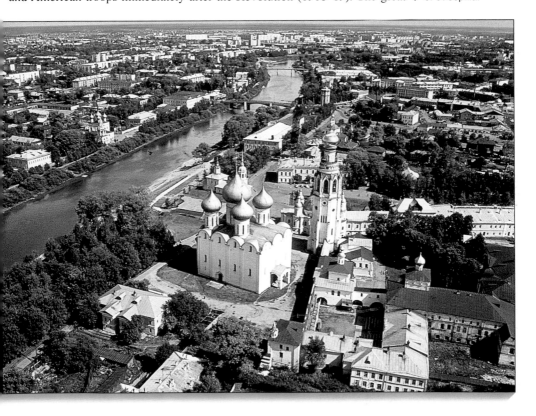

Russian scientist and poet Mikhail Lomonosov was born close to the town. Thirty km (18 miles) outside Arkhangelsk is the open-air **Muzei-zapovednik Derevyanova Zodchestva** (Wooden Architecture Museum Reserve; open 10am–5pm; closed Tues) at **Malye Karely** ➒. The forests make an effective backdrop for wooden churches, *izby* (cottages) and outhouses, many of them superbly decorated with carved window surrounds, eaves and crests running along the roof. The museum also holds concerts and provides a home to craftsmen.

Solovetsky Islands

Arkhangelsk is a departure point for the **Solovetskiye Ostrova** (Solovetsky Islands) in the White Sea, familiarly known as Solovki. This name has a particular ring to those whose relatives were imprisoned or died in the Solovetsky Special Purpose Camp, one of the camps the writer Solzhenitsyn called the "gulag archipelago". **Solovetsky Monastyr** (Solovetsky Monastery) ➓ was a medieval fortress and major border post, and this can be seen in its grim, grey aspect, defensive walls and towers rising above the White Sea. The high windows recall embrasures, and the two 16th-century cathedrals were once linked by secret underground passages containing huge vaults for food and a hidden water supply in case of siege. Political and religious opponents were despatched here from the Middle Ages onwards. They were held in cells in the walls and towers and beneath the cathedrals.

The area is of outstanding natural beauty and this particular part of the White Sea has a comparatively moderate climate. You can take a tour on a small boat around the islands. The church on **Golgotha Hill** ⓫ on **Ostrov Anzersky** (Anzersky Island) is a good place from which to look over the whole archipelago.

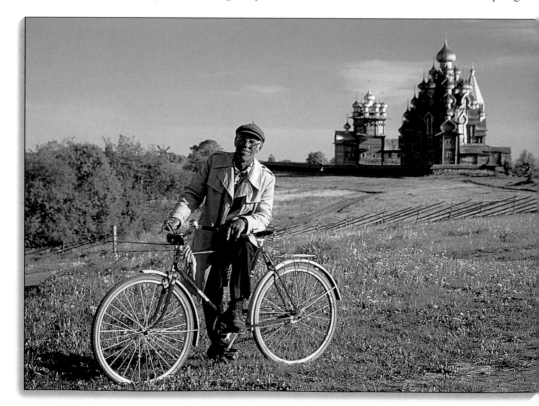

Exploring Kareliya

The western side of the region, northeast from St Petersburg, is the Autonomous Republic of **Kareliya**, with its richly forested, flat landscape dotted with lakes. To see what the area has to offer, take a five-day trip on a river boat. The tours start from St Petersburg (longer cruises from Moscow) and take in the Valaam Islands on Ladozhskoye Ozero (Lake Ladoga), Petrozavodsk (capital of Kareliya) and Ostrov Kizhi (Kizhi Island). On the boat tour, the **Valaam Islands** come into view early on the second morning. Energetic passengers are advised to skip the organised tour and lecture and walk the 5 km (3 miles) through the woods to **Valaamsky Monastyr** (Valaam Monastery) ⓬. Returned to the Orthodox Church's possession in 1990, the monastery is an active religious community, with a farm and workshops, and tourism is now big business. The buildings, outlying cells and chapels, are being restored: major damage to the frescoes in the **Preobrazhensky Sobor** (Cathedral of the Transfiguration) was caused not by years of neglect but by over-officious guardians covering them with Perspex, thus trapping moisture and causing the paint and plaster to flake off.

The port of **Petrozavodsk** ⓭ on the banks of Onezhskoye Ozero (Lake Onega) was founded in 1703 to serve a cannon foundry nearby. Despite the destruction wrought during World War II, Petrozavodsk is an attractive town, built on a series of plateaux rising from the water. The neoclassical **Kruglaya Ploshchad** (Round Square) survived the Nazis. About 70 km (43 miles) north of the town of Petrozavodsk is **Bodpad Kivach** (Kivach waterfall), the best of many on the River Suna, set in the midst of a vast nature reserve.

Petrozavodsk is a good springboard for exploring the northern reaches of Lake Onega and the island of **Kizhi** ⓮, a unique museum of wooden architec-

Map on page 212

TIP

Karelia is home to some of the oldest volcanic rock and soil in the world – almost 3.3 billion years old. Petrozavodsk's Geological Research Institute in the Karelian Science Centre organises tours.

BELOW: Valaam Island, Lake Lagoda.

THE VANISHING FORESTS

The Republic of Karelia (pop. 800,000), which borders Finland, is three-quarters covered with forest, and the logging and paper industries account for most of its economy. But Karelia is only now learning that it needs to respect its environment to ensure a healthy and prosperous future. During Soviet times, these forests were only partly exploited as the area bordering Finland was left untouched to minimise the country's contact with the decadent West. Since the collapse of the USSR, however, the Russian economy has become a free-for-all and Russian *biznessmeni* along with their Western partners are taking advantage of the country's weak legal system to exploit the forests for all they're worth. About 9 percent of Karelia's forests are virgin old-growth areas, considered the oldest and most biologically diverse in Europe. They are protected by Russian and international law. In the first half of the 1990s, parts of these forests were not merely destroyed, but almost no effort was made to replant. In 1996, foreign timber companies agreed to a Greenpeace-sponsored moratorium on the purchase of old-growth timber from Karelia. By 1998, however, timber companies, with the support of Karelia's newly-elected governor, said they were intent on resuming cutting.

Modern Murmansk's role in World War II is highlighted in the Muzei Militarny Severnogo Morskogo Flota (Museum of the North Sea Fleet), Ulitsa Tortseva 15 (open Thurs–Mon 9am–5pm).

BELOW: ecologists ring an elder at the Barents.

ture. The 22 domes of the **Preobrazhenskaya Tserkov** (Church of the Transfiguration), 1714, are made entirely of wood and without the use of nails. The iconostasis inside the church is also of interest, not least because it is curved rather than straight. The interiors of some houses look much as they did when they were still home to local peasants.

Murmansk and the far North

Heading north, you come to **Belomorsk 15**, from where it is possible to take a trip to the Solovetsky Islands. If you are intending to go to **Murmansk 16**, the journey north takes in some stunning scenery at any time of the year. And if one should be brave enough to go during the cold, dark winter months, you might be lucky enough to see the Northern Lights. To members of the older generation, Murmansk is equated with the Allied Forces who defended the town and port during World War II. It was through here that supplies from the West reached the rest of Russia. The port was founded in 1916 with British assistance (even the first houses were brought over from England) on the Barents Sea, which does not freeze thanks to the North Cape Stream. It rests between two low hills by the mouth of the River Kola and it is here, 68.5° north, that you really appreciate the meaning of a long winter night: the sun does not rise for 52 days.

The Leningrad Region

The area around St Petersburg, still known as the **Leningrad Region**, is well worth exploring if you get the chance. Northwest of the city, between (Lake Ladoga) and the Gulf of Finland, the landscape is dominated by country houses (*dachas*) belonging to residents of St Petersburg. Part of the region belonged to

Finland until 1940, and some of the best houses here were Finnish built. Now the area is dotted with sanatoria and wooden houses, often huddled round picturesque lakes. It is ideal for cross-country skiing in winter.

The last town on the Russian side of the border is the Swedish-Finnish medieval city of **Vyborg** ⓱. This area changed hands many times between the 13th and 20th centuries. It may not seem very Russian, for many of its buildings are left over from Finnish rule. **Vyborgsky Zamok** (Vyborg Castle) dates largely from the 16th century, and there are defensive towers from the 14th, but buildings from all periods survive, and the early 20th-century art nouveau buildings are especially striking. If you like follies, then the early 19th-century castle burial vault will be of interest. The peace and quiet of Vyborg has been disrupted since the late 1980s, as this has become the main crossing point for Finnish and Russian tourists and business people, and a busy freight route.

Petrokrepost ⓲, famous to those familiar with Russian history as Schlusselberg, lies 30 km (18 miles) east from St Petersburg, towards Lake Ladoga. The town's main claim to fame is the **krepost** (fortress) which was used as a prison in pre-Revolutionary times. Peter the Great's sister was imprisoned here, and in 1887 Lenin's brother, Alexander Ulyanov, was executed in the yard for his role in an attempt on Alexander III's life. **Staraya Ladoga** ⓳, 100 km (60 miles) along the south side of the lake, is noted for its 12th-century **Tserkov Gioraya Pobedonostsa** (Church of St George) filled with marvellous frescoes, and other 17th-century buildings. Sixty km (37 miles) to the southeast is **Tikhvin** ⓴, worth a visit for its 16th- and 17th-century monuments and the **Dom Muzei Rimskovo-Korsakova** (Rimsky-Korsakov House Museum).

Going west along the south bank of the Gulf past Petrodvorets and the impe-

Map on page 212

BELOW: river fish drying in the wind.

rial summer palaces, you come to the closed city of **Sosnovy Bor** ㉑, best known for its nuclear power station. On reaching the border with Estonia at **Narva** ㉒, jump out on the Russian side, which is called **Ivangorod**, and take a look around the fortress there. Also, notice the strong difference in lifestyle between the Russian and Estonian sides of the border.

South of St Petersburg

In times of war, Novgorod withheld supplies of salt from its enemies, and used it as a powerful bargaining tool.

Novgorod and Pskov ruled the roost when the Tatars took over the rest of ancient Rus, building up trading links with the Hanseatic League and protecting themselves against attacks by the Poles and Livonians with heavy fortifications. Rich merchants built themselves churches galore.

When Russia was united under the rule of the Moscow princes at the end of the 15th century, Ivan III invited Pskov and Italian architects and craftsmen to help in the building of the churches in the Moscow Kremlin. The local monasteries were centres of learning, and Novgorod's historical chronicles and texts, scratched on pieces of dried birch bark, are known to historians all over the world.

The area suffered appallingly from the Nazi occupation. Whole villages were burned, complete with all their inhabitants. Buildings of interest that have survived or have been restored are concentrated in the two main towns.

BELOW: Cathedral of St Sophia in Novgorod.

Novgorod ㉓ has a rich past. At its height, the principality ruled from here spread all the way up to the White Sea and west to present-day Poland. Its power did not always work to the city's good, however. In 1570, for example, Ivan the Terrible butchered some 60,000 of Novgorod's citizens when they rebelled against his rule. Nowadays the town itself lacks great beauty, but is

Novgorod

redeemed by its numerous monuments. The **Kremlin** Ⓐ built on the bank of the River Volkhov is at the heart of the old city. It is dominated by the magnificent 11th-century **Sofiysky Sobor** (Cathedral of St Sophia) Ⓑ. Inside are 12th-century frescoes, including a portrait of Constantine and Helen, and the remains of 11th-century mosaics. One of the most surprising things to be found here is the east portal, with 12th-century bronze doors made at Magdeburg, taken – according to legend – from the fortress of Sigtunain in 1187. They are a superb example of Western European Romanesque metalwork tucked away in the heart of Russia. **Khudozhestveno Muzei Novgoroda** (Novgorod Museum of Art) Ⓒ (open 10am–6pm; closed Tues) is also housed here. It has a wealth of icons and church utensils. The monument outside the building, erected to commemorate the millennium of Russia in 1862, is by the sculptor Mikhail Mikeshin.

On the opposite bank of the river is **Yaroslavovo Dvorishche** (Yaroslav's Court) Ⓓ, a pretty ensemble of 12th- to 16th-century churches. It was thought to have been the residence of the princes of Yaroslav until the end of the 14th century. There are plenty of other churches in town, some in the most unexpected places. If you count fewer than 30 as you wander round you have missed a fair number. Outside the town, only a short bus trip away, are two more sights. The **Yuriev Monastyr** (St George Monastery) is still being restored, but work is coming along nicely (open 10am–5pm; closed Tues), and there is the excellent **Muzei Arkhitektury i Drevnykh** (Museum of Architecture and Ancient Monuments) just across the road.

South of Novgorod, on the other side of Ilmen Ozero (Lake Ilmen) at the confluence of two rivers, is **Staraya Russa** ㉔. More intimate than Novgorod, the town is also rich in churches, for this was the centre of salt production. Fyo-

Maps:
Area 212
City 220

The countryside south of Pskov forms the backdrop for much of Pushkin's writing. His family estate is near Pushkinskiye Gory.

BELOW: residents of Novgorod, 1880.

Map on page 212

dor Dostoyevsky and his family spent their summers in Staraya Russa from 1872, and part of *The Brothers Karamazov* is set here. His house is now a museum: the **Dostoyevskovo Muzei** (Dostoevsky Museum; open 10am–6pm; Sat, Sun 10am–5pm; closed Mon).

For many people outside Russia, all they know about **Pskov** ㉕ is that it was here, in the royal train, that Nicholas II signed his abdication. Lake Chudovo, where the hero of Eisenstein's film *Alexander Nevsky* defeated the Teutonic Knights in the famous battle on the ice in 1242, is not far from the city.

Like Novgorod the town is dominated by its fortress and churches. They played a bigger defensive role than those in Novgorod, because of the ever-present danger from across the nearby border. Pskov's **Kremlin** is more fairytale in appearance than that of Novgorod. Instead of square red-brick towers, here we have heavy, round, squat towers with wooden roofs.

The **Troitsky Sobor** (Trinity Cathedral), built in 1669, still dominates any view of the town. This white structure was not only a church, but also the place where the state council sat in session and where important state documents were kept. The **Kutekrom Bashnya** (Tower) in the corner of the Kremlin walls was where the poet Pushkin liked to look down over the river.

Outside the old town are yet more religious buildings. The magnificent **Spaso-Preobrazhensky Sobor** (Cathedral of the Transfiguration) in the Mirozhsky Monastyr, decorated in the 12th century by Greek masters and their Russian apprentices, is a world in itself. The frescoes definitely merit a visit.

About 30 km (18 miles) along the main road to the west of Pskov, you find **Izborsk** ㉖. The village is built around the remains of a medieval fortress. Another 20 km (12 miles) further on, nestling in a deep ravine, is the 16th-century **Pskovo-Pcherskaya Lavra** (Monastery of the Caves) at **Pechory** ㉗, its picturesque beauty matched only by the strangeness of its underground caves, used as burial vaults for monks. Of particular note is the **Uspensky Sobor** (Cathedral of the Assumption), erected on the site of an ancient cave church. The monastery is still a religious institution, and it is possible to come here for a retreat.

Pushkin's estate

Even Russians indifferent to the medieval history of the Pskov area do not remain unaffected by its connection with the poet Alexander Pushkin (1799–1837). The **Mikhailovskoye** estate at **Pushkinskiye Gory** (Pushkin Hills) ㉘, 130 km (80 miles) south of Pskov, belongs to an ensemble of three estates and the nearby **Svyatogorsky Monastyr**. The estates were restored after the war and the parks returned to their former glory. Amble slowly round the grounds and drop into Pushkin's study, where he worked during his exile, then take a peek into the small cottage where his old nanny lived (open 9am–4.30pm; closed Mon and last day of month).

The other estates here, **Petrovskoye** and **Trigorskoye**, are all reflected in Pushkin's poetry and prose. Mikhailovskoye and Trigorskoye form the background to *Evgene Onegin*, and the monastery features in *Boris Godunov*. ❑

BELOW: country life. **RIGHT:** dressed in national costume for the midsummer festival of Ust-vym.

Map on page 212

THE SOUTHWEST

The cathedrals, fortresses and war memorials of the southwestern steppes bear witness to the region's many rulers. It was here that Ivan Turgenev found inspiration

PRECEDING PAGES: whooper swans. **BELOW:** Smolensk's Bogoyavlensky Cathedral.

The perennial question of whether Southwestern Russia is Asian, Western or unique is a relevant today as ever it was. Never more so than in a region that has struggled through 1,100 years of being sniped at, ravaged and plundered, from all directions. Yet despite countless changes of ruler, Southwestern Russia remains fundamentally *russkiy*. It was here that the Russian Empire was forged.

Kievan Rus, which covered western Russia and parts of present-day Ukraine and Belarus, emerged after the 860s when the Varangians (Vikings) arrived to lord over and protect the Slavic tribes. It was as Rus that the area gained its Slavic identity and from this word we get *russkiy*, which refers to the Russian people and all matters personal, homely and non-imperial.

From 1054, Kievan Rus was divided into principalities. These lasted into the 12th century from which point the history of **Smolensk ㉙** offers a typical catalogue of the tumultuous battles and power struggles which have marked Russian history, causing Rus to expand into imperial Rossiya in an attempt to survive.

From the 12th century to the 20th, Smolensk and its region have passed from Kievan to Tatar, Lithuanian, Muscovite, Polish, Russian, French, German, Soviet and now finally back to Russian rule. Situated on the upper River Dneiper (Dnepr), "the gate of Russia" was first mentioned in 863. It soon became an important centre along the trade route between Moscow, 390 km (242 miles) to the northeast, and the West. Indeed, the town gets its name from the Russian word for tar, *smola*, because it was here that the river traders tarred their boats.

At the centre of the old town is Cathedral Hill on which the vivid green and white **Uspensky Sobor** (Assumption Cathedral) stands, on ground hallowed since 1101. The most remarkable features of this 18th-century church are the gilded interior and the wooden iconostasis carved by the Ukrainian, Sila Trusitsky. The town's three 12th-century churches – SS Peter and Paul, St John the Divine and the Archangel Michael – are also worth a visit.

The main attraction of Smolensk is the **city wall**. Built by 300,000 people between 1596 and 1602, the 15-km (9-mile) long, 15-metre (49-ft) high wall was known as "the precious necklace of Russia". Precious indeed, considering that regent Boris Godunov forbade anyone in Russia, to build themselves a stone edifice during its six years of construction.

For art lovers, the **Kartinnaya Galereya** (Art Gallery; open 10am–6pm; closed Mon), Ulitsa Krupskaya, has a valuable collection of icons and the **Muzei S. T. Konenkova** (Sculpture Museum; open 10am–6pm), Ulitsa Mayakovskaya 7, has some fun exhibits, including *matryoshka* dolls.

City in the forest

Founded in 985 on the River Desna by Prince Vladimir, **Bryansk** ㉚, 325 km (200 miles) southwest of Moscow, lies in the heart of a 12,000 square-km (4,630-sq mile) forest and has a rich and brutal history.

The forest has ensured the survival of the inhabitants of Bryansk on many occasions, most notably during World War II when 60,000 people fled from the invading Germans and lived in huts in the woods, forming a formidable partisan movement. The Bryansk fighters are remembered at **Partizanskaya Polyana** (Partisan Field) on the Orel road, just outside Bryansk where there is a museum (open 10am–5pm; closed Mon), preserved huts, and a wall on which are recorded the names of the 8,000 partisans who died. You may also spot some of the wild boar, brown bears and elks which roam the forest.

South of the city, the working **Svensky Monastyr** (Sven Monastery) is a reminder of the days when Bryansk was also a significant trading town. Furs and jewellery were sold here at the Sven Fair, which reached its zenith in the 17th century. The huge **Uspensky Sobor** (Assumption Cathedral), commissioned by Ivan the Terrible has not withstood the test of time, but the two gate churches are relatively intact (entry on request). The view from here is splendid.

The region has been home to many artistic heroes. In **Ovstug** ㉛, 48 km (30 miles) northwest of Bryansk, the picturesque estate of nature poet Fyodor Tyutchev makes an interesting day trip (open daily; closed Tues). The village of **Spasskoye Lutovinovo** ㉜ – 70 km (43 miles) north of Orel and 340 km (211 miles) south of Moscow – is where Ivan Turgenev wrote *Fathers and Sons* and *A Nest of Gentlefolk* in the 1850s on his family estate. It is well worth a visit (museum open 10am–5pm; closed Tues). ❑

A memorial to the World War II Battle of Kursk – Belgorod road, 115 km (71 miles) south of Kursk – features a museum (open 10am–5pm; closed Mon), T-43 tank, TaK fighter plane, trenches and a wall, out of which are sculpted the faces of tank crews.

BELOW: the city wall, Smolensk.

ALONG THE VOLGA

The mighty Volga, Europe's longest river, has played a major role in the development of Russia, as the ancient towns and villages along its banks testify

Map on page 230

For many centuries the Volga has been like a mother feeding the Russian nation. It has witnessed numerous battles and wars, and has always stirred strong feelings in Russian hearts. It rises in Valdayskaya Vozvyshennost (the Valdai Hills), not far from the picturesque Lake Seliger, and flows 3,530 km (2,195 miles) south to the Caspian Sea.

From time immemorial, people have gravitated to the river. One of the best preserved of the early settlements is **Veliky Bulgar** (Great Bulgar), the former capital city of the Volga Bulgars, near **Posileniye Bulgar** (Bulgar Village) in Tatarstan. Other great sites include the remnants of Itil and Sarai, former capital cities of the Golden Horde, not far from Volgograd and Astrakhan.

The **Povolzhye** (Volga Region) comprises the middle and lower parts of the river from Kazan to Astrakhan. **Kazan ❶** (pop. 1.1 million) is the capital city of Tatarstan, a sovereign republic in the Russian Federation. It was founded in the second half of the 13th century, and in the mid-15th century became the capital of the Kazan khanate. In the second half of the 15th and in the early 16th centuries Moscow princes besieged the city repeatedly. In 1552 it became part of the Russian state and in the 18th century developed into a major administrative, trade, industrial and cultural centre.

The **Kazan Kremlin** is a marvellous ensemble of 16th-century architecture. Particularly handsome are the towers. They include the **Spasskaya Bashnya**, a 45-metre (147-ft) high clock-bearing tower begun in 1555, the seven-tier 55-metre (180-ft) high **Suyumbiki** with its stone dome and gate leading to the Sovereign's yard, and the **Tainitskaya** towers.

Kazan is famous for its **university**, which is one of the oldest and most respected in Russia. Its students have included illustrious scholars, writers and politicians, notably Lenin, Lobachevsky and Leo Tolstoy. Kazan is also the native town of Tatar poet Musa Jalil and Russian singer Fyodor Chaliapin.

Around 74 km (46 miles) downstream, travelling southwest from Kazan, the Volga joins the Kama, its largest tributary. Just south of here is the town of **Ulyanovsk ❷** (formerly Simbirsk), pop. 650,000, occupying both banks. It was founded in 1648 to protect the southeastern outskirts of the Russian state from incursions. It is perhaps most famous for being Lenin's birthplace, hence its name: Lenin's original surname was Ulyanov – "Lenin" was one of the many revolutionary *noms de guerre*.

Another 125 km (78 miles) downstream from Ulyanovsk, a truncated cone of the Karaulny mound and the Kabatskaya hill rise on its right bank. This is where the **Zhiguli Hills** begin, the most beautiful part

LEFT: fisherman grapples with a sturgeon.
BELOW: flooded willows.

Along the Volga

where the **Zhiguli Hills** begin, the most beautiful part of the Volga. On the left bank of the river, opposite the village of **Usolye**, stands **Tolyatti** ❸ at the bottom of the Zhiguli Hills. A modern city, it is well known for its **Volzhsky Avtozavod** (Volga Car Factory), which produces Zhigulis, Ladas, Sputniks and Samaras.

Further downstream, approximately half-way down the Volga's entire length, stands the town of **Samara** ❹ (known as Kuibyshev between 1935 and 1991), extending for dozens of kilometres along the bank. A broad staircase leads from the bank to the city centre, and a cast-iron grille adorns a riverside park. Named after the Samara River which flows into the Volga at this point, the town was built in 1586 as a fortress on the Volga's left bank. The easternmost town on the protected trade routes along the Samara bend. The town was an important crossing point, and used for monitoring the nomads' movements around the Trans-Volga's steppes. By the early 19th century Samara had grown considerably, and only its centre was confined by the disintegrating fortress. Though known as an industrial town throughout its history, Samara is especially proud of its theatre, which is one of the best local theatres in Russia. Samara's Drama Theatre, **Teatr imeni Gorkogo**, named after Maxim Gorky, can be found on Ploshchad Chapayeva.

After Samara the Volga turns sharply to the west. The landscape here is stunningly beautiful. The right bank with its steep and high cliffs is mountainous while the left bank is a lowland of emerald-green meadows.

Trading centre

After Samara comes **Saratov** ❺ (pop. 1 million), a modern industrial town, founded on the left bank of the Volga in 1590. In 1674 the town was moved to the right bank, to a sloping hollow surrounded by the **Lysaya, Altynnaya** and **Uvekskaya Mountains**. In the first 100 years of its existence it was little more than a small fortress designed to protect river trade routes from the raids of nomads. During the reign of Peter the Great, the city's central square was called Gostinaya, on account of the **Gostiny Dvor** (rows of shops) built for merchants. The **Sobor Svyatoi Troitsi** (Trinity Cathedral) was built in Gostinaya Square in 1695. In the 18th century Saratov emerged as a major trading centre. The production of salt on **Elton Ozero** (Lake Elton) boosted the city's development. The first industrial enterprises date from that time. In the late 18th century grain became a key commodity, along with salt and fish.

In 1798 Saratov was made the centre of a *guberniya* (a pre-Revolution term equivalent to "province", which has now been reintroduced) and awarded a coat of arms. Like many other Russian towns, Saratov was a wooden town and as a result, it often suffered from fires. There was a particularly devastating fire in 1810, which prompted new city planning. In 1865 a new theatre was built of stone; this has survived as the **Teatr Operi i Balleta** (Opera and Ballet Theatre) on Teatralnaya Ploshchad 1 (Theatre Square).

Also here is the **Muzei Iskusstv imeni Radishcheva** (Art Museum), Ulitsa Radischeva, which opened in 1885 (open 10am–6pm; closed Mon). It contains rich collections of paintings, sculptures, porcelain and furniture. The city's main street, Moskovskaya Ulitsa, leads to Muzeinaya Ploshchad (Museum Square), a remnant of old Saratov. Its major feature is the **Stary Sobor** (Old Cathedral) and, nearby, the former theological seminary, with arcades and columns. The **Muzei Kraiyevedeniya** (Museum of Local Lore), Ulitsa Lemontova, is worth a visit (open 10am–4pm; closed Wed).

Volograd's eternal flame burns in memory of those who lost their lives here during World War II.

Some 394km (244 miles) downstream from Saratov stands the town of **Volgograd ❻** (pop. 1 million). During the 13th century the area was occupied by the Golden Horde. When the Kazan and Astrakhan khanates eventually col-

BELOW: Volga embankment, Volgograd.

NIZHNY NOVGOROD

Perhaps the most successful city after Moscow in terms of economic development in post-Communist Russia, is Nizhny Novgorod (known as Gorky in the Soviet era after the writer Maxim Gorky who was born here). Situated 250 km (155 miles) upstream from Kazan, Nizhny (pop. 1.6 million) is historically closer to the towns of the Zolotoye Koltso (Golden Ring), but is nevertheless seen as a major city of the Volga Region and indeed Russia. Two giants of Soviet engineering have their roots here: MiG, the soviet aircraft manufacturer, and GAZ, the Gorky Avto Zavod (Gorky Car Plant), producer of the Volga saloon car. In the mid-1990s, GAZ alone had 350,000 employees.

The city became infamous for being the place of exile for the dissident, physicist and Nobel prize winner, Andrey Sakharov in the 1980s. His flat is now a museum, **Muzei A. D. Sakharova**, Prospekt Gagarina 214 (open Sat–Thurs, 9am–6pm). Nizhny Novgorod was founded in the early 13th century. Its **Kremlin** houses the **Arkhangelskoye Sobor** (Cathedral of the Archangel Michael), built in 1631 and the 19th-century governor's house, now the **Khudozhestvenny Muzei** (Art Museum; open 10am –5pm; Wed noon–7pm; closed Tues). Many of the city's churches are undergoing restoration.

The Mother Russia memorial of Mamaev Kurgan in Volograd was built to commemorate the Battle of Stalingrad, 1942.

BELOW: field of flax on the banks of the Volga near Rzhev.

lapsed in the second half of the 16th century, a new town called Tsaritsyn was built on the island where the Tsaritsyn River flows into the Volga. It was designed to protect the country's southeastern borders.

The town suffered numerous raids by nomads, and the Don Cossacks, who rose in rebellion against the ruling regime, entered the town more than once. Peter the Great attached great importance to the town and built a barrage more than 60 km (38 miles) long and a rampart about 12 metres (40 ft) high. In 1765, Catherine the Great issued a decree allowing foreigners to settle in Russia. Among Tsaritysyn's newcomers from western Europe was a sizeable colony of Germans, whose neighbourhood became known as Sarepta.

By the 19th century the town had lost its function as a fortress and become a trading and industrial centre. With the introduction of railways, industry developed rapidly, and soon saw-mills and cast-iron foundries were operating.

In the winter of 1942–43 the town (then called Stalingrad) was the focus of the key battle which marked the turning point in World War II. Fierce fighting lasted for 200 days and nights; some 300,000 of Hitler's crack troops lost their lives and the whole town lay in ruins.

After the war, the town was built anew. It extended along the Volga for nearly 100 km (60 miles). New factories, houses and parks were built. The memorial on **Mamaev Kurgan** (Mamaev Mound) by the sculptor Vuchetich and architect Belopolsky was built to commemorate the battle. It depicts a group of grieving citizens carrying wreaths to put on the heroes' graves. Behind the sculpture is a ramp paved with granite slabs and on both sides of the ramp are granite blocks resembling anti-tank teeth; they are engraved with the dates of all the major battles that took place near the town. The ramp ends with an 11-metre

Map
on page
230

(36-ft) high sculpture of a warrior with a submachine-gun and a grenade in his hand. Behind him, near the terrace with red flowers, rises a wide staircase with high walls on both sides showing the town's ruins. The staircase leads to a gigantic sculpture of a female figure symbolising the **Mother Russia**, a sword high in her hand.

There are extensive views of the city and the river from the bottom of the main monument and from the top of the mound. Try and visit the **Muzei Izobrazitelnykh Iskusstv** (Fine Arts Museum), Ulitsa Port-Saida, to see its collection of Russian paintings and Palekh boxes (open 10am–5pm; closed Mon). The **Planetary** (Planetarium), Ulitsa Gagarina 14, was presented to Volgograd by Germany. It is one of the few of its kind in the country (shows every hour, 10am–4pm).

Cultural crossroads

Downstream from Volgograd, the river turns to the southeast, flowing along the sandy-clay steppe of the lower Volga area. The right bank of the river near **Astrakhan** ❼ (the last town on the Volga) is 12 metres (40 ft) high. Astrakhan lies in the Volga's delta, straddling 11 islands separated by channels and rivulets and has a population of approximately half a million. In the 18th century Astrakhan was on the Caspian Sea; today the sea falls short by some 200 metres (218 yards).

In the 8th century, 10–12 km (6–7 miles) upstream on the Volga's right bank stood **Itil**, the capital city of the Khazar (Turkic-speaking nomadic tribes). The name "Astrakhan" was first used in the 13th century. In 1558 Ivan IV's troops captured Astrakhan without a fight and annexed it to Moscovy. Another turning

BELOW: Astrakhan, in the Volga delta.

point in the town's history was 1558, when New Astrakhan was founded on the opposite, left bank. The first wooden fortifications were built here. Between 1582 and 1589 they were replaced by a stone fortress: the **Astrakhan Kreml** (Kremlin) **A**. This has seven towers, three of them with gates. **Krasnie** and **Nikolskie** gates, located in the Kremlin's northwestern part, led to the Volga. The third **Prechistenskaya Bashnya**, with a bell tower incorporated in the eastern wall, led to the suburb **Bely Gorod** (White Town).

Close to the Prechistensky Gate is the **Uspensky Sobor** (Cathedral of the Assumption) **B**. The cathedral is a marvellous monument built by the serf-architect, Dorofei Myakishev, in 1698. From all sides, it is surrounded by a two-tier gallery decorated with filigree carved stone, creating an impression of light and air. The upper church with five graceful domes rises from this unusual, seemingly weightless pedestal. The Cathedral of the Assumption together with the place of execution and a high bell tower, built in the 19th century, make up a majestic architectural ensemble. The pseudo-Russian details overload the facades of the structure, but its tiers, evenly diminishing as they rise, make the bell tower look austere.

The **Troitsky Sobor** (Trinity Cathedral) **C**, built between the late 16th and 18th century on the opposite side of the Kremlin territory, looks modest compared with the Cathedral of the Assumption. But in terms of craftsmanship, it is a large and intricate complex.

Many of the Kremlin's architectural structures date from the 19th century. Of particular interest are the Guard House (1807) and the **Kirillovskaya Chasovnya** (Chapel). In the early 19th century, the chapel's original 17th-century structure was enclosed in a classical shell. The main portal (17th-century) is hidden behind the short massive Doric columns.

Another architectural structure that has survived on the territory of the former Bely Gorod is the Tower of the **Preobrazhensky Monastyr** (Transfiguration Monastery) **D**. Its snow-white octahedron, adorned with multi-coloured belts and insets and crowned with a dome, is magnificent.

Not far from the Preobrazhensky Monastery there is the **Demidov Homestead** **E**, at Ulitsa Sverdlova 55, another architectural legacy of the 17th and 18th centuries. It was the largest and the most important home in the town. The Demidovs were an ancient merchant family in Russia. The size of the building was immense and even today it occupies half the block.

Among the churches that have survived outside the Kremlin's boundaries is the **Ioann Zlatoust** (St John Chrysostom) **F**, Ulitsa Volzhskaya 14. It was built in 1763, and its octahedron-on-tetrahedron composition was common in Central Russia. The church was reconstructed more than once, the final version in the form of a cross, incorporating the decor associated with classicism. The entrance to the church is adorned with a figure of Christ. The bent figures of angels on the western façade of the belfry express grief.

Buildings in classical style became a regular feature in towns after 1769. The early 19th century gave rise to such imposing and outstanding buildings as the **City Technical School** **G** and the **Department**

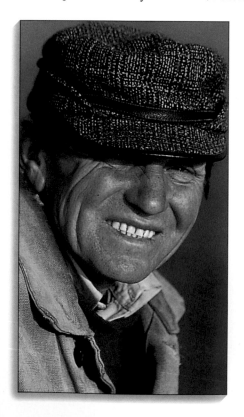

BELOW: boatman on the Volga River.

for the Supervision of the Kalmyk People ⓗ at Ulitsa Volodarskoga 22. Stone structures were built not only in the centre of Astrakhan but in the outskirts, too. A striking example is the surviving building of the hospital on Parobichev Hill. Eastern merchants, who enjoyed extensive privileges, settled in Astrakhan. They built their trade rows and lived in tight-knit communities in the centre of Bely Gorod. The surviving structures of the Indian and Persian homesteads were built in the 19th century.

Foreign merchants also built their own religious institutes, hence the **Belaya Mechet** (White Mosque) ⓘ, Ulitsa Zoi Kosmodemyanskoi 41, and the **Chernaya Mechet** (Black Mosque) ⓙ, Ulitsa Musy Dzhaliya Ulitsa 26, erected by Strakhan Tatars in the mid-19th century. In the eastern part of town, at the confluence of the Kutum River and the canal stands a Roman Catholic church, **Katolicheskaya Tserkov,** dating from the 18th century. Such architectural imports form a magnificent contrast to Astrakhan's other buildings.

Equally impressive are the commercial buildings that served the merchants. The merchants' estates on the Kutum's northern bank also illustrate the luxury of the times. One of the most interesting features of Astrakhan's architecture of the 19th century is the elaborate metalwork. A strong Oriental influence is evident in the fancy grilles, balconies, arches and gates.

The **Kartinnaya Galereya B.M. Kustodieva** (Kustodiev Art Gallery) ⓚ (open 10am–6pm; closed Sun), Ulitsa Sverdlova 81, is named after Astrakhan's most famous native resident, Boris Kustodiev, a graphic artist and colourist. It contains works by artists from the 18th and 19th centuries and modern masters.

The city is still expanding. New buildings are constantly appearing, both in the centre and on the outskirts. The best of these complement the the old town. ❑

TIP

Boat tours of the Volga delta reserve can be arranged through Intourist in Astrakhan (Sovietskaya Ulitsa). Don't miss the red lotuses which bloom in August.

THE URALS

Marking the border between Europe and Asia, the Ural Mountain region is the industrial heartland of Russia, where modern cities rise out of a landscape of forests and lakes

Map on page 240

To picture the Urals, imagine smokestacks, factories and heavy industry. That is how leaders of the old USSR envisaged this mountain chain, and they proceeded to transform it into a succession of massive state-owned industrial enterprises. The region has never attracted many tourists, partly because Soviet leaders declared most of the Urals off-limits to foreigners – bans that were lifted only in the *perestroika* years. Today, foreigners in the area are generally businessmen sifting through the tattered remains of Soviet industry in search of investment opportunities.

There are still some areas of outstanding natural beauty where lakes and hiking paths dot the landscape, but the lack of tourist facilities make them inaccessible for everyone except the experienced traveller in Russia. The 2,000-km (1,250-mile) long Ural Mountain range – stretching between the Kara Sea in the north and Kazakhstan in the south – is not the insuperable geographical barrier one imagines: it is less than 2,000 metres (6,500 ft) at its highest point and has never been a serious obstacle to invasion from either direction. But in the absence of any other geographical feature it has long been taken to mark the divide between European Russia and Siberia, and by extension, between Europe and Asia.

The Ural Mountains date back 250 million years. Until the 15th century they were sparsely inhabited by a variety of local tribes. By contrast, today's Urals accommodate more than 20 million inhabitants, covering five regions: Sverdlovsk, Perm, Chelya-binsk, Orenburg, Kurgan, and two republics, Udmurtiya and Bashkortostan. The Urals' rich reserves of iron ore, coal, precious minerals and ferrous and non-ferrous metals eventually attracted large-scale European migration in the 18th century. Between 1752 and 1762 alone, 55 factories were built in the region, and industrial centres sprouted up in Yekaterinburg, Perm and Orenburg.

Industry moves in

Russia's devastation during World War II brought a boom to the Urals. After the German army roared across much of the European part of the USSR, Stalin moved 1,300 factories and hundreds of thousands of people to beyond the Urals for protection – not only from ground troops, but also from the Luftwaffe. The new Ural industrial base tripled capacity and was able to supply 40 percent of the Soviet Union's military needs for the war. The German armies never came close to the Urals, and historians cite Stalin's relocation of Soviet industry as a decisive factor in the outcome of World War II. Today, of course, distance is no

PRECEDING PAGES: the Ilych Reserve at Pechora. **LEFT:** Yekaterinburg. **BELOW:** selling *tvorog* (curd cheese) at the Central Market in Yekaterinburg.

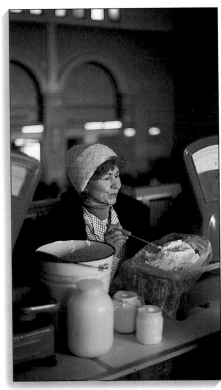

Yekaterinburg was named after Catherine the Great. During Soviet times it was known as Sverdlovsk after the Bolshevik leader Yakov Sverdlov who is said to have arranged the execution of Tsar Nicholas II.

barrier, as Gary Powers showed in 1960 in his U2 spy plane. He was however, shot down over Yekaterinburg. Today's American-produced jets are less likely to be shot down as they fly into the city's increasingly busy international airport.

Following the war, Soviet authorities continued to expand heavy industry and the manufacturing of weapons. Traditional rural life in the region changed permanently as people flocked to the cities to work. Between 1940 and 1979, the Urals' urban population more than doubled. Even though the Urals still has one of the lowest population densities in Russia, it claims one of the highest outputs in heavy industry and defence sectors.

By the final years of Soviet power, the Urals accounted for a third of the country's steel production and a quarter of its cast iron. "The economic region of the Urals plays an important role in building the material and technical base of Communism," the country's main encyclopaedia enthused. The intense industrialisation has also made the Urals one of the most polluted regions in the world, resulting in staggering health problems for local inhabitants.

Capital of the Urals

Yekaterinburg ❶ (pop. 1.5 million), omitted from many tourist maps until 1990, is the Urals' most important urban centre and is Russia's third city (a popular claim of many large Russian cities). It is the first major Russian city in Asia; 40 km (25 miles) to the west along the highway, a 4-metre (13-ft) high memorial marks the Asian-European border. The city spreads out around the Iset River and is surrounded by taiga (forests).

The winter here lasts for about five months, from November to April, and the temperature may fall to –40°C (–40°F). The summer, which normally

BELOW: at work on the production line.

lasts no more than two months, maintains an average temperature of 20°C (68°F).

Like most major cities in the Urals, Yekaterinburg's history has been closely associated with industry. The city was founded in 1723, and within five years the area had set up an ironworks, the first of many industrial enterprises attracted by the abundant raw materials of the region. It remained modestly populated for many decades with just 10,000 people at the start of the 19th century, but the population exploded under socialism, climbing from 100,000 in 1917 to four times that number at the end of World War II. The war triggered an industrial boom in the city, and the area became one of the Soviet Union's most important manufacturing centres for years afterwards. With its solid industrial base, Yekaterinburg is one of the few towns outside European Russia to make real progress in market reform.

Yeltsin's home town

Modern Yekaterinburg is best known for its political sons, the president of the Russian Federation, Boris Yeltsin, and Nikolai Ryzhkov, prime minister during Gorbachev's presidency. Yeltsin was born into a poor family some 150 km (93 miles) from Yekaterinburg, in **Butka**. He spent most of his life in Yekaterinburg, first studying at the Urals Polytechnic (now the Urals State Technical University), then building a career in the construction industry while rising through the ranks of the Communist Party.

Many remember Yeltsin as a tough but popular leader, and locals still recall the day that party officials came to visit in 1985. Yeltsin was later summoned to the capital to become chief of the Moscow party, effectively taking up the post of mayor of the city. With Gorbachev's blessing he used this post as a power-

Map on page 240

A remarkable sight in modern Yekaterinburg are the old wooden houses, complete with carved window frames and other details. Many of these are still used as homes and offices.

BELOW: a cross marks the site of Tsar Nicholas II's execution at Yekaterinburg.

DEATH OF A TSAR

Yekaterinburg is most famous in the history books not for its industry, but for its role in the execution of Tsar Nicholas II following the Bolshevik Revolution. After seizing power in 1917, the Communists imprisoned Nicholas and his family, moving them to several locations before bringing them to Yekaterinburg in April, 1918. The family was confined to a brick home formerly belonging to a local businessman, Ipatyev. Accounts of the royal family's end were wrapped in secrecy throughout the Soviet period, but historians believe that guards treated the family cruelly during their final days. In July the Bolsheviks decided to dispose of the tsar once and for all, to avoid him being recaptured by the anti-Bolshevik forces that were then threatening the town. The tsar was moved into the basement of the house and informed that he was about to die. The historian William Henry Chamberlain wrote: "The tsar did not understand, and began to say 'What?' whereupon Yurovsky shot him down with his revolver. This was the signal for the general massacre. The other executioners emptied their revolvers into the bodies of the victims." The bodies were taken into the surrounding woods and left in a shallow grave. In 1998 their remains were removed to St Petersburg for reburial.

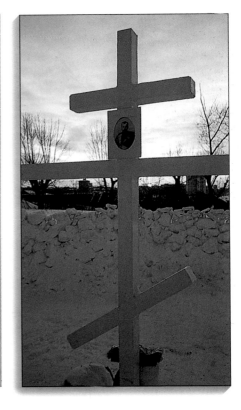

base for reform at the heart of the Soviet Empire. He did not know that he would be staying on in Moscow as president of a new Russian state.

Exploring Yekaterinburg

Town planners have thankfully kept most of the industry outside the town centre, creating instead pleasant wide avenues lined with trees and modern apartment blocks and offices.

Start your sightseeing by walking south, away from Prospekt Lenina (Lenin Avenue), the city's main street, along Ulitsa Karl Liebknecht. The first major sight – a few minutes' walk, to the right – is the **Istorichesky Muzei** (Regional History Museum) **A**, Ulitsa Malisheva 46 (open 11am–5pm; closed Tues). Here you'll find an interesting historical collection starting with late tsarist rule and continuing through to the present. Highlights include pre-Revolutionary photographs and objects from Yekaterinburg, a photographic record of the men who killed Tsar Nicholas II and his family, and objects connected with the original inhabitants of the Ural region, including tents, hunting implements, and fur garments.

The **Muzei Molodyozhi** (Youth Museum) **B**, Ulitsa Karl Liebknecht 32 (open 9am–7pm, Sat 1–7pm; closed Sun), once belonged to the Komsomol Communist youth organisation. The museum now takes an imaginative look at Soviet history and has opened a radical exhibition on Soviet life. Displays include a maze of mirrors, said to illustrate the futility of Soviet bureaucracy, and a man walking through a glass wall, showing how Russians are looking forwards and backwards at the same time. In another room there is an artist's rendition of what the world would look like after nuclear war.

A folk display in Yekaterinburg's History Museum.

BELOW: a selection of hors d'oeuvre known as *zakuski*.

Yekaterinburg

Map on page 242

A five-minute walk north back up Ulitsa Karl Liebknecht is the site of Tsar Nicholas II's and his family's final home, the former **Dom Ipatyeva** (Ipatyev House) **C**, now surrounded by concrete fencing. A small wooden *chasovnya* (chapel) has been erected as a makeshift shrine while local people gather enough money to rebuild the house as a museum. Twice the local governor has attempted to raise funds and twice they have been insufficient.

In the decades following the execution, many Russians came to the house to peer quietly into the last link with former times. But in 1977 the Kremlin, increasingly worried that Dom Ipatyeva could become a place of worship, ordered the local party boss, Boris Yeltsin, to remove it. A few days later the bulldozers were driven up to the house in the middle of the night. By the next morning, nothing was left of the building.

There are several museums a few blocks west of Prospekt Lenina. In an area that is the site of the city's original settlement is the **Muzei Iskusstva** (Art Museum) **D**, Ulitsa Voyevodina 5 (open 11am–6pm, closed Mon), home to mostly Russian paintings. The large building's centrepiece is a 4.5-metre (15-ft) high iron pavilion crafted in an intricate Oriental style for display in Paris in 1900. Other highlights include local metal sculptures, a popular and traditional art form of the area.

The **Geologichesky Muzei** (Geological Museum) **E**, Ulitsa Kuybysheva 39 (open 10am–5pm, closed Sun, Mon), houses an interesting collection of some 600 minerals found in the Urals, including malachite, topaz, a 748-kg (1,650-lb) crystal and meteorites.

If you return to Prospekt Lenina and walk one block to the east, you'll come to **Ploshchad 1905** (1905-Square) **F**, Yekaterinburg's main square and the home to **Dom Gorodskogo Pravitelstva** (City Hall) **G**, Prospekt Lenina 24, which was built between 1947 to 1954 by German prisoners captured during World War II. Here you will find a large statue of Lenin erected in 1957.

On the east side of town, where Prospekt Lenina starts, is the **Uralsky Gosudarstvenny Tekhnichesky Universitet** (Urals State Technical University) **H**, the largest university in the Asian part of Russia, which once had 20,000 students, 7,000 teachers and employees and occupied several blocks of town with its own hospital, hostels and hotels. Known for its strong science and engineering departments in particular, the school has produced a series of prominent Soviet and Russian officials, including Boris Yeltsin and his wife, Naina, who met as students here. At one time 12 graduates of the school were on the Central Committee of the Communist Party. More recently the university has experienced harder times, since local industry has cut back its need for university-level engineers.

Although hardly worth a tourist visit, **Uralsky Mashinostroitelny Zavod** (Urals Factory of Heavy Machine Construction), Ploshchad 1 Pyatiletki, on the north part of town is famous throughout Russia and once ranked as one of the largest factories in the world. A machine tool and heavy plant factory, "Uralmash" once employed a staggering 50,000 people in the area. As a Soviet publication of 1991

BELOW: Urals State Technical University.

stated: "For many decades, this name was the symbol of the newest, most powerful, most progressive technology in the country." The introduction of market economics to Russia gave this factory, and many others, a harsh slap in the face. Output fell dramatically, and Uralmash management reduced the number of workers to 29,000.

Steel city

A name virtually synonymous with Soviet industrialisation, **Magnitogorsk** ❷ (pop. 450,000) is also one of the world's most polluted cities. Ironically, this most Soviet of places, 113 km (70 miles) into Asia from the European divide, was designed by an American firm. When the Soviet government decided to increase exploitation of the Urals' rich iron ore deposits, which had already been mined for hundreds of years, they turned to the McKee corporation of Cleveland, Ohio (at the time selected US businesses were free to co-operate with the new but underdeveloped Soviet state). McKee was called upon to help in the design of Magnitogorsk, and it drew its inspiration from the US steel plant in Gary, Indiana, which was at the time the largest iron and steel plant in the world. The American firm was paid US$2.5 million in gold for its services. The construction of Magnitogorsk began in 1929; pig iron was already in production by 1932, and steel was being manufactured by the following year.

The initial name of the plant launched during the USSR's first Five-Year Plan was the Stalin Magnitogorsk Metallurgy Kombinat. Workers in this model industrial project settled in an area called Sotsgorod, a Russian-language abbreviation for "The Socialist City". The city's population rapidly expanded to 146,000 by 1939, and it soon became one of the country's major industrial

BELOW: Central Market in Yekaterinburg.

Map on page 240

centres. The area still stamps out huge quantities of steel: in 1990 Magnito-gorsk produced 25 percent of all Soviet goods containing metal.

Accidents and experiments

Founded in 1736 as a defensive fortress, **Chelyabinsk ❸** (pop. 1.2 million) is the administrative centre of the southern Urals. It grew rapidly in the 19th century as a trading centre along the railway. Located 200 km (125 miles) southeast of Yekaterinburg, the city is an important industrial centre for the manufacture of cast-iron products such as tanks, and other metal products.

The Chelyabinsk area is also the site of two of the worst nuclear accidents in the post-war period. In September 1957, a mechanism designed to cool nuclear waste failed in nearby **Kyshtym** and contaminated the area with radioactive material. For years the incident was shrouded in secrecy. From 1951 to 1961, the Mayak (Lighthouse) nuclear bomb plant 100 km (80 miles) northwest of Chelyabinsk dumped huge quantities of radioactive waste into a local lake. The lake has since evaporated, but the radioactive dust remains a lethal threat. Intourist arranges tours, including visits to a biophysics centre specialising in treatment of the victims of radiation, and meetings with local scientists specialising in nuclear and energy problems.

In Chelyabinsk, the main sights are the **Geologichesky Muzei** (Geology Museum), highlighting Ural minerals, Ulitsa Truda 98; the **Kartinnaya Galereya** (Picture Gallery), Ulitsa Truda 92, containing work by Russian and foreign artists from the 15th to the 20th centuries, and the **Muzei Prikladnykh Iskusstv** (Applied Art Museum), Ulitsa Revolutsii 1, showing off the best of local masters.

Orenburg ❹ (pop. 500,000), an industrial centre founded in 1735, is located near the site of one of the most grotesque experiments of the Cold War. According to recent press accounts, in 1954 the Red Army exploded an atomic bomb near the city during military exercises. Subsequently, local villagers suffered a 50 percent increase in cancer, and of the 44,000 soldiers who participated only 1,000 are still alive. Orenburg is home to the military aviation academy where Yury Gagarin, the first human being in space, studied. A jet which he used is located at the entrance to the academy.

In and around Perm

On the European side of the Urals, **Perm ❺** is another large industrial centre (pop. 1 million). It was founded in 1723 as a village around a factory. From 1940 to 1957, Perm was renamed Molotov, in honour of the Soviet foreign minister who signed the non-aggression pact with Nazi Germany in 1939. Perm's highlight is the **Gosudarstvennaya Kartinnaya Galereya** (State Picture Gallery), Komsomolsky Prospekt 4, with its fine display of 16th–19th-century icons, sculptures and Russian and foreign paintings (closed Mon). The **Etnografichsky Muzei** (Ethnographic Architecture Museum) at **Khokhlovka**, 45 km (28 miles) north of Perm, preserves examples of pre-20th-century rural life. ❑

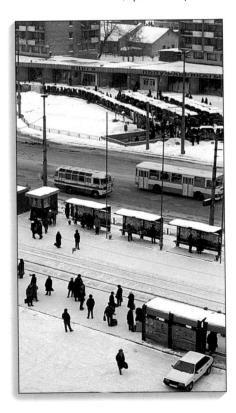

BELOW: waiting for public transport.

THE EUROPEAN SOUTH

This is Russia with a southern flavour. Here, you can soak up the sun in the Black Sea resort of Sochi or sample the curative mineral waters of the Caucasian Mountains

Map on page 250

The European South, or Northern Caucasus as it is also called, stretches across the south of the Russian Federation, bounded by the Black and Sea of Azov to the west and the Caspian Sea to the east. The scenery is diverse: from the fertile black-earth steppe of the Don to the north, to the snow-capped Caucasian mountains to the south; from the subtropical Black Sea coast to the semi-desert areas by the Caspian. The vegetation is equally varied: coniferous forests at the foot of the mountains, subtropical vegetation along the shores, high meadows carpeted with mountain flowers and rush-filled river valleys.

Both the subtropical climate and the mineral-rich soil in the Northern Caucasus make it an extremely fertile area and a wide variety of fruits and vegetables grow in abundance. Just north of Sochi at **Dagomys ❶** are the most northerly tea plantations in the world, producing Krasnodarsky tea, a large percentage of which goes for export. Tobacco, including rare oily kinds, is another important resource. Despite the harsh legislation during Mikhail Gorbachev's anti-alcohol campaign when nearly one-sixth of the Soviet Union's vineyards were destroyed, the northern part of the Caucasus is still renowned for its vineyards. In the small town of **Abrau-Dyurso**, west of the Black Sea port of Novorossiysk, vintners have been producing one of Russia's best champagnes for more than 150 years.

The Caucasus has been home to dozens of different peoples over time, resulting in the ethnic diversity which characterises the region to the day. It covers more than six autonomous republics and is home to Ukrainians, Russians, Caucasians (Circassians, Adygeis, Kabardians, Balkars, Ossets), Greeks, Abkhazians, Georgians, Armenians and Estonians.

The Kuban Cossacks (named after the river which runs through Krasnodar) and their descendants live on the plains to the north of the Caucasus. Their capital is **Krasnodar ❷** (pop. 630,000). Before the Revolution, Krasnodar was called Yekaterinodar – from *Yekaterina* (Catherine) and *dar* (gift). Catherine the Great gave this city to the Kuban Cossacks in return for conquering southern lands for the Russian crown. Today it is the capital of the **Krasnodarsky Kray** region, an area rich in minerals, especially oil, and famous for its wheat.

The Black Sea coast

The Black Sea is an internal and virtually isolated body of water, which is contaminated below 200 metres (656 ft) with hydrogen sulphide. Although marine life is sustainable only in the top 200 metres, the Black Sea supports a variety of different fish, three species of dolphin and more than 13 types of jelly-

PRECEDING PAGES: the Caucasian Mountains. **LEFT:** a wild iris. **BELOW:** raising lambs in the hills.

Triumphal Arch at Novocherkassk, the 19th-century capital of the Don Cossacks near Rostov-on-Don.

fish. It is fed by a large number of rivers, which dilute the salt content and keep the sea clean. **Novorossiysk ❸** is southern Russia's principal port. It has become especially important since Ukraine gained independence and Russia's naval base in the Crimean port of Sevastopol moved in part to Novorossiysk. Another vital Black Sea port is **Tuapse ❹**, south of Novorossiysk, where most of the Russian oil tankers berth.

Sochi

Russia's most popular beaches stretch along the east coast of the Black Sea from Tuapse to Georgia. The best known resort is **Sochi ❺**. Like the rest of the coast, Sochi is protected from cold northerly winds by the Caucasus and enjoys a subtropical climate. The area around Sochi has evidence of habitation dating back to prehistoric man. The first official Russian settlement on the River Sochi was the coastal fortress of Aleksandria, founded in 1838 to prevent Ottoman expansion in the area. The fortress came under constant attack, not by the Turks but by the local Caucasian peoples and 15 years later it was evacuated by the Russian garrison as the Crimean campaign began. Russian troops returned in 1864 and by 1866 the local inhabitants had been subdued. Alexander II ordered that the region be "settled" by Russians and Ukrainians.

Sochi began developing as a tourist destination in the late 19th century. In the Soviet period it became a popular holiday destination among Russians and their leaders. You can still see the *dachas* (country houses) of some the politicians – Stalin, Khrushchev, Brezhnev – who spent holidays here. Indeed, Khrushchev was on holiday at his Black Sea *dacha* just along the coast in Pitsunda (now in the Republic of Abkhazia) when he was removed from power in 1964.

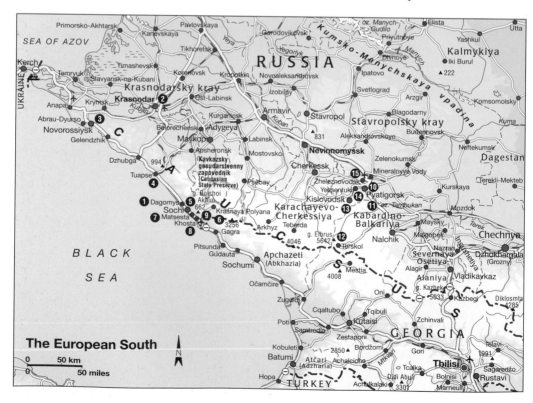

The European South

Sochi's popularity is further boosted by its numerous *sanatorii* (therapeutic hotels) and *doma otdykha* (rest-houses), which offer cures and treatments for various illnesses using local spa therapies. Many Soviet trade unions had therapeutic hotels in Sochi to which their members could come on holiday with their families. A number of these *sanatorii* still exist and you can generally arrange to stay at one by turning up at the door. Sochi remains a favourite destination for conferences, and hosts an annual international film festival in June.

Like all the Russian Black Sea beaches, those in Sochi are pebble rather than sand. They drop away steeply into the sea making them excellent for swimming. You can walk most of the coast along the romantic seafront promenades and through the parks lush with magnolia palm and cypress. Most popular of Sochi's parks is the botanical garden, **Park Dendrarii Ⓐ**, with more than 1,600 different types of trees. Next to Drendariy Park you will find the **Derevo Druzhby** (Tree of Friendship). Although it looks similar to an orchard, it is in fact one tree to which, in honour of visiting foreign representatives, 40 different citrus fruits have been grafted – Japanese tangerines, Italian lemons, American oranges and Indian grapefruits, to name a few.

Kurortny Prospekt Ⓑ is the main street in Sochi, where most of the major hotels are situated. The prospekt begins in the north at Platanovaya Alleya (Plane Alley, named for the plane trees which line it) at **Park Rivyera Ⓒ** and traverses the length of Sochi crossing several small rivers. In the evening, life shifts from the seafront cafés to restaurants and cafés along Kurortny.

Sochi has a number of museums including a good art gallery, **Muzei Izobrazitelnykh Iskusstv** (Sochi Art Gallery) Ⓓ at Kurortny Prospekt 51, which features a collection of paintings, drawings and sculpture from the 17th to the

Maps:
Area 250
City 252

TIP

The best time to visit Sochi is in autumn when there are long hours of sunshine and the humidity is low. Spring comes early to the coast and flowers bloom in late March.

BELOW: *borshch* (beetroot soup), a popular dish in the Caucasus.

A TASTE OF THE CAUCASUS

The cuisine of the northern Caucasus and the Black Sea coast is influenced both by the bordering country of Georgia and by the local inhabitants. Here you will find Ukrainian *borshch* (beetroot soup) alongside Georgian *kharcho* (a spicy meat and tomato broth). You can try Russian *pelmeni* (a type of ravioli served with sour cream or vinegar) and Georgian *khinkali* (a larger spicier version of *pelmeni*). As well as traditional Russian breads there are Armenian *lavash* (a soft pancake-thin unleavened bread) and Georgian *khachapuri* (a delicious hot cheese-filled bread). On the beach vendors often come by selling hot corn on the cob, roasted hazelnuts and *semochki* (sunflower seeds). Another unusual seaside snack is *chukchela*, a Georgian sweet made of hazelnuts or walnuts strung on a piece of string and coated with hot grape juice, which solidifies as it cools. An integral part of summer picnics is *shashlyk*, a type of marinated kebab cooked on long skewers over charcoal embers. The Armenian version is wrapped in *lavash* and cheese. In the seafront cafés try locally caught trout in delicious Georgian *bazha* (walnut and coriander sauce), and finish your meal with an excellent Turkish or Greek-style coffee and a *paklava* (pastry) made with fresh mountain honey.

A pleasant half-day excursion can be made from Sochi to Dagomys Tea Farm to sample the local brew in attractive surroundings.

20th century (open 10am–5.30pm; closed Mon). **Muzei Istori Goroda-kurorta Sochi** (Sochi History Museum) **E**, Ulitsa Ordzhonikidze 29, contains exhibits from the earliest evidence of prehistoric habitation through to the modern day (open 9am–6pm; closed Mon).

The **Muzei Pisatelya Nikolaya Ostrovskogo** (Ostrovsky Literary Museum) **F** (open 9am–6pm; closed Wed) is dedicated to Nikolai Ostrovsky, a revolutionary writer who fought in the Civil War following the October Revolution. Unable to hold a pen as a result of his injuries, he dictated his novels to his wife. The museum has three sections: a house-museum dedicated to Ostrovsky and a literary collection at Pavla Korchagina 4; and at Krasnaya Polyana, 50 km (34 miles) into the mountains, a house-museum (open 10am–5pm; closed Wed) dedicated to the Estonians who settled in the Caucasus in the 19th century, in particular the writer Tommsaare.

The foothills of the Caucasus

Most compelling of all is the countryside around Sochi. If you don't have a car, there are plenty of tour operators located on Kurortny who arrange moderately-priced bus trips into the mountains surrounding Sochi. One of the most spectacular routes is the journey to the mountain village of **Krasnaya Polyana** **G** (Beautiful Glade), 50 km (30 miles) from Sochi and 600 metres (1,970 ft) above sea level. The road up to Krasnaya Polyana snakes along ledges cut into steep mountain gorges providing breathtaking views. Along the way, look out for two crowbars sticking out of the rock, a memorial to the workers who died while building this treacherous road between 1897 and 1899. A fork in the road takes you to a place called **Medvezhy Ugol** (Bears' Corner), an allusion to the

BELOW: Black Sea port of Sochi.

Maps:
Area 250
City 252

brown bears that roam these parts, along with wild boar and deer. There is also a Narzan mineral water spring. Archaeological finds suggest that the area was inhabited first in the Stone Age. At the turn of the 20th century it was a hunting preserve for the tsar and his family. Today, as the **Caucasian State Preserve**, it is famous for its herd of bison.

Krasnaya Polyana is surrounded by snowy mountain peaks, at the foot of which are dense forests. Footpaths lead to an arboretum and the remains of the tsar's hunting lodge, and to river valleys, waterfalls and alpine meadows. There are several places to stay that make a good base for hiking trips in the summer months and skiing in the winter.

Matsesta ❼, 12 km (7 miles) southeast of Sochi, is the region's main spa town. In local Circassian, *matsesta* means "fire water". The sulphur waters turn bathers' skins bright red; they also help to treat systemic disorders, ulcers, and skin diseases. The marble *banya* (baths) date from tsarist times.

About 25 km (15 miles) from Sochi is **Khosta** ❽, another spa with hot mineral springs. It can be reached by train, bus, or boat. The pleasant beaches here are less populous than those in the centre of Sochi. Three kilometres (2 miles) inland is a forest preserve containing trees as old as 800 years. Here, too, are all that remains of an 11th-century fortress believed to have been built by Genoans. Nearby is a collection of cork oaks brought from Portugal, France, Spain and Algeria.

Mt Bolshoi Akhun ❾ with a 662-metre (2,171-ft) observation tower, is 20 km (12 miles) inland from Sochi. From the top of the tower there is an excellent view of the snow-topped peaks of the high Caucasus, the coastline beyond Sochi, and even the Abkhazian resort of Pitsunda. A little way from the tower

BELOW: carrying water from the well.

LITERARY HERO

Mikhail Yurevich Lermontov (1814–41) is one of Russia's leading romantic writers whose life and works are integral to the Caucasus. He is best known for his novel, *Hero of our Time*, a large part of which is based in Pyatigorsk. As a child, Lermontov visited the region on several occasions and his earliest poems refer to the local landscape and culture. Lermontov was exiled to the Caucasus in 1837 for writing a poem alleging that the tsarist regime was to blame for Pushkin's death. A year later he returned to St Petersburg, where his reputation as a writer grew. His work was characterised by his cynical views on contemporary society and his criticism of the tsarist regime. In 1840 he was exiled to the Caucasus again, this time to a military post. The following year, strangely reminiscent of the plot of *Hero of Our Time*, Lermontov quarrelled with another officer and was killed in a duel just outside Pyatigorsk. You can still visit the Academic Gallery, Bulvar Gagarina, where the character "Pechorin" first sees "Princess Mary", and the Spa Research Institute, Prospekt Kirova, site of the fashionable balls in the novel. The author's cottage can be seen at the Lermontov Museum Reserve, Ulitsa Lermontova (open 10am–5pm; closed Tues and last Thurs in month).

Map on page 250

The Caucasians are famous for their curative mineral water springs, reputed to improve the heart and vascular systems, nervous system, stomach ailments, gynaecological problems and skin diseases.

BELOW: abundant tomato harvest. **OPPOSITE:** southern gentlemen.

are the **Agurskiye vodopady** (Agur waterfalls). There are good restaurants at the foot of the tower and by the waterfalls serving Caucasian food and wine.

Spa towns of the northern Caucasus

Kavkazskiye Mineralnyye Vody (Caucasian Mineral Waters) is a resort region made up of four main towns: Kislovodsk, Pyatigorsk, Zheleznovodsk, and Yessentuki, all of which are connected by trolleybuses. The area is located on the northern spur of the central Caucasus. Summers are warm, 20° to 25°C (68°–77°F) and long, winters are mild and the sun shines nearly 300 days a year. The marvellous climate, curative waters, lush vegetation and mountain scenery have lured the health-conscious for nearly two centuries. The region is also known for its abundance of fruits and vegetables, dry and sweet wines, cognacs and, of course, drinking waters. Today there are a few Intourist hotels as well as the numerous *sanatorii*.

Pyatigorsk (Five Peaks) ❿, the region's oldest spa, was founded 200 years ago on the southern slopes of **Mt Mashuk** (993 metres/3,257 ft). It has 43 mineral springs and its own research institute for the development of new cures. You cannot visit Pyatigorsk without coming across reference to the Russian poet and author Mikhail Lermontov (1814–41) who died here fighting a duel (*see box on page 253*). The **Lermontovskaya Galereya** (Lermontov Gallery) is situated in the town's central park among the mineral springs and grottoes. **Ozero Tambukan** (Lake Tambukanskoye) ⓫, 11 km (6 miles) from Pyatigorsk, is renowned for its mud, which is said to improve muscle tone and blood vessels.

Gora Elbrus (Mt Elbrus) ⓬, Europe's highest peak, is a 168-km (104-mile) drive south. The region is noted for its horse farms. Races are held at the local hippodrome from May to September).

Kislovodsk ⓭ (Sour Waters), 40 km (25 miles) southwest of Pyatigorsk, claims to have the best climate in the region. Founded in 1803, Kislovodsk is renowned for its Narzan mineral water. In the local language, *narzan* means "drink of the gods"; it is used in medicinal baths. The town is surrounded by beautiful landscapes, including a 12-hectare (30-acre) artificial lake. Nearby is a strange rock formation known as the **Zamok Kovarstva i Lyubvi** "Castle of Perfidy and Love" from which, the story goes, a young shepherd boy and wealthy local girl who were in love but forbidden to marry made a pact to throw themselves to their deaths. The shepherd jumped, but the girl did not. Here you'll find the Caucasian restaurant **Zamok** (Castle). Order the delicious fresh trout.

Halfway between Pyatigorsk and Kislovodsk is **Yessentuki** ⓮, named after a local mineral water that is prescribed for stomach, intestinal, and urological disorders. Built in the early 19th century, the spa is known for its Gothic and Greek-style architecture and for its mud baths. **Zheleznovodsk** ⓯ (Iron Waters), the smallest of the four spa towns, is 630 metres (2,066 ft) above sea level. It was built at the recommendation of the General Aleksei Yermolov who fought in the Caucasian war. Local sites include the Mauritanian-style **Ostrovsky Baths** (1893), the **Emir of Bukhara's palace**, and the **permafrost caves**. ❑

SIBERIA AND THE FAR EAST

Siberia may seem awesome in size, but the delights of Irkutsk's wooden houses, the rugged mountains of Altay and the wonders of Lake Baikal are easily accessible by plane or train

Map on page 260

In 1982, Russian geologists exploring a remote region of the Siberian taiga near Gornaya Khasiya, found a family of *raskolniki* (Old Believers) who had been living in hiding since tsarist times and knew nothing of the fall of the tsar and the rise of Soviet rule. Such is the vastness of the great Siberian plain.

Exploring Siberia measures up to a lifetime's ambition, not a vacation. But for a determined and hardy traveller, much of the flavour of this remote part of the world can still be savoured in the Russian and Soviet-era outpost towns that dot the vast Siberian taiga from the Urals to the Pacific, the Arctic Ocean to Mongolia.

Travel in Siberia tends to take two forms: stop-offs along the Trans-Siberian Railway and city-jumping on Aeroflot internal flights. With the easing of travel restrictions during the 1990s, even more exotic excursions are also possible: deep tundra snow-mobiling, boat cruises up the Yenisey and Lena rivers with a helicopter shuttle in between, and hunting and fishing expeditions.

Adventurous travelling requires careful planning, with the help of private Russian travel agencies. In Siberia, the best of the new agencies are located in Irkutsk, but be warned: where amenities are concerned, Siberia makes Moscow seem like Paris. Many towns have no restaurants or hotel rooms. A hefty dose of patience is as important to a traveller as bottled water.

The region's geography

Covering 12.5 million sq km (4.8 million sq miles), Siberia is a geo-political invention rather than a physical, geographical identity. The name Siberia comes from the Mongolian *sibi*, which means "sleeping land". It encompasses a wide range of terrain, related by little more than the remoteness of European Russia to the west and China and Mongolia to the south. The Buryats in Ulan-Ude consider themselves residents of Siberia just as much as the Yakuts living near the Bering Strait.

A journey from west to east Siberia starts at the rolling Urals and passes immediately on to the great primeval forests of the taiga. The taiga is almost equal in size to the whole of Western Europe. It stands pretty much as it has for millions of years, since logging is economically impractical in the remote forests.

Further east is the River Ob, running north from the Altai Mountains through Gorno-Altaysk to Barnaul, Novosibirsk, just missing Tomsk and then meandering north towards the Arctic Circle where it enters the Obskaya Guba. This is Russia's longest river, 5,410 km (3,362 miles), and the first of a network of rivers flowing north to the Arctic Ocean. The others

PRECEDING PAGES: Siberian reindeer. **LEFT:** Nentsy mother and child. **BELOW:** Siberian tiger on the prowl.

Siberia and the Far East

include, from west to east, the Yenisey, Angara and Lena. To the south of the taiga is the world's biggest bog, the Urmany. The region has some of the richest oil reserves in the world, which, together with oil rigs in the Severnoye More (North Sea), once accounted for 95 percent of the Soviet Union's hard currency earnings. Foreign oil workers are beginning to explore the region, but roads cannot be built over the soft ground. Further east is Ozero Baykal (Lake Baikal), "the Pearl of Siberia", and the boundary between Siberia and the Russian Far East. To the north, Siberia hugs the Arctic Circle, passing over the diamond-rich region of Yakutiya and on to the Bering Strait. Siberia peters out on the island of Big Diomede, within sight of the United States's island of Little Diomede, seven time zones away from where it starts.

Map on page 260

A little history

Though sporadic fur-trading was underway by the 11th century, the process of "opening" Siberia to Russia did not really begin until 1552 – the year Ivan the Terrible liberated Kazan from the Tatars and created a gateway for expansion.

Siberia has endured two great waves of exploration and settlement. The first occurred during the expansion of tsarist Russia, when Russian explorers reached the coast of California. Expansion was characterised by brutal suppression of native peoples followed by waves of exiles and serfs seeking freedom. The explorer credited with doing most to open up Siberia is the Cossack Yermak, an outlaw who travelled with a band of mercenaries in the hope of winning the tsar's favour and pardon. Yermak was killed in 1564, but not before founding the fortress of Tomolosk on the River Ob. Successive explorers and settlers continued to arrive right up to the time of the Bolshevik Revolution in 1917.

BELOW:
Siberian portrait.

The greatest wave of Siberian settlement came with Stalin's first Five-Year Plan in 1929, which called for the rapid transformation of Russia from an agrarian to an industrial society. This daring, ultimately brutal programme led to the founding of thousands of small and medium-sized industrial towns across Siberia.

Industrial expansion led to ecological disasters for many regions, as improper care was taken to guard the delicate environment. Today, Siberia is littered with leaky oil pipelines, ill-conceived reservoirs, nuclear waste disposal sites, and blighted by short-sighted logging and thousands of smoke-spewing factories. The only thing that has protected Siberia from environmental ruin is its vastness.

During this period of settlement, enthusiastic *komsomoltsy* (young Communists) were encouraged to go to Siberia to work on one of the hundreds of large industrial projects designed to transform Russia into a modern, industrial power. It was a heroic undertaking, embarked upon in the most idealistic years of Soviet rule. Many elderly Russians who took part speak fondly of those hard and heady achievements of their youth.

The Trans-Siberian Railway

The world's longest continuous train journey, the Trans-Siberian Railway, crosses seven times zones along its 9,299-km (5,778-mile) route from Moscow

TIP

Since travel restrictions to Siberia have been lifted, it is more likely that a visitor will be invited into a local home than hassled about his or her camera. But both events occur and it is important to have all your documents in order, including a visa valid for all destinations.

to Vladivostok, passing from a stretch across the north Gobi Desert to a 4,000-metre (13,125-ft) high mountain pass in the remote Amur Mountains. It actually comprises three routes: the Trans-Siberian, the Trans-Mongolian and the Trans-Manchurian railways, the last two making the connection to Beijing.

The railway was built to counter Western Europe's commercial shipping fleets and to break their monopoly on trade with the Orient. Tsar Alexander III dreamed of creating a faster route to the Orient. Due to political upheavals this aim was never achieved, but the Trans-Siberian railway did support Russia's expansion into Central Asia and allowed it to keep a grip on its Far East holdings as far south as Vladivostok.

The ability of Russia to transport troops and weapons quickly to these remote areas allowed the country to become the world's largest empire. Construction began in 1890. At the time, it was the world's most ambitious engineering project. The entire stretch from St Petersburg to Vladivostok was finished in 1905. (See *Insight On The Trans-Siberian Railway*, page 124.)

Western Siberia

Siberia's second largest city, **Omsk ❶**, approximately equidistant at 800 km (498 miles) from Yekaterinburg in the northwest and Novosibirsk in the southeast, is also one of its oldest. It was founded in 1716 as a fort city and later became a place of exile. Among those banished here was the writer Fyodor Dostoyevsky, who spent four years in Omsk until 1854.

Before the 18th century, Omsk traders supplied Asian markets with slaves, which were kept on **Katonsky Ostrov** (Katon Island) until they could be sold. Two forts can still be visited: **Stary Krepost** (Old Fort), built in 1716, and

BELOW:
the gate to an Old Believers' enclave.

Novy Krepost (New Fort), built by the Russians at the end of the 18th century. Today, Omsk is the administrative centre of Western Siberia with a population of 1.2 million. It is regarded as has having one of the best museums of fine art in Siberia, **Muzei Izobrazitelnykh Izkusstv**, Ulitsa Krasny Putch 55, featuring a collection of 7,000 works (open daily; closed Mon).

From Omsk there are day tours to **Tara ❷**, a Siberian fort town 300 km (186 miles) north, founded in 1594. It is also possible to visit **Krutinskiye Ozera** (Steep Lakes) ❸, comprising three beautiful natural lakes (Ik, Saltaima and Tenisa), 200 km (125 miles) to the northeast of Omsk. During the warm summer months, these lakes and the surrounding area are popular among local families as a weekend getaway for hiking and swimming.

Novosibirsk ❹, Siberia's largest city, 700 km (435 miles) east of Omsk, is the quintessential, dull Soviet city. It was built predominantly as an industrial centre. Indeed, the city is a virtual monument to Stalin's single-minded drive to industrialise Russia. Its airport is Siberia's hub, and nearly all flights between Moscow and the Far East refuel here. Attached to the city is the research centre of **Akademgorodok** (Academic Town), a prestigious Soviet-scale think-tank that was badly affected by the brain-drain of the early 1990s.

Novosibirsk has the usual array of theatres and worthy museums, but one museum does stand out: the **Istorichesky Muzei** (Local History Museum), Vokzalnaya Magistral 11 (open 10am–6pm; closed Sat, Sun), which does an excellent job of documenting the history, geography and ethnic make-up of Siberia. It even includes the requisite woolly mammoth display.

The town of **Tomsk ❺**, 400 km (248 miles) northeast of Novosibirsk, is perhaps best known for its academic prowess: it has more professors per head than

Map on page 260

Negotiate the price of your journey with the taxi driver before setting off. Official taxis don't always use their meters.

BELOW: travelling on the Trans-Siberian railway.

The countryside around Tomsk is beautiful, but harsh: beware of ticks in the summer (June–July) as tick-borne encephalitis can be a real danger.

any Russian city, the oldest university in Siberia and its **Botanical Gardens** is thought to be one of the finest in the country.

Rich pickings

At the centre of the **Kuzbass** coal-mining region, **Kemerovo ❻** is politically and economically critical to Russia. It is the prime supplier of the country's coal. Founded in 1918, the modern Soviet-era city is now ringed by seven large coal mines, which employ nearly every inhabitant in the town. The only reason for tourists to come to Kemerovo is to see a genuine Russian coal mine (the mines are working mines, not tourist attractions, but a day trip can be arranged privately), although the city **Kemerovsky Istoriko-Arkhitekurny Muzei Krasnaya Gorka** (Regional Museum of Nature, History, Architecture and Ethnology) has some interesting exhibits (open 10am–6pm; closed Mon). It is possible to arrange a train trip from here across the taiga to the **zapovednik** (nature preserve) 50 km (31 miles) to the south of Tomsk.

Krasnoyarsk ❼, 1,000 km (620 miles) from Novosibirsk and 600 km (370 miles) east of Kemerovo, is one of the latest Russian cities to open its arms to foreign tourists, though it's hard to imagine there will be much of a rush to visit it. Founded in 1628 along the River Yenisey, Krasnoyarsk became a place of political exile. Today it is choking in industry: iron, aluminium, heavy machinery and agricultural equipment are all manufactured here. The pride of the town is the 18th-century **Pokrovskaya Tserkov** (Church of the Protection of the Virgin), Ulitsa Mira. However, the city does have several museums, including the **Krasnoyarsky Kulturnno-istorichesky Tsentr i Muzeiny Kompleks** (Krasnoyarsk Cultural and Historical Centre and Museum Complex). The *Saint Niko-*

BELOW: the shores of Lake Baikal.

lai, the ship on which Lenin is supposed to have sailed into exile in Sekhushenskoye in 1897, is on Ulitsa Dubrovinskoyo. Vasily Surikov, the 19th-century artist, was born and lived in Krasnoyarsk and his house, **Muzei-usadba V. I. Surikova**, Ulitsa Lenina 98, can be visited (open 10am–6pm; closed Monday).

Map on page 260

Wood and water

Founded in the late 1600s by Cossacks, **Bratsk ❽**, 600 km (373 miles) east of Krasnoyarsk, has been overtaken by progress – literally. The old city is now under the reservoir of the **Bratsk Hydroelectric Station**, once the largest in the world. New Bratsk, founded in 1955 as the logging and wood processing centre of central Siberia, is an ecological nightmare where production targets have taken precedence over all other concerns. The extent of the ecological disaster is clearly evident on a drive out to the taiga. Winds whip over vast, denuded expanses of land where no replanting has taken place.

Bratsk, however, is not without attractions. Before the basin that held Old Bratsk was flooded, workers transported all the historic buildings to a nearby hillside. The result is a wonderful **Otkryty Muzei Etnografii** (open-air museum; open 10am–5pm; closed Mon) devoted to the wood-working skills of Bratsk's first residents. Several *logizby* (peasant cottages), barns, and *bani* (bathhouses) have been constructed here. The highlight is a wooden church, built without a single nail.

The tourist office in Krasnoyarsk offers trips along the Yenisey River; outings to the striking rock formation of Krasnoyarskiye Stolby (Krasnoyarsk Pillars), as well as hunting packages.

Altay Mountains

The territory of Altaisky Kray, in the south of Western Siberia, bordering Kazakhstan and the Respublika Altay (Republic of Altay), is an ideal place for

BELOW: winter weather.

Theatres, opera houses and concert halls provide popular entertainment throughout Siberia and the Far East.

the adventure tourist to experience the Russian outback. What with its natural beauty – one-third of the territory is covered by woods – mountains, low rainfall and pleasant summer temperatures of around 20°C (68°F), it makes an ideal centre for hiking, rafting and climbing.

The starting point for exploring the region is **Barnaul** **9**, the administrative centre of the territory, founded in 1730. It lies 230 km (143 miles) southeast of Novosibirsk on the River Ob and is accessible by plane, train and bus from Novosibirsk. There are two museums worth seeing in town: **Altaisky Krayevoi Muzei Hstorii** (Altay Museum of Regional Studies and History), Ulitsa Polzunova 46, was founded in 1823 and claims to be the oldest in Siberia. It pays homage to Barnaul's most famous citizen, the inventor Ivan Polzunov (open 10am–6pm; closed Mon, Tues). **Gosudarstvenny Khudozhestvenny Muzei Altaiskogo Kraya** (Altay State Art Museum), Prospekt Lenina 88, is the region's main art gallery containing Russian works from the 16th to 20th centuries (open 10am–6pm; closed Mon).

In the resort of **Belokurikha** **10**, 200 km (124 miles) to the south, the combination of the local spring waters and pure mountain air creates an ideal atmosphere for the Russian sanitorium and indeed it is home to several specialised *doma otdykha* (rest homes, similar to Western health farms). Here, you can ski, trek, make use of the medical facilities or simply enjoy the scenery.

Lake Baikal

A trip to Siberia is not complete without seeing the "Pearl of Siberia," **Ozero Baykal** (Lake Baikal) **11**, the 636-km (395-mile) long stretch of water which lies 66 km (41 miles) east of Irkutsk. One of the world's great lakes, Baikal is

Map on page 260

more than simply Siberia's top tourist attraction, it is a force of nature. For once, Russian statistics are not gratuitous. The lake holds 20 percent of the world's fresh water and its maximum depth plunges to 1,637 metres (5,370 ft). (See *Insight On Lake Baikal*, page 272.) Lake Baikal offers so many endemic species (1,500) and so much geological diversity that the study of the lake has created a new scientific discipline: Baikology.

Its most famous indigenous species is the *nerpa*, the world's only fresh-water seal. Sturgeon and *omul* (similar to salmon and trout) feature among the marine life. The lakeside village of **Listvyanka** ⓬ makes an interesting day-trip from Irkutsk, where the extraordinary ecology of the area is best explained in a small museum at the **Muzei Baikolovedeniya Limnologicheskogo Instituta** (Baikal Limnological Institute).

Whatever the season, weather on Baikal is unpredictable. The lake is ruled by a micro-climate in which storms may rise and fall without passing over the shoreline. Weather often bears little relation to that in Ulan-Ude or Irkutsk. Even on the lake, it may change drastically in minutes. The first snow appears in early October, and the lake is frozen from January to May. In the summer, Baikal is warm enough for swimming. The best beaches can be found near the entrance to **Ostrov Olkhon** (Olkhon Island) ⓭ on the lake's west shore, about one and a half hours northeast by car from Irkutsk.

Port Baykal ⓮ is a charming village 65 km (40 miles) southeast of Irkutsk, a former crossroads on a now dead-end line of the Trans-Siberian Railway. Timber, coal and sand from around the lake is ferried to the port where it is loaded onto rail cars which leave once a day. There are no tourist facilities to speak of, but a stroll through the town gives a delightful sense of what life on Baikal is like for the locals.

Well worth a visit is Muzei Zodchestva i Etnografii (the Museum of Wooden Architecture and Ethnography) in Taltsy, 47 km (30 miles) south of Irkutsk on the road to Baikal (open 10am–5pm).

Irkutsk

Irkutsk ⓯ (pop. 600,000) is arguably the most appealing Siberian city and the one best developed to accommodate tourists, mainly as a result of being the launching point for excursions to Lake Baikal. It is located along the Angara River, about 30 minutes by car north of the southernmost tip of the lake.

It was founded in 1662 by Russian Cossacks, as a place of exile on the crossroads to Mongolia and China. Its most famous residents were the Decembrists, who were exiled there following an unsuccessful coup against the tsar in December 1825. A museum dedicated to the Decembrists is located in **Dom Volkonskhyx** (the house of Count Sergey Volkonsky), Pereulok Volkonskogo 10 (open 10am–5.30pm; closed Mon).

For many years a centre of the defence industry, the city is undergoing enormous change as it retools itself in the post-Cold War period. The growing tourism industry is seen as a possible saviour for the depressed region. The fur trade, the timeless Siberian standby, is also growing in importance. Irkutsk's largest factories are a tannery, shoe and fur factory. Other manufacturing industries include heavy machinery, timber and building materials. The population is a comfortable mixture of Russians and

BELOW: carved lintel decorates a Siberian home.

assorted peoples, including about 20 percent Buryats, the Mongolian Buddhist descendants who settled Lake Baikal's southern shore. The city has expanded to cover both banks of the Angara River, but the historical and commercial centres are located on the west bank. Though the central districts are characterised by the usual Soviet-era concrete blocks and monuments to the Great Patriotic War (World War II), the older outer districts still feature wood-frame homes, even Russian log *izby*.

Izba, the peasants' wooden cottage, is traditionally made from five walls and a roof. The fifth wall divides the building in two for either the expanding family or livestock, whichever the more pertinent.

A beautiful **riverside park** has been constructed along Ulitsa Gagarina, across from the Intourist Hotel, and this is the best starting point for a tour of the city. Begin at Ulitsa Karla Marksa and proceed to the bridge at the city's promenade. Looping back, take Ulitsa Lenina, making sure you stop by at the city's **central market**. This four-storey indoor bazaar of clothing, electronics and other soft goods draws enthusiastic Siberians from hundreds of miles.

Most of the shops in Irkutsk can be found between the central market and Ulitsa Karla Marksa. From Ulitsa Karla Marksa, proceed back to the river, passing the delightful **Krayevedchesky Muzei** (Local History Museum), across from the large concrete obelisk. The museum has several departments across town – the central building on Ulitsa Karla Marksa houses the Departments of History and Natural History (open 10am–6pm; closed Mon). There is also an exhibition hall in the **Spasskaya Tserkov** (Church of our Saviour) on Ulitsa Sukhe-Batora (open 10am–6pm; closed Tues).

Other places to see when in Irkutsk include: the **Muzei Izkusstv imeni Sukhacheva** (Art Museum), Ulitsa Lenina 5, named after Sukachev – it also has exhibition halls at Ulitsa Karla Marksa 23 (open 10am–6pm; closed Mon). For plays and concerts check out the **Irkutsk Dramatichesky Teatr** (Irkutsk Drama

BELOW: a Buryat Lamaist monk.

SEAT OF BUDDHISM

The greatest attraction of Ulan-Ude is the Ivolginsk Datsan, the seat of Buddhism in Russia, 30 km (19 miles) west of the town. The temple was opened in the 1960s ostensibly to show the world that religious tolerance existed in the Soviet Union. In reality, it was all a charade. The KGB had secretly sent a dozen agents to Ulan Bator, Mongolia, to become sufficiently familiar with the rituals of Buddhism to open the datsan. The KGB agents enjoyed large *dachas* in the mountains and were driven to the temple each day in *Zil* limousines. In the late 1980s the pretence became reality as more and more curious Buryats attended the temple. The temple, modest by the standards of Tibet or other Buddhist centres, is in a splendid setting with snow-capped peaks towering over the plain and a small mountain stream running nearby. Its colourful interior contains numerous images of the Buddha, Buryat paintings and a museum. Today, it may be visited without official supervision. Follow the path along the datsan's inside walls: the prayer wheel (spin it gently as you pass) is said to write a prayer 1,000 times for each spin. You may visit a service at the main temple – generally held in the morning – but keep to the rear of the building as the main part is reserved for the lamas.

Theatre), Ulitsa Karla Marksa 14 (tel: 3952 24 11 24); and the **Irkutsk Filar-moniya** (Philharmonic), Ulitsa Dzerzhinskogo 2 (tel: 3952 24 11 00).

Map on page 260

Republic of Buryatia

On the east side of Baikal, the capital of the Republic of Buryatiya, **Ulan-Ude** ⑯, is beginning to discover its identity having been closed to foreigners until 1988. Perhaps no city in Russia today shows the diversity of the Russian empire better than Ulan-Ude. Buryat culture and language, which bear a close resemblance to those of Mongolia, were nearly extinguished under Soviet rule. Today, though 50 percent of the population has the appearance of Buryats, few people can speak Buryat. However, young people are beginning to show an interest in Buddhism and the Dalai Lama has visited Ulan-Ude on several occasions to encourage the re-education of the Buryat people.

Ulan-Ude lies on the badly polluted Selenga River, which winds its way through Mongolia to Lake Baikal. To the south, a desert stretches to the Mongolian border. To the north a range of mountains frames the southern shore of Lake Baikal. It is laid out like the archetypal Soviet city. The central square, an enormous stretch of empty asphalt, is overlooked by what is surely the biggest head of Lenin in the world. On the outskirts, wooden homes are common, reminders of the city's status as a Cossack frontier town.

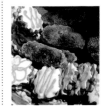

Cakes on sale in a Siberian market.

Diamond-studded Yakutia

In theory you could reach Yakutsk from Baikal by water; in practice it would, at best, be very difficult. The mighty Lena river meanders north from Baikal around the Udokan Mountains towards the Verkhoyansky Mountains where it

BELOW: at work in all weather on a natural gas plant.

Today, visitors to Vladivostok can stroll along the docks and freely shoot pictures of the naval fleet – a stark contrast to the days when a careless photo could trigger an international incident – but the locals may still scold you for doing so.

BELOW: prisoner in Sakhalin, 1894.

widens and continues north to the Arctic Ocean. Where the Lena widens, the town of **Yakutsk** , which dates from the first wave of Russian exploration in 1632, can be found. It is best reached by air on regular flights from Moscow, Irkutsk and Vladivostok.

Like most outposts of its kind, Yakutsk was founded by Cossacks, working to please the tsar, who permitted them freedom in an empire of serfs. Later it became one of the cruellest places of exile, notorious for its brutal cold.

The city might have remained a simple outpost had it not been for the discovery of enormous mineral riches in the region, including diamonds. Today Yakutsk is the capital of the Yakutiya Republic, a swathe of far northern Siberia covering more than 2.6 million sq km (1 million sq miles).

Yakutsk itself is a dull Soviet city, but it offers an excellent base for exploring the native Yakut and Evenki villages on the tundra. There is a fine **Muzei Istorii i Kultury Severnikh Narodov** (Museum of North Peoples), Prospekt Lenina 5/2, providing a glimpse of how Yakutiya's native peoples lived before the Soviet era. You can take a hydrofoil to **Lenskiye Stolby** (Lena Pillars), giant rock formations about an hour upstream from Yakutsk. Cruises on the Lena and a trip to **Derevnya Yakutsk**, the old village of Yakutsk, are also offered.

Far Eastern ports

Nakhodka ⑱ was a Soviet-era solution to the problem of closing Vladivostok to foreign shipping in the 1950s. It was the commercial port and the end of the Trans-Siberian Railway line, while Vladivostok was the naval port.

Taking a plane or train further east will bring you to **Vladivostok** ⑲ at the base of the Sikhote-Alin Mountains, bordered by China to the west and the Sea of Japan to the east. Vladivostok is sometimes called the "San Francisco of Russia", a reference to its Pacific location and its steep streets. But that's as far as the comparison goes with this Soviet naval city, which was completely closed to foreign shipping between 1958 and 1991. It was first taken from the Chinese in 1860 and has since become the country's main port in the Far East.

The twists and turns over the steep streets offer visitors many beautiful views of the city and the ocean. The climate is pleasant with summer temperatures reaching 20°C (68°F) and winter lows rarely dipping below –15°C (5°F).

Volcanic isles

The **Kurilskiye Ostrova** (Kurile Islands) ⑳, a chain of volcanic islands extending from Kamchatka to the northern Japanese island of Hokkaido, would probably be unheard of outside Sakhalin if they were not the subject of a territorial dispute between Russia and Japan over the South Kuriles, which Japan claims, but which Russia took in World War II.

The islands are stunningly beautiful all year round, with towering volcanoes sloping into violent seas. The Russians have done very little to develop them, except for creating a number of small fishing villages and a naval base situated on Shikotan. The journey by sea takes one and a half days from the closest port,

Korsakov **㉑**, on the island of Ostrov Sakhalin. Ships also leave daily from Vladivostok, weather permitting, and take three days.

With a population of 6,000, **Yuzhno-Kurilsk ㉒**, a fishing village on the island of **Ostrov Kunashir**, is the capital of the Kurile chain, and the most accessible destination in the group. At its southern tip, the island is within 12 km (7 miles) of Japan, whose hills are clearly visible from most points on the island. The village itself is little more than a maze of rickety huts and a fishing plant.

The island has a small **Muzei Yestestvoznaniya** (Museum of Natural History) in the town square. At the entrance a Japanese face is carved into a stone, a compelling reminder of the island's former landlords. From Yuzhno-Kurilsk it is possible to arrange boat trips to nearby **Ostrov Shikotan ㉓**, the most beautiful island in the chain, with a sunny micro-climate.

Russia's Alaska

The island of **Ostrov Sakhalin ㉔** has long held an exotic allure for Russians as a remote land of possibilities. Rich in natural resources such as oil, gas and non-ferrous metals, it is Russia's Alaska. Passed between Japan and Russia during the 19th and 20th centuries, Russia finally occupied Sakhalin in the last days of World War II. The capital of **Yuzhno-Sakhalinsk ㉕** was founded in 1881 at the base of Mount Bolshevik. Surrounding the city are virgin forests blanketing mountainous terrain, which provide a spectacular backdrop.

It is difficult to imagine what would draw a foreign tourist to **Magadan ㉖**, a remote gulag centre in northeast Siberia where winter temperatures can plummet to –65°C (–85°F). It was first named on maps in 1939 and it relies on building materials manufacture and a small fishing industry. ❑

TIP

The best time to visit Yakutsk is between June and August. On 25 June the city hosts the Ysykh festival, a colourful celebration of native Yakut culture.

BELOW: a young resident in remote Yakutsk.

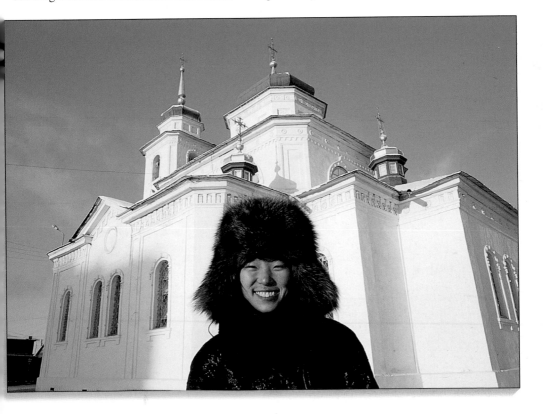

LAKE BAIKAL – THE PEARL OF SIBERIA

The most beautiful jewel in Siberia's crown is Baikal Ozero, the world's deepest lake, which attracts scientists and tourists alike to its shores

Lake Baikal's crystal clear waters cut a north-south swathe through the mountains and taiga of Siberia, creating a rich habitat for a flora and fauna unique to this region.

Baikal is roughly the size of Belgium. It covers 32,000 sq km (12,352 sq miles), holds one-fifth of the world's fresh water and is more than a mile deep (1,637 metres/5,370 ft).

SPECIES OF THE LAKE

The lake's most renowned resident, the *nerpa* (Baikal seal), is believed to have been trapped here when the last Ice Age retreated. The seal then slowly adapted to the freshwater environment of its new home. Today, the grey-coloured *nerpa* is a protected species, but the Russian authorities still allow 6,000 to be slaughtered each year for their fur and blubber. About 60,000 *nerpas* inhabit Baikal.

More than 50 species of fish can be found in the waters. Among the more interesting fish is the *golomyanka*, which lives up to 1.5 km (1 mile) below the surface and gives birth to living young. The highly-prized Baikal sturgeon can produce up to 9 kg (20 lb) of caviar on reaching maturity, and the *omul*, a member of the salmon family, often appears on the menu as a local speciality.

◁ **HOME FROM HOME**
Wooden homes are typical of the lakeside villages. The Museum of Wooden Architecture near Irkutsk contains fine examples of Siberian buildings.

△ **FINE BALANCE**
The construction of the Irkutsk hydroelectric station in the 1950s led to a rise of 1 metre (3 ft) in the depth of water and caused serious ecological problems.

⊲ WHAT'S IN A NAME?

The word Baikal is derived from the Turkish word Bai-Kul, meaning "a rich lake". The lake has been designated a UNESCO World Heritage Site.

△ OBSERVATION POSTS

For the past 50 years Irkutsk State University has been making observations of the Baikal biota at Bolshyie Koty and on the Angara biostation.

▽ MAKING A LIVING

Fishing, forestry and fur farming are the main occupations. The climate around the lake is ideal for mink and sable; fox and beaver trapping is common.

▷ ICY WATERS

Lake Baikal is fed by more than 300 rivers, and drained by just one, the Angara. For five months of the year it is frozen to a depth of 10 metres (30 ft).

▽ LAKE RESIDENT

The sturgeon *Acipenser baeri* inhabits the shallows of Lake Baikal. It takes between 18 and 20 years to reach maturity.

OUT AND ABOUT ON THE LAKE

Helicopter trips, horse-riding, hiking and fishing are just some of the summer excursions on offer around Baikal, while in winter, troika rides, skiing and skating top the list – but don't expect anything sophisticated. Irkutsk is the best launching point for trips. Hydrofoils and ferries make regular journeys to lakeside settlements in summer, and travel agencies such as Irkutsk-Baikal Intourist can tailor packages to suit. The southwestern side of the lake is the most accessible. One of the best places to view what is said to be the oldest lake in the world (20 million years) is from the hill behind the Limnological Institute at Listvyanka, 66 km (41 miles) east of Irkutsk. For the more adventurous, a trip to the Khamar-Daban mountains south of Baikal offers the chance to explore taiga, alpine tundra and glacial lakes. Heading northwest is Olkhon Island, a favourite holiday spot for Russians where the *nerpa* seals can be glimpsed off its north coast.

BELARUS AND UKRAINE

These two independent states share their roots with Russia in the once grand principality of Kievan Rus

Belarus and Ukraine have always been considered close cousins to Russia. Their languages are close enough to be almost mutually comprehensible. Their political fates have been interwoven for centuries. Kiev, the "Mother of Russian cities", was at the heart of the first Eastern Slavic state of Kievan Rus. With the rise of Muscovy, much of Belarus and Ukraine was brought under Tsarist control and ruled from St Petersburg. Next to Belarus (White Russia), Ukraine became known as "Malorossiya" (Little Russia), an epithet that illustrated its provincial and dependent status. More recently, the three countries formed the core of the Soviet Union, making up half of its population and a much greater proportion of its leaders.

Yet to see Belarus and Ukraine only as adjuncts to the powerful Russian state is to see only a part of the story. This historic borderland has two faces; one looks towards Moscow and the east, but the other – smaller but still recognisable – is turned to the west and towards Europe. Much of the history of Ukraine and Belarus, and the origins of many current difficulties, can be found in the unfinished dialogue between the two sides of their national characters.

With independence in 1991, Ukrainians and Belarusians had the opportunity to take charge of their own affairs, maybe even to move out from under Russia's shadow. It was not a comfortable experience. By 1995, Belarus had retreated back towards the margins of the continent with its brand of Soviet-style authoritarianism. Ukraine, on the other hand, remained caught between east and west, unsure of its vocation and hesitant in its actions. Ukrainian nationalists in the west of the country argued with Russian-speakers in the east, a small band of market reformers found themselves consistently out-manoeuvred by the old Soviet administrators, the government found itself at odds with Moscow over the question of Crimea – since 1954 part of Ukraine – and the large naval base at Sevastopol. Yet through it all, and despite a collapsing economy, Ukraine was able to address its problems without bloodshed. This, more than anything, was an important step towards the future.

Meanwhile, the visitor will find much of interest: Orthodox cathedrals, Tatar palaces, Polish castles and elegant Hapsburg frontier towns sit side by side with grandiose Soviet developments and monuments to the fallen of two World Wars. Kiev is a thriving modern city and cultural centre; hiking, fishing and *dacha* life are features of the countryside; and in season the Black Sea resorts buzz with holiday atmosphere. The bureaucrats might appear a little frosty, but the legendary hospitality of the people can still be experienced at home among the families of Belarus and Ukraine. ❑

PRECEDING PAGES: the trident is the symbol of Ukrainian independence; Yalta's waterfront, Crimea. **LEFT:** the dramatic Lastochkino Gnezdo (Swallow's Nest), near Yalta, was built in 1912 for a German oil magnate.

BELARUS AND UKRAINE: A SHORT HISTORY

The history of these two countries is both longer and initially grander than that of Russia, which subsequently overwhelmed them

Belarus and Ukraine owe their origins to strategic geography, specifically rivers. The Varangians (Vikings) who opened up trade links between the Baltic and the Black Sea in the 9th century rowed rather than walked, and the most convenient route was along rivers from the Baltic. The Dvina was the most heavily travelled river, as it put traders within porterage distance of the Dnipro (Dneiper) for the journey to Byzantium.

The Varangians acted as catalysts for the development of the early Slav settlements along these rivers. Those settlements on the first leg of the outward journey, the most notable being the principality of Polatsk, were the nucleus of the future Belarus. The Dnipro leg was dominated by Kiev, and it was on the territory of present-day Ukraine, with a fusion of Scandinavian and Slav influences, that the first great regional political entity was formed in the 9th century, Kievan Rus.

Kievian Rus

In its heyday before the Mongol invasion in the 13th century, Kievan Rus had a place in the first rank of European states. Remarkably soon after Prince Volodymyr's (Vladimir's) conversion to Christianity in 988, Kiev boasted a cathedral modelled on the Hagia Sophia in Constantinople and more than 400 churches.

Long claimed by the Russians as their own, the ownership of this glorious part of the eastern Slav heritage continues to be a matter for dispute. The geographical inheritance rests with the independent Ukrainian state that takes Kiev as its capital, but many Russians find a history without any substantial connection to what they called the "Mother of Russian cities" difficult to accept (*see* A Question of Identity, *page 286*).

The later roots of the organised Russian state

reach back to the northern Rus principalities, such as Novgorod, which began to break from Kiev in around 1050. The entire region then fell under the "Tatar Yoke", the wave of Mongol invaders that swept across the steppes in

the 13th century. A declining Kiev was also sacked by the Mongols in 1240, and only St Sophia's and a couple of hundred houses were left standing.

The traditions of Kievan Rus were absorbed by the principalities of Galicia and Volhynia, whose location further to the west allowed them to escape such close Tatar attention. These regions, now in western Ukraine, have been crucial through the centuries in maintaining Ukrainian cultural and political traditions.

The decline of Kievan Rus in the 13th and 14th centuries coincided with the rise of neighbouring Lithuania and Poland to the north and west, and Muscovy (Russia) to the east.

PRECEDING PAGES: *The Battle of Balaklava, 25 October 1854*, lithograph by E. Walker and O. Norrie. **LEFT:** Ukrainian musicians. **RIGHT:** Tatar couple.

From that time up until the present, and apart from brief periods of self-assertion, the fate of Ukraine (the "borderland") and Belarus was in the hands of these and other foreign powers.

The Cossacks

Incorporation within the Lithuanian state and then the Polish dominated commonwealth did much to expose Ukraine and Belarus to Western European influences. Poland, ardent champion of the Roman Church, did its utmost to bring Ukraine and Belarus within the Catholic fold.

A compromise between Catholicism and Orthodoxy eventually emerged in the shape of

the "Uniate" (Greek Catholic) Church, which retained the Orthodox ritual while acknowledging the temporal power of the Pope, but this development did nothing to ease the religious tensions with Eastern Orthodoxy. Many Ukrainians and Belarusians remained to take up the new faith and to work under the Polish landlords; others escaped to the periphery of the commonwealth, to the plains of the Dnipro basin and the home of the Ukrainian Cossacks.

The Ukrainian Cossacks were originally a collection of outlaws and fugitives, surviving by hunting, fishing and by grazing cattle along the dangerous border territories between the Polish Commonwealth, Russian Muscovy and the Ottoman Tatars to the south. With time they took on forms of political organisation, including the self-governing entity formed beyond the *porozhy* (rapids) of the Dnipro, which became known as the Zaporizhean Sich. Social and religious resentment at Polish rule provided the catalyst, and it was from Zaporizhe in 1648 that the Cossack leader, Bogdan Khmelnitsky, launched the great Ukrainian offensive that succeeded in driving the Poles from Ukraine.

Khmelnitsky's dream of a Ukrainian state – the Cossack Hetmanate – was threatened from the west by a Poland eager to reverse its stunning defeat, and was also vulnerable to Tatar incursions from the south. So it was in 1654, by an agreement concluded at Pereyaslav, that Khmelnitsky proceeded to carve a somewhat ambiguous niche for himself in Ukrainian folklore by turning to Muscovy for assistance.

The rise of the Russian Empire

The assurances of autonomy included in the Pereyaslav agreement were undermined as Moscow extended its control. At first Ukraine was split along the line of the Dnipro, with the left (east) bank under Russian control, and the right (west) bank, along with most of Belarus, remaining under the Polish Commonwealth.

However, Poland was subject to partition three times at the end of the 18th century, and Catherine the Great delighted in "recovering" Belarus and most of Ukraine. The exception was Galicia which became part of the Austro-Hungarian Empire, a fact that explains the very different architectural styles in such western Ukrainian cities as Lviv and Chernivtsi.

Catherine's attention was also drawn to the strategic goal of securing access to the Black Sea. With the help of Alexander Suvorov, Russia's most successful general, Ottoman forces were pushed out of southern Ukraine and Crimea became part of the Russian Empire.

Under the Russian Empire, the Ukrainian and Belarusian lands lost many traces of their former national distinctiveness. The territories were reorganised into provinces governed from St Petersburg, a programme of conversion to Russian Orthodoxy was launched, and any signs of national feeling were dealt with harshly by the tsarist authorities.

At the westernmost edge of the Empire, Belarus, in particular, was in the front-line of any conflicts with other European powers. In the 19th century the territory had to withstand the invading armies of Napoleon, 140 years later it bore the brunt of Hitler's "Operation Barbarossa" against the Soviet Union. Therein lies the explanation for the singular lack of historical buildings in Belarus.

The Crimean War

In the middle of the 19th century Ukraine's Crimea became a focus of a long and bitter war between Russia on the one side and Britain, France, Turkey, Piedmont and Austria on the other. The

THE LIGHT BRIGADE

Theirs not to reason why,
Theirs but to do and die:
Into the valley of Death
Rode the six hundred.
    — ALFRED, LORD TENNYSON

British army, the 11th Hussars, whose singular misfortune was to be under the command of two of the biggest asses in the British army, Lord Cardigan and Lord Lucan. It was Lord Cardigan who misunderstood an order and sent 600 men straight into the barrels of the Russian guns which lined three sides of the contested valley. Almost half of them were killed on the spot.

Another figure to gain immortality through the war was Florence Nightingale, whose noble nursing in the most appalling conditions led to

Crimean War reflected the Western powers' distrust of Russian expansionism and in particular Tsar Nicholas' designs on Ottoman Turkey.

The Allies expected a swift victory over the Russian forces, but in the event the war was protracted and hard won.

One of its most famous episodes was the misguided Charge of the Light Brigade during the Battle of Balaklava, immortalised by Alfred Tennyson's haunting refrain about the futility of the charge (*see above*). The 600 in question were the most brightly-plumed troopers in the

LEFT: a 17th-century engraving of a Cossack.
ABOVE: nursing the wounded in the Crimean War.

a reappraisal of provisions for humanitarian treatment of soldiers.

The 20th century

Despite tsarist oppression, the influence of nationalism spread also to the lands of the Russian Empire. In Ukraine, this found expression in the use of the national language and through the writings and poetry of such figures as Taras Shevchenko and Lesia Ukrainka.

As the Russian Empire collapsed during World War I, these national movements in both Ukraine and Belarus attempted to move towards independence. They faced formidable obstacles; their lands were being pressed from all sides by competing armed forces and ideologies, the movements themselves were weak and poorly organised. Yet in all the chaos of revolution and war, Ukrainians received their first taste of modern self-government with the proclamation of the Ukrainian National Republic in 1918, governed from Kiev, and a Western Ukrainian National Republic based on the territories that had been part of the Austro-Hungarian Empire. The republics even agreed to unify in 1919, but by then the tide of events was already turning against independence.

As the Bolsheviks consolidated their hold within Russia, so Poland was reasserting its historical claim to western Ukraine and Belarus. Fighting between these two ancient adversaries was concluded only with the Treaty of Riga in 1921. The western Ukrainian and Belarusian regions became part of Poland. The Ukrainian Soviet Socialist Republic (SSR), with its capital in Kharkiv in the east, and the Belarusian SSR became in 1922 founding members of the Union of Soviet Socialist Republics (USSR).

Starvation and deportation

Between the wars the reinstalled masters of Ukraine and Belarus did everything in their power to suppress any independent national instincts. In particular, Stalin's genocidal instincts wreaked havoc in Soviet Ukraine. After a period of calm in the 1920s when Ukrainian language use grew, Stalin's assumption of power coincided with a vicious offensive against the two social bases of Ukrainian nationalism, the peasants and the educated classes.

The cost of the remarkable pace of Soviet industrialisation under the first five-year plans was borne by the peasantry. While iron and steel furnaces and hydroelectric plants were being built, the forced collectivisation of agriculture destroyed traditional country life. Opposition to collectivisation was answered with the imposition of impossible production quotas, enforced at gunpoint. Forced to give up all their food to the state, seven million Ukrainians died in the famine of 1932 and 1933.

Another part of this intentional tragedy was the campaign against all signs of "nationalist deviation" among Ukrainian leaders. These purges resulted in the repression or execution of four-fifths of the Ukrainian cultural elite.

A QUESTION OF IDENTITY

Questions of Ukrainian and Belarusian identity lead straight back to their complex national histories. For much of the last 100 years they would not have called themselves Ukrainians or Belarusians at all, but *Rusyny* (Ruthenians). This identified them with the lands and religion of Kievan Rus, the original East Slavic state. However, as Muscovy grew in power it came to claim also the historical rights to the legacy of Kiev, and the image of Rus became intertwined with the growth of the Russian state.

This was a crucial transformation, since it was on this basis that Moscow took up the imperial mission to reunite all the "Russian" lands. The *Rusyny* were deemed to be Russian – whether Little Russians (Ukrainians), or White Russians (Belarusians) – and any cultural differences ascribed to the period of "forced" separation and the influence of the hostile Catholic Poles. This interpretation underpinned tsarist and Soviet policies of russification, and today some Russians still deny that Ukraine and Belarus are "real" nations. Many Ukrainians and Belarusians take a different view. The idea that Ukraine and Belarus have their own histories and cultures comes from the 19th century, and most Ukrainians and Belarusians today, even those who would not call themselves nationalists, still readily volunteer an opinion on how they differ from the Russians.

Stalin's brutal hand made significant numbers of Ukrainians and Belarusians ready to regard Hitler as a liberator, but this illusion quickly disappeared as the reality of German rule became clear. Far from satisfying demands for self-rule, the Nazis regarded the Ukrainians and Belarusians as fit only for servitude, and millions were transported to the Reich as slave labour to support the German war effort.

Those who remained were caught in the middle of the direct clash between Nazi and Soviet forces. More than 8 million Ukrainians and Belarusians were killed amid total material destruction – and hostilities did not end with the Nazi defeat. Hundreds of thousands of real and alleged Nazi collaborators, former German prisoners of war and repatriated slave workers, Ukrainian "bourgeois nationalists", and others suspected of disloyalty were sent to concentration camps in Siberia. The Ukrainian Insurgent Army, based in western Ukraine, continued its guerrilla activity against the Soviet authorities until the 1950s.

The road to independence

Following World War II, the western borders of Ukraine and Belarus took on the shape that they have today, the only subsequent addition being the "gift" of Crimea to Ukraine made by Khrushchev in 1954. Ukraine's role in the post-war USSR was second in importance only to Russia's. At 600,000 sq km (232,000 sq miles) and with a population of 51 million, it remains a large country by European standards. The renowned fertility of its black soil accounted for nearly a quarter of Soviet agricultural production, and its industrial contribution was of the same order. Ukrainian politicians even took senior positions in the Kremlin.

Belarus, the poorest part of the Russian Empire at the turn of the 20th century, was paraded as the quintessential Soviet success story. Not only were its new industries conspicuously efficient by Soviet standards, but the people of Belarus had seemingly followed the blueprint for Soviet Man, eschewing atavistic national instincts in favour of socialism.

Conventional wisdom failed to take adequate stock of undercurrents of discontent in both

Ukraine and Belarus. As in Russia itself, intellectual dissidents made the running, but resentment in Ukraine was channelled also through the working class, notably those who could not forget the pre-war repression.

Discontent in Belarus was more muted, before the Chernobyl (Chornobyl) disaster in 1986 gave Ukrainians and Belarusians common cause. The doomed nuclear plant was 97 km (60 miles) from Kiev, and only the prevailing winds saved the Ukrainian capital from lethal deposits. Nevertheless, any number of villages had to be abandoned and vast tracts of agricultural land, particularly in southern Belarus,

were made unusable for further crop production. Belarus was yet again the unhappy victim of a neighbour's malice or misfortune.

As Mikhail Gorbachev tried to salvage the remains of the Soviet Union with preparations for a new Union treaty, both Ukraine and Belarus took steps to increase their autonomy from Moscow. After the failure of the 1991 coup, they signed the death warrant for the Union by declaring independence.

With the collapse of the Soviet Union in 1991, and for the first time ever, the people of Belarus and Ukraine were in a position to shape their own destiny in peacetime. History casts a long shadow over their efforts. ❑

LEFT: vast numbers of Ukrainians were deported to Siberian labour camps following World War II.
RIGHT: a reminder of Soviet rule in Belarus.

LIFE TODAY IN BELARUS AND UKRAINE

The transition from Soviet rule has not been easy: Belarus has played safe with a Soviet-style economy while Ukraine struggles with the free market

On one of the roads leading out of Kiev, a set of huge factory gates used to bear the legend *Zarya Kommunisma* – the Dawn of Communism. In 1992, in keeping with the spirit of the times, the factory managers recognised the need for a change: they removed the *Kommunisma*. Passers-by are now promised a new dawn, but the problem is that no one seems to be able to say exactly what it will bring.

Ukraine and Belarus were not ready for the collapse of the Soviet Union. Although many supported the idea of independence – more than 90 percent of Ukrainians voted in favour during a referendum in 1991 – few had any vision of what life after Communism would look like. Hungarians and Czechs could, however vaguely, be united in 1989 by the notion that their countries were returning to their rightful places in Europe. Ukrainians and Belarusians, on the other hand, did not seem sure where their rightful place might be.

Independence brings uncertainty

Mykhailo Hrushevsky, the first President of Ukraine during its brief and chaotic period of independence after World War I, was sure of the root of the problem. In his vast *History of Ukraine-Rus* he relates countless instances where the honest ordinary folk were betrayed by fickle leaders always ready to sell out the national interest to the Poles or the Russians.

Whether or not you agree with Hrushevsky's diagnosis, the period since he wrote it has hardly been conducive to a cure. Stalin's purges of the 1930s decimated the Belarusian and Ukrainian intelligentsia, creating along the way an instinctive preference for conformity among the post-war generations. While some intellectuals continued to speak out, notably in the

Helsinki groups that tried to monitor and publicise the Soviet Union's record on human rights, it was easier to keep your head down.

What about the ordinary Belarusians and Ukrainians? As Mikhail Gorbachev relaxed

the grip of the totalitarian regime in the late 1980s, you could see them joining environmental organisations to protest against the Chornobyl (Chernobyl) nuclear plant disaster, beginning to emerge into the public sphere where their opinions had so long been assumed but not asked for.

Yet they, too, had been changed by Soviet rule. The collectivisation of agriculture and the famine that followed had targeted the traditions of rural life at the core of Belarusian and Ukrainian identity. Post-war Communism brought some gloomy certainties into people's lives, but at the cost of undermining their capacity for initiative and enterprise.

PRECEDING PAGES: facade of Shevchenko University, Kiev.
LEFT: children at play, Platz Jakub Kolas, Minsk.
RIGHT: young woman from Odessa.

When the Soviet Union collapsed, some in the West thought that the transition would be a relatively straightforward affair. What was to stop countries such as Belarus and Ukraine, with their well-educated population, large industrial base and fertile land, from prospering under the new system? As it turned out, the biggest obstacles were in people's minds.

The Belarusian model

The experience of Belarus and Ukraine – and Russia as well – shows that democracy and the market need some cultural and behavioural roots that cannot grow overnight. The countries

lessly played on nostalgia for the Soviet Union.

As good as his word, he proceeded over the next two years to rebuild both an autocratic system of government and to resurrect the planned economy, drawing up the wagons for a last defence of the Soviet system. Lukashenka's plans did bring protesters out onto the streets of Minsk, but the sad fact was that his instincts were probably in line with those of the majority of the Belarusian people.

Lukashenka's disdain for democracy earned him international isolation, but for a while his economy seemed to be performing a great deal better than that of Ukraine. The "Belarusian

of Central Europe had a huge advantage: a Pole might remember the business that his family used to run before the Communist takeover; a Czech would recall her country's parliamentary debates from the inter-war years. Belarusians and Ukrainians were left to chart their future without any living memories of democracy and the market to guide them.

Instead, the formative influences that were left were those inculcated by the Soviets, and the regime of Alexandr Lukashenka in Belarus showed that they could be difficult to shake off. Lukashenka, an eccentric but politically astute former collective farm director, was elected in 1994 after a campaign in which he shame-

model" – which for all intents and purposes meant the Soviet one – was held up in Minsk as a genuine alternative to the market, and while Belarus was ridiculed from further abroad for being out of step with the times, many Ukrainians and Russians could only look on in envy as state employees received their pay cheques on time.

Ukrainian indecision

If the Belarusian approach to transition was not to approach, then the Ukrainians had a different problem – indecision. The first president after 1991, the avuncular Leonid Kravchuk, was a master at appearing all things to all people, a flexibility which served him well in Ukrainian politics, but which eventually brought the economy close to collapse. His attempts to use government funds as a solution to all ills kept the money presses working overtime, and led to the hyperinflation of 1993 which wiped out the savings of millions of Ukrainians.

His successor in 1994 was Leonid Kuchma, the former director of the Pivdenmash rocket factory, which had terrorised the capitalist world with its production of Soviet military hardware. His administration began with the promise of a firm and realistic approach to Ukraine's economic woes. He also received plaudits – and credits – for concluding Ukraine's commitment to give up the nuclear arsenal inherited from the Soviet Union. Yet, despite getting a grip on the currency, successive administrations under Kuchma's presidency became stuck under the weight of conflicting demands and interests.

On one side were the advocates of market reform, whose political influence came not from their numbers but rather from their ability to unlock the big international funds. Then there were the regional elites from smoky industrial cities like Donetsk, Dnipropetrovsk and Kharkiv, all with impeccable political connections and big business interests, all competing for control over energy distribution networks and the profitable state factories. Finally, there were the vociferous and still-powerful Communists, who formed the largest single group in each of Ukraine's two parliaments elected since independence.

Faced with a choice, the Ukrainian government operated by the maxim "if you see a fork in the road, take it". The result was to leave two or three economies trying to coexist: the remnants of the planned system being fought over by the well-connected business clans, the market left struggling to find gaps where it could. In trying to satisfy all its constituencies, the government ended up pleasing very few.

It was not difficult to spot the few who did well. The status symbols were those recognisable from Moscow, the same sharp suits and tinted-glass Mercedes cars. In Kiev you could also see the beginnings of a new middle class, but the truth was that the spoils of the Ukrainian market were being divided very unevenly.

For the vast majority however, life in Ukraine was as hard as ever, as they waited months or even years to receive their meagre wages or pensions from the state. When the state fails them, Ukrainians have the blessing of being able to turn to a more reliable safety net – the *chornozem* (black earth) that once earned the

> **HARD FACTS**
>
> Forty percent of the population of the Ukraine were living below the poverty line in 1998 – almost twice as many as in Belarus.

country the epithet "bread-basket of Europe". Although the huge and wasteful collective farms still dominate the countryside, all the other available private land is cultivated, from plots attached to *dachas* (country retreats) to impossibly awkward strips along roadsides and railway embankments. From here families grow the food they need for the long winter months, as well as the chance to earn money at the local markets.

Living off the land

Ukrainians and Belarusians have been surviving this way for centuries, a life of subsistence based on the land. It is here that you can get a

---

LEFT: workers in Belarus spread hay before winter.
RIGHT: newlyweds pose for a photograph in front of the war memorial in Platz de Sieges, Minsk.

taste for the remaining traditions of rural life, and also settle down for an acquaintance with such exotica as *salo*, cured pig fat that is one of the most hallowed delicacies. If this is not to your taste, and don't be surprised if it isn't, then some fine alternatives would be *borshch*, the national soup made from beetroot and other vegetables, and sometimes topped with *smetana* (sour cream), or *varenyky*, dumplings which can be filled with anything from potatoes to fruits. You should not have to wait long before also seeing the appearance of the vodka (*horilka* in Ukrainian).

Claims of legendary Slavic hospitality can ring a bit false when you are faced with an uncooperative shop assistant or obstructive bureaucrat, but an introduction to a Ukrainian or Belarusian family usually does more than enough to compensate.

The *dacha* is the usual place for the family to spend the warm spring and summer weekends, and conversations turn with the seasons. September is the month for mushrooms, and the early morning mushroom-picking expeditions are a particular passion in Belarus.

Fishing trips can be taken all year: in summer you will find enthusiasts waiting for a catch along the river banks; in winter the same char-

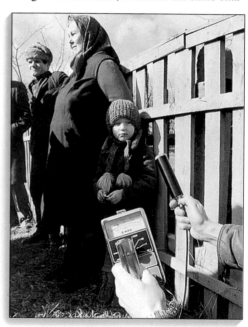

CHORNOBYL CATASTROPHE

Since April 1986, Ukraine and Belarus have been indelibly associated with a nuclear power station near their common border. Nearly 9 tonnes of radioactive material were released when an experiment with a reactor at Chornobyl in Ukraine went catastrophically wrong. The Soviet authorities evacuated 135,000 people; thousands more were exposed to radiation as the prevailing wind blew north across Belarus. While 32 people at or near the plant died within days, the longer term effects are still being felt in radiation-related illnesses and cancers. The reactor itself was covered with concrete and the plant surrounded by a 30-km (19-mile) exclusion zone.

acters, now bundled up and fortified with *horilka*, move out to huddle over holes drilled in the ice. These retreats to nature are sacred, one of the only ways that ordinary Ukrainians and Belarusians could get away from crowded apartment buildings and factory floors. Some in southern Belarus may even have supposed that these oases of private space would forever be out of the reach of the government, until this notion was cruelly disabused by the contamination from the ruined reactor at Chornobyl.

The language issue

It was in the villages that the Ukrainian and Belarusian languages survived the Soviet period. Both of these, and Russian as well, are lineal descendants of the Slavic language used in Kievan Rus. Over the centuries they gradually grew apart. Ukrainian and Belarusian are still widely used in the countryside, and you will increasingly come across them in the towns as well.

There are also regional divisions: in the Ukrainian west, attempts to speak Russian may well be met with feigned incomprehension; across in the eastern towns of the country

VOICE OF COMMUNISM

When Khrushchev declared at the State University in Minsk in 1959 that "the sooner we all start speaking Russian, the faster we shall build communism" he was simply rephrasing a customary prejudice against the "peasant dialects" of Belarus and Ukraine.

around two-thirds of the schools in the country were teaching in Belarusian. By 1998 that figure was down to around one-third, a development attributed to the doggedly pro-Russian Lukashenka. By contrast, Ukrainian has been promoted as the language of instruction throughout the country, although Russian is still widely used in the east. This can be an uncomfortable experience for some, particularly for parents who grew up speaking Russian, but whose

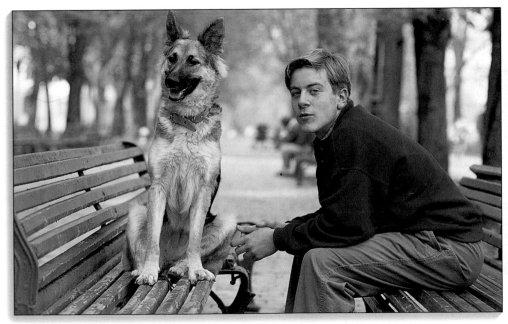

Ukrainian will be the rarity. They are used interchangeably in Kiev, with Ukrainian generally being the language of politics and education and Russian still often used for business and commerce.

Russian was promoted as the language of advancement during tsarist and Soviet times, and the question for the new states is whether and how to support their national languages, which for so long were considered subordinate. Belarus decided not to; after independence

FAR LEFT: the ruins of the Chornobyl nuclear plant.
LEFT: Ukrainians are tested for radiation.
ABOVE: relaxing in the Black Sea resort of Odessa.

children are now encouraged to talk in a different language. Yet people can come to terms with the change: President Kuchma, who hails from the eastern city of Dnipropetrovsk, had to take Ukrainian lessons when running for office in 1994, but once elected it was rare to hear him speak anything else.

Opportunities for the young

With all their problems and their troubled inheritance, it is not surprising that a lot of hope for Belarus and Ukraine is invested in the generations that have grown up since 1991.

Even in Belarus, where Lukashenka kept the official media on a short leash, young people were more exposed to outside influences than at any time before. In Ukraine, local cable networks and the Internet brought in a quantity and variety of information that was bewildering to an older age group. Bootleg copies of the latest blockbusters were available on the streets of Kiev within weeks of their release. Students flocked to new courses being offered in marketing, finance, business administration; many picked up English or other foreign languages along the way.

Yet the opportunities that Belarus and Ukraine provided for their young were still few and far between. Most state enterprises were businesses, but the authorities' residual mistrust of private enterprise made this a tortuously complicated and expensive process.

Those businesses which actually made it off the ground still found their fate in the hands of venal local officials.

Economic freefall

By 1998, even the limited progress that had been made in putting the economy back together seemed under threat. Ukraine looked on in dismay as the *hryvna*, whose stability since its introduction two years earlier had been one of the only economic achievements,

not an attractive prospect for bright school-leavers, and government service was both poorly organised and poorly paid. There were some jobs available in the new financial sector, but memories of old rouble accounts made worthless by inflation and sad stories of bogus investment schemes meant that few put too much trust in the local banks.

Some managed to find work with the growing number of foreign firms, but many ended up having to scrape a living from small-scale trading, braving the rapacious customs police to bring in clothes from Turkey, hi-fis from Abu Dhabi, or cars from Western Europe. What they needed was the chance to set up their own followed the rouble downhill. From abroad, the financial crisis of 1998 looked like a reminder of how far Russia, Belarus and Ukraine still had to go in creating a functioning market system. But many in the countries themselves, watching their savings lose their value as prices began to rise, continued to wonder whether it was worth the effort. Perhaps the Western way was not for them; perhaps there was another model that might be more in keeping with their national traditions.

ABOVE: primary schoolchildren in Odessa, Ukraine.
RIGHT: Lenin's statue stands guard over a boulevard in Yalta on the southern shores of Crimea.

This was certainly what was in the mind of President Lukashenka. Belarus escaped comparatively unscathed from the financial rubble – it did not have far to fall – and he was quick to claim this as a resounding endorsement of his Soviet-style economy. Away from the market and democracy, Lukashenka's vision was shaped instead by the possibility of relief through a new union, this time a Slavic one.

Should the Slavs unite?

The idea of Slav unity has a pedigree in Russian thought stretching back to the 19th century, and its combination with nostalgia for the Soviet times made for a potent brew. Much of the talk of integration since 1991 was motivated by the mission to bring the Eastern Slavs back under a single roof. For his part, Lukashenka's grandiose dream was to become their new leader.

Earlier attempts at Slav unity at the start of the 20th century, including the Slav peoples of central Europe, foundered on nationalist rivalries between them and on Russia's desire to be first among equals.

Proposals for a new post-Soviet union have had to cope with exactly the same tensions. Even in Belarus, which appeared to have made its choice for eternal partnership with Russia, actual progress towards union was not as clear-cut as the rhetoric. When the moment came, neither Moscow nor Minsk were prepared to give anything up.

Ukraine has been more adamant in its opposition to the idea, preferring to control its own fate even if not certain what this should be. With politicians unable to agree, it was left to other national institutions to give the country a focus. In Ukraine this means the football teams: the mighty Dynamo Kiev and the national team, often one and the same.

When the Russians arrived in 1998 to take part in the first post-independence derby game, Ukrainians looked up just for a moment from the business of surviving to take notice. They might even have taken heart from their team's 3–2 victory.

Sometimes by default, sometimes by intent, the colours of Belarus and Ukraine are working themselves back into their people's minds and back into the fabric of Europe. ❏

The area where you might see the fewest signs of Ukrainian cultural life is Crimea, which was an autonomous region in the USSR before World War II, and then spent nine years as part of Russia before being transferred to Ukraine in 1954 – ostensibly to mark the 300th anniversary of Ukrainian "union" with Russia from the times of Bogdan Khmelnitsky.

Following the collapse of the USSR, Crimea became a touchstone for Russian sensitivity at the loss of empire. Although rumblings from the Crimean ethnic Russian community, which forms a majority on the peninsula, died down after 1995 this is still a potentially divisive issue.

In all the discussions over Crimea, it is easy to forget that its largest population before 1944 was that of the Crimea Tatars. Identified by Stalin as guilty of collaboration with the Nazis, the entire Tatar population was deported, mostly to Central Asia. This act of calculated barbarism was acknowledged as "groundless" even by the Soviets themselves in 1967, but it was to be another 20 years before the Tatars were allowed to begin returning home. The early returnees managed to rebuild homes while their Soviet roubles still had some value; more recent arrivals have had to settle in makeshift houses around Crimea's capital, Simferopol.

BELARUS

*At the crossroads between Poland and Russia, ravaged by
warring armies, Belarus has survived as a nation in its own right
with much of historical interest to offer the visitor*

Map on page 302

Most visitors arriving in Belarus from the West arrive through the border town of **Brest ❶**, a town that used to be one of the busiest thoroughfares in Eastern Europe. Its name in the 20th century is irrevocably linked with the conduct of war. It was in Brest-Litovsk at the end of World War I in March 1918 that revolutionary Russia agreed a separate peace with the German High Command, surrendering control over Ukraine, the Baltic States, Finland and Poland in exchange for an end to hostilities. This treaty was annulled with the final defeat of the Central Powers in November of the same year.

A more celebrated episode in Brest's modern history was its valiant resistance to Hitler's invading army of 1941. This is immediately apparent to those arriving by railway who see the commemorative plaque within the station building, all the more so to those who venture out of the city centre to the site of the old Brest fortress. Here the garrison of Soviet soldiers held on for six weeks after the Nazi invasion, persuading the German army commanders that the main body of their forces would have to bypass Brest in order to press on towards Minsk. The fortress, **Brestskaya Krepast**, was badly damaged in 1941, and was reduced to rubble as the retreating Nazis fought against the Red Army in 1944. Now partially rebuilt, it houses a museum honouring its Soviet defenders (open Wed–Sun, 9.30am–6pm).

PRECEDING PAGES: square in Minsk. **LEFT:** World War II memorial, Brest. **BELOW:** central Minsk.

Beyond Brest

On leaving Brest, the road to the east passes through the **Belovezhskaya Pushcha Nature Reserve ❷**, 85,000 hectares (210,000 acres) of unspoiled deep forest of the sort that once covered much of Europe. It is now the main sanctuary of the European bison, which was almost extinct by the mid-20th century but is now numbered by the thousand in this area alone. The quantity and variety of wildlife made this forest the favourite hunting ground of the Polish and then the Russian royal families; one remarkable Russian 12-day shoot produced a tally of 36 elks, 53 stags, 325 roebuck, 42 of the famed bison, and 138 wild boar.

Further to the north, nestling near the borders with Poland and Lithuania, is the town of **Hrodno ❸**. Although sacked by Tatars and Teutonic Knights in the 13th and 14th centuries, Hrodno managed to avoid the contemporary fate of towns like Brest, being taken with relative ease by the advancing Nazis in 1941. This means that while Hrodno may not have "hero-city" status, it does offer some rare clues as to what pre-war Belarus must have looked like. Of the many historic buildings left standing, the modest 12th-century **Barysahlyebskaya Tserkva** (Church of SS Barys and Hlyeb) is one of the oldest Belarusian structures left

TIP

Brest has the unexpected distinction of hosting one of the finest Indian restaurants in the former Soviet Union. The Restoran Indija is at the junction of Karl Marx and Hoholja streets.

from the times of Kievan Rus. The castle overlooking the Neman river was originally built by the Lithuanians in the 14th century, and the baroque **Farny Sabor** (Farny Cathedral) in the town centre is a reminder of later Polish rule.

One of the most powerful influences in the Hrodno region were the Radziwills, a family of Lithuanian magnates that rose to prominence when Barbara Radziwill secretly married the Polish King Sigismund II in 1547. Although Barabara died four years later, allegedly poisoned by Sigismund's mother, the Radziwills continued to play a leading role in Polish politics until the 20th century. The family owned large tracts of land in western Belarus, and built the imposing castle at **Mir ❹** and the palace and fortress at **Njasvich ❺**.

Another more infamous product of the local Polish nobility was Felix Dzerzhinsky, the fanatical Bolshevik revolutionary who went on to set up the first Soviet secret police organisation, the Cheka, in 1917. Dzerzhinsky authorised and supervised the arbitrary terror meted out against real and imagined enemies of the young Soviet state, thereby installing the machinery that was later to become the KGB. The town of **Dzerzhinsk ❻**, near his birthplace to the west of Minsk, was named in his honour. Ironically, the previous name for this town, Koydanovo, referred to a Mongol commander who had also brought fear into the hearts of the local populace six centuries earlier.

The capital city of Minsk

The Belarusian capital, **Minsk ❼**, was a massive casualty of World War II, and anything that looks older than 1945 has been heavily restored or rebuilt. Minsk has grown dramatically since the war and its population has tripled since 1970, but even with its parks and pleasant open spaces it is still difficult to discern many traces of the old town. The 17th century **Bernardzinskaya Tsarkva** (Orthodox cathedral of the Bernadine monastery) **Ⓐ** and some renovated houses along **Troitskaya Naberezhna** (Trinity Embankment) by the Svislach River hint at a more distant past, but these now look strangely out of place among the monumental Soviet boulevards and apartment buildings.

Among the lost features of Minsk, as indeed of Belarus, are the Jews who became subjects of the Russian Empire as it expanded its borders in the 18th century. Tsarist restrictions on their rights meant that they were confined to the "Pale of Settlement", land along the western edge of the empire and the Black Sea coast. The Russian census of 1897 showed that 5 million Jews were living in the "pale". A hundred years of conflict and persecution, and the possibility of emigration to Israel, has meant that Jews now make up only 1 percent of Belarus's 10.4 million inhabitants. It is difficult to underestimate the effect that World War II has had both on the landscape and on the Belarusian psyche. The **Muzey Istorii Byalikay Aychynnay Vayny** (Museum of the Great

Maps
Area 302
City 304

Instead of the usual array of national heroes, notes of the national currency feature government buildings and wild animals, including the hare (zaichik) *that has become the currency's nickname.*

BELOW: Brest Fortress has been partially rebuilt since its ruination in World War II.

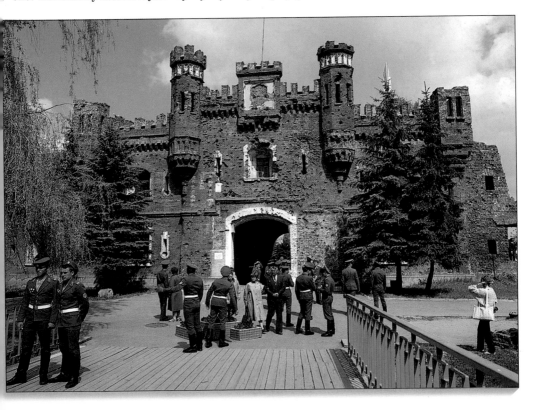

Patriotic War **B**; open 11am–6pm; closed Mon), along the central Skaryna Prospect at number 25, is a grim reminder of the horrors visited upon the country during the war, but in a country full of memorials the most impressive is still the complex at **Khatyn 8**, 60 km (37 miles) north of Minsk. It was built on the site of a village which was destroyed by the Nazis in 1943 as a reprisal for the murder of German soldiers. Only one person survived when the villagers of Khatyn were locked in a single burning building, and the statue of this survivor, Yuzif Kaminsky, dominates the centre of the complex. Accompanied by solemn funereal music, Khatyn also commemorates the hundreds of other Belarusian villages ruined by war and the quarter of the population that lost their lives between 1941 and 1945.

The tragic impression left by Khatyn is both compounded and compromised by the memory of another similar-sounding episode in Soviet history, the murder of thousands of Polish officers by the NKVD (forerunner of the KGB) in the Katyn forest near Smolensk in Russia in 1940. For many years the Soviet government falsely claimed that the killings were perpetrated by the Nazis, and it was only in 1992 that the Russian government released documents which proved the complicity of the Soviet authorities in the massacre and cover-up. A few years earlier, in 1988, Belarusians became aware of the atrocities committed by their own government, with the discovery of mass graves in the Kurapaty forest near Minsk containing at least half a million victims of Stalin's terror.

Ancient Belarus

Such wholesale destruction inflicted by modern conflicts means that very little remains of the country's earliest origins, when most of Belarus formed part of

TIP

A sensible precaution to take against the small risk of food contamination is to avoid wild mushrooms and berries, which retain radiation longer than other vegetation, and to steer clear of locally produced milk.

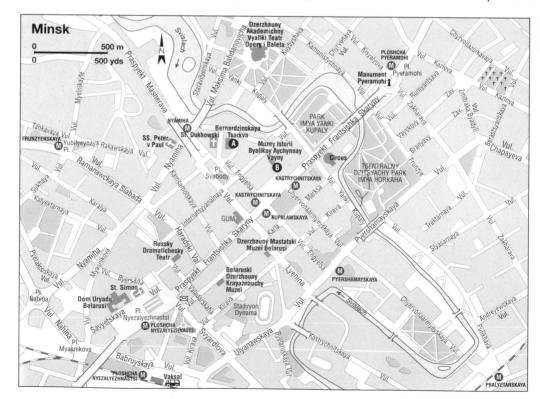

the kingdom of Kievan Rus, trading goods along the river grid that linked Byzantium with the Baltics.

The main exception is the quiet northern town of **Polatsk** ❾, whose location along the Dvina river made it the dominant regional centre from the 10th until the 12th centuries. The **Saphiyskyy Sabor** (Cathedral of St Sophia), originally modelled on the great cathedral in Kiev, was built during this period, although it was substantially rebuilt in baroque style under Polish rule. Polatsk remained influential into the Middle Ages, its ruling élite making enough money from agriculture to send their sons to study at the great European universities.

The influx of Renaissance and humanist influences into Belarus is apparent in the work of Frantsysk Skaryna of Polatsk. He held degrees from the universities of Cracow and Padua, and editions of his translation of the Bible into Belarusian in the 16th century were the first printed books not only in Belarus, but in the whole of eastern Europe. His and other achievements are celebrated in Polatsk's **Muzey Belarushka Knihadrukavanni** (Museum of Historical Books and Printing; open 10am–5pm; closed Sun, Mon).

Belarus was rarely promoted in Soviet times as a holiday destination and the resulting lack of attention given to tourism make it an occasionally challenging place to explore. Visitors have been put off by worries over the Chornobyl catastrophe whose effects were felt most strongly in southern Belarus, although Western organisations maintain that the risks associated with short stays in the country are insignificant. The national authorities have yet to put much effort into promoting an attractive external image. Yet in return for some patience and perseverance Belarus provides a fascinating portrait of a country that has seen the worst that the 20th century could offer, and survived. ❑

Minsk, along with such cities as Kiev and Odessa, was renowned as a major centre of Jewish influence and culture during the 18th and 19th centuries.

BELOW: market place, Minsk.

A COMMONWEALTH IS BORN

In December 1991 the once-mighty Soviet Union was laid to rest in the Belovezhskaya Pushcha Nature Reserve near Brest. In a lodge in the forest, the elected leaders of Russia, Ukraine and Belarus – Yeltsin, Kravchuk and Shushkevich – agreed to replace the USSR with a looser association, the Commonwealth of Independent States (CIS). They proposed Minsk as the administrative centre of the CIS, giving the Belarusian capital a chance to become the Brussels of eastern Europe. As it turned out, the commonwealth has been almost entirely ineffective. Twelve of the 15 former Soviet republics regularly attend CIS meetings, but they have yet to agree on exactly what the organisation should be doing in their name. Russia has been arguing for a closer confederation that could help to restore Moscow's global authority. Other countries, including Ukraine, have been more wary. On the rare occasions when everyone reaches agreement, such as in 1994 on the introduction of free trade, little is implemented. Those who mourn the passing of the Soviet Union have denounced the creation of the CIS as an act of criminal irresponsibility, but even those glad to see the Union behind them still have few kind words to say about the unloved organisation that was born in Belovezh.

UKRAINE

Evidence of Ukraine's chequered history abounds. The Tatars, Genoese, Poles, Hapsburgs and Russians have all left their mark on ancient Kievan Rus

Generations of Poles and Russians can attest to the difficulty in holding and keeping the borderlands of Ukraine. The lands are flat and famously fertile, broken only by the Carpathian mountains to the west, and by the Crimean peninsula in the south. The region has been a crossroads of migration paths, trade routes and imperial ambitions for centuries, and the evidence left behind goes far beyond the Russian hegemony of the last 300 years. Ukraine includes the frontier towns of the Hapsburg Empire, as well as Polish castles, Tatar palaces, and the remains of old Greek and Genoese trading posts along the Black Sea coast.

Ukraine is also rediscovering its own history, and one of the best examples is Kiev **1** itself. From the glorious period at the heart of Kievan Rus when only Constantinople could compete in importance, Kiev was almost completely destroyed by Batu Khan and the Tatars in 1240. It was to take six centuries before Kiev's population reached the same level again, during which time the city was fought over by Lithuanians, Poles and then Russians. It barely survived the chaos and destruction of two world wars in the 20th century, but history is now turning full circle and Kiev is beginning to reassert itself as one of the great European capitals.

PRECEDING PAGES:
Opera and Ballet
Theatre, Kiev.
LEFT: St Sophia's
Cathedral.
BELOW: the
monastery of
Kievo-Pecherskaya.

The upper town of Kiev

The story of early Kiev revolves around the achievements of two men, Volodymyr (Vladimir) the Great and his son Yaroslav the Wise, and a walking tour of the upper town begins at the junction of two streets bearing their names, Vulitsya Volodymyrska and Yaroslaviv Val. This is the site of the **Zoloti Vorota** (Golden Gate) **A**, the ancient entrance to the city that is now a block away from the Kiev Opera and Ballet Theatre. The gate was built by Yaroslav in the 11th century as part of the fortifications of the upper town and was given its name by the golden dome of the Church of the Annunciation which stood on top. Both the gate and the church were ruined by the Tatars in 1240; what you see today is a 1982 restoration supposedly true to the original design. You can visit the museum inside to find out more about ancient Kiev and for some fine views across the modern city (open Mar–Nov: 10am–5.30pm; closed Thur).

From the Golden Gate, **Misto Yaroslava** (Yaroslav's Town) **B** is reached by walking north up Vulitsya Volodymyrska, passing the austere SBU **building** – the Ukrainian successor to the KGB – on your right at number 33. This gives way a little further on to the open square in front of **Sofiysky Sobor** (St Sophia's Cathedral) **C**, and to the left the gold and green domes of the cathedral itself. This is Yaroslav's

most enduring memorial, completed in 1031 in honour of his victory in battle against the nomadic Pechenegs. Its Byzantine layout and design, as well as the name taken from the Hagia Sophia in Constantinople, reflect all the authority and prestige that Kievan Rus enjoyed at the time. It was the spiritual heart of the early Rus state and remains a treasure of Eastern Slav civilisation.

The cathedral was restored and enlarged at the end of the 17th century, when many of the external intricacies were added in Ukrainian baroque style. As the models just past the cathedral entrance make clear, the original 11th-century building consisted of the nave and four parallel aisles, each ending in semicircular apses, its 13 cupolas representing Christ and the Apostles. The striking central mosaic of the Virgin Mary also dates from the 11th-century, as do some of the frescoes on the north wall of the nave. The marble tomb of Yaroslav himself lies in the northeast corner.

The exit from St Sophia's is through the 18th-century bell tower, past the grave of Patriarch Volodymyr to your left (*see page 314*), and out across the newly-paved square. It was here that the citizens of Kiev turned out in their thousands in 1648 to welcome the Cossack regiments of Bogdan Khmelnitsky after their victory over the Poles. The **statue of Bogdan Khmelnitsky** on horseback in the centre of the square was added only much later, in 1888.

The upper town has been threatened with ruin on many occasions, but in the 20th century a new menace appeared: the Soviet planners. When the Ukrainian SSR joined the Soviet Union in 1922, the Bolsheviks feared that Kiev was too infected with nationalism to be a trustworthy capital, and this honour was granted instead to the eastern city of Kharkiv. By the 1930s Kiev was back in favour, but the authorities still felt that the city was not suitably equipped to

Map
on page
312

On the last weekend in May, the capital celebrates the "Days of Kiev". By this time the chestnuts are in full bloom and the city looks at its best after the long winter.

BELOW: Ukrainian entertainers aboard a cruise ship.

house the new generation of Soviet administrators. As a result, they decreed that the entire area from St Sophia's past **Mikhailivska Ploshcha** (St Michael's Square) be cleared to make way for a triumphant new avenue of government buildings. The onset of World War II meant that the plans could not be implemented in full, but this "reprieve" came too late for the 12th-century Golden-Domed Monastery of St Michael, which was demolished in 1935 and 1936.

Gradually the damage done during the Soviet era is being repaired. The white marble figure of Princess Olha, who privately converted to Christianity 33 years before her grandson Volodymyr the Great, returned to the centre of the square in 1996 after a break of 77 years, flanked by Saints Cyril, Methodius and Andrew. They stand next to the rebuilt bell tower and new golden domes of **Mikhailivsky Sobor** (St Michael's Cathedral) **D**. The only reminder of the Soviet plans is the neoclassical bulk at the northwest of the square, built in 1937, which now houses the **Ukrainian Ministry of Foreign Affairs**.

A small exhibition on the history of the Monastery of St Michael – including the Soviet plans for reconstruction of the area – can be seen in the cathedral's new bell tower.

Volodymyr's Town

Beyond the ministry to the left, down **Vulitsya Desyatynna**, you move into **Misto Volodymyra** (Volodymyr's Town) **E**. It was Volodymyr who first formed the lands of Rus into a coherent political entity in the 10th century, and it was his momentous decision in 988 to adopt Eastern Christianity as its official religion. The **Desyatynna** (Tithe Church), so called because Volodymyr gave up one-tenth of his income to have it built, was the first stone church in Rus. Its foundations are visible in the park across from the end of Vulitsya Desyatynna, next to the grey building of the **Ukrainsky Istorychny Muzey** (Museum of Ukrainian History **F**; open 10am–6pm, closed Wed and last Thur in month). The Tithe Church was founded in 989 and was the burial place of Volodymyr; it was also the refuge for hundreds of Kievans who retreated onto its roof to escape Batu Khan in 1240. The roof collapsed, the survivors were left to the mercy of the Tatars.

Andriivska Tserka (St Andrew's Church) **G** provides the perfect antidote to the tales of destruction from early Kiev. Balancing at the top of the hill of the same name, the church was designed with exquisite grace by Rastrelli, the Italian architect who shaped 18th-century St Petersburg. It marks the entrance to one of Kiev's most likeable streets, the **Andriivsky Uzviz** (Andrew's Descent), which winds its way down to the Podil region by the river. This is Kiev's Montmartre, full of artists and cafés, and the best place to shop for souvenirs.

Just beyond the 19th-century **Zamok Richarda Levove Sertse** (Castle of Richard The Lion Heart) **H**, you can take the wooden steps up to the right to reach an observation platform giving excellent views over the **Podil O**. This was traditionally the trading region of Kiev which grew around the main port along the Dnipro (Dnieper). A little further down the street, at No. 13, is a museum dedicated to the writer **Mikhail Bulgakov J** (open 10am–6pm, closed Wed). His novel *The White Guard* remains the best account of the chaos and uncertainty of life in Kiev at the end of World War I. Descending into the Podil, you can return to the upper town by taking the **funicular**, built in 1905, that leaves from the **Poshtova Ploshcha**. You can reach this square by walking to the right along Vulitsya Petra Sahaydachnoho, Podil's main street.

The 18th-century St Andrew's Church dominates Kiev's skyline above Podil.

Central Kiev: Kreshchatyk

Vulitsya Kreshchatyk is modern Kiev's central street, famous for the rows of chestnut trees that soften the lines of its post-war architecture. The city authorities gave the street a facelift in 1998, and despite its six lanes of traffic it still enjoys a relaxed atmosphere. The northern end of the street towards the river is **Evropeyska Ploshcha** (European Square) set against the backdrop of the Soviet arch built in 1982 to celebrate the eternal union of the brother Slavs. The same year also saw the completion of the **Ukrinsky Dim K** formerly the Lenin Museum, now a Ukrainian cultural centre. The view is improved by the reopened **Filarmoniya** (Philharmonia) **L**, originally constructed in 1882 as the Kiev Merchant's Association, which holds regular concerts and recitals. The ticket office is down the steps to the left of the building. Visitors to this spot in 1892 would have witnessed the first electric tram in the Russian Empire as it trundled down the hill towards the Podil.

Back along Kreshchatyk, past the distinctive electric clock tower of the Trades Union centre, is the **Maidan Nezalezhnosti** (Independence Square) **M**, Kiev's central square. Although the individual buildings are unremarkable, the square gets its life from the crowds of Ukrainians that gather by the fountains in summer. The plinth in front of the 1960s **Hotel Moskva** used to support a large statue of Lenin, and in 1990 he stayed just long enough to witness the hunger strikes and demonstrations that forced the resignation of the then prime minister. In the south-

BELOW: the hub of modern Kiev, Kreshchatyk.

Hydropark, an island park in the middle of the Dnipro, has Kiev's main beaches and is a great place to see how young Ukrainians spend their summer days and evenings.

east corner of the square you see the columns of the **Konservatoriya imeni Chaikovskoho** (Tchaikovsky State Conservatory) .

In the times of Kievan Rus, the Kreshchatyk valley lay outside the city walls and got its name – meaning crossed or crossroads – from the many ravines that marked the hills on either side. Even in the mid-19th century, most of the area on the left-hand side of Kreshchatyk was a country estate belonging to the Mering family. Towards the end of the century it was developed and contains some fine townhouses, as well as the **Dom Horodetskoho** (House of Gargoyles) that now stands opposite the Presidential Administration on Vulitsya Bankova.

The **Bessarabsky Rynok** (Bessarabian Market) marks the end of Kreshchatyk. From here you can walk up the **Bulvar Tarasa Shevchenko** in the direction of Kiev's university. Although the first library in Kiev was founded by Yaroslav the Wise in the 11th century, Ukraine had to wait until 1615 before it had its first institute of higher education, the **Kiev-Mohyla Academy** in the Podil. The distinctive red building of the **Kyivsky Universitet imeni Shevchenka** (Kiev State University) appeared in the mid-19th century. Further down the boulevard on the right is another splendid 19th-century addition, the neo-Byzantine **Volodymyrsky Sobor** (St Volodymyr's Cathedral) .

The Pechersk Monastery

BELOW: Monument to the Defence of the Motherland, known locally as the "steel wench".

About 3 km (2 miles) southeast of the town centre is the resplendent **Kievo-Pecherska Lavra** (Kiev Pechersk Monastery) , a complex of churches, caves and museums founded in 1051 where you can easily spend a whole day. It is reached by heading up from **Evropeyska Ploshcha** (European Square) along Vulitsya Mykhayla Hrushevskoho, passing the **Natsionalny Khudozhny**

UNORTHODOX RESTING PLACE

As the totalitarian regime started to crumble in the late 1980s, one of the most visible signs of change was the revival of interest in religion. As with most things in Ukraine, this has not been without its moments of controversy. In 1993, members of a cult calling itself the White Brotherhood had to be forcibly prevented from occupying St Sophia's Cathedral. Two years later there was a more dramatic, and tragic, encounter on the same site. Political independence reawakened a split in the Orthodox church in Ukraine between those in favour of a separate Ukrainian branch of Orthodoxy and those giving allegiance to the patriarch in Moscow. When the patriarch of the independent Ukrainian Orthodox church, Volodymyr, died in 1995, his followers wanted to bury him in the grounds of St Sophia's. The cathedral still belonged to the state as a museum, but with the Ukrainian government seemingly unwilling to make a decision the situation was left to escalate out of control when the funeral procession carrying Volodymyr's body was stopped by security forces. During a running battle on St Sophia's Square the patriarch was laid to rest in a hastily-dug hole in the pavement by the bell tower, where his tomb – proclaiming him the patriarch of all Ukraine-Rus – remains to this day.

Muzey Ukrainy ❶ (Museum of Ukrainian Fine Arts; open 10am–6pm; closed Friday) and the white **Kabinet Ministriv** (Cabinet of Ministers) building on the right, and the **Ukrainian Verkhovna Rada** (Supreme Council) on the other side. Set back in a park behind the Rada, is the baroque **Mariinsky Palats** (Mariinsky Palace) ❶, restored in 1868 for the arrival of Tsar Alexander II and Empress Maria (book tours at Muzey Istorii Mista, Vulitsya P. Orlyka 8; open 10am–6pm, closed Fri). At the Arsenalna metro station, the street becomes Vulitsya Sichnevoho Povstannya (Street of the January Uprising), which leads to the monastery. Trolleybus No. 20 follows this route from the Kreshchatyk.

The monastery spreads down to the River Dnipro, and the crowd of domes and cupolas poking above the woodland slopes is one of Kiev's most memorable sights. The name "Pechersk" comes from the subterranean passages, chapels and caves (*pechera*) that have been dug into the rock. The monastery barely survived the onslaught of the Tatars in the 13th century, but remained an important site of pilgrimage for Orthodox Christians throughout the Middle Ages. In the 18th century it acquired its present Ukrainian baroque appearance, and under the Soviets it was turned into a museum. Since 1988 most of the monastery has been returned to the Orthodox Church (open 9.30am–6pm, closed Tues).

The main entrance to the upper part of the monastery is through the elaborately painted **Troitska Nadbramma Tserkva** (Trinity Gate Church), beyond which the interior is dominated by the 96-metre (315-ft) bell tower of the **Uspensky Sobor** (Cathedral of the Assumption). The tower gives a grand perspective over the Dnipro and the left bank, as well as southwards towards the rigid features of the huge **Monument to the Defence of the Motherland**, or the "steel wench" as she is more colourfully known. The magnificent Uspensky

Map on page 312

Bessarabsky Market, at the southern end of Kreshchatyk, presents a colourful show of fruit, flowers and vegetables.

BELOW: Rainbow Arch, Kiev.

TIP

Tickets for the main museums of Pechersk Monastery, and for the bell tower and caves (where you buy a candle instead of a ticket) are available only at the respective entrances, not at the main ticket office.

Cathedral that once accompanied the bell tower is now being rebuilt. The original was destroyed during World War II. The large golden-striped dome to the east of the tower belongs to the **Trapezna Tserkva Antoniya ta Feodosiya** (Refectory Church of St Anthony and Theodosius). The upper monastery includes the **Museum of Historical Treasures**, (open for tours in Russian and Ukrainian; English tours, in summer only at hourly intervals, require pre-booking) which has a collection of ancient Scythian jewellery, and the quirky Miniatures Museum featuring such oddities as the world's smallest book.

The lower part of the monastery contains the entrances to the caves themselves. Their origins, and the origins of the monastery, are linked with the extraordinary life of Anthony of Pechersk, who in 1028 became a monk at the monastery of Esphigmenon on Mount Athos in Greece. He returned to Kiev with the mission to bring the monastic tradition to his native Rus, a tradition which emphasises asceticism and separation from society as a means of moving closer to God. After settling in a cavern by the Dnipro his fame as a holy man began to attract followers, who in turn started to carve the religious labyrinth into the hillside. When the number of monks reached 15, Anthony retired from the **Dalny Pechera** (Further Caves) and found solitude again in a new grotto, the **Blyzky Pechera** (Nearer Caves). Like the other monks, he is buried underground. In 1051 Kievan Rus ceded the hillside to the monks, and Anthony laid the foundations of the monastery of the caves, the **Kievo-Pecherska Lavra**.

The riches of Chernihiv

One of the richest cities of Kievan Rus, **Chernihiv ❷** is about 140 km (87 miles) to the northeast of the capital along the main Odessa to St Petersburg

BELOW: frescoes at the Kievo-Pecherskaya Monastery.

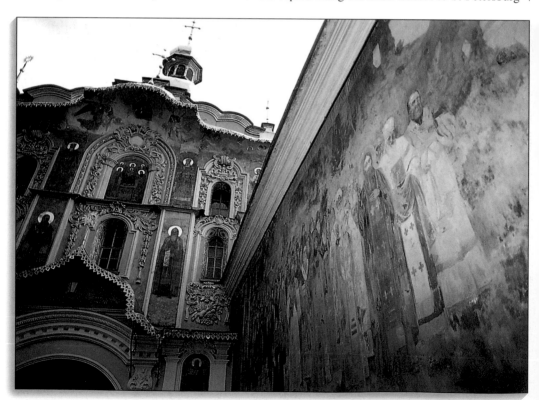

highway. The city was founded in the early 8th century on the River Desna, part of the "water road from the Varangians to the Greeks" that supported its early trading wealth. It reached pre-eminence in the 11th and 12th centuries, and its most valuable sites date from this period. After being sacked by the Tatars in 1239 Chernihiv lost its former importance, and fell to both Lithuanians and Poles before coming under Russian sway in the 17th century.

Approaching Chernihiv from the south you first catch sight of the five golden domes of **Tserkva Sv. Kateryny** (St Catherine's Church). Completed in the 18th century, this church is now a museum of local arts and crafts (open 10am–5pm, closed Wed). Behind St Catherine's lies the **Dytynets**, the historic site of ancient Chernihiv. Most of the Dytynets is now included within a park named after Mikhailo Kotsiubinsky, a classic name in Ukrainian modernist writing who lived in Chernihiv from 1898 until his death in 1913.

The **Kotsiubinsky Park** includes two outstanding monuments to the times of Kievan Rus. The **Spaso-Preobraszhensky Sobor** (Spassky Cathedral) dates originally from 1017, and its two sharp conical towers make it stand out from the more gentle contours that define most Orthodox buildings. It was built at the behest of Prince Mstyslav the Brave, who had challenged his brother Yaroslav the Wise for control of Kievan Rus after Volodymyr's death in 1015. Mstyslav was granted all the lands east of the Dnipro in an attempt to avoid another round of the fratricidal blood-letting that had already cost the lives of three of their brothers. It was only after Mstyslav himself died in 1036 – he is buried in the cathedral – that Kievan Rus was united to enjoy its "golden age" under the rule of Yaroslav. The nearby **Borysohlibsky Sobor** (Cathedral of SS Boris and Hlib) is slightly younger, dating from the 12th century, but retains a much more

Map on page 310

TIP

If you are planning a day trip to Chernihiv you may wish to take a picnic lunch. There aren't many decent eateries around the town's historic centre.

BELOW: before the start of a church service.

traditional design. There is, however, a family connection. Borys and Hlib were two of the three brothers killed in the feuding that followed Volodymyr's death (killed by another brother, Sviatopolk the Damned), and they were later canonised by the Orthodox Church.

The cannons lining the embankments at the southern end of the park point out across the River Desna and its tributary, the Strizhen. Looking out from near the monument to Taras Shevchenko, you can see the Ukrainian baroque outlines of the **Yeletsky Monastery** to the right, and further in the distance the imposing 58-metre (190-ft) bell tower of the **Troyitsky Monastery**. This hill contains the **Pechera Antoniya** (Anthony Caves), named after Anthony of Pechersk; more than 300 metres (984 ft) of underground passages connect five well-lit chapels, most of them constructed before the 14th century.

Lviv and western Ukraine

Travelling west through Ukraine the landscape is gradually transformed as spires and steeples start to appear among the bulbous Orthodox cupolas. These western lands were brought behind the Soviet border only with World War II, and retain many affinities with the central European empires and countries that once held sway here. These are also the parts of Ukraine that feel their national identity most strongly, with Ukrainian spoken as a matter of course.

Lviv ❸ was founded in the 13th century by Prince Danylo of Galicia, and its strategic position controlling the passes across the Carpathian mountains has ensured it a turbulent history. Foreign travel has not been essential for the inhabitants of Lviv; their bitter experience has been that time will bring the foreign countries to visit. A 90-year-old woman who has lived in Lviv all her life would

BELOW:
a Kievan woman
in festive spirit.

Map on page 310

have been born in the Hapsburg Empire, then after a spell in the ephemeral Western Ukrainian Republic after World War I (and a few weeks of Bolshevik rule in 1920) she would have settled down in Poland. In 1939 the Soviets arrived again, only to be driven back by the invading Nazis two years later. From 1941 until 1944 she had to endure the German-controlled General Government of Poland, before again joining the Soviet Union. From 1991 she would have survived to see an independent Ukraine.

The wide boulevard in the centre of Lviv is **Prospekt Svobody**, with the **Teatr Opery ta Baletu** (Opera and Ballet Theatre) commanding its northern end. This tree-lined promenade has always been a popular meeting place, and there will often be knots of Ukrainians having earnest and occasionally heated discussions around the **statue of Taras Shevchenko**. The old town is just to the east, and you can reach it by turning left off Prospekt Svobody after the monument to the Polish poet **Adam Mickiewicz**. This brings you to Lviv's **Katolytsky Sobor** (Roman Catholic Cathedral), whose tower is one of the city's most distinctive landmarks. Construction began here soon after the city first fell under Polish control in the mid-14th century, although much of the intricate interior work is more recent. Be sure to visit also the exquisitely carved **Boyim chapel**, built by a wealthy Hungarian merchant in the 17th century, just across from the cathedral on the opposite side from the tower.

Just past the cathedral you enter the elegant **Ploshcha Rynok** (Market Square), with the 19th-century building of the Lviv town hall in its centre. Soviet power always sat uneasily in this part of Ukraine, and when controls were relaxed in the 1980s the local authorities in Lviv were at the forefront of calls for an end to the totalitarian system. The fate of the Lenin statue, invari-

For souvenir shopping in Lviv, go to the open-air arts and crafts market in the square behind the Ukrainian Drama Theatre, to the right of the opera house.

BELOW: Opera and Ballet Theatre, Lviv.

Hapsburg influence: Lviv's Grand Hotel.

BELOW:
flower sellers
in Lviv market.

ably a useful barometer of local opinion, is instructive: it had been removed from its perch in front of the Opera already in September 1990, the first such instance in the entire Soviet Union.

To the east of Ploshcha Rynok, along Vulitsya Ruska, you can see the three-tiered bell tower of **Uspenska Tserkva** (Renaissance Uspensky Church), the traditional focus of the local Orthodox community, with the delicate **Kaplitsya Trox Svyatyteliv** (Three Saints Chapel) clinging to its base. Next door to the north is the dome of **Kostol Dominikana** (Roman Catholic Dominican Church). It was the meeting of these two faiths, when parts of Orthodox Rus came under Polish Catholic control, that produced the hybrid Ukrainian Catholic (known also as Greek Catholic or Uniate) Church in the 16th century. Under the Union of Brest-Litovsk in 1596 parts of the Ukrainian church agreed to unite with Rome as long as they be allowed to keep their traditional Orthodox rites. The concessions to Rome were bitterly opposed by many Orthodox believers, and as the region came under Russian and then Soviet control, so Ukrainian Catholics were subject to campaigns of forced conversion and persecution. In 1946 a fraudulent synod even proclaimed their formal "union" with Russian Orthodoxy, but priests in western Ukraine continued to minister in secret.

In the autumn of 1989 a quarter of a million Ukrainian Catholics demonstrated in Lviv for the legalisation of their faith, and in 1990 the spiritual centre of Ukrainian Catholicism, **Sobor Svyatoho Yura** (St George's Cathedral) in Lviv, was returned to them. This baroque cathedral is 20 minutes' walk to the west of the old town on **Ploshcha Svyatoho Yura** (St George's Square).

Lviv is the major city of western Ukraine, but by no means its only attraction, and the Carpathians and the regions to the southwest are fascinating areas to explore. This is the historic borderland between populations – eastern Slavs, western Slavs, Romanians and Hungarians – and empires, and every place presents its own mix of cultures. The Soviets arrived only with the outbreak of World War II, and towns such as **Uzhhorod** and **Chernivtsi** ❹ have kept much of their inheritance from the Hapsburgs, as well as from the inter-war period when they formed part of Czechoslovakia and Romania respectively.

Chernivtsi, the main city of the historic region of Bukovina, was developed by the Austrians after being ceded to them in 1775 by the retreating Ottomans. **Teatr Musyky ta Dramy** (Music and Drama Theatre) was a gift from the Hapsburg monarchy, and designed by the same Viennese architects who had built the opera in Odessa 20 years earlier. The late-19th-century palace, now the main university building, is an intriguing blend of architectural styles. Further to the west, as the road from Chernivtsi to Kamyanets-Podilsky crosses the Dniester river, is the beautifully reconstructed fortress at **Khotyn** ❺, which served as the stronghold of successive local powers from the Kievan Rus principality of Galicia to the Cossacks and the Poles.

Map on page 310

Ukraine's national anthem begins with the rather curious line "Ukraine is not dead yet", only comprehensible in the context of the country's long and difficult history.

The Black Sea port of Odessa

A visit to the southern lands along the Black Sea coast introduces a new cast of characters, including ancient Greeks, Crimean Tatars, Genoese traders and even French noblemen, to the story of Ukraine. **Odessa** ❻ and Crimea were not part of the territory of Kievan Rus, and were conquered by the Russian Empire as the armies of Catherine the Great moved south at the end of the 18th century.

In May 1794, the Russian empress moved to consolidate her gains by founding a port on the site of a coastal village called Khadzhibei. The new town

BELOW: choir in full voice, Armenian Church, Chernivtsi.

took its name from the ancient Greek settlement of Odessos, which was wrongly supposed to be nearby, and quickly grew into a thriving commercial centre. Even during the Soviet period Odessa retained the open outlook of a port city, and its natives take credit for the country's funniest jokes and most popular songs. Long stretches of sandy beach (away from the city but accessible by boat or public transport) and plenty of local restaurateurs also make it a very popular place to relax.

TIP

If the accommodation in Odessa itself does not match up to what you are looking for, there are often hotel ships moored in the port at the bottom of Potemkin Steps.

A tour of Odessa begins on the majestic terrace of **Prymorsky Bulvar Ⓐ**, by the statue to the city's first governor the **Duke de Richelieu**. It was under his progressive administration that Odessa was transformed in the early 19th century, and after the duke's return to France in 1814 (where he become prime minister after the defeat of Napoleon) a city honoured him with a spot overlooking one of Odessa's most treasured symbols, the **Potyomkinskaya Lestnitsa** (Potemkin Steps) Ⓑ. Built between 1837–41 they were immortalised in Eisenstein's classic film about the 1905 Russian Revolution, *The Battleship Potemkin*. The steps are best seen from below, without the discordant backdrop of the modern sea port, and from where the unique tapered design – the bottom step is 9 metres (30 ft) wider than the top – plays tricks with the perspective.

Arriving back at the top of the steps turn left along the boulevard, past the plush **Hotel Londonska**, towards the **statue of Pushkin Ⓒ**. The famous Russian poet spent a year of exile in Odessa, 1823–24, keeping himself busy by starting work on his epic poem *Evgene Onegin* and also by having an affair with the wife of Count Vorontsov, the new governor. Nearby is a cannon captured from the British frigate *Tiger*, a trophy from the Crimean War claimed during an Anglo-French naval assault on the city in 1854.

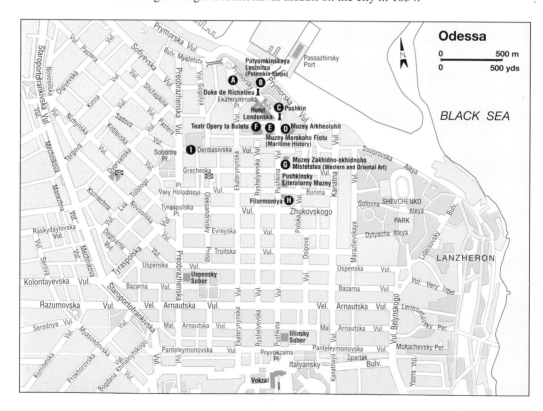

The road heading away from the seafront is **Pushkina Vulitsya** and immediately on your left you come to the **Muzey Arkheolohii** (Museum of Archaeology) **D**, which has a fine collection of relics from the early civilisations that lived around the Black Sea (open 10am–5pm, closed Mon). Opposite, behind the **Muzey Morskoho Flotu** (Museum of Maritime History **E**; open 10am–6pm, closed Thurs), is the marvellously ornate late-19th-century **Teatr Opery ta Baletu** (Opera and Ballet Theatre) **F**, whose style is a blend of Italian Renaissance, Viennese and classical baroque. Music lovers may also like to wander further down Pushkina Vulitsya, past the **Muzey Zakhidno-skhidnoho Mistetstva** (Museum of Western and Oriental Art **G**; open 11am–4.30pm, closed Wed) to the **Filarmoniya** (Philharmonia) **H**, where the Odessa Philharmonic Orchestra has been given a new lease of life under the energetic direction of their American conductor, Hobart Earle.

The central street of Odessa, which crosses Pushkina Vulitsya past the Opera, is another reminder of French influence over the early city. De Ribas masterminded the military campaign which won this part of the coast from the Turks in the late 18th century, and **Deribasivska Vulitsya** **I** was named in his honour. The street is one of Odessa's most vibrant, best enjoyed in the summer from one of the many bars and cafés that spill out onto the pavements. From here, Vulitsya Ekaterynynska takes you back down towards the Potemkin steps.

Crimea peninsula

The **Crimea peninsula** **7**, jutting out into the Black Sea, contains the most dramatic scenery in Ukraine, where the steppe finally gives way to three parallel ranges of limestone mountains along the rocky southern coast. Its strategic

Maps:
Area 310
City 322

BELOW: Prymorsky Bulvar, Odessa.

Map
on page
310

importance for control of the Black Sea has made it a prize that is still disputed, and generations of settlers and conquerors arriving from all points of the compass have left their mark on the landscape.

Yalta 8, the main resort of the Crimea, has been the favoured retreat of the Russian elite ever since the imperial family began resting at nearby Livadia in the 1860s. It has a magical reputation across the former Soviet Union for its sunshine, fine wine and fine living, so much so that some locals interpret the very act of arrival as an implicit surrender of the right to get value for money. Nonetheless, it is an exceptional location and an evening stroll along the waterfront remains a wonderfully un-Soviet experience.

Just outside the town to the west is the **Livadyysky Dvovets** (Palace of Livadia) **9** which was built in 1911 for Nicholas II. In February 1945, it hosted the conference of Allied leaders – Stalin, Churchill and Roosevelt – which became synonymous with the post-war division of Europe after Stalin failed to keep a promise to hold free elections in the countries of central and eastern Europe. The ground floor of the palace is devoted to an exhibition about the conference, and upstairs is a series of rooms taking you back to its tsarist past (open 8am–7.30pm June–October; 9am–4.30pm rest of year). A little further along the coast is the **Lastochkino Gnezdo** (Swallow's Nest). The castle, balancing on a promontory and now containing an Italian restaurant, is best reached by the regular boat service from Yalta.

The city of **Sevastopol 10**, which until 1996 was closed to foreigners, offers a completely different set of attractions. Still home to the Russian Black Sea Fleet, which leases bays and infrastructure from the Ukrainians, Sevastopol has a record of heroic resistance to sieges in both the Crimean War and then during World War II, commemorated in various monuments and the vast 115-metre (377-ft) panorama hall.

Southwest of the city are the ruins of the ancient Greek colony of **Chersonesus**, founded in 421 BC, and where the Kievan prince Volodymyr the Great is said to have been baptised in 988.

The Greeks were not the only Mediterranean settlers along the shores of the Crimea. Genoa's alliance with Constantinople – the Treaty of Ninfeo of 1261 – opened up the Black Sea area to the Italian city state, and the Genoese set up large trading posts in Kaffa, now **Feodosiya 11** and **Sudak 12** in eastern Crimea which grew rich on commerce along the Silk Route to China and Central Asia. City defences from these times remain, and the walls and towers of the fortress overlooking Sudak have been completely restored.

The fate of the Genoese was sealed in 1453 when Constantinople fell to Mehmed II. Their trade now had to pass through the Turkish-controlled straits, and by 1475 an alliance of Ottoman Turks and Crimean Tatars had squeezed them off the peninsula. The Tatars, settlers who from the times of the Golden Horde, agreed to Ottoman suzerainty and continued to control the Crimea until the Russian conquests of the 18th century. The seat of their khanate was in the town of **Bakhchysaray 13** and the Khan's Palace, originally built in 1519, is a poetic reminder of the diversity of Crimean history. ❏

BELOW: Russian Orthodox Church in Yalta, Crimea.
RIGHT: boat trip on the Black Sea.

EXPLORING THE CRIMEAN COAST

Even with its fading tourist infrastructure, the Crimea is still the best choice for seeing the sunnier side of Ukraine

The Crimea has almost everything you could ask for in a tourist destination: dramatic mountains plunging down to the sea, a tropical climate, a remarkable and rich history. The only piece missing has been the tourist industry itself, which adapted very quickly to Western price levels after 1991, but had more problems with delivering similar levels of service and accommodation. This has already begun to change, and a fascinating region is now navigable for the foreign traveller. The naval base of Sevastopol was opened up to foreigners in 1996, and a brief tour along the coast towards Yalta is enough to illustrate the variety of Crimea's attractions.

EXCURSIONS AWAY FROM THE COAST

Just outside Sevastopol, the ruins of the ancient Greek colony of Chersonesus lead on towards the port of Balaklava, in whose defence the Light Brigade was decimated during the Crimean War. Foros, with its nine-domed church high on the cliffs above you, is where Gorbachev was held captive in his *dacha* during the failed putsch of 1991, and from there it is not far across the vineyards to the Russian aristocratic palaces at Alupka and Livadia.

Visitors to Crimea will find that interest is not limited to the coastal areas. Inland, near the Tatar palace at Bakhchysaray, is the cave city of Chufut-Kale, inhabited from the 6th to the mid-19th centuries in turn by Christians, Muslim Tatars and Karaite Jews.

◁ **ANCIENT AND MODERN**
Yalta's 19th-century churches draw their inspiration from past ties with Armenia and the Byzantine Empire.

△ **CRIMEAN TATARS**
The resting place of the former rulers of the Crimea, the Tatar khans, is their "garden palace" at Bakhchysaray.

◁ GREATER YALTA
Hemmed in by the Black Sea and the soaring Crimean mountains, the modern resort town of Yalta now stretches out across the slopes that lead up from the pebbly beaches and the town's seafront.

△ BEACH LIFE
From June until September, Crimea's beaches are packed with Ukrainians and Russians of all ages, shapes and sizes. The best and sandiest beaches can be found around Yevpatoriya and Feodosiya.

HEADING FOR THE HILLS

The Crimea attracts climbers and hikers from across Europe and beyond, and offers some spectacular trails along its mountainous southern coast. There are some English-language walking guides – Frith Maier's *Trekking in Russia and Central Asia* has a chapter covering Crimea – but it is always worth asking locally for guidance on the most suitable routes and campsites. For day trips around Yalta there is good walking around the Uchansu waterfall and Lake Karagol, both just off the mountain road to Bakhchysaray. For a stroll through a vast variety of Crimean flora, try the Nikitsky Botanical Gardens, accessible by boat and road 5 km (3 miles) to the east of Yalta on the way over towards Hurzuf.

▽ SOVIET STYLE
Members of the Soviet élite knew how to relax in style. Brezhnev used to take his holidays in this delightful lodge near Yalta.

▷ FORTIFICATIONS
Feodosiya has long been a fortified city, and parts of the defences from 13th-century Genoese trading posts survive to this day.

▷ HOME COOKING
Some of the best food in Ukraine comes from the family oven and an invitation to dinner should not be refused.

INSIGHT GUIDES

TRAVEL TIPS

Simply travelling safely

American Express Travellers Cheques

- are recognised as one of the safest and most convenient ways to protect your money when travelling abroad

- are more widely accepted than any other travellers cheque brand

- are available in eleven currencies

- are supported by a 24 hour worldwide refund service and

- a 24 hour Express Helpline service provides assistance and information when travelling abroad

- are accepted in millions of shops, hotels and restaurants throughout the world

Travellers Cheques

CONTENTS

Getting Acquainted

RUSSIA

Area 17.1 million sq km (6.6 million sq miles). Land boundaries: 20,139 sq km (12,514 miles). Coastline: 37,653 km (23,397 miles).
Population 147.8 million (growth rate –0.001%).
Ethnic mix Russian 81.5%, Tatar 3.8%, Ukrainian 3%, Chuvash 1.2%, Bashkir 0.9%, Belarusian 0.8%, Moldavian 0.7%, others 8.1%.
Major languages Russian.
Government Russia is a federation consisting of 89 regions. It adopted a new constitution in December 1993.
Capital city Moscow (pop. 9 million).
Communications 893,000 km (555,000 miles) of roads, 145,000 km (90,050 miles) of railways. Number of airports with permanent surface runways: 565.

Climate

Russia spans a range of climatic zones, from the arctic tundra of northern Siberia to the steppes of Central Asia. Almost everywhere is extremely cold in winter, the exception being a small area along the Black Sea coast, where January temperatures remain above freezing. By contrast, most places average around -20°C (-4°F), with the cold intensifying to the northeast. In northeast Siberia, winter temperatures are usually somewhere near -50°C (-57°F), and have been known to plummet as low as -68°C (-90°F). The Pacific coast, European Russia, Belarus and Ukraine are milder; Moscow has January daytime temperatures of around -9°C (16°F), St Petersburg -7°C (19°F).

Most of the country experiences warm summers, the exceptions being the arctic north and the Pacific coasts, where cold ocean currents keep temperatures down. Across much of Siberia summer daytime values are around 20°C (68°F), but can sometimes rise to 38°C (100°F). In Moscow, July daytime temperatures average 23°C (73°F), but vary widely from year to year. Southern Russia and Ukraine have hotter and more humid summers. Most of Russia has a summer maximum of rainfall, with thunderstorms common in early summer. Eastern regions are drier.

Mountain areas include the Carpathian mountains in Western Ukraine and the Caucasus, where the climate is broadly similar to that of the Alps, albeit with colder winters.

Economy

Although Russia is a vast country with a wealth of natural resources, a well-educated population, and a diverse industrial base, it has found it difficult to shift the emphasis from the old centrally planned economy to a market driven one.

Under the current regime, it has made some progress towards a market economy by freeing most prices, slashing defence spending, unifying foreign exchange rates, and launching an ambitious privatisation programme. But output has fallen and unemployment has risen (to as many as 4 million, according to unofficial estimates).

Political instability and the inherent dependence on the international development effort has lead to periods of hyper-inflation and devaluation of the rouble. Poor management of the privatisation plan and the concentration of power and money in a few hands exacerbates the situation.

The crime rate has increased with the influence of the Russian mafia being felt in many areas. Some, with justification, refer to modern Russia as the "Wild West".

Industries include the complete range of mining and extractive activities producing coal, oil, gas, chemicals and metals; all forms of machine building from rolling mills to high-performance aircraft and space vehicles; shipbuilding; road and rail transportation equipment; communications equipment; agricultural machinery, tractors, and construction equipment; electric power generating and transmitting equipment; medical and scientific instruments; and consumer durables.

The main agricultural products are grain, sugar beet, sunflower seeds, meat, milk and vegetables.

Time Zones

Russia has eight time zones. Moscow and St Petersburg are three hours ahead of Greenwich Mean Time. Moscow time is adopted nearly everywhere west of the Urals.

When it is 3pm in Moscow, it is 5pm in Yekaterinburg, 7pm in Novosibirsk, 8pm in Irkutsk, 9pm in Chita, and 10pm in Vladivostok.

By then, the inhabitants of Petropavlovsk-Kamchatsky on the far eastern Kamchatka Peninsula have just started a new day and the polar bears on the frozen Chukchi Sea in the far northeast are already an hour into the new day. Moscow time is shown on the station clocks along the Trans–Siberian Railway.

Religion

In Russia and the eastern region of the Ukraine and Belarus, the Russian Orthodox Church is the most influential faith. Western regions of Ukraine and Belarus are more influenced by the Roman Catholic Church.

Baptists, Adventists and other Protestant branches are also quite influential, though under attack from nationalist elements in the political and religious establishment.

Islam is the main faith in the Caucasus and among the Tatar population of the lower and middle Volga. Many Jews have emigrated and there are fewer than 100 synagogues. Buddhism is practised by the Buryats near Lake Baikal and the Kalmyks of the lower Volga.

BELARUS

Area 207,600 sq. km (80,150 sq. miles). Land boundaries: total 3,098 km (1,925 miles). Coastline: none.
Population 10.4 million. Growth rate: 0.3%.
Ethnic mix Belarusian 78%, Russian 13%, Polish 4%, Ukrainian 3%, Jewish 1%, other 1%.
Major languages Russian, Belarusian.
Government Independent republic. The constitution adopted in 1996 has not been recognised as legitimate by the West.
Capital city Minsk (pop. 1.7 million).
Communications 98,200 km (61,000 miles) of roads, 5,570 km (3,460 miles) of railways.
Climate Mild continental. Average temperatures: January –7°C (20°F); July 17°C (63°F).
Time zone Minsk time is GMT plus 2 hours.
Religion Mainly Russian Orthodox.

Economy

Belarus, one of the better developed former Soviet states, has a diverse machine building sector and a healthy agriculture sector. It also serves as a transport link for Russian oil exports to the Baltic states and Eastern and Western Europe. Compared with Russia, there has been very little privatisation and the state still plays a large part in the economy. High inflation was one of the consequences of independence and harsh austerity measures were introduced to combat it. Belarus's principal exports are machinery and transport equipment, chemicals and foodstuffs.

UKRAINE

Area 603,700 sq. km (233,100 sq. miles). Land boundaries: total 4,558 km (2,832 miles). Coastline: 2,782 km (1,729 miles).
Population 50.7 million.
Ethnic mix Ukrainian 73%, Russian 22%, other 5%.
Major languages Ukrainian is the official language; Russian is still widely spoken.
Government Independent republic. A new constitution was adopted in 1996.
Capital city Kicv (pop 2.6 million).
Communications 273,700 km (170,000 miles) of roads, 23,350 km (14,500 miles) of railroads.
Climate mild continental, closer to sub-tropical along the southern Crimean coast. Average temperatures: January –7°C (20°F) in the northeast, 4°C (40°F) on the Crimean coast; July 19°C (66°F) in the northeast, 25°C (77°F) on the Crimean coast.
Time zone Kiev time is GMT plus 2 hours

Economy

Ukraine's economy had been second only to Russia's within the former Soviet Union, producing more than three times the output of the next-ranking republic. Its fertile black soil generated more than a quarter of Soviet agricultural output, its farms provided meat, milk, grain and vegetables to other republics, and its diversified heavy industry supplied equipment and raw materials to industrial and mining sites. Following independence, it suffered the same economic cycle as Russia, with high inflation, countered by austerity measures leading to a decline in industrial output. This hampered its intended privatisation programme.

Planning the Trip

What to Bring

Clothing

Today Russia, Belarus and Ukraine are are visited by people from many different countries with many different styles of dress. You may dress as you would normally dress at home.

Coming to Russia, Belarus and Ukraine in the cold months (November to March), you should not be surprised to meet temperatures of 25° to 30°C below zero (–13°F to –22°F) and will need to dress accordingly, not forgetting a hat and gloves. It's best to dress in layers of clothing to cope with the variations in temperature between the frozen outdoors and the centrally-heated indoors. Waterproof shoes are a necessity in winter, since the legendary Russian frost is often interrupted by periods of thaw. For business meetings, formal dress is obligatory. The dress code is as rigorously enforced as in the West and compliance is an important matter of status.

Electricity

Electrical current in tourist hotels is normally 220 V AC, but don't count on it. In some remote places you will also find 127 V. Sockets require a continental-type two-pin plug. It is best to take adaptors with you.

Money Matters

RUSSIA

It used to be the case that most financial transactions undertaken by tourists were made in foreign currencies. This situation has

Visas and Passports

Russia

You will need a valid passport, an official application form, confirmation of your hotel reservations (for business travellers and tourists) and three passport photographs, to obtain your visa from a Russian embassy or consulate. If you apply personally, rather than through a travel agency, allow ample time, as it might take a month or so.

According to new regulations, this term can be shortened to 48 hours if an applicant is a business traveller, or if he or she has an officially recognised invitation (telex, fax and email are accepted) from a Russian host. However, fees for this express service are correspondingly higher, reflecting the convenience.

The visa is not stamped into the passport, but produced as a separate sheet of paper consisting of three sections. The first part is removed on entry to the country, and the last is taken out on leaving the country. You are obliged to have your passport and visa registered within three days of arrival, failure to do so may result in a heavy fine upon departure.

There are transit visas (for up to 48 hours), tourist, ordinary and multiple entry visas (for two or more visits).

If you go to Russia on the invitation of relatives or friends, you will get a visa for a private journey which presupposes that no hotel reservation is needed. Independent tourists should organise their trip through an Intourist accredited agent or their Russian hosts. They need an itinerary, listing in detail, times, places and overnight reservations.

It is sensible to carry your passport and visa at all times while you are in Russia, since the police have the right to check your identity at will. Without them you may be asked to go to a police station and you might be prohibited from entering your

hotel, the embassy of your country and many other places.

Hotels will give you a hotel card that serves as a permit to enter the hotel and use its restaurant and currency-exchange office.

Belarus

Visas are issued by Belarusian embassies abroad provided that you can produce evidence of an official invitation or confirmation of booked accommodation through Belintourist (the Belarusian equivalent of Intourist), or a sponsor. Travellers who do not have a visa cannot register at any hotel. Visas are not issued on arrival and airlines have instructions not to board anyone without a visa. Fees fluctuate wildly. Transit visas are issued on the train to people who have a Russian visa and are travelling to Moscow via Belarus.

Ukraine

A valid passport and visa are required. Visas are obtained from Ukrainian embassies or consulates worldwide. A letter of invitation from a person, company, or organisation in Ukraine or a tour company voucher is required to obtain a visa.

Travellers from countries where there is a Ukrainian embassy or consulate cannot obtain visas at airports or border crossings. Travellers must therefore ensure that the proper visa is obtained before arriving in Ukraine. Travellers who intend to visit Russia from Ukraine must also have a Russian visa. All visitors must register on arrival with the local law enforcement authorities.

For those travelling from Kiev to Moscow, it is now possible to pick up transit visas to Russia from the Russian Embassy in Kiev, but it is still advisable to arrange all Russian visas before arriving in Kiev. People have been charged more than $350 for trying to leave Moscow on a Ukrainian visa.

completely changed. It is illegal to make payments in foreign currencies; they should be made in roubles or with credit cards. A new rouble (worth 1,000 old roubles) was introduced in January 1998.

There is no limit to the import of hard currency, but the sum must be declared on entry. The amount exported should not exceed the amount declared when entering the country. If you are carrying less than US$500 you may enter the country via the Green Corridor at Moscow's Sheremyetovo airport. Unspent roubles should be changed back into hard currency before you leave the country.

The black market has largely disappeared as there are many banks and exchange points. Do compare rates before changing currency, as they vary considerably.

All large hotels have an official exchange counter where you can buy roubles with hard currency cash, travellers' cheques and credit cards. You will need your customs declaration form, on which all your money transactions must be recorded. Keep this form as you will need to show it when leaving the country.

ATMS These can be found in major cities on main thoroughfares and at central metro stations.

Credit cards Most tourist-related businesses and restaurants accept major credit cards.

BELARUS

The currency is the Belarusian Rubel (BR). The exchange rate has fluctuated considerably in recent years; in autumn 1998 the official rate stood at around 55,000 BR to the US dollar, the unofficial or "street" rate was more than 100,000.

Travellers' cheques are not widely accepted. Most tourist hotels accept either American Express or Visa credit cards. The Planeta Hotel in Minsk provides cash from Visa and credit cards during business hours, but ATMS are not generally in use in Belarus.

More colour
for the world.

HDCplus. New perspectives in colour photography.

http://www.agfaphoto.com

AGFA

Probably the <u>most</u> <u>important</u> TRAVEL TIP you will ever receive

Before you travel abroad, make sure that you and your family are protected from diseases that can cause serious health problems.

For instance, you can pick up *hepatitis A* which infects 10 million people worldwide every year (it's not just a disease of poorer countries) simply through consuming contaminated food or water!

What's more, in many countries if you have an accident needing medical treatment, or even dental treatment, you could also be at risk of infection from *hepatitis B* which is 100 times more infectious than AIDS, and can lead to liver cancer.

The good news is, you can be protected by vaccination against these and other serious diseases, such as *typhoid*, *meningitis* and *yellow fever*.

Travel safely! Check with your doctor at least 8 weeks before you go, to discover whether or not you need protection.

Consult your doctor before you go... not when you return!

SmithKline Beecham

V A C C I N E S

Produced as a service to public health

UKRAINE

In late 1996, Ukrainians introduced the hryvna to replace a temporary currency – the karbovanets (which means rouble in Ukrainian). After being stable for two years at around 3.2 hryvna to the UK pound and 2 hryvna to the US dollar, the currency lost value in the financial crisis of 1998.

Ukraine has a cash economy, but travellers' cheques and credit cards are gaining wider acceptance in larger cities. Use of credit cards is limited to better hotels, tourist-restaurants, international airlines and select stores. Changing US dollars or any other currency is legal only at banks, currency exchange desks at hotels, and at licensed exchange booths.

Getting There

RUSSIA

Until recently, foreigners could only enter Russia through special entry points whose number could be counted on the fingers of one hand. Although today the number of these "doors" is virtually unchanged, all the procedures, including customs formalities, are much simpler.

By Air

More than 30 international airlines connect Moscow's Sheremetyevo II airport with the rest of the world. Flights take about nine to 10 hours from New York, four hours from London, Paris and Rome; from Frankfurt it takes three hours, two hours from Stockholm, six from Delhi and eight hours from Peking.

In addition to Moscow, some international carriers also fly to Pulkovo-2 in St Petersburg and some are now increasing their coverage to include towns such as Nizhny Novgorod, Saratov and Yekaterinburg.

Aeroflot's destinations include Anchorage, Chicago, London, Los Angeles, Miami, Montreal, New York, San Francisco, Seattle, Shannon (Ireland), Stockholm and Washington DC.

By Sea

Several Russian ports accept international passenger liners. St Petersburg on the Baltic Sea is connected with London, Helsinki, Gothenburg, Stockholm and Oslo. Nakhodka, on the Japan Sea coast, is connected with Yokohama in Japan, Hong Kong, Singapore and Sydney, Australia. Additional information about sea routes, schedules and bookings can be obtained from travel agencies, Russian tourist agencies or Morflot.

By Rail

Railways are the most important means of passenger transport within Russia and connect the largest cities (Moscow, St Petersburg, Kiev, Minsk) with Western European capitals. Visitors who have the time can travel in a comfortable first-class sleeping-wagon (SV), the pride of the Russian railways.

Passengers in transit through Belarus to Russia do not need a Belarus visa, but those in transit through Ukraine need a Ukrainian transit visa, which must be obtained before departure. A double-transit visa is needed if the return journey is on the same route.

From Western Europe the train takes two to three days to Moscow, with a change of gauge on reaching Russia.

The most popular rail routes for international traffic are Helsinki to St Petersburg (departing 1pm and arriving at 9pm) and Helsinki to Moscow (departing 5pm and arriving at 9.30am the next morning).

By Road

During the past few years marked changes have taken place in the quality of services along Russian roads. Moscow now has new service and repair stations for non-Russian cars. However, you should still be cautious of travelling through Russia by car. It can be dangerous and road borders take hours to cross due to delays at customs. Outside towns petrol stations are, on average, 100 km (60 miles) apart.

You can bring your own car by sea through St Petersburg, Tallinn in Estonia, Odessa on the Black Sea and Nakhodka in the Far East.

There are no international bus lines direct to Russia, but specially organised bus tours operate from the UK, Germany and Finland.

BELARUS

By Air

Lufthansa was first off the mark with flights to Minsk from Frankfurt, and Austrian Airlines fly from Vienna. Polish Airlines also fly to Minsk. The national carrier, Belarus, flies to most Western European capitals and major US cities. British Airways now fly five times a week from Gatwick.

By Rail

In addition to the traditional rail links with Russia, there is an overnight train from Tallinn, Estonia.

Public Holidays in Russia

- **January** New Year's Day (1); Russian Orthodox Christmas Day (7).
- **February** Defenders of the Motherland Day (23).
- **March** International Women's Day (8).
- **May** Victory Day (9).
- **June** Russian Independence Day (12)
- **November** Great October Socialist Revolution Anniversary (7).

UKRAINE

By Air

Kiev can now be reached through an increasing number of Western airlines. There are flights from most Western European capitals, with Austrian Air, Swissair, KLM, British Airways and Lufthansa among the regular flyers. Air Ukraine International also has connections to the main European cities.

The main airport, Borispil, is a 40–minute car journey from Kiev city centre. Austrian Air and Lufthansa also fly direct to Odessa.

By Rail

A slower option is to take the train. From Moscow, Kiev is only a night's ride away. In the evening trains depart almost every half–hour from Moscow's Kiev station. From the West, Kiev is on the main train routes from south Central Europe.

By Sea

Odessa on the Black Sea is on the itinerary of liners travelling from many European ports, with the most regular services being to Istanbul.

Customs

When entering Russia you must fill in the customs declaration. It must be returned to the customs office, along with another customs declaration which you fill in on leaving the country.

Russian customs regulations have been revised several times in the last few years. Customs authorities want to find a compromise between conforming to international standards of customs regulations and preventing the export of large batches of cheap goods bought in Russian shops for resale in other countries.

The latest edition of the Russian customs regulations prohibits the import and export of weapons and ammunition (excluding approved hunting tackle), and also drugs and devices for their use. It is prohibited to export antiquities and art objects except for those imported and declared on entry.

As customs regulations change frequently, it is best to check with the Russian consulate or embassy in your home country about restrictions and limitations before travelling.

A 30 percent duty is required to export any personal items worth more than $10,000. Export duties may be imposed on any items which are determined by customs officials at the point of departure to be of commercial use. Certain items,

such as caviar, medications, jewellery, precious and semi-precious stones or metals and fuel may be exported duty-free in limited amounts only.

Computers, electronic notebooks and related hardware must be presented for scanning at the airport at least two hours prior to departure.

Samovars, carpets from Central Asia and icons often carry export restrictions requiring you to have them priced by the Ministry of Culture. If export permission is given, a 100 percent export duty on the estimated value is often applied upon departure.

In Ukraine, you are exempt from customs formalities if you are carrying less than US$1,000 (or equivalent) and less that US$250 worth of jewellery and valuables. Otherwise you have to fill in a declaration.

Health Regulations

Visitors from the US, Canada, European countries and Japan do not need a health certificate, but vaccinations against tetanus and diphtheria are recommended. It is also advisable to be inoculated against Hepatitis A. Visitors from regions suspected to be infected by yellow fever, especially some African and South American territories, require an international certificate of vaccination against yellow fever. Travellers who intend to stay in Russia or Belarus for more than 90 days, or Russian visitors who have multiple entry visas, must have a certificate showing that they are HIV negative.

Practical Tips

Security

Don't carry all your cash in one place, and avoid displaying large sums of money. Be especially careful while buying souvenirs from street vendors – thieves may be watching to see where you keep your money. Tuck your bag and camera firmly under your arm while shopping. The rule to observe is to behave sensibly and be aware that street crime here is as rife as it is in any big city in the world.

Unless you've acquired adequate conversational Russian, it's a good idea to carry a card which says, in Russian, where you are staying and the telephone number. If you get lost, seek assistance in any western-standard hotel where they are likely to speak English, or hail a taxi and show the driver the card.

When travelling by train always try and book in advance, never buy tickets from the casual person apparently returning an unwanted ticket at the railway station, and ensure that your ticket reflects your passport details as you will be required to show it to the conductor.

In both Russia and Ukraine, incidences of crime against foreigners have increased in recent years. Belarus is safer to visit, although common street crime is still a problem especially at night and in or near hotels frequented by foreigners. Be sure to lock your door securely if on an overnight sleeper train.

Road Safety

Many Russian drivers are reckless, so don't expect them always to stop if you misjudge when crossing the road – they'll expect you to jump

When you're
bitten by the travel bug,
make sure you're protected.

Check into a British Airways Travel Clinic.

British Airways Travel Clinics provide travellers with:

- A complete vaccination service and essential travel health-care items
- Up-dated travel health information and advice

Call **01276 685040** for details of your nearest Travel Clinic.

BRITISH AIRWAYS
TRAVEL CLINICS

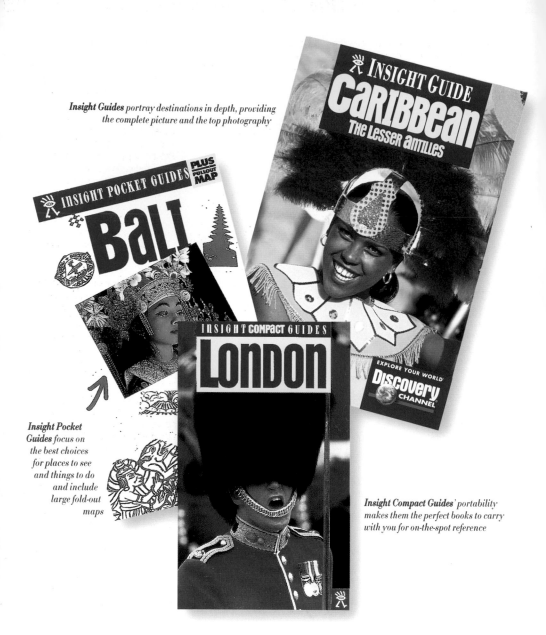

Insight Guides portray destinations in depth, providing the complete picture and the top photography

Insight Pocket Guides focus on the best choices for places to see and things to do and include large fold-out maps

Insight Compact Guides' portability makes them the perfect books to carry with you for on-the-spot reference

Three types of guide for all types of travel

INSIGHT GUIDES Different people need different kinds of information. Some want *background information* to help them prepare for the trip. Others seek *personal recommendations* from someone who knows the destination well. And others look for *compactly presented data* for on-the-spot reference. With three carefully designed series, Insight Guides offer readers the perfect choice. Insight Guides will turn your visit into an experience.

The world's largest collection of visual travel guides

out of their way and are likely to hit you if you don't understand this convention. Unfortunately, even drivers who have a licence may not be that experienced or safe on the roads so when hailing a cab try to stop a registered taxi: in Moscow the taxis are easily recognisable by their bright yellow, New York-style cab colour.

While walking, be aware of a traditional Russian hazard still very much in evidence: the manhole without a cover. And don't expect heavy doors, typical of the underground, to have dampers fitted – they're likely to swing towards you with enough force to knock you off your feet.

Medical Treatment

Apteki (pharmacies) in the major cities are usually well-stocked with domestic and imported medicines, although in times of financial crisis they may be short of foreign medicines. Most pharmacists will understand the English pronunciation of a drug, not brand names. If you need special medication it is best to bring it with you. Doctors and hospitals often expect immediate cash payment for

health services. Medical insurance is essential, preferably with supplementary medical insurance with specific overseas coverage, which includes repatriation.

Pharmacies in Moscow
American Medical Center Drugstore
Shmitovsky Proyezd
tel: (095) 956 3366
Drugstore
Sadko Arcade Krasno–gvardeysky Proyezd
tel: (095) 253 9592
Anna Import–Export NV
Priyutsky Per.3
tel: (095) 978 1073
Dina–Medica
Kashirskoye Shosse 44/1
tel: (095) 323 6510
Diplomatic Polyclinic Drugstore
Dobryninsky 4th Pereulok 4
tel: (095) 237 4034
Eczacibasi Drugstore
Ulitsa Maroseyka 2/15
tel: (095) 928 9189, 921 4048
International Pharmacy
Ulitsa Kozhevnicheskaya 13
tel: (095) 235 7583
Pharmacy Central Enquiry Office
tel: (095) 927 0561

Take Precautions
It is recommended that you wash fruit and raw vegetables before you eat them. Likewise, you should not drink unfamiliar tap water because a different and unfamiliar mineral composition can easily produce an upset stomach. It is particularly important not to drink St Petersburg's tap water, even in small quantities. Bottled mineral water is available everywhere.

Be careful when buying alcohol from kiosks. It's been known for brand-name bottles to be emptied of their original contents and refilled with homebrew of dubious quality.

Doctors
Your hotel service bureau will find a doctor to come to your hotel room or will refer you to the nearest clinic. Medical standards in Russia are good and in the big cities there are specialists available for every kind of illness. Medicines and hospital treatment must be paid for in roubles.

In Moscow, the following hospitals offer good levels of service:
International Medical Centre
Grokholsky Pereulok, 31, 10th floor
tel: (095) 280 8374 or 280 8388

St Petersburg Police Alert

Crime should be the least of your worries when visiting St Petersburg – according to official statistics, very few crimes are committed against foreigners. The "crime-fighters", however, *are* a cause for concern. A growing number of innocent foreigners have been harassed and beaten by the local police.

In general, Russians accept police brutality as a part of life since there are few controls on the police force, which is a federal ministry, and the local civil rights organisations are still quite weak.

The St Petersburg police force (*militsia*) is considered, even by its own leadership in Moscow, to be one of the most corrupt and inefficient forces in Russia. The

problems all begin with a routine document check in the street. According to law, all Russians are required to carry their internal passport with them at all times, while foreigners, too, are supposed to carry their passport. In most cases, those stopped by the police are allowed to go if their documents are in order. If not, or if they are not carrying their passport, or if they are even slightly drunk, then the police can take them to the station. Many of those detained are beaten and robbed.

Practical Advice If you see police walking down the street, cross to the opposite side. If you are stopped, be polite and do what they say. If they wish to detain you,

say the word "*konsulat*" (consulate) so that they know you wish to speak with your country's consulate. In most cases, though, the police do not allow people to call. Be polite but firm, insisting that they have to let you go, or they will have big problems when you contact your consulate.

How to Find Help If you are abused by the police, there is almost no recourse, except to complain to the *St Petersburg Times*, tel: (812) 325 9595, 325 6080, which, unfortunately, regularly publishes such stories. If you are the victim of abuse or a crime, it is best first to contact your consulate and ask them to assist in speaking to the police.

European Medical Centre
2-ya Tverskaya-Yamskaya 10
tel: (095) 251 6099, 250 0730.
emergencies (095) 956 7999.
American Medical Center and Pharmacy
2-ya Tverskaya-Yamskaya 10
tel: (095) 956 3366.
Assit-24, Delta Consulting Group
tel: (095) 229–6536.
Athens Medical Centre
Michurinsky Prospekt 6
tel: (095) 147 9322.

In St Petersburg:
24-Hour Medical Centre for Foreigners
22 Moskovsky Prospekt
tel: (812) 316 6272.
Although the clinic is open from 8:30am–8pm, it does have a 24-hour emergency ambulance service.
American Medical Center
10 Serpukhovskaya Ulitsa
tel: (812) 326 6272.
It is much more expensive than the centre above, so bring a credit card.

Health Spas

The healing properties of the mineral waters in the Kavkazskiye Mineralniye Vody Region (Caucasian Spa District) have been known for centuries. This area, and the customs of resort people, were described by the writer Mikhail Lermontov, author of *A Hero of Our Time*, who was killed in a duel in the spa town of Pyatigorsk.

Emergency Numbers

All Russian cities have unified emergency telephone numbers which can be dialled free from public telephones:
Fire (*Pozharnaya okhrana*)   01
Police (*Militsia*)   02
Ambulance
(*Skoraya pomoshch*)   03
Gas Emergency
(*Sluzhba gaza*)   04
Information (*Spravochnaya*)   09

Officials responding to these calls will speak little English, so a knowledge of Russian is needed to make yourself understood.

Pyatigorsk mineral waters are still popular and are used to treat bowel complaints, the neural system, dyspepsia, pathological metabolism, and vascular, gynaecological and skin problems. Other spas in this region – Essentuki, Kislovodsk and Zhelez-novodsk – are just as famous as Pyatigorsk. However, it's no more safe to venture into the area on your own than it was in Lermontov's time: plane hijacks and kidnappings have been common in recent years, and several tourist groups were abducted and held for ransom in the late 1990s.
Sochi and Matsesta are also in the vicinity of the Kavkazskiye

Mineralniye Vody Region, on the Black Sea coast close to the spa of Tskhaltubo.

Newspapers

Foreign language press
In Moscow, you will find the informative *Moscow News*, and the more recent and authoritative *Moscow Times*. Both are translated into English, and are on sale in most major hotels and at kiosks. The off–Broadway *Exile* bi-weekly carries valuable restaurant and nightlife tips.
When you arrive in Moscow, try to find a copy of the *Moscow Business Telephone Guide*, the city's most detailed telephone directory. Updated on a monthly basis, it is available free of charge at major hotels and restaurants and is on sale throughout the city.
In St Petersburg, the twice-weekly newspaper, *St Petersburg Times*, and the monthly magazine, *Pulse*, will give you important information on local events. If you are staying in the country for some time, a copy of *The Traveller's Yellow Pages*, which can be bought at hotels in Moscow and St Petersburg, is useful.

Russian language press
Izvestya, one of the best known Russian newspapers in the West, is no longer the "official paper of the Communist party", but owned by a

Tips for Women Travelling Alone

1 Avoid walking around a city centre alone at night. Russian friends will often insist on walking you either part of the way, or all the way home. Refusal of this offer could offend your Russian friend.
2 Russian men often behave chivalrously, in a way that some Western women might find offensive. Do not be shocked if they open the door for you, take you by the arm when crossing the street, or stepping off a bus. Refusal of this offer could also offend your Russian friend.

3 Be careful who you smile at. Smiling at a man is often taken to mean that you like him, and so do not be surprised if he starts following you.
4 If you go anywhere with a man, he will want to pay for you, and any attempt to pay for yourself is a serious insult to his honour.
5 If, at any time, an unpleasant situation does arises in a dark and secluded area, make it clear you are a foreigner, simply by speaking English. Troublemakers take advantage of the fact that Russian

women are usually ashamed of violence against them and are unlikely to report a violent incident to the police, but they know that a Western woman is more likely to press for her rights and file charges.
6 In general, be firm and strong with troublemakers, though not rude and aggressive. Most of them are cowards and in some strange way, Russian men have an ingrained respect of women because of their mothers – they respect a strong women, which is the Russian mother.

leading capitalist, Vladimir Potanin and his financial-industrial empire, Unexim Group. Most national and local papers are financed by leading financial and industrial corporations. *Argumenty i Facty*, a national weekly newspaper, has a circulation of 20 million. The liberal daily *Komsomolskaya Pravda* has a circulation of more than 12 million. Also popular, but with smaller circulation are *Kommersant Daily* and *Segonya*. The most widely read St Petersburg newspaper is the *Sankt–Petersburg Vedomosti* (140,000).

In Ukraine, the better papers are *Den*, *Kievskie Vedemosti* and the weekly *Zerkalo Nedeliy*. In Minsk look out for *Svaboda*, the best of the remaining independent papers, which has been forced to print abroad and is not sold through official outlets.

Postal Services

Post offices are generally open 9am–6pm Monday–Saturday; they often close at midday for an hour. They are closed on Sundays. Some post offices, however, work only one shift a day, 9am–3pm or 2–8pm.

The mail service in Russia provides an increasing variety and standard of services. Not all post offices accept international mail bigger than a standard letter.

International postal delivery can be slow – it may take two or three weeks for a letter from Moscow to

Dialling Codes

International codes
Russia – 7
Belarus – 7
Ukraine – 380
City prefixes
Moscow – 095
St Petersburg – 812
Minsk – 0712
Kiev – 44
Odessa – 482
If you are trying to make a call within the CIS, then dial 8 before the city code.

reach Western Europe and sometimes even a month or more to reach the US.

Couriers

If you have important documents or packages to send abroad, you should consider using a courier service. There are a number of international and Russian courier services available in Moscow:
DHL, 3rd Samotechny Pereulok, 11/2, tel: (095) 941 8732, 956 1000, 961 1000
TNT, Express Worldwide, Denezhny Pereulok, 1, tel: (095) 201 2585
UPS, Bolshoi Tishinsky Pereulok, 8, tel: (095) 961 2211, 253 1937
Pony Express, tel: (095) 930 2080

The following services are available in Kiev:
DHL, tel: (44) 264 7200
TNT, tel: (44) 277 1411
UPS, tel: (44) 290 0000

Cables & Telegrams

Cables to addresses within Russia can be sent from any post office. The same applies to international cables. It may be simpler, but more expensive, to send a cable from a hotel.

Telephone

The telephone system is improving all the time, but it is still not as good as in the West.

There are two types of street phones, one using brown-coloured tokens and the other plastic cards, both available at metro stations. Opt for the tokens if you don't need to make too many calls.

Place a token, bought in the metro, or from a kiosk, in the slot on top of the phone. When answered, depending on the type of telephone, the token may drop by itself (good for three minutes – you can place the next token as soon as the first one drops), or on touchtone phones push the # button to connect the call.

Quite often you will be misconnected, so never buy a single token, and the line will be

Internet Access

You are now able to access the Internet, or send and receive email at the following Internet cafés in Moscow:
Virtual World
Volgogradsky Prospect 1
tel: (095) 742 5000
Open 10am–9pm, free
Neolit
Zemlyanoi Val 36/38
tel: (095) 974 7484
Open 24 hours; entrance fee
Screen
Novocherkassky Boulevard 19a
tel: (095) 349 1920
Open noon–8pm daily; entrance fee
Agmar
Moscow House of Youth, Komsomolsky Prospect 28
tel: (095) 245 8496
Open 10am–10pm
Russian Exhibition Centre
Prospect Mira, pavilion 69
tel: (095) 974 7484
Open 10am–7pm; entrance fee
IRPO
Ulitsa Chernyakhovskogo 9, office 108
tel: (095) 152 7331
Open 9am–9pm; entrance fee
Chevignon Internet Café
This café can be found inside the Chevignon store in Stoleshnikov Pereulok (downtown).

Also check out your hotel's business centre.

bad so be prepared to shout.

To dial further afield, go to a post office. As this whole process can be complicated and time-consuming, it is simpler but more expensive to phone from your hotel.

You can now dial the UK and the US direct from Moscow and Kiev. To call the UK from a private address in St Petersburg, you will have to book your call in advance through the international operator. A direct call can be made through a hotel service bureau.

Tipping

Though Russia has been socialist for more than 70 years, tipping, one of the capitalist sins, is still an accepted practice. Waiters, porters and taxi drivers have always appreciated tips. Ten percent is the accepted rule, although some Western-managed restaurants will inform you that you are not supposed to tip. Porters will take what's acceptable anywhere else in the world. Guides and Interpreters will appreciate small souvenirs or gifts from home rather than tips, in addition to their fee.

Embassies and Consulates

Moscow
Canada
Starokonyushenny Peryulok 23
tel: (095) 956 6666
Ukraine
Leontevskiyper
tel: (095) 229 1079
United Kingdom
Sofiyskaya Nab 14
tel: (095) 956 7200
United States
Novinsky Boulevard 15
tel: (095) 252 2451

St Petersburg
Canadian Consulate
Malodestkoselskiy Prospekt 32
tel: (812) 325 8448.
France
nab. Moiki 15
tel: (812) 314 1443, 312 1130
Germany
ul. Furshtatskaya
tel: (812) 327 3111
Italy
Teatral'naya pl. 10
tel: (812) 312 3106
Sweden
10th line (VO),
1/3 Malaya Konnushnaya
tel: (812) 329–1430
United Kingdom
Proletarskaya Diktatury 5
tel: (812) 325 6036
Open 10am–5pm, Monday–Friday
United States
ul. Furshtatskaya 15

tel: (812) 275 1701; emergency after hours: 274 8692
Open 9:30am–1pm, Monday–Friday

Minsk
France
Pl. Svobody 11
tel: (0712) 102 548
Germany
Ulitsa Zakharova 26
tel: (0712) 233 0752
United Kingdom
Karla Marxa 37
tel: (0712) 229 2969
United States
Starovilenskaya 46
tel: (0712) 231 5000

Kiev
Canada
Yaroslaviv Val. 31
tel: (44) 212 2235
France
Vyl. Reiterska 39
tel: (44) 228 8728
Germany
Vyl. Chkalova 84
tel: (44) 216 7498
Russia
Vozdukhnoflotskiy Prospekt 27
tel: (44) 244 0961
United Kingdom
Vyl. Desytatinna 9
tel: (44) 462 0011
United States
Vyl. Yuria Kotsyubinskoho 10
tel: (44) 244 3745

Religious Services

Russian Orthodox
Most churches are now open for services in Moscow and St Petersburg. The main service usually starts around 9 or 10am. Women should always cover their heads. Note that hands in pockets is taken as a sign of disrespect. Observe the etiquette of the locals around you. The service in English at 10am on Sundays at **St Catherine's**, Ulitsa Bolshaya Ordynka 60/2, Moscow, tel: (095) 238 8334, is worth a visit.

Roman Catholic
Chapel of Our Lady of Hope
Kutuzovsky prosp. 7/4, korp. 5, kv. 42, Moscow
tel: (095) 243 9621
Church of the Immaculate Conception
Ulitsa Malaya Gruzinskaya 27, Moscow
tel: (095) 252 3911
The Catholic Church
Kovensky Pereulok 7, St Petersburg

Baptist
Seven Day Adventist and Baptist Church
Ulitsa Danilovskaya 37, Moscow
tel: (095) 126 8767, 468 6500
The Baptist Churches
29a, Bolshaya Ozernaya Ulitsa, St Petersburg

Muslim
The Mosque
Vypolzov per. 7, Moscow
tel: (095) 281 3866
Mechel
7 Kronversky Prospekt, St Petersburg

Jewish
The Synagogue
Bolshoi Spasoglinischevsky Peryulok 10, Moscow
tel: (095) 924 2424.

Overseas Missions

Russian Missions Abroad
Canada
285 Sharlotta Street, Ottawa
tel: (613) 235 4341;
fax: 236 6342
Visa Department
tel: (613) 236 7220; fax: 238 6158
United Kingdom
5, 13 & 18 Kensington Palace Gardens, London W8 4QG
tel: (0171) 229 3828
Consulate, 58 Melville Street Edinburgh, EH3 7HL
tel: (0131) 225 7098
United States
Embassy, Wisconsin Avenue, N.N. Washington DC 200007
tel: (202) 298 5700
fax: 298 5749
Consulate, 9E 91st Street, New York, NY 10128

tel: (212) 328 0926
fax: 831 9162
Visa Department, 1825 Phelps
Place NW Washington DC
tel: (202) 939 8907
fax: 939 8909

Belarusian Missions Abroad
France
38, Boulevard Suchet, 75016 Paris
tel: (01) 40 50 10 66
fax: 45 25 64 00
Germany
Fritz Schaffer Str. 20, 53113 Bonn
tel: (0228) 26 54 57
fax 26 58 60
United Kingdom
1 St Stephens Crescent,
London W2 5QT
tel: (0171) 221 39 41
fax: 221 39 46
United States
1619 New Hampshire Ave., NW,
Washington, DC 20009
tel: (202) 986 1606
fax: 986 1805

Ukrainian Missions Abroad
Canada
331 Metcalfe Street, Ottawa
tel: (613) 230 2961
fax: 230 2400
France
21 Avenue de Saxe, 75007 Paris
tel: (01) 43 06 07 37, 43 06 04 11
fax: 43 06 02 94
Germany
Rhcinhochenweg 101, 53424
Remagen-Oberwinter
tel: (0228) 94 18 60
fax: 94 18 63.
Also consulates general in Munich
and Dusseldorf
United Kingdom
78 Kensington Park Road,
London W11 2PL
tel: (0171) 727 6312
fax: 792 1708
United States
3350 M Street NW, Washington,
DC 20007
tel: (202) 333 7507
fax: 333 7510
Also consulates general in Chicago
and New York

Airline Offices
Moscow
Air Algerie
Korovy Val 7, Section 11
tel: (095) 237 5257, 237 7486
Open Monday–Friday 9am–1pm;
2pm–5pm
Air France
Korovy Val 7,
tel: (095) 234 3377, 237 3344
Open Monday–Friday 9am–1pm,
2–6pm
Alitalia
Ulitsa Pushechnaya 7
tel: (095) 923 9840, 923 9856
Open Monday–Friday
9.30am–1.30pm and 2–6pm,
Saturday 9.30am–1pm
Austrian Airlines
Zolotoye Kolsto Hotel, Smolenskaya
Ploschad 5, floor 6,
tel: (095) 258 2020
Open Monday–Friday 9am–6pm,
Saturday 9am–1pm
British Airways
Sovincenter, Suite 1905,
Krasnopresnenskaya Nab. 12,
floor 19, Office 1905
tel: (095) 258 2492; flight
enquiries, tel: (095) 578 2923
Open Monday–Friday 9am–6pm
British Airways
Sheremetyevo II airport
tel: (095) 578 2923/2736
Delta Air Lines
Sovincenter, Suite 1102a,
Krasnopresnenskaya Nab. 12,
floor 11
tel: (095) 258 1288
Open Monday–Friday 9am–5.30 pm,
Saturday 9am–1pm
Finnair
Kuznetsky Most 3
tel: (095) 292 8788, 292 1758
Open Monday–Friday 9am–5pm
Japan Airlines
Kuznetsky Most 3
tel: (095) 921 6448, 095 921 6648
Open Monday–Friday 9am–6pm.
KLM (Royal Dutch Airlines)
Krasnopresnenskaya Nab. 12, floor
13, Office 1307
tel: (095) 258 3600, 258 3605
Open Monday–Friday 9am–5pm
LOT (Polish Airlines)
Korovy Val 7
tel: (095) 238 0003, 238 0313
Open Monday–Friday 9am–6pm,

Chambers of Commerce
**Russian Chamber of Commerce
and Industry**
6 Ilyinka (Kuybyshev) St,
Moscow 101000
tel: (095) 929 0009
**American Chamber of
Commerce**
Riverside Towers,
Kosmodamianskaya Nab. 52,
Building 1b, floor 8
tel: (095) 961 2141
fax: (095) 961 2142
**Russo-British Chamber of
Commerce**
42 Southwark Street,
London SE1 1UN
tel: (0171) 235 2423
Moscow office: 1904, 19th Floor,
World Trade Centre
12 Krasnopresnenskaya Nab.,
Moscow 123610
tel: (095) 253 2554
**French-Russian Chamber of
Commerce**
22 Ave Franklin D. Roosevelt,
75008 Paris
tel: (01) 422 59710
Moscow office: Apt. 3, 4
Pokrovsky Blvd, Moscow 101000
tel: (095) 207 3009
**Italian–Russian Chamber of
Commerce**
5 Via San Tomaso, Milan
tel: (2) 481 6725.
Moscow office: 7 Denezhny
Pereulok, Moscow 121002
tel: (095) 241 5729

Saturday 9am–5pm
Sabena (Belgian World Airlines)
Krasnopresnenskaya Nab. 12,
floor 17, office 1701
tel: (095) 258 1193, 258 1888
Open Monday–Friday 9am–1pm,
2–6pm
SAS (Scandinavian Airlines)
Kuznetsky Most 3
tel: (095) 925 4853, 095 925 4747
Open Monday–Friday 9am–5.30pm
Swissair
Krasnopresnenskaya Nab. 12,
floor 20, Office 2003
tel: (095) 253 1888
Open Monday–Friday 8.30am–
5.30pm
Transaero

Smolensky 2nd Pereulok 3
tel: (095) 241 4800/7676

St Petersburg
Austrian Airlines
57 Nevsky Pr
tel: (812) 325–3260
Open Monday–Friday 9am–5pm
Air France
Pulkovo-2
tel: (812) 104–3433
35 Bolshaya Morskaya Ul
tel: (812) 119 8252
Open Monday–Friday 9am–5pm
British Airways/Deutsche BA
1/3 Malaya Konnushnaya
tel: (812) 329 2565
Open: Monday–Friday 9am–5:30pm
Delta Airlines
36 Bol. Morskaya Ul
tel: (812) 311 5820, 311 5819
Open Monday–Friday 9am–5.30pm
Finnair
19 Mal. Morskaya Ul
tel: (812) 325 9500
KLM
Zagorodnyy Pr 5
tel: (812) 325 8989
Lufthansa
7 Voznesensky Pr
tel: (812) 314 4979
SAS
57 Nevsky Pr
tel: (812) 325 3255
Open Monday–Friday 9am–5pm
Swissair/SAS/Austrian Airlines
57 Nevsky Pr
tel: (812) 325 3255/3250
fax: (812) 164 7873
Swissair
57 Nevsky Pr
tel: (812) 325–3250
Open Monday–Friday 9am–5pm

Kiev
Air France
Vyl. Bolshaya Zhitomirskaya 6/11
tel: (44) 229 1395
British Airways
Yaroslaviv Val 5
tel: (44) 247 6644
KLM
Vyl. Esplanadna, 20
tel: (44) 220 1614
Lufthansa
Khreshchatyk 14
tel: (44) 229 6297

Swissair/Austrian Airlines
Vyl. Chervonoarmiiska 9/2
tel: (44) 244 35 40/41/42
Transaero
Shevchenko Blvd 10
tel: (44) 246 3737
Ukraine International
Prosp. Peremohy 14
tel: (44) 216 6730

International Travel Agents

United Kingdom
American Express
6 Haymarket, London SW1Y 4BS
tel: (0171) 930 4411
P & O Cruises
77 New Oxford Street, London WC1
tel: (0171) 800 2222
Page and Moy
136–140 London Road,
Leicester, LE2 1EN
tel: (0116) 250 7114

United States
Four Winds Travel
175 Fifth Ave, New York, NY 10010
tel: (212) 777 7637
Russian Travel Bureau
245 E 44th St, New York, NY10017
tel: (212) 986 1500

See also Independent Operators,
page 344.

Russian National Tourist Offices

Canada
1801 McGill Avenue, Suite 930,
Montreal, Quebec H3A 2NA
tel: (514) 849 6394
fax: 849 6743
United Kingdom
Russian National Tourist Office
Orchard House,
167–169 Kensington High Street,
London W8 6SH
tel: (0171) 937 7210/7207
fax: (0171) 938 2912

United States
800 Third Avenue, Suite 3101, New
York, NY 10022
tel: (212) 758 1162
fax: 758 0933

Getting Around

By Train

With some 145,000 km (90,050
miles), the railway system of Russia
is the longest in the world. It is a
means of transport used for
4 billion individual trips per year.
The busiest lines in European
Russia connect Moscow with
St Petersburg and Kiev in the
Ukraine, where a train leaves
almost every hour. You may prefer
to travel to St Petersburg and back
by train, leaving late at night and
arriving the next morning.

In overnight sleeping cars, tea is
always served and trains travelling
for more than eight hours have a
restaurant car attached during the
day. Commercial trains running on
these lines offer a very comfortable
service with food and bed linen
included in the price. Economy
tickets may not include these
services so be prepared to pay
extra for your bedding.
Reservations You should make your
reservation several days ahead as
reserved train seats are in short
supply, especially 2nd class tickets,
which are cheap but fairly
comfortable. You can reserve your
seat through a travel agent; at the
Intourist counter at the station; or
at the Intourtrans Office, Ul.
Petrovka 15, Moscow, tel: (095)
929 8743, 929 8848, 921 8968,
929 8741.

There are booking offices in the
railway stations of every major city.
The ticket must have a cover and a
coupon (it is valid only with both
these components).
General Inquiries For inquiries
about train arrivals and departures
from all stations, tel: (095) 266
9000, (095) 266 9333. Ticket

booking to all destinations, tel: (095) 266 8333, (095) 262 0319.

In St Petersburg, the telephone number for all inquiries about arrivals and departures of trains is (812) 168 0111.

By Car

Car Rental

Western car companies can be found in the major cities and you will find branches at international airports. Cars can also be hired with a driver. Check up-to-date details before you leave, or at hotels, which advertise such companies. Before you hire a car, read the advice printed under "*Routes*" below.

Budget, tel: (095) 915 5237
Eurodollar, tel: (095) 298 6146
Eurocar, tel: (095) 253 1369, 578 3878, 155 0170
Hertz, tel: (095) 578 5646

Routes

If you intend to visit Russia by car you should first contact Intourist, or a specialist tour operator as they have worked out a number of routes that can be easily negotiated with your own vehicle. Road conditions off these routes are very poor.

The ideal route through European Russia means entering the region from Finland, driving via St Petersburg and Moscow to the Caucasus and the Black Sea, ferrying the car across to Yalta or Odessa and then crossing Ukraine to the Czech and Slovak republics or Poland.

Sovinterautoservice
Institutski per., 2/1, Moscow
tel: (095) 101 496
The specialist for car travel in Russia. It can solve nearly every problem a foreigner may have on Russian roads.

Rules of the Road

Russia is a signatory to the International Traffic Convention. Rules of the road and road signs correspond to international standards. The basic rules, however, are worth mentioning.
1 In Russia vehicles are driven on the right side of the road.
2 It is prohibited to drive a car after consuming any alcohol, even the smallest amount. If the driver shows a positive alcohol test, the consequences may be very serious. It is also prohibited to drive a car under the effect of drugs or any powerful medicine.
3 The driver must have an international driving licence and documents verifying his or her right to drive the car. These papers must be in Russian and are issued by Intourist. You can also obtain a temporary International Drivers Licence from your automobile

Trans-Siberian Railway

This rail link from Europe to the Orient is one of the most exotic train trips in the world, and the longest. Over a period of nine days the train crosses seven times zones from Moscow to Vladivostok, passing through much of the diversity of Siberian Russia. It makes many scheduled stops along the way, but never lingers longer than 15 minutes. If you want to explore further than a few hundred yards from the tracks, you must disembark and rejoin a later train. Stop-offs should be scheduled ahead of time, especially if travelling first class, since you could easily lose your cabin.

The port of Vladivostok was opened to foreign tourists in 1992. It is now possible to begin or end a Trans-Siberian rail trip in Yokohama, near Tokyo in Japan. A two-day cruise connects Vladivostok with Yokohama.

Adding to the network is the Baikal-Amur Mainline (BAM), which connects Tayshet to Komsolmolsk. Located just 66 km (41 miles)

from Lake Baikal, Irkutsk is the most popular stopover for Trans-Siberian travellers. A typical Trans–Siberian train trip would include a two-day stop in Irkutsk, from which excursions to Lake Baikal are easily arranged.

Other popular stopovers are Novosibirsk, Listvyanka (on Lake Baikal), Bratsk (by air or train from Irkutsk) and Khabarovsk.

Train accommodation is available in first-class (two-person compartments) and second-class (four-person compartments). Ask the conductor to lock your compartment whenever you leave it, as theft is rampant on Russian trains. Most embassies also recommend that foreign travellers speak as little as possible on the train so as not to attract attention.

The train plying the route, the Rossiya, is of slightly better quality than most Russian trains. The food is also better than normal: soups are usually good, and tea is always available from the conductor at a nominal charge. The best strategy is to do like the Russians: pack

your own food and eat it in your own carriage. Bed linen and towels are provided and there is a toilet and wash basin at the end of each carriage.

If nine days on a train doesn't appeal to you, it is possible to disembark somewhere along the route and fly the rest of the way. Taking the train from east to west as far as Irkutsk and connecting to Moscow by air would include the most exotic portion of the train journey and leave time to tour the capital as well.

There are also trans-continental rail routes, such as those from Moscow to Peking in China and Ulan Baatar in Mongolia. They demand an adventurous spirit and a willingness to spend a week in the train contemplating the endless Trans-Siberian landscapes before you.

Miners demanding back pay have adopted the practice of blocking the Trans-Siberian every once in a while to voice their grievances, so it's wise to listen to the news before boarding the train.

association at home. In the UK the AA can issue this for a small fee and one passport size photo.

4 Vehicles, except for Intourist cars, must carry the national registration code and a national licence plate.

5 The use of the horn is prohibited within city limits except in emergency situations.

6 Seat belts for the driver and front seat passenger are compulsory.

7 The speed limit in populated areas (marked by blue coloured signs indicating "town") is 60 kph (37 mph); on most arterial roads the limit is 90 kph (55.5 mph). On highways the limit can differ, so look out for road signs specifying other speeds.

8 You can insure your car in Russia through Ingosstrakh, the national insurance company, or through a private insurance company.

By Boat

Many rivers in European Russia are open to navigation during the spring and autumn. You can travel along the Dnieper, Volga, Oka, Moskva, Don, Dniester, Neva and other rivers. The cities on the banks of the rivers are connected by passenger ships and hydrofoils (Raketa and Kometa Class).

If you plan a trip along one of these routes, you can make a reservation through Intourist or directly at the Moscow River Station (Rechnoy Vokzal).

River Stations
Moscow
Mostourflot
tel: (095) 459 7140
Intourist
tel: (095) 156 8019
Severny Rechnoy Vokzal
Leningradskoe shosse 51
tel: (095) 457 4050.
St Petersburg
Rechnoy Vokzal
Prosp. Obukhovskoy Oborony 195
tel: (812) 262 1318 (information)
262 5511 (booking office)
Kiev
Rechnoy Vokzal
Poshtova Pl
tel: (44) 416 1268

Cruises
Intourist offers organised river cruises on comfortable river liners which are relaxing and interesting, but quite expensive. These cruises are sold through foreign travel agencies that sell Intourist tour packages. Intourist has started to offer trips along the Lena, and soon the Ob and the Yenisey will also feature on its programme.

By Plane

Aeroflot, once the world's largest airline, has been broken up, and each republic now runs its own airline. The name Aeroflot is still used by the Russian airline. It flies to many remote and outlying areas, sometimes using helicopters and small hopper planes. Many of its aircraft have been designed primarily for military purposes and lack the comfort of Western carriers, but it has recently bought a fleet of European Airbuses.

As with most airlines, the cheapest fares cannot be bought from Aeroflot direct but from consolidators. Fares within Russia can be reasonable, though flights have to be booked far in advance since demand exceeds capacity. Check-in at Aeroflot counters starts one and a half hours before departure and ends half an hour beforehand. Foreigners have to pay for their tickets in hard currency and sometimes at grossly unfavourable rates.

In Ukraine and Belarus, the former Soviet fleet now makes up the core of Air Ukraine and Belavia respectively.

Aeroflot offices
Moscow
Leningradskiy Prospekt 37, bldg 9
tel: (095) 155 8019; ticket information, tel: (095) 155 5045
St Petersburg
7–9 Nevsky Prospekt
tel: (812) 311 8093 (Russia travel); 315 0072 (international travel)
Khabarovsk
5 Amursky Boulevard
tel: (421) 332 071

City Maps

Particularly recommended for Moscow and St Petersburg are the German Falk plan maps, available from most large bookshops.

Minsk
18–28 Karl Marx Street
tel: (0712) 224 232
Kiev
66 Boulevard Shevchenko
tel: (44) 774 4223

Aeroflot Offices Abroad
London
70 Piccadilly, London W1V 9HH
tel: (0171) 355 2233
New York
235 West 48th Street, NY 10036
tel: (212) 245 1100
Paris
33, Avenue des Champs Elysées
tel: (01) 42 25 43 81, 42 56 19 30

City Transport

MOSCOW
Buses and trolleybuses
Buses and trolleybuses are slow, because of traffic conditions, but extremely cheap. Most maps show routes, and bus stop are clearly marked by yellow boards indicating route number and terminus. Buy tickets from the driver.

Taxis
There is a central taxi service and you can book a cab by calling (095) 927 0000, or (095) 923 8052, day or night. Waiting time is about an hour. Never take unlicensed cabs at night. Instead of taking a taxi from the airport, pre-book a transfer with your tour operator.

Taxis usually cost about $100 for this run. A pre-booked taxi should cost around $50. The express mini-bus service can be off-putting for first-timers to Moscow. It is, however, a marked improvement on the city's bus service. It runs past both terminals of Moscow's main airport and is ideal for the economy traveller.

Taxi prices in Moscow are

exorbitant if you take a cab from in front of your hotel. Just a couple blocks away you will probably be able to catch one for half the price, so it's worth walking a short distance. You should be able to get to the city centre for the rouble equivalent of US$5 to $10 and to anywhere in Moscow for $10 to $20 – throw in another couple dollars at night.

Chauffeur-driven cars

A chauffeur-driven car can save time and hassle and need not be that expensive, especially if you use one of the private individuals who advertise in the classified columns of the *Moscow Times*. For a more official, possibly more comfortable arrangement, check out:
Intourist, tel: (095) 215 6191
InNis, tel: (095) 927 1187
Autosan, tel: (095) 280 3600

The Metro

The Moscow Metro system is famous for its fabulous architecture. It is also fast, reliable and cheap and the best way to travel around in Moscow. Buy tokens from the ticket windows in the entry halls or, if you can, buy a monthly pass. Each station, including those which are at the same location but on different lines, has its own name.

ST PETERSBURG

Buses, trams and trolleybuses

These run from 6am–1am the following morning. To make full use of the system, it is essential to have a special map called *Marshruty Gorodskovo Transporta – Trolleibus, Avtobus i Tramvai* (Town Transport Routes for Trolleybuses, Buses and Trams). Ask your hotel receptionist where to buy a copy.

Stops marked by an "A" sign serve buses, while stops marked "T" serve trolleybuses. The latter are less crowded than buses during rush-hour. Tram signs hang from wires above the middle of the road.

Taxis

Taxis in St Petersburg are cheap. Cabs are pale yellow with a "T" sign. Those which congregate outside hotels inflate their prices considerably, so it is cheaper to flag down a vehicle in the street. As in Moscow, determine the price of a journey before setting out. It's advisable to pre-book a taxi from the airport through your tour operator, it should cost about $50.

The Metro

Like St Petersburg's buses and trams, the Metro runs from 6am–1am, and like the Moscow Metro it is famous for its architecture and murals. This is the fastest way to get around St Petersburg, and it is well worth trying to get to grips with routes and Cyrillic signs.

KIEV

The three lines of the Kiev Metro are very reliable and cheap. Use of the metro requires *zhetony* (tokens)

Kiev Metro

which are sold from booths by the stations entrance.

MINSK

The Minsk Metro has two lines open between 6am–12.30am. *Zhetony* (tokens) can be purchased from attendants at the station. Trolley buses and trams run between 5.30am–1am and cover areas that can not be reached by the metro.

Tour Operators

Intourist, the former state travel agency, was privatised at the beginning of 1993. It continues to offer services in all the large Russian cities, but it no longer has the monopoly on the Russian travel business. Tours, which include cruises from Moscow to St Petersburg, city breaks, business trips and conferences, can still be booked through Intourist offices in main cities.

INTOURIST OFFICES

London
Intourist House, 219 Marsh Wall, London E14 9FJ
tel: (0171) 538 8600/5961
fax: (0171) 538 5967
email: info@intourus.demon.co.uk
website:
http://www.intourus.demon.co.uk
New York
630 Fifth Avenue, Suite 868
tel: (212) 757 3884
Paris
7, Boulevard de Capucines
tel: (01) 47 42 47 40
Sydney
Underwood House,
37–49 Pitt Street
tel: (02) 277 652

INDEPENDENT OPERATORS

United Kingdom
Voyages Jules Verne
21 Dorset Square,
London NW1 6QG

tel: (0171) 616 1000
website: http://www.vjv.co.uk
Offers cruises and more expensive, specialist tours.
Noble Caledonia
11 Charles Street,
London W1X 8LE
tel: (0171) 409 0376
Offers cruises.
Cox & Kings Travel
Gordon House, 10 Greencoat Place,
London SW1P 1PH
tel: (0171) 873 5000
Arranges luxury train journeys throughout Russia on the Bolshoi Express.
Regent Holidays
15 John Street, Bristol BS1 2HR
tel: (0117) 921 1711
website:
http://www.regent-holidays.co.uk
Provides cheap flights, bespoke tours, trips on the Trans-Siberian Railway and will book hotels all over Russia.
The Russia Experience
Research House, Fraser Road, Perivale, Middx UB6 7AQ
tel: (0181) 566 8846
fax: (0181) 566 8843
email: russ–exp@compuserve.com
website:
http://www.trans-siberian.co.uk
Organises informal trips for individuals featuring family stays, trans-Siberian trips and trekking.

United States
Russiatours
13312 North 56th Street,
Suite 102, Tampa, Florida 33617
tel: (813) 987 2477
fax: (813) 988 6420
email: Russiatour@aol.com
Aims to provide clients with American–style service.

Australia
Passport Travel
Suite 11A, 401 St Kilda Road,
Melbourne 3004
tel: (3) 9867 3019
fax: (3) 9867 1055
email: passport@werple.net.au
Website: www.travelcentre.com.au
Arranges homestays in Russia; Trans-Siberian, Trans-Manchurian and Trans-Mongolian rail journeys; and individual tours through China.

Minsk Metro

УСХОД
USKHOD

МАСКОЎСКАЯ
MASKOWSKAYA

ПУШКІНСКАЯ
PUSKINSKAYA

ПАРК ЧАЛЮСКІНЦАУ
PARK CHALYUSKINTSAU

МАЛАДЗЁЖНАЯ
MALADZYOZHNAYA

АКАДЭМІЯ НАВУК
AKADEMIYA NAVUK

ФРУНЗЕНСКАЯ
FRUNZYENSKAYA

ПЛОШЧА ЯКУБА КОЛАСА
PLOSHCHA YAKUBA KOLASA

НЯМІГА
NYAMIHA

КУПАЛАЎСКАЯ
KUPALAWSKAYA

ПЛОШЧА ПЕРАМОГІ
PLOSHCHA PYERAMOHI

КАСТРЫЧНІЦКАЯ
KASTRYCHNITSKAYA

ПЕРШАМАЙСКАЯ
PYERSHAMAYSKAYA

ПЛОШЧА НЕЗАЛЕЖНАСЦІ
PLOSHCHA NYEZALYEZHNASTSI

ПРАЛЕТАРСКАЯ
PRALYETARSKAYA

ИНСТЫТУТ КУЛЬТУРЫ
INSTYTUT KULTURY

ТРАКТАРНЫ ЗАВОД
TRAKTARNY ZAVOD

Interchange

Metro Line and Stations

Where to Stay

Choosing a Hotel

Accommodation continues to improve, particularly in Moscow and St Petersburg. Foreign-run hotels and joint ventures between Russian and Canadian and Finnish operators in particular are helping to push up standards. A number of grand old hotels and wonderful art nouveau establishments have been lavishly restored, but these tend to be at the expensive end of the range. Intourist-run hotels can usually be relied upon to provide a fairly consistent, though not necessarily inspiring service. At the budget end of the price spectrum, facilities will be basic.

Russia

Owing to inflation and constant fluctuations in the rouble-dollar rate, these price bands are approximate and will serve as a guide only. Some hotels have been discounting rooms to attract foreign visitors, and others offer more favourable rates for group tour bookings. It is worth checking what's on offer with a reliable tour operator before booking.

MOSCOW

Luxury

Baltschug Kempinski Moskau
Balchug Ul 1
tel: (095) 230 6500
Website:
http://www.kempinski-moscow.com
Located just across the river from the Kremlin, this hotel has a superb view. Kempinski is a well-known chain of German luxury hotels. **$$$$**

Metropol
Teatralny Proyezd 1–4
tel: (095) 927 6000
Website:
http://www.moscow-guide.ru
The most famous hotel in Moscow. This is the place to stay if you can possibly afford it. It has been beautifully renovated and is elegant, luxurious and, of course, expensive. **$$$$**

Marriott Grand Hotel
Tverskaya Ulitsa 26
tel: (095) 935 8500
US President, Bill Clinton, stayed here on a visit to Moscow. **$$$$**

National
Ulitsa Mokhovaya 15/1
tel: (095) 258 7000
Like the Metropol, the National is an old trademark Moscow hotel which has recently been renovated. It is next door to the Kremlin. **$$$$**

Expensive

Radisson Slavyanskaya
Berezhkovskaya Nab 2
tel: (095) 941 8020
This is a luxury hotel with several fine restaurants and bars. It has a good view of the river. President Clinton stayed here several times before he switched to Marriott. Avoid the Kievsky railway terminal area next door. A three-stop metro ride into the city centre may be much quicker than an expensive hotel cab in the rush hour. **$$$**

Sheraton Palace Hotel
Ulitsa Tverskaya–Yamskaya 1st 19
tel: (095) 931 9700
email: palacehotel.sales@ns.co.ru
Website: http://www.sheraton.com
This is a Western–style hotel on Moscow's main thoroughfare. **$$$**

Aerostar
37 Leningradsky Prospekt
tel: (095) 213 9000
A Canadian-Russian hotel with an excellent seafood restaurant. It's about a 15-minute journey from the city centre. **$$$**

Savoy
Rozhdestvenka 3
tel: (095) 929 8500/8555/8590
This hotel was the first Western-Soviet joint venture into the hotel business. Its standards are first class. **$$$**

Price Guide

Prices are based on the cost of a room for two, including breakfast.

$$$$ Luxury over US$280
$$$ Expensive US$150–$280
$$ Moderate US$35–$150
$ Budget US$10–$35

Arbat
Plotnikov Pereulok 12
tel: (095) 244 7635
In New York parlance this hotel is in a "downtown off–Broadway" location. **$$$**

Tverskaya
Ulitsa Tverskaya–Yamskaya 1st 34
tel: (095) 290 9900, 258 3000
Located in the city centre, right on Tverskaya, this hotel has been recently renovated. **$$$**

Art Sport
Ulitsa Peshchannaya 3rd 2
tel: (095) 955 2300
email: artsport@glasnet.ru
Located in a quiet area, relatively close to the centre. **$$$**

Sofitel Hotel Iris
Korovinskoye Shosse 10
tel: (095) 488 8000
email: sofitel.iris.moscow@co.ru
Website: http://www.sofitel.com
A quality Western-style hotel, a long way from the city centre. **$$$**

Mir
Devyatinsky Bolshoi Pereulok 9
tel: (095) 290 9518/04
The Mir is next door to the American embassy. **$$$**

Novotel
Sheremetyevo II airport
tel: (095) 926 5900
A fine hotel, useful for the airport, but quite a way from the city. **$$$**

Renaissance Moscow
Olimpiysky Prospekt 18/1
tel: (095) 931 9000/9833
This hotel offers a good service, but it is some distance from the centre. **$$$**

Le Meridien
Nakhabino Moscow Country Club
tel: (095) 926 5911
Le Meridien, 30 km (19 miles) from Moscow, offers reasonable long-stay rates. **$$$**

Moderate

Intourist
Ulitsa Tverskaya 3/5
tel: (095) 956 8400/8426/
8430/8304
Just around the corner from
National, close to the Kremlin, the
strategic location makes up for
Soviet-style architecture and
second-rate service. **$$**

Moskva
Ulitsa Okhotny Ryad 2
tel: (095) 292 1100
Redolent of the Soviet era but
convenient for the Kremlin. **$$**

Rossiya
Ulitsa Varvarka 6
tel: (095) 232 5000
Another hotel with a lingering Soviet
flavour, right next door to the
Kremlin and Red Square. **$$**

Cosmos
Prospect Mira 150
tel: (095) 215 6791, 234 1587
(See entry below.) **$$**

Mezhdunarodnaya
Krasnopresnenskaya
Naberezhnaya 12
tel: (095) 253 1391/2103
Service matches that offered by
Intourist, Moskva and Rossiya
hotels but both the Cosmos and
Mezhdunarodnaya are a 20-minute
journey from the city centre. **$$**

Budget

Budapest
Petrovskiye Linii 2/18
tel: (095) 924 8820, 921 1060
The Budapest is in a nice downtown
location. **$**

Belgrad
Ulitsa Smolenskaya 8
tel: (095) 248 2841
Further from the city centre than
the Budapest Hotel, but the service
is comparable. **$**

Ukraina
Kutuzovsky Prospect 2/1
tel: (095) 243 2596/3030
This is one of Moscow's "wedding
cake" buildings. It has a superb
river view. **$**

Izmaylovo
Izmaylovo 71
tel: (095) 166 3627/2763
A modern hotel, 15 minutes by
metro from the city centre, with
friendly English-speaking staff. It is

a bit out of the way, but there is a
flea market next door which attracts
souvenir-hunters. **$**

ST PETERSBURG

Luxury

Astoria
39 Bolshaya Morskaya Ulitsa
tel: (812) 210 5757
A grand and luxurious hotel
opposite St Isaac's Cathedral. The
old wing retains its art nouveau
features. **$$$$**

Grand Hotel Europe
1–7 Mikhailovskaya Ulitsa
tel: (812) 329 6000
Another upmarket option,
resplendently restored and centrally
located. **$$$$**

Nevsky Palace
57 Nevsky Prospekt
tel: (812) 275 2001
Centrally located, restored,
upmarket and expensive with first-
class restaurants. **$$$$**

Price Guide

Prices are based on the cost of a
room for two, including
breakfast.

$$$$ Luxury over US$280
$$$ Expensive US$150–$280
$$ Moderate US$35–$150
$ Budget US$10–$35

Expensive

Pribaltiskaya
14 Ulitsa Korablestroiteley
tel: (812) 356 3001
The Pribaltiskaya is a modern hotel
about 7 km (4 miles) from the
centre, overlooking the Gulf of
Finland. **$$$**

Pulkovskaya
1 Ploshchad Pobedy
tel: (812) 123 5102
This hotel is a long way from the
centre, on the road to the airport.
Comfortable and often used by
tourist groups. **$$$**

Moderate

St Petersburg (formerly Leningrad)
5/2 Pirogovskaya Naberezhnaya
tel: (812) 542 9101

A short metro ride away from the
centre, overlooking the cruiser
Aurora and the Neva River, with
adequate rooms. **$$**

Moskva
2 Ploshchad Alexandra Nevskovo
tel: (812) 274 3001
Centrally located opposite the
Alexander Nevsky Monastery, which
compensates for the poorly-
maintained rooms. **$$**

Sovietskaya
43 Prospekt Lermontovo
tel: (812) 329 0181
A joint Finnish-Russian venture, only
a short bus ride from the centre
along the Fontanka River. **$$**

Karelia
27/2 Ulitsa Marshala
Tukhachevskaya
tel: (812) 226 3515
Inexpensive hotel used by Intourist,
10 km (6 miles) from the centre. **$$**

Budget

Cheaper options, where the
standard will be basic, go for about
US$10–$30 a night. These include:

Hotel Druzhba
4 Ultisa Chapygina
tel: (812) 234 1844 **$**

Dvoretz Molodyozhy
47 Ulitsa Professor Popov
tel: (812) 234 3278 **$**

Vyborgskaya
3 Ulitsa Torzhkovskaya
tel: (812) 246 9141 **$**

Hotel Sputnik
34 Prospekt Morisa Toreza
tel: (812) 552 5632, 356 8504 **$**

Matisov Domik
3/1 reki Pryazhki Naberezhnaya
tel: (812) 219 5445 **$**

THE GOLDEN RING
Yaroslavl

Hotel Youbileinaya
11 A Reka Kotoroselnaya
Naberezhnaya
tel: (0852) 224159
This hotel was built in 1973 on the
river near the Monastery of the
Transfiguration. It is popular with
foreign tourists. **$$**

Kotorosl
87 Bolshaya Oktyabrysky
tel: (0852) 212 415, 211581
A modern, five-storey hotel with

restaurant, sauna and gym, two tram stops from the town centre. **$**

Vladimir
Zarya
36 A Studenaya Gora
tel: (0922) 291441
This central hotel/business centre overlooks the River Klyazma. It can accommodate 300 people and has a bar, banquet hall and casino. **$$**
Vladimir
74 Ulitsa III Internatsionala
tel: (0922) 227381
This small Western-standard hotel is located in the historic centre, a short walk east from the Cathedral of the Assumption and 400 metres (0.25 mile), from the railway station. **$$**
Zolotoye Koltso
Ulitsa Chaikovsky
tel: (0922) 248807
This modern tourist complex can accommodate 380 people. It not only has a restaurant and sauna, but also has a dentist, acupuncturist, lawyer and faith-healer. **$$**

Suzdal
Suzdal Tourist Complex
tel: (09231) 20908
email: gtk@tcsuz,vladimir.ru
The complex contains a 300-room hotel and a 200-room motel, swimming pool, sauna, cinema and conference hall. **$$**

THE EUROPEAN NORTH
For those travelling under their own steam, finding Western-standard hotels is not going to be possible, so you have to take what is on offer. The best option is to stay in one of the larger urban centres and journey out from there. An alternative option, if possible, is to stay in one of the monasteries, such as Solovetsky.

Arkhangelsk
Belomorskaya
3 Ulitsa Timme
tel: (8182) 263208, 469075
email: belhotel@arkhangelsk.ru
Modern, nine-storey hotel with 190 rooms. Located in city centre. **$$**

Northern Cruising
If you are on a cruise around the European North of Russia you will not require a hotel or a restaurant. The Western-run tour boats have excellent facilities, while the Russian ones are also pleasant, if limited on the choice of food. Both provide evening entertainment, a dance in the café, or a dubbed American film.

Purnavolok
88 Severnaya Dvini Naberezhnaya
tel: (8182) 432 389
The hotel is centrally located with fine river views. It has 78 rooms, a sauna and a restaurant, where a dinner will cost you about $8. **$**

Murmansk
Arctica
Ploschad Pyat Uglov
tel: (8152) 57293
The best hotel in this area. **$$**

Vologda
Oktyabrskaya
25 Ulitsa Oktyabrisky
tel: (8172) 20145
A modern hotel, comprising 738 rooms. **$$**

Vyborg
Druzhba
5 Zheleznodorozhnaya Ulitsa
tel: (278) 25744
Built by the Finns, this very modern hotel has a restaurant with Russian cuisine. **$$**

Novgorod
Beresta Palace
Rajon 3, Studentscheskaja Ulitsa
tel: (8162) 34747
Located centrally on the east of the river: a luxury hotel with 202 rooms, swimming pool, tennis courts and facilities for the disabled. **$$$**
Intourist
tel: (8162) 75089
This is a mid-priced hotel on the west of the river just north of the Kremlin. **$$**

Petrozavodsk
Hotel Severnaya
21 Prospect Lenina
tel: (81422) 76420, 70703
Located in the city centre, about 700 metres (half a mile) from the railway station. This three-storey modernised hotel was built by the Finns in 1937. It comprises 189 rooms, a restaurant and café. **$$**
Karelian Tourist Centre
2 Naberezhnanya Gyllinga
tel: (81422) 52306, 53113
Located in the city centre on the shores of Lake Onega, about 2 km (1.2 miles), from the railway station. The 10–storey centre was built in 1978. It has 280 beds in single or triple rooms. **$$**

Pskov
Rizhskaya
25 Rizhsky Prospekt
tel: (81122) 62223
Modest but quite adequate hotel west of the Velikaya River. **$$**

SOUTHWESTERN RUSSIA
Kursk
Kursk
Ulitsa Lenina, near corner of Ulitsa Mozhayskovo
tel: (0712) 26980
The Hotel Kursk has a decent restaurant. **$$**
Tsentralnaya
2 Krasnaya Ploshchad
tel: (0712) 569048
An old hotel with a reasonable restaurant. **$$**

Orel
Rossia
37 Ulitsa Gorgovo near Ploshchad Lenina
tel: (086) 267550
If you are desperate for someone to speak English to you, rather than snarling Russian, this is the hotel to try. The food served in the restaurant is satisfactory, but unremarkable. **$$**

Bryansk
Bryansk
Prospekt Lenina, north end
tel: (0832) 466844.
The Bryansk offers both standard

rooms and de luxe rooms and has two bars and a restaurant. **$$**

Desna
Ploshchad Lenina
tel: (0832) 740135
A moderately priced hotel without a restaurant. **$**

Smolensk

Rossia
23/2 Ulitsa Dzerzhinskovo
tel: (081) 2296651/33970
The most modern hotel in Smolensk. **$$**

Tsentralnaya
Corner of Ulitsa Konenkova and Ploshchad Lenina
tel: (081) 2233604
The oldest hotel in Smolensk, but it has a decent restaurant. **$**

Price Guide

Prices are based on the cost of a room for two, including breakfast.

$$$$ Luxury over US$280
$$$ Expensive US$150–$280
$$ Moderate US$35–$150
$ Budget US$10–$35

ALONG THE VOLGA

Kazan

Tatarstan
Ulitsa Pushkina 4
tel: (8432) 316603
This three–star Intourist hotel is not the city's most centrally located, but its better quality service and clientele make it the most attractive. **$$**

Samara

National
Ulitsa Frunze 91/37
tel: (8462) 370422
(See below.) **$$**

Rossia
Ulitsa Maxima Gorkogo 82
tel: (8462) 390311
Both the Rossia and National are Intourist hotels. The National is the better of the two and is consequently more expensive but neither is extortionate. **$$**

Saratov

Slovakia
Ulitsa Lermontova 30
tel: (8452) 267618/28
A three–star Intourist hotel not far from the Volga embankment. **$$**

Volga
Nemetskaya Ulitsa 34
tel: (8452) 243645/35
A less expensive hotel. **$–$$**

Volograd

Intourist
Ulitsa Mira 14
tel: (8442) 337713
A good a choice as any. **$$**

Astrakhan

Lotus
Ulitsa Krimlovskaya 21
tel: (8512) 229500
This local Intourist hotel is still probably the best place in town to stay. **$$**

THE URALS

Yekaterinburg

Magistre
8-Marta Ulitsa 50
tel: (3432) 224206
Excellent and unobtrusive service at a very reasonable price. Big single rooms, well equipped and centrally located. Great breakfast. **$$**

Ural
8-Marta Ulitsa 45
tel: (3432) 223391
Just down the road from the Magistre, slightly more expensive and in a more Soviet style. **$$**

Oktyabrskaya
Ulitsa S. Kovalevskoi 17
tel: (3432) 445146
A Finnish-built brick building, this former Communist Party hotel is one of the best hotels in town. There are 69 pleasantly clean rooms all with well-kept bathrooms. It's situated in a quiet environment just outside the centre, a few blocks from the Urals State Technical University. **$$**

THE EUROPEAN SOUTH

Sochi

Sochi has a huge variety of accommodation on offer, from private flats (try the bureau by the station) to large hotels.

Expensive

Radisson SAS Lazurnaya
Kurortniy Prospekt 103
tel: (8622) 975974
fax: (8622) 956 1704
The Radisson is located about a 10-minute drive from the centre of Sochi and 20 minutes from the airport. It offers suites and a limited number of villas in addition to rooms. There are three restaurants, a fitness centre and an outdoor pool. Reasonable weekend deals are often available out of season, but if you can't afford to stay, splash out on breakfast and spend the rest of the day by the pool. **$$$**

Primorskaya
Sokolova 1
tel: (8622) 925743
fax: (8622) 924006
A well situated seafront hotel with great views onto the Black Sea. It has a bar and restaurants. **$$$**

Moderate

Zhemchuzhina
Chernomorskaya 3
tel: (8622) 924355
fax: (8622) 928797
A large 3-star hotel (960 rooms), 27 km (17 miles) from the airport, on the seafront in the centre of Sochi. Facilities include restaurants, bars, sea-water swimming pools, tennis courts and sauna. **$$**

Budget

Moskva
Kurortniy Prospekt 18
tel: (8622) 923617
fax: (8622) 923410
Located on the main prospekt, the Moskva has adequate rooms and is a good budget option. Bar and sauna. **$**

Dagomys Tourist Complex
Leningradskaya 7
tel: (8622) 322400, 606060
The Tourist Complex is in Dagomys, 18 km (11 miles) from the centre of Sochi and 45 km (28 miles) from the airport. The complex comprises three hotels – the Dagomys,

Olimpiiskaya and Meridian (motel). Facilities include an indoor and outdoor pool, sauna, fitness room, restaurants and bars. **$–$$**

Krasnaya Polyana
Peak Hotel
Zashitnikov Kavkaza
77 Krasnaya Polyana
tel: (8622) 963600/(7095) 255 3805
fax: (8622) 963645
A cosy, high-quality mountain hotel located in Krasnaya Polyana which provides an excellent base for climbing and winter sports. Indoor and outdoor pools, fitness centre, sauna, bar. **$$**

SIBERIA
Bratsk
Taiga
Ulitsa Mira 35
tel: (3993) 443978
This simple, Intourist-run, 2-star hotel provides an adequate base for touring the region. **$$**

Irkutsk
Intourist
Ulitsa Gagarina 44
tel: (3952) 290167, 290273
The Intourist is situated on the Angara River, a short walk from the centre of town. **$$**
Angara
Ulitsa Sukhe–Batora 7
tel: (3952) 255106, 255105
A central hotel. **$$**
Krasnoyarsk
Oktyabrskaya Hotel
Prospekt Mira 15
tel: (3912) 221916, 276968
A favourite haunt of Communist Party guests in the Soviet era. Prices here are generally higher than those elsewhere in Siberia. **$$**

Lake Baikal
Baikal
Listvyanka
tel: (3952) 290391
The Baikal is the only hotel on the lake. It offers splendid views and a good restaurant – the local perch is delicious. Even if you're staying in Irkutsk, it's worth coming to the restaurant for lunch. Many of the

Intourist packages include a lunch stop here. **$$**

Novosibirsk
Sibir
Ulitsa Lenina 21
tel: (3832) 231215, 233381
The best hotel in Novosibirsk is the modern Intourist-run Sibir. **$$**

Ulan Ude
Geser
Ulitsa Ranzhurova 11
tel: (30122) 28151
fax: (30122) 25925
Centrally located, with good business services and a sauna. **$$**

Vladivostok
Amursky Zaliv
Ulitsa Naberezhnaya 9
tel: (4232) 225520
The best hotel in town is this maze-like, huge, depressing, Soviet-style hotel. However, its great location on Amur Bay makes up for the architecture. **$$**
Hotel Vladivostok
Ulitsa Naberezhnaya, 10
tel: (4232) 222246
The Vladivostok is situated opposite the Amursky Zaliv with views of the bay. Be warned: both hotels are overrun with prostitutes who may knock on your door at any time of the night. **$$**

Yakutsk
Ontario
Vilyushkyy Trakt
tel: (4112) 422066
The best hotel in Yakutsk is the 3-star Ontario, 6 km (3.5 miles) north of the town, in the style of a Yakut log building. **$$**
Sterkh
Prospekt Lenina 8
tel: (4112) 242701
For the comforts of the inner city life try the 3-star Intourist-run Sterkh. **$$**

ALTAY REPUBLIC
Barnaul
Sibir
Sotsialisticheskiy Prospekt 116
tel: (3852) 255170
Built in 1967, the Sibir is in the

centre of Barnaul, near the railway terminal and 30 minutes from the airport. It has five floors and 156 rooms. **$**
Belokurikha
Pensionat Belokurikha
Altaisky Krai, Belokurikha
tel: (277) 20196
This is the central rest home in the town from where guests can set off skiing, or trekking, make use the medical facilities on offer or simply enjoy the surrounding beauty and fresh air. **$**

Belarus
Hotel accommodation in Belarus has changed little from Soviet times, and Western notions of service have yet to appear over the horizon. Nonetheless, the following are the best available. The prices are calculated at the official exchange rate.

Minsk
Yubileinaya Hotel
19 Prospekt Masherova
tel: (0712) 269 024
One of he two main Intourist hotels in the capital. **$$**
Planeta
31 Prospekt Masherova
tel: (0712) 238 587
The other Intourist hotel, a little further up the road. **$$**
Minsk
11 Prospekt Skaryny
tel: (0712) 200 132
A slightly cheaper option. **$$**

Brest
Intourist
Vyl. Maskouskaya 15
tel: (01622) 52 083
A 1970s hotel. **$$**

Hotels in Kiev
Kiev has lagged behind in upgrading the variety and quality of its places to stay. Construction projects started in 1998 should soon improve the situation. The business hotels in the city centre still tend to be overpriced and the tourist hotels rather basic.

Hrodno
Hotel Belarus
Vyl. Kalinovskoho 1
tel: (0152) 441 674
Comfortable and good value. **$**

Ukraine

Kiev
BUSINESS HOTELS
Dnipro
Khreshchatyk 1/2
tel: (44) 229 8287
Central, and one of the better of the
Soviet–era hotels. **$$$**
Khreschatyk
Khreshchatyk 14
tel: (44) 229 7339
Centrally located just off the main
square. A cheaper hotel, although
far from picturesque. **$$$**
Kyivska
Gospitalna 12
tel: (44) 220 4144
A former Intourist hotel that has
been renovated. Pricey. **$$$**
Rus
Gospitalna 4
tel: (44) 220 4226
Situated just down the hill from the
Kyivska, but costing around $50

less per room. **$$**
Domus
Yaroslavska, 19
tel: (44) 462 51 20/1/2/3
Located in the Podil area of the city,
this is a new hotel which is clean
and bright even if the rooms are
quite small. **$$–$$$**

Price Guide

Prices are based on the cost of a
room for two, including
breakfast.

$$$$ Luxury over US$280
$$$ Expensive US$150–$280
$$ Moderate US$35–$150
$ Budget US$10–$35

Ukraina
Shevchenko Blvd. 5
tel: (44) 229 28 07
Renovated and conveniently located
just off Kreshchatyk, Kiev's main
street. **$$**

TOURIST CLASS
Andriivskyi Complex
Vozdvizhenska 60 (in the courtyard

just off Andriivskyi Uzviz 24)
tel: (44) 416 2256
Well–placed but erratic. Check for
booking fees. **$$**
St Petersburg
Shevchenko Blvd. 4.
tel: (44) 225 7101
Vyl. Volodymyrska 36.
tel: (44) 229 5943
One of Kiev's oldest hotels. **$$**

Other tourist hotels with basic
rooms can be found on the left
bank of the river.
Bratislava
Vyl. Malyshka 1
tel: (44) 559 69 20
Close to metro Darnitsa **$$**
Slavutych
Vyl. Entuziastiv 1
tel: (44) 555 38 59 **$$**
Tourist
Vyl. Okipnoi 2
tel: (44) 517 88 32. **$$**

Lviv
Grand
Pr. Svobody 13
tel: (0322) 724 042
This is the best bet, with Habsburg
architecture and a good Ukrainian

Youth Hostels

The non-profit national Russian
Youth Hostel Association (also
known as Hostelling Russia,
Russian Youth Hostels and RYH)
was founded in 1992.
In addition to building a network
of budget accommodation within
Russia, Russian Youth Hostels also
has close ties to many Hostelling
International national associations
such as DJH – German YHA, SRM –
Finnish YHA, and the Baltic Youth
Hostel Associations.
Through this large network of
associations, it is now possible to
stay in youth hostels in all the
countries lying on the Baltic Sea.

Moscow
Heritage Hostel
Kosmonavtov ul, 2
tel: (095) 975 3501
fax: 975 3610
email: evgen@az–tour.msk.ru **$**

Travellers Guest House
Bolshaya Pereyaslavskaya, 50,
10th floor
tel: (095) 971 4059
email: tgh@glas.apc.org **$**
G&R International Hostel
Yunosty St. 5/1, block 6, off 35
tel: (374) 5731, 7430 **$**

St Petersburg
St Petersburg International Hostel
3rd Sovetskaya Ulitsa, 28,
St Petersburg, 193036
tel: (812) 329 8018
fax: 329 8019
email: ryh@ryh.spb.su
Postal address (to Russia via
Finnish post): St Petersburg
International Hostel, PO Box 8,
SF–53501, Lappeenranta, Finland.
This is a Russian-American joint
project with English-speaking staff.
The renovated 19th-century
building contains a cybercafé and

shows nightly movies. **$**
Hostel Holiday
1 Mikhailova Ulitsa, St Petersburg
195009
tel: (812) 542 7364
Central location near Finland
Station with river views.
MasterCard is accepted. **$**
Summer Hostel
Baltiyskaya Ulitsa 26
tel: (812) 252 5381, 252 7563
Bunk goes for around $12. **$**

Novgorod
Novgorod Hostel
Komsomolskaya Ulitsa (Novo-
Luchinskaya Ulitsa) 27A
tel: (816) 714 58, 720 33 **$**

Irkutsk
Baikalcomplex, 664029 – 29,
PO Box 3598
tel: (3952) 46 2437 **$**

restaurant on the ground floor. **$$$**

George
1 Mickiewicz Square
tel: (0322) 725 952
A former Intourist hotel, which was built by an Englishman at the end of the 19th century. Faded grandeur makes this a fun place to stay. **$$**

Dniestr
Vyl. Mateika 6
tel: (0322) 720 783
Slightly more austere than the George, but with more convincing plumbing. **$$**

Chernivtsi

Cheremosh
13a Komarova
tel: (03722) 487 77
The best tourist hotel in town, 3.5 km (2 miles) from the centre. **$$**

Odessa

Londonskaya
11 Prymorsky Blvd.
tel: (0482) 225 019
One of the finest hotels in Ukraine. The best rooms are the old ones facing out towards the sea, but these are also very expensive. **$$$**

Krasnaya
Vyl. Pushkina 15
tel: (0482) 227 220
The substantial Krasnaya is the best of the rest of the hotels. **$$$**

Grand Moscow
Vyl. Deribasivska 29
tel: (0482) 224 016
There are a number of slightly decrepit but worthwhile places along the main Vyl. Deribasivska, of which the Hotel Grand Moscow is the most notable. **$$**

Chorne More Hotel
52 Rishelevska
tel: (0482) 242 028
Offers standard Intourist fare. **$$**

THE CRIMEA

The southern Crimean coast has plenty of tourist rooms, but little has been done since 1991 to upgrade them or promote them to visitors.

Yalta

Oreanda
Lenin Embankment 35/2
tel: (0654) 328 166
The Oreanda, at the western end of the Lenin Embankment, is the best place to stay. **$$–$$$**

Yalta
Vyl. Dryazhinskoho 50
tel: (0654) 350 150
The huge Yalta with more than 2000 beds dominates the other end of the town. **$–$$**

Palas
Chekhova 8
tel: (0654) 324 380
The Palas is a smaller and more pleasant place nearer the centre. **$–$$**

Sevastopol

Sevastopol
Nakhimova 8
tel: (0692) 523 671

Language Centres

An inexpensive way to visit Russia is through institutes that run Russian language courses. Among these are the Lomonosov and Lumumba universities and the Pushkin Institute of Russian Language in Moscow, the University of St Petersburg, the Shevchenko University in Kiev and other universities and linguistic co-operatives. They are all able to arrange visas and inexpensive accommodation during the period of studies.

To communicate directly with the universities you should contact the cultural attaché of the Russian embassy or consulate. It is rather more difficult to make contact with the co-operatives since they are not represented abroad.

When selecting courses, care should be taken to ensure that the teaching is on a professional level. It is also worth contacting the Russian departments of universities at home. Many are now running short (one- or two-week) overseas study tours (including flight to Russia, accommodation and transport within Russia, and tuition fees) for the general public.

Hotel accommodation in Sevastopol is limited, but this is a reasonable bet. **$**

Sudak

Horyzont
Vyl. Turistikoyu
tel: (06566) 334 882
Situated behind the fortress, this hotel is worth trying. **$**

Where to Eat

What to Eat

Most of the different ethnic groups populating the CIS pretend to have their own national cuisine, and some of them genuinely have. Within this diversity, Russian, Georgian and Ukrainian cuisines are said to be the best.

Russian

The most famous dishes are beef Stroganov and Beluga caviar. Russian cuisine includes popular dishes like *bliny* (pancakes served with butter and sour cream, caviar, meat, jam etc), *shchi* (sour cabbage soup with meat pepped up with mustard), *pelmeny* (boiled dumplings with meat) and *kasha* (a type of gruel or porridge made of different grains).

Georgian

Georgian food has always been popular in Russia, and several Georgian restaurants have recently opened in Moscow to compete with the venerable but Soviet-style monopolist Aragvi on Tverskaya and the Tbilisi in St Petersburg. Georgian cuisine is famous for its *shashlik*, *tsyplyata tabaka* (chicken fried under pressure), *basturma* (spicy salted and smoked meat), *suluguni* (salted cheese), green and red *lobio* (beans), specially cooked aubergines, and *satsyvi* (chicken). It can be served with *lavash* (a special kind of bread), or with *khachapuri* (a roll stuffed with cheese) flavoured by various spices such as *tkemali* or with a delicious *bazha* sauce.

Ukrainian

Ukrainians have traditionally been known to eat a lot – but also tastily. Specialities include *borshch* (beetroot soup with cabbage, meat, mushrooms and other ingredients), *galushky* (small boiled dumplings) and *varenyky zvyshneyu* (curd dumplings with red cherries served with sugar and sour cream). Known and served around the world is chicken Kiev (or Kiev cutlet), prepared with different spices and garlic. Loved by everyone in the Ukraine is *salo* (salted raw lard spiced with garlic) served with black bread. Also very popular is *kolbasa* (assorted smoked sausages).

Where to Eat

Inevitably the following list of restaurants concentrates on Moscow and St Petersburg where choice is continually expanding. In other cities and towns, it is often best to ask around when you arrive. In the current climate, restaurants often open and close within the space of weeks. At some restaurants, you should take your own alcoholic drinks as these may not be available, or you may not like the overwhelmingly sweet champagnes and wines.

MOSCOW

All national cuisines are well represented, with the big hotels incorporating several excellent restaurants. Booking is not usually necessary. If you opt for an old Soviet-style restaurant and don't want to arrive to a table laden with hors d'oeuvres, specify a "*chisti stol*" (a "clean table") when booking. However, unlike several years ago, there are hundreds of fine restaurants to choose from, check out the *Moscow Business Telephone Guide* and *Exile*.

RUSSIAN

Praga
Arbatskaya Ploshchad
tel: (095) 290 6171
Open noon–3pm; 6pm–4am
Probably Moscow's most famous restaurant since the 19th century, expensive. $$$

Samovar
Ulitsa Myasnitskaya 13
tel: (095) 924 4688
Open noon–11pm
A quiet, elegant restaurant. Myasnitskaya means "meat dealers' street", so check out the *pelmeny*. The orthodox *pelmeni* mix should contain beef, pork and mutton, but there are plenty of kinds to choose from. $$$

Sudar
Zubovsky Proyezd 2
tel: (095) 247 1157
Open noon–midnight
Lively restaurant, great food. $$$

U Babushki
Ulitsa Bolshaya Ordynka 42
tel: (095) 230 2797
Open noon–11pm
Excellent food. $$$

U Yuzefa
Ulitsa Dubininskaya 11/17
tel: (095) 238 4646.
Open noon–midnight
A Jewish restaurant with a Russian touch. $$$

Bochka ("Barrel")
Ulitsa 1905 Goda
tel: (095) 252 3041
Open round the clock
The barbecue is as hot as things got here in 1905 and, indeed, 1993. $$$

Margarita Cafe
Ulitsa Malaya Bronnaya 28,
Patriarch's Ponds
tel: (095) 299 6534
Open 1pm–midnight
The food is not exceptional, but the café, named after the enchantress from the famous Mikhail Bulgakov book, *Master and Margarita*, offers a different kind of local flavour – live trendy music. This is the Moscow students' haunt, it may be a little crowded. $$

Mesto Vstrechy ("The Tryst")
Maly Gnezdnikovsky Pereulok 9/8
tel: (095) 229 2373
Open 10am–5am
(See the following entry.) $$

Mefisto
Shmitovsky Proyezd 10
tel: (095) 259 6497
Open 10am–6am
Both Mesto and Mefisto are

fashionable "cellar" restaurants serving tasty, not always strictly Russian, meat and seafood dishes. At Mefisto, you can watch your pork ribs or a mutton leg being grilled as you work on the appetisers. **$$**

Gvozdi ("Nails")
Bolshaya Nikitskaya 19
Open noon–5am
More egalitarian than the rest and less cosmopolitan. Here you can sample real Russian cuisine. **$$**

GEORGIAN

U Pirosmani
Novodevichy Proyezd 4
tel: (095) 247 1926
Open noon–11pm
Named after a famous Georgian painter, this is probably the finest (and most expensive) Caucasian restaurant in town. It has a beautiful interior and a good view. Quiet live music. **$$$**

Suliko
Bolshaya Polyanka 42/2
tel: (095) 238 2601
Open noon–midnight
This restaurant serves great *shashlik* and aubergine. Tasteful live music. **$$**

Tiflis
Ostozhenka 32
tel: (095) 290 2897
Open noon–midnight
Tiflis offers a wide variety of Georgian dishes.
Wine note: You will find authentic Georgian wine at Pirosmani, Suliko and Tiflis. **$$**

Guria
Komsomolsky Prospect 7/3
tel: (095) 246 0378
Open 7am–11am, noon–2:30pm, 5:30 pm–10:30pm
(See the following entry) **$**

Mama Zoya
Sechenovsky Pereulok 8
Open noon–10pm
Both Guria and Mama Zoya serve excellent *khachapuri, satsivi, shahlik, lobio* and aubergine. Service may be a little sloppy, but the atmosphere is warm, friendly and gregariously Georgian. Be prepared for some really loud live ethnic music. **$**

EUROPEAN

The following Western restaurants are expensive, but provide good service and most offer Russian cuisine.

El Dorado
Ulitsa Polyanka 1/3
tel: (095) 238 9154
Open 11:30am–11:30pm. **$$$**

Casanova
Kudrinskaya Ploschad 1
tel: (095) 255 4228
Open 6pm–5am. **$$$**

Grand Imperial
Gagarinsky Pereulok 9/5
tel: (095) 291 6063
Open 11:30am–1:30 am
Exorbitant. **$$$**

Price of a Meal

The following restaurant categories are based on the price of a meal for one. They serve as a guide only, due to fluctuations in the rouble-dollar exchange rate.

$$$ Expensive: more than US$50
$$ Moderate: US$20–$50
$ Budget: less than US$20

Savoy
Ulitsa Rozhdestvenka 3, Hotel Savoy
tel: (095) 929 8600
Open 1pm–11pm. **$$$**

Le Club
Ulitsa Radishchevskaya 20
tel: (095) 915 1042
Open noon–2am Sunday–Thursday, noon–5am Friday and Saturday. **$$$**

Teatro Mediterraneo
Teatralny Proyezd 1/4, Hotel Metrolpol
tel: (095) 927 6069
Open 11am–2am. **$$$**

Le Gastronome
Kudrinskaya Ploshchad 1
tel: (095) 255 4433
Open noon–11pm. **$$$**

Amalteya
Stremyanny Pereulok 28, korpus 1
tel: (095) 236 0256
Open 11am–midnight. **$$**

AMERICAN

Starlite Diner
Ulitsa Bolshaya Sadovaya 16
tel: (095) 290 9638
Korovy Val 9
tel: (095) 959 8919
Open round the clock. **$$**

American Bar and Grill
Ulitsa Tverskaya–Yamskaya 32/1
tel: (095) 251 7999
Open round the clock; also at Zemlyanoi Val 59
tel: (095) 912 3615
Open noon–3am. **$$**

B.B. King
Ulitsa Sadovaya–Samotyochnaya 4/2
tel: (095) 299 8206
Open noon–midnight
Features live blues and other music, with American Cajun cuisine. **$$**

T.G.I. Friday
Ulitsa Tverskaya 18
tel: (095) 209 3601
Open 11am–1:30am
Okhotny Ryad shopping mall
Open noon–midnight. **$$**

Moosehead
Ulitsa Bolshaya Polyanka 54
tel: (095) 230 7333
Open noon–5am. **$**

Papa John's
Ulitsa Myasnitskaya 22
tel: (095) 755 9554
Open 6pm–morning. **$**

ST PETERSBURG

The city has a wide selection of restaurants to choose from, representing most of the world's major cuisines.

Svir
Hotelship Peterhof, Makarov Emb
tel: (812) 325 8888
An elegant restaurant on the Neva serving international, Russian and seafood. Live music. **$$$**

Admiralty
Nevskij Palace Hotel, 57 Nevsky Prospekt
tel: (812) 275 2001
Russian and seafood specialities served in a maritime setting. **$$**

Brasserie
Grand Hotel Europe
1 7 Mikhailovskaya Ulitsa/Ulitsa

Brodskovo
tel: (812) 329 6000
An elegant Italian restaurant. **$$**
Europa
Grand Hotel Europe
Nevsky Prospekt
tel: (812) 329 6000
This leading Russian and
continental gourmet restaurant has
a striking art nouveau setting. **$$**
Golden Dragon
62 Dekabristov Ulitsa, near the
Mariinsky Theatre
tel: (812) 114 8441
Not surprisingly serves Chinese and
Southeast Asian cuisine. **$–$$**

Price of a Meal

The following restaurant
categories are based on the
price of a meal for one. They
serve as a guide only, due to
fluctuations in the rouble-dollar
exchange rate.

$$$ Expensive: more than
US$50
$$ Moderate: US$20–$50
$ Budget: less than US$20

Mollie's Irish Bar
36 Rubinshteina Ulitsa
tel: (812) 319 9768
Open 11am–3am
Guinness on tap and hearty pub
food; live music. **$$**
Nikolai
52 Bolshaya Morskaya
tel: (812) 311 1402
Situated next to St Isaac's Square,
Nikolai serves European cuisine
with salmon specialities from
Finland. **$$**
Patio Pizza
182 Nevsky Prospekt
tel: (812) 271 7792
Italian food and salad bar – a rarity
in Russia. **$$**
Polonaise
45 Bolshaya Morskaya Ulitsa
tel: (812) 315 0319
Russian cuisine in a historic
18th–century building. **$$**
Tandoor
2 Voznesensky Prospekt
(near St Isaac's Cathedral)
tel: (812) 312 3886

An Indian menu with a good, varied
vegetarian selection. **$$**
Tinkov's
Kazanskaya Ulitsa
This centrally–located restaurant is
one of the coolest and largest in
town. It has its own micro-brewery.
$–$$
Tschaika
14 Kanal Griboedova
tel: (812) 312 4631
For those longing to sample five
kinds of German beer to the sounds
of jazz. **$$**
Idiot
82 Naberezhnaya Moika
tel: (812) 315 1675
The pseudo-bohemian decor and
atmosphere is popular with tourists
and ex-pats. **$**
La Cucharacha
39 Naberezhnaya Reki Fontanki
tel: (812) 110 4006
This is one of the few genuine
Mexican restaurants in town;
centrally located just off of Nevsky
Prospekt. **$**
Tbilisi
10 Sytninskaya Ulitsa
tel: (812) 232 9391
Serves Georgian cuisine. **$**

THE GOLDEN RING
Yaroslavl
Kotorosl
87 Bolshaya Oktyabrysky
tel: (0852) 211536
Medved
40/2 Ulitsa Svobody
tel: (0852) 223628

Vladimir
Zolotoye Koltso
tel: (0922) 47208
Lada
23 Prospekt Lenina
tel: (0922) 23274

Suzdal
Pokrovskaya Hotel
in the Motel Suzdal complex
Trapeznaya
in the town Kremlin

THE EUROPEAN NORTH
Arkhangelsk
Yubileiny
52 Troitsky Prospekt
tel: (8182) 432880

Murmansk
Thanks to the number of foreign
sailors in town, restaurants here
are better than might be expected.
Darya Morya
26/9 Prospekt Lenina
tel: (8152) 72335
Good venue for seafood.
Polyarniye Zari
17 Ulitsa Knipovicha
tel: (8152) 54360
Worth trying.

Novgorod
Fortress
The best place to eat, particularly if
you are here only for the day, is in
the fortress itself (roubles and
dollars), which provides warming
sustenance in winter and has an
open veranda for the hot summer
days. It has the best location.
You can also try:
Café Posad
14 Ulitsa Bolshevikov
tel: (8162) 94849
Good value.
Intourist Hotel
16 Ulitsa Velikaya
tel: (8162) 94288
Open until midnight.

Pskov
Kavkaz
10 Oktyabrisky Prospeckt
tel: (8112) 24637
Pskov
5a Ulitsa Yana Fabritsusa
tel: (8112) 28758

Vologda
Oktyabrskaya
25 Ulitsa Oktyabrisky
tel: (8172) 63138

Vyborg
Even though this is a small town,
you can eat your heart out in a
variety of grill bars and restaurants,
including the restaurant at:
Hotel Druzhba
5 Zheleznodorozhnaya Ulitsa
tel: (278) 94464

SOUTHWEST RUSSIA

Kursk

The following two hotels have reasonable restaurants:

Tsentralnaya
2 Krasnaya Ploshchad
tel: (0712) 569048 **$$**
Kursk
Ulitsa Lenina, near corner of Ulitsa Mozhayskovo
tel: (0712) 26980 **$$**
Grim Restaurant
For simple fare, try this unfortunately named restaurant near Hotel Kursk. **$**

Bryansk
Hotel Bryansk
Prospekt Lenina
tel: 007 0832 46 68 44
The hotel's restaurant is worth trying. **$$**

Orel
Café Aktyor
Ploshchad Lenina, southeast of Turgenev Theatre.
Serves standard Russian café fare – bread, cakes, biscuits and hotpots. **$**

Smolensk
Lapatinski Sad
Ploshchad Lenina
A good place for a basic, filling meal. **$$**

THE URALS

Yekaterinburg
Hotel Oktyabrskaya
Ulitsa S. Kovalevskoi 17
tel: (3432) 445146
This is the best option for eating.
Hotel Sverdlovsk
Chelyuskintzev 106
Offers sporadic choice and as well as quality.
Restaurant Kharbin
Ulitsa Kyibisheva 40D
tel: (3432) 226325
This is an unusually appealing Chinese restaurant for Russia, with authentic Chinese chefs. Hanging lanterns and elaborately decorated rooms add to the atmosphere. Reservations in advance are essential.

THE EUROPEAN SOUTH

Most hotels have good restaurants which are priced according to the level of the hotel.

Sochi
Lubava
Hotel Zhemchuzhina
Chernomorskaya 3
tel: (8622) 992976
Open 8am–2am (café service from 9pm)
The Lubava serves Russian food.
Kanyon
Kazachii Brod
tel: (8622) 448189
Open 11am–midnight
The Kanyon is a good traditional Greek restaurant.
Kavkavskiye Aul
tel: (8622) 970817
Located near the Agurskie waterfalls, this restaurant serves excellent Caucasian food.

SIBERIA AND THE FAR EAST

Irkutsk
Intourist
Ulitsa Gagarina 44
tel: (3952) 290167, 290273
The hotel offers a choice of restaurants. The second-floor restaurant is the best in town, though the music is too loud and the menu irregular. As in most state restaurants, the menu diminishes as the night goes on, so arrive early. The Peking restaurant charges in hard currency and serves a dreadful imitation of Chinese food. However, on the fourth floor of the hotel there is a delightful little tea shop that serves tea and caviar blinis.
Baikal
Ulitsa Khmelnitskogo 1
Serves Russian cuisine.
Arktika
Ulitsa Marksa 26
Offers good seafood, especially perch, fresh from Lake Baikal.
Tsentralny
Ulitsa Timirjazeva
Serves Russian specialities.

Eating Out in Crimea

Some of the best places to eat in Yalta on the Crimean coast are along the Lenin embankment. In summer open-air restaurants and bars line both sides of the walkway.
Oreanda Hotel
Lenin Embankment 35/2
tel: (0654) 328 166
The restaurant at the Oreanda is good value.
Espagnola
tel: (0654) 320 043
An interesting restaurant beached opposite the Oreanda in an old-style galleon.
Kafe Sochi
A large restaurant to be found further along the Lenin embankment from the Oreanda.

Yakutsk
Ontario
Vilyushkyy Trakt
tel: (4112) 422066
The Ontario restaurant, a joint venture, is Yakutsk's best. **$$**

UKRAINE

Ukraine is famous for several dishes: chicken Kiev and *borshch* being best known. The first – the white meat of chicken stuffed with garlic and butter – is almost invisible on the menus of the cities' restaurants. The second, a cabbage, beetroot and potato soup, is available everywhere and often the best thing on the menu. Also good are *vereniki*, small dumplings filled with curd cheese.

Kiev
Tsarskoe Selo
Vyl. Sichnevoho Povstannya 42/1
tel: (44) 573 9775
For excellent Ukrainian food, make your way to this restaurant, set in a reconstructed indoor Ukrainian village up by the Pechersk Monastery. You are well advised to book in advance.
Skhody (Lesnitsa in Russian)
Hrinchenka 7
tel: (44) 229 8629
This restaurant, just off

Independence Square, is worth trying for Ukrainian cuisine.

Kureni
Parkova Aleya 4
tel: (44) 293 4062
An open-air restaurant for the summer months.

Arizona
Nab. Kreshchatynska 25
tel: (44) 416 2438
A fine Mexican restaurant in the Podil.

Tequila House
Spaska 8
tcl: (44) 417 0358
Another good Mexican eaterie in the Podil.

San Tori
Sahaidachnoho 41
tel: (44) 462 4994
San Tori serves excellent but pricey Thai and Japanese food.

Other good central restaurants include:

Studio
Museiny per. 4
tel: (44) 228 7208

Pantagruel
1 Vyl. Lysenko
tel: (44) 228 8142
Close to the Golden Gates.

Lviv

Grand Hotel
Prosp. Svobody 13
tel (0322) 722 936
The restaurant in the Grand Hotel has traditional Ukrainian dishes at very reasonable prices.

Hotel Dniester
Vyl. Mateika 6
tel: (0322) 797 008
The Dniester also offers a good spread.

Of the restaurants in Lviv, among the best are:

Pid Levom
19 pl. Rynok
tel: (0322) 726 813

Kniazhy Lviv
Vyl. Hnatiuka
tel: (0322) 729 086

Odessa

Londonskaya Hotel
Prymorsky Blvd.
tel: (0482) 250 488

The Londonskaya has a wonderful courtyard for summer lunches and dinners.

Valday
Ploshchad Potemkynstiv
The Valday is among the best of the many small restaurants that dot the centre of Odessa.

Galactica
Preobrazhenska 23
Perhaps one of the oddest restaurants, where standard Ukrainian dishes are presented under bizarre stellar titles.

Pivdenna Palmira
tel: (0482) 684 477
If you are down at Arcadia beach, it's worth stopping here.

What to Drink

Everyone knows what they drink in Russia: vodka, and tea from the samovar. This is only half the truth. There are numerous other drinks within different national cuisines. The Ukrainian traditional alcoholic drink is *gorilka* which resembles vodka. But more popular, and more refined, is *gorilka z pertsem*, i.e. gorilka with a small red pepper. The traditional non-alcoholic drink is *uzvar* (made of stewed fruit).

Georgians drink different dry and semi-dry wines, such as *Adzhaleshi*, *Kindzmarauli*, *Akhasheni*, *Tsinandali*, *Mukuzani*, *Kinzmarauli*, *Alazan Valley*, and *Tvishi* (reported to have been the favourite wine of Stalin). Non-alcoholic drinks from Georgia are represented by the best in Russian mineral water such as *Borzhomi* and *vody Lagidze* (mineral water with various syrup mixtures).

In summer Russians prefer to drink *kvas*, a refreshing drink prepared from bread fermented with water and yeast.

Nightlife

Nightlife in Moscow

Nightclubs

Alexander Blok
Krasnopresnenskaya Naberezhnaya
tel: (095) 255 9284/78
This club is in a boat by the Mezhdunarodnaya hotel.

Alexander's No.1 Club
Ulitsa Pushkinskaya 1
tel: (095) 292 0272

Arbat Blues Club
Filippovsky Pereulok 11, Bldg. 2
tel: (095) 291 1546

Bulgakov
Ulitsa Bolshaya Sadovaya 10
tel: (095) 209 9914/9723
Open 7pm–7am.

Beverly Hills
Kudrinskaya Ploshchad 1
tel: (095) 255 4228
Open 6:30pm–6am
Chuck Norris's famous Moscow venture.

Night Flight
Ulitsa Tverskaya 17
tel: (095) 229 4165

Monte Carlo
Ulitsa Balchug 3/2
tel: (095) 232 9394

Up and Down
Zubovsky Blbd 4
tel: (095) 201 5291

Music

The following is a list of venues for Moscow's best jazz, reggae and rock concerts.

Four Rooms
Raushskaya Naberezhnaya 4/5
tel: (095) 231 7895

Vermel
Address and telephone as for Four Rooms, above.

Hermitage Club
Karetny Ryad 3
tel: (095) 299 1160/7519

Jazz Art

Ulitsa Begovaya 5
tel: (095) 191 8320
Open 7pm–11pm Tuesday,
Wednesday, Friday and Sunday.
Krizis Zhanra
Prechistensky Pereulok 22/4
tel: (095) 243 8605
Open 11am–11pm.
Nostalgie Art Café
Chistoprudny Boulevard 12a
tel: (095) 916 9478
Open 8am–11:30 pm.

Casinos

Casino Arbat
Arbat restaurant
Ulitsa Novy Arbat 21
tel: (095) 291 1134
Casino Gabriela
Ulitsa Tverskaya 3/5
tel: (095) 956 8448
Casino Metropole
Metropole Hotel
Teatralny Proyezd 1/4
tel: (095) 927 6950
Open round the clock.
Casino Moscow
Kalanchovskaya 21/40
tel: (095) 975 1967
Cherry Casino (Metelitsa)
Novy Arbat 21
tel: (095) 291 1170
Golden Dragon
3rd Ulitsa Yamskovo Polya 15
tel: (095) 975 5566/03

Shopping

What to Buy

Goods are plentiful throughout the
CIS, except in times of financial
crisis, and many Western chains
have opened stores in Moscow and
St Petersburg. Apart from at
markets, bargaining does not take
place. In the large cities, shopping
hours are now more in line than
those of the West, especially in the
large malls. Standard opening
hours elsewhere are
Monday–Saturday 10am–7pm,
many smaller shops take a lunch
break from 2–3pm.

Souvenirs

Inexpensive souvenirs, toys and
other knick-knacks abound on
Russian streets.

The "must see" street in
Moscow is the Arbat, where
Moscow painters and wood carvers
sell their works. Prices are quite
high, so don't be in a hurry to buy a
set of Russian *matryoshkas* (the
wooden dolls which fit inside one
another). The same set may be
found much cheaper somewhere
else. The Izmailovo market in the

city's northeastern suburb (metro
Izmailovsky Park) is worth a trip.

There are places similar to Arbat
in St Petersburg (Ostrovsky
Ploshchad), in Kiev (on October
Revolution Square) and in other big
cities. More upmarket souvenirs
can be bought in special shops, art-
salons and curio shops. But beware
of the problems waiting at customs:
according to new Russian
regulations, antiquities, precious
metals and art works may not be
exported without prior approval. The
risk of confiscation is real. Customs
officials are particularly strict about
antique icons. Permits can be
obtained from the government
offices on Neglinnaya Street 8–10,
2nd floor, room 29, Moscow, tel:
(095) 921 3258. Many art galleries
will provide the necessary
documentation.

Outside Moscow and St
Petersburg, look out for lace,
jewellery (Veliky Ustiug), painted
wooden objects (Archangelsk) and
carved ivory (especially in the
village of Lomonosovo, near
Archangelsk).

Russian and Ukrainian crafts and
traditional goods are similar
therefore items common to both
countries, such as fur hats, can just
as easily be bought in Kiev. A
particularly good place to buy is the
huge weekend market at the central
Republican stadium.

Ukraine's crafts include painted
wooden boxes, plates and spoons,
earthenware pottery, embroidered
cloths and linen and woollen rugs.

Moscow's Food Shops

Food shops now abound in
Moscow. You will find dozens of
shops on every street carrying
domestic and imported
foodstuffs. Caviar is stocked by all
the major food outlets. Here is a
selection:
Yeliseyevsky Gastronom
Unitsa Tverskaya 14
Novoarbatsky Food Store
Ulitsa Novy Arbat 11
Gastronoom No. 20
Ulitsa Bolshaya Lubyanka 14

Good for chocolates and
champagne.
Food Island
Leningradsky Prospekt 50
Foodland
Krasnopresnenskaya
Naberezhnaya 9
Global USA
Ulitsa Tverskaya 6
Sovhispan S.A.
Novinsky Boulevard 7/1
Expo-EM
Ulitsa Fersmana 9

Photography

Photographic equipment is easily obtainable in Moscow, St Petersburg and Kiev and quick film-developing services are available. Generally speaking, taking photographs in galleries, museums and exhibitions is permitted, but visitors should take care not take photographs of military installations or anything else that might be seen as a security object.

Though souvenir shops are quite common in Kiev, the best selection is available at Andriivsky Uzviz.

Where to Shop

MOSCOW

Department Stores

GUM (State Department Store)
Krasnaya Ploshchad 3 (Red Square)
This famous arcade has been commandeered by branches of foreign stores, and you won't find many Russian goods here although you will find some Russian handicrafts and souvenirs. Foreign-made goods will probably be more expensive than at home. However, it is worth visiting, if only for the fabulous decor.
Detsky Mir (Children's World)
Teatralny Proyezd 5
This store sells everything from toys and clothing to buggies.
TsUM (Central Department Store)
Ulitsa Petrovka 2
You'll find plenty of kitsch here in addition to traditional Russian goods, such as amber and coral jewellery, samovars, rugs and furs.
Petrovsky Passage
Ulitsa Petrovka 10
Another magnificent arcade. It is as expensive as GUM.
Tishinka Trading Centre
Ulitsa Bolshaya Gruzinskaya 50
Cheaper than the central shopping centres, Tishinka houses a supermarket, a market and a restaurant.

Fur Shops

Ars
Ulitsa Malaya Bronnaya 4
Alina Salon
Prospekt Vernadskogo 39
Bogumin
Zheleznodorozhny Proyezd 6
Claude Litz
Ulitsa Kuznetsky Most 14
Salon Ekaterina
Ulitsa Bolshaya Dmitrovka 1
Furs and Leather Shop
Chistoprudny Boulevard 21
Gornostai
Aptekarsky Pereulok 10A
Intermekh
Ulitsa Petrovka 2
Russian Fur
Ulitsa Dokukina 10
Sovmehkastoria
Ulitsa Bolshaya Dorogomilovskaya 14

Speciality Shops

Russkiye Souveniry
Kutuzovsky Prospekt 9
The place to shop if you are interested in upmarket souvenirs, such as lacquer boxes, silverware and ethnic costumes.

Jewellery Shops

Afran
National Hotel, Ulitsa Mokhovaya 15/1
Almaz
Komsomolsky Prospekt 49
Centre Yuvelir #1
Ulitsa Petrovka 24/1
Check the *Moscow Business Guide* for other Centre Yuvelirs.
Imperator
Berezhkovskaya Naberezhnaya 2
Jewels
Ulitsa Pushechnaya 7/5
Russian Gold
Ulitsa Lesnaya 43

Antiques Shops

Aktsia
Ulitsa Bolshaya Nikitskaya 21/18;
Raritet
Ulitsa Arbat 31
Starina
Ulitsa Petrovka 24

ST PETERSBURG

One of the best places to buy souvenirs is at the three bridges, next to the cathedral of Our Saviour on the Blood, right on Kanal Griboyedova.

Department Stores

Gostinny Dvor
35 Nevsky Prospekt
Most famous of St Petersburg's department stores.
Passage
48 Nevksy Prospekt
Another big department store; specialises in women's clothing.

Books, Maps, Music

Isskust
16 Nevsky Prospekt
Art books, posters and postcards.
Dom Knigi
28 Nevsky Prospekt
Posters, postcards and maps.
Antikvarnaya Kniga
18 Nevsky Prospekt
Second-hand books.
Melody
32/34 Nevsky Prospekt
Music store.
Mir
13 Nevsky Prospekt
Books in English.
Rhapsody
13 Ulitsa Bolshaya Konnushennaya (Zhelyabova)
Sheet music and records.
Bukinist
59 Liteyny Prospekt
Second–hand books.

Jewellery

Yantar (Amber)
24 Ulitsa Gertsena
Jewellery shop occupying the former Fabergé building.

Language

Language Tips

Modern Russian has no established and universally used forms of addressing. The old revolutionary form "*tavárishch*" (comrade), still used among some party members, lacks popularity among the rest of the population. One way is to say: "*Izviníti, skazhíte pozhálsta...*" (Excuse me, tell me, please...) or "*Izviníti, mózhna sprasít...*") or "*I ozhálst*" (Excuse me, can I ask you...).

If you want to look original and show your penetration into the depths of history of courteous forms, you can address the man as *gospodin* (sir), and the woman as *gospozha* (madam). Many people want to restore these pre-Revolutionary forms of address in modern Russian society. If you know the name of the father of the person you are talking to, the best and the most neutral way is to use both these when addressing him or her. The English forms of address – Mister or Sir – will also be accepted quite well.

You can hear common parlance forms *Maladan heelavék!* (Young man!) and *Dévushka!* (Girl!) to a person of any age and also *Zhénshchina!* (Woman!) to women in the bus, in the shop or at the market. These forms should be avoided in conversation.

Transliteration

There are four systems of transliteration of Russian words into English (see: *The Transliteration of Modern Russian for English Language Publications* by J.T. Shaw, the University of Wisconsin Press,

1967). If necessary, the systems can be combined so that one letter or a group of letters is transliterated according to one system and the other according to another. To transliterate some Russian letters, English letter combinations are used:

ж = zh, x = kh, ц = ts, ч = ch, ш =sh, щ = shch, ю = yu, я = ya, ё = yo. The Russian letter combination кс is transliterated both as *ks* and as *x*. Russian letters are transliterated (with a few exceptions) in a similar way: й, ы = y, e, ё = e.

To transliterate Russian soft sign between the consonants and before no-vowel, the apostrophe is used, or the soft sign is ignored, as before vowels. The transliteration of nominal inflections has a number of peculiarities: ый, ий = y, ие, ье = ie, ия = ia.

If the traditional English spelling in names differs from their letter-by-letter transliteration they are mostly translated in their English shape: Moscow (city), but river Moskva.

The Genetive inflections in the names of the streets and the other objects are translated according to their pronunciation, and not their spelling: площадь Горького, (*ploshchad' Gór'kogo*) = pl. Gorkovo in this book. The transliteration in this section shows the way to pronounce Russian words and therefore does not correspond exactly with their spelling.

The city maps and their captions use Russian words and abbreviations: ul. (*úlitsa*), means street; per. (*pereúlok*) – lane; prosp. (*prospékt*) – avenue; pl. (*plóshchad'*) – square; *alléya* – alley; *bul'vár* – boulevard; *magistrál* – main line; *proézd* – passage; *shossé* – highway; *spusk* – slope.

The Russian system of mentioning house numbers is as follows *prosp. Kalinina 28* (*28 Kalinin Avenue*).

English/Russian

From a linguistic point of view, Russian belongs to the Slavonic branch of the Indo-European family of languages. English, German,

French, Spanish and Hindi are its relatives.

It is important when speaking Russian that you reproduce the accent (marked here before each stressed vowel with the sign ') correctly to be understood well.

Historically Russian can be called a comparatively young language. The evolution of the language to its present shape on the basis of the spoken language of Eastern Slavs and the Church-Slavonic written language is thought to have occurred between the 11th and 14th centuries.

Modern Russian has absorbed a considerable number of foreign words. Very few tourists will be puzzled by Russian words like *telefon, televizor, teatr, otel, restoran, kafe, taxi, metro, aeroport*.

The thing that intimidates people making their first acquaintance with Russian is the Russian alphabet. In fact the alphabet can be remembered easily after a few repetitions and the difference with the Latin alphabet is only minimal. An understanding of the Russian alphabet permits one to make out the names of the streets and the shop signs.

The Russian (or Cyrillic) alphabet was created by two brothers, philosophers and public figures Constantine (St Cyril) and Methodius, both born in Solun (now Thessaloniki in Greece). Their purpose was to facilitate the spread of Greek liturgical books in Slavonic speaking countries.

Today the Cyrillic alphabet with different modifications is used in the Ukrainian, Belarusian, Bulgarian and Serbian languages, as well as a few others.

The Alphabet

The first two columns show the printed letter in Russian upper and lower case. The third column shows how the Russian letters sound and the fourth column shows the name of the letter in Russian.

А а **a**, archaeology **a**
Б б **b**, buddy **be**

В	в	**v**, vow **v**	
Г	г	**g**, glad **ge**	
Д	д	**d**, dot (the tip of the tongue close to the teeth, not the alveoli) **de**	
Е	е	**e**, get **ye**	
Ё	ё	**yo**, yoke **yo**	
Ж	ж	**zh**, composure **zhe**	
З	з	**z**, zest **ze**	
И	и	**i**, ink **i**	
Й	й	**j**, yes **jot**	
К	к	**k**, kind **ka**	
Л	л	**l**, life (but a bit harder) **el'**	
М	м	**m**, memory **em**	
Н	н	**n**, nut **en**	
О	о	**o**, optimum **o**	
П	п	**p**, party **pe**	
Р	р	**r** (rumbling – as in Italian, the tip of the tongue is vibrating) **er**	
С	с	**s**, sound **es**	
Т	т	**t**, title (the tip of the tongue close to the teeth) **te**	
У	у	**u**, nook **u**	
Ф	ф	**f**, flower **ef**	
Х	х	**kh**, hawk **ha**	
Ц	ц	**ts**, (pronounced conjointly) **tse**	
Ч	ч	**ch**, charter **che**	
Ш	ш	**sh**, shy **sha**	
Щ	щ	**shch**, (pronounced conjointly) **shcha**	
ъ		(the hard sign)	
Ы	ы	**y** (pronounced with the same position of a tongue as when pronouncing G, K) **y**	
ь		(the soft sign)	
Э	э	**e**, ensign **e**	
Ю	ю	**yu**, you **yu**	
Я	я	**ya**, yard **ya**	

Useful Words and Phrases

Numbers

1	*adín*	один
2	*dva*	два
3	*tri*	три
4	*chityri*	четыре
5	*pyat'*	пят´
6	*shes't*	шесть
7	*sem*	семь
8	*vósim*	восемь
9	*d'évit'*	девять
10	*d'ésit'*	десять
11	*adínatsat'*	одиннадцать
12	*dvinátsat'*	двенадцать
13	*trinátsat'*	тринадцать
14	*chityrnatsat'*	четырнадцать
15	*pitnátsat'*	пятнадцат´
16	*shysnátsat'*	шестнадцать
17	*simnátsat'*	семнадцать
18	*vasimnátsat'*	восемнадцать
19	*divitnátsat'*	девятнадцать
20	*dvátsat'*	двадцать
21	*dvatsat' adin*	двадцать один
30	*trítsat'*	тридцать
40	*sórak*	сорок
50	*pidisyat*	пятьдесят
60	*shyz'disyat*	шестьдесят
70	*s'émdisyat*	семьдесят
80	*vósimdisyat*	восемьдесят
90	*divinósta*	девяносто
100	*sto*	сто
200	*dv'és'ti*	двести
300	*trísta*	триста
400	*chityrista*	четыреста
500	*pitsót*	пятьсот
600	*shyssót*	шестьсот
700	*simsót*	семьсот
800	*vasimsót*	восемьсот
900	*divitsót*	девятьсот
1,000	*tysicha*	тысяча
2,000	*dve tysichi*	две тысяч и
10,000	*d'ésit' tysich*	десятьтысяч
100,000	*sto tysich*	сто тысяч
1,000,000	*milión*	миллион
1,000,000,000	*miliárd*	миллиард

Pronouns

I/we
ya/my
я/мы

You
ty (singular, informal)/
vy (plural, or formal singular)
ты/вы

He/she/they
on/aná/aní
он/она/они

My/mine
moj (object masculine)/
mayá (object feminine)/
mayó (neutral or without marking the gender)/
maí (plural)
мой/моя/моё/мои

Our/ours
nash/násha/náshe/náshy (resp.)
наш/наша/наше/наши

Your/yours
tvoj etc. (see My)
vash etc. (see Our)
твой/ваш

His/her, hers/their, theirs
jivó/jiyó/ikh
его/её/их

Who?
khto?
Кто?

What?
shto?
Что?

Greetings & Acquaintance

Hello!
zdrástvuti (neutral, and often accompanied by shaking hands, but it is not necessary)
Здравствуйте!

zdrástvuj (to one person, informal)
Здравствуй!

alo! (by telephone only)
Алло!

priv'ét! (informal)
Привет!

Good afternoon/Good evening
dóbry den'/dobry véchir
Добрый день/Добрый вечер

Good morning/Good night
dobrae útra/dobraj nóchi (= Sleep well)
Доброе утро/Доброй ночи

Good bye
dasvidán'ye (neutral)
Досвиданья

ciao! (informal)
Чао!

paká! (informal, literally "until")
Пока!

Good luck to you!
shchislíva!
Счастливо!

What is your name?
kak vas (tibya) zavút?/kak váshe ímya ótchistva? (the second is formal)
Как вас (тебя) зовут?/Как ваше имя иотчество?

My name is.../I am...
minya zavut.../ya...
Меня зовут...Я...

It's a pleasure
óchin' priyatna
Очень приятно

Good/excellent
kharashó/privaskhódna
хорошо/отлично

Do you speak English?
vy gavaríti pa anglíski?
Вы говорите по-английски?

I don't understand/I didn't understand
ya ni panimáyu/ya ni pónyal
Я не понимаю/Я не понял

Repeat, please
pavtaríti pazhálsta
Повторите, пожалуйста

What do you call this?
kak vy éta nazyváiti?
Как вы это называете?

How do you say...?
kak vy gavaríti...?
Как вы говорите...?

Please/Thank you (very much)
pazhálsta/(bal'shóe) spasíba
Пожалуйста/(больпюе) спасибо

Excuse me
izviníti
Извините

Getting Around

Where is the...?
gd'e (nakhóditsa)...?
Где находится...?

beach
plyazh
...пляж

bathroom
vánnaya
...ванная

bus station
aftóbusnaya stántsyja/aftavakzál
...автобусная станция/автовокзал

bus stop
astanófka aftóbusa
...остановка автобуса

airport
airapórt
...аэропорт

railway station
vakzál/stántsyja (in small towns)
...вокзал/станция

post office
póchta
...почта

police station
...milítsyja
...милиция

ticket office
bil'étnaya kássa
...билетная касса

market place
rynak/bazár
...рынок/базар

embassy/consulate
pasól'stva/kónsul'stva
...посольство/консульство

Where is there a...?
gd'e z'd'es'...?
Где здесь...?

currency exchange
abm'én val'úty
...обмен валюты

pharmacy
apt'éka
...аптека

(good) hotel
(kharóshyj) atél'/(kharoshaya) gastínitsa
...(хороший)отель/(хорошая)гостиница

restaurant
ristarán
...ресторан

bar
bar
...бар

taxi stand
stayanka taxí
...стоянка такси

subway station
mitró
...метро

service station
aftazaprávachnaya stantsyja/aftasárvis
...автозаправочная станция

news stand
gaz'étnyj kiósk
...газетный киоск

public telephone
tilifón
...телефон

hard currency shop
val'útnyj magazín
...валютный магазин

supermarket
univirsám
...универсам

department store
univirmák
...универмаг

hairdresser
parikmákhirskaya
...парикмахерская

jeweller
yuvilírnyj magazin
...ювелирный магазин

hospital
bal'nítsa
...больница

Do you have...?
u vas jes't'...?
У вас есть...?

I (don't) want...
ya (ni) khachyu...
Я (не) хочу...

I want to buy...
ya khachyu kupít'...
Я хочу купить...

Where can I buy...
gd'e ya magú kupít'...
Где я могу купить...

cigarettes
sigaréty
...сигареты

wine
vinó
...вино

film
fotoplyonku
...фотоплёнку

a ticket for...
bilét na...
...билет на...

this
éta
...это

postcards/envelopes
atkrytki/kanv'érty
...открытки/конверты

a pen/a pencil
rúchku/karandásh
...ручку/карандаш

soap/shampoo
myla/shampún'
...мыло/шампунь

aspirin
aspirn
...аспирин

I need...
mn'e núzhna...
Мне нужно...

I need a doctor/a mechanic
mn'e núzhyn dóktar/aftamikhánik
Мне нужен доктор/автомеханик

I need help
mn'e nuzhná pómashch'
Мне нужна помощ́

Car/plane/trains/ship
mashyna/samal'yot/póist/karábl'
машина/самолёт/поезд/корабль

A ticket to...
bil'ét do...
билет до...

How can I get to...
kak ya magu dabrátsa do...
Как я могу добраться до...

Please, take me to...
pazhalsta atvizíti minya...
Пожалуйста, отвезите меня...

What is this place called?
kak nazyváitsa eta m'ésta?
Как называется это место?

Where are we?
gd'e my?
Где мы?

Stop here
astanavíti z'd'es'
Остановите здесь

Please wait
padazhdíti pazhalsta
Подождите, пожалуйста

When does the train [plane] leave?
kagdá atpravl'yaitsa poist [samalyot]?
Когда отправляется поезд (самолёт)?

I want to check my luggage
ya khachyu prav'érit' bagázh
Я хочу проверить багаж

Where does this bus go?
kudá id'yot état aftóbus?
Куда идёт этот автобус?

Shopping

How much does it cost?
skól'ka eta stóit?
Сколько это стоит?

That's very expensive
eta óchin' dóraga
Это очень дорого

A lot, many/A little, few
mnóga/mála
много/мало

It (doesn't) fits me
eta mn'e (ni) padkhódit
Это мне (не) подходит

At the Hotel

I have a reservation
u minya zakázana m'esta
У меня заказана комната

I want to make a reservation
ya khachyu zakazát' m'esta
Я хочу заказать место

A single (double) room
adnam'éstnuyu (dvukhmestnuyu) kómnatu
одноместную (двухместную) комнату

I want to see the room
ya khachyu pasmatrét' nómer
Я хочу посмотреть номер

Key/suitcase/bag
klyuch/chimadán/súmka
ключ/чемодан/сумка

Eating Out

Waiter/menu
afitsyánt/minyu
официант/меню

I want to order...
ya khachyu zakazat'...
Я хочу заказать

Breakfast/lunch/supper
záftrak/ab'ét/úzhyn
завтрак/обед/ужин

the house speciality
fírminnaya blyuda
фирменное блюдо

Mineral water/juice
minirál'naya vadá/sok
минеральная вода/сок

Coffee/tea/beer
kófe/chai/píva
кофе/ чай/пиво

What do you have to drink (alcoholic)?
shto u vas jes't' vypit'?
Что у вас есть выпить?

Ice/fruit/dessert
marózhynaya/frúkty/disért
мороженое/фрукты/десерт

Salt/pepper/sugar
sol'/périts/sákhar
соль/перец/сахар

Beef/pork/chicken/fish/shrimp
gavyadina/svinína/kúritsa/ryba/kriv 'étki
говядина/свинина/курица/рыба/креветки

Vegetables/rice/potatoes
óvashchi/ris/kartófil'
овощи/рис/картофель

Bread/butter/eggs
khleb/másla/yajtsa
хлеб/масло/яйца

Soup/salad/sandwich/pizza
sup/salát/butyrbrót/pitsa
суп/салат/бутерброд/пицца

A plate/a glass/a cup/a napkin
tar'élka/stakán/cháshka/salf'étka
тарелка/стакан/чашка/салфетка

The bill, please
shchyot pazhalsta
Счёт, пожалуйста

Delicious/Not so good
fkúsna/ták sibe
вкусно/так себе

I want my change, please
zdáchu pazhalsta
Сдачу, пожалуйста

Money

I want to exchange currency (money)
ya khachyu abmin'át' val'yutu (d'én'gi)
Я хочу обменять валюту (деньги)

Do you accept credit cards?
vy prinimáiti kridítnyi kártachki?
Вы принимаете кредитные карточки?

Can you cash a traveller's cheque?
vy mózhyti razminyat' darózhnyj chek?
Вы можете разменять дорожный чек?

What is the exchange rate?
kakój kurs?
Какой курс?

Time

What time is it?
katóryj chas?
Который час?

Just a moment, please
adnú minútachku
Одну минуточку

How long does it take?
sköl'ka vrémini eta zanimáit?
Сколько времени это занимает?

Hour/day/week/month
chas/den'/nid'élya/m'ésits
час/день/неделя/месяц

At what time?
f kakóe vrémya?
В какое время?

This (last, next) week
eta (próshlaya, sl'édujshchiya) nid'elya
эта (прошлая, следующая) неделя

Yesterday/today/tomorrow
fchirá/sivód'nya/záftra
вчера/сегодня/завтра

Sunday
vaskris'én'je
воскресенье

Monday
panid'él'nik
понедельник

Tuesday
ftórnik
вторник

Wednesday
sridá
среда

Thursday
chitv'érk
четверг

Friday
pyatnitsa
пятница

Saturday
subóta
суббота

The weekend
vykhadnyi dni
выходные дни

Signs & Inscriptions

вход/выход/входа нет
fkhot/vykhat/fkhóda n'et
Entrance/exit/no entrance

туалет/уборная
tual'ét/ubórnaya
Lavatory

Ж (З)/М (М)
dlya zhén'shchin/dlya mushchín
Ladies/gentlemen

зал ожидания
zal azhidán'ya
Waiting hall

занято/свободно
zánita/svabódna
Occupied/free

касса
kassa
booking office/cash desk

медпункт
mitpúnt
Medical services

справочное бюро
správachnae bzuro
Information

вода для питья
vadá dlya pit'ya
Drinking water

вокзал
vakzál
Terminal/railway station

открыто/закрыто
atkryta/zakryta
Open Closed

запрещается/опасно
zaprishchyaitsa/apásna
Prohibited/danger

продукты/гастроном
pradúkty/gastraným
Grocery

булочная/кондитерская
búlachnaya/kan'dítirskaya
Bakery/confectionery

закусочная/столовая
zakúsachnaya/stalóvaya
Refreshment room/canteen

самообслуживание
samaapslúzhivan'je
Self-service

баня/прачечная/химчистка
bánya/práchichnaya/khimchístka
Bath-house/laundry/dry cleaning

книги/культтовары
knígi/kul'taváry
Books/stationery

мясо/птица
m'ása/ptítsa
Meat/poultry

овощи/фрукты
óvashchi/frúkty
Green-grocery/fruits

универмаг/универсам
univirmák/univirsám
Department store/supermarket

Further Reading

History

The Blackwell Encyclopaedia of the Russian Revolution, edited by H. Shukman (Blackwell, 1989).
Catherine the Great, by J.T. Alexander (Oxford University Press, 1989).
Comrades 1917 – Russia in Revolution, by Brian Moynahan (Hutchinson, 1992).
History of Soviet Russia, by E.H. Carr (Pelican). In three volumes, first published 1953.
A History of the Soviet Union, by G.A. Hosking (Fontana/Collins, 1990).
The Icon and the Axe, by James Billington (Vintage US).
The Last Tsar, by Edvard Radzinsky (Hodder & Stoughton, 1992).
The Making of Modern Russia, by L. Kochan and R. Abraham (Penguin, 1983).
A People's Tragedy, by Orlando Figes (Pimlico).
Nicholas II: Emperor of all the

Russians, by Dominic Lieven (John Murray, 1993).
Paul I of Russia, by Roderick E. McGrew (Oxford, 1993).
Peter the Great: His Life and Work, by Robert K. Massie (Abacus).
Soviet Colossus: History of the USSR, by Michael Kort (M.E. Sharp, 1993).
Stalin, Man of Contradiction, by K.N. Cameron (Strong Oak Press, 1989).
Stalinism and After: Road to Gorbachev, by Alec Nove (Routledge, 1993).

Politics

Glasnost in Action, by A. Nove (Unwin Hyman, 1989).
Lenin's Tomb, by David Remnick (Viking, 1993).
The Other Russia, by Michael Glenny and Norman Stone (Faber and Faber, 1990).
Voices of Glasnost, by S. Cohen and K. van den Heuvel (Norton, 1989).

Biography/Memoirs

An English Lady at the Court of Catherine the Great, edited by A.G. Gross (Crest Publications, 1989).
The Gulag Archipelago, by

Russian Literature

A Hero of Our Time, by Mikhail Lermontov (Penguin).
And Quiet Flows the Don and **The Don Flows Home to the Sea**, by Mikhail Sholokhov.
Children of the Arbat, by Anatoli Rybakov (Hutchinson, 1988).
Crime and Punishment, The Brothers Karamazov, The Devils, by Fyodor Dostoyevsky. Penguin.
Dead Souls Diary of a Madman and Other Stories, by Nikolai Gogol.
Doctor Zhivago, by Boris Pasternak (Penguin).
Eugene Onegin, by Alexander Pushkin (Penguin).
Fathers and Sons, On The Eve, Sportsman's Sketches, by Ivan Turgenev (Penguin).

Lady with Lapdog and Other Stories, by Anton Chekhov (Penguin).
The Master and Margarita, by Mikhail Bulgakov.
The Penguin Book of Russian Short Stories, edited by David Richards (Penguin, 1981).
War and Peace, Anna Karenina and **The Death of Ivan Ilyich and Other Stories**, by Leo Tolstoy (Penguin).
We, by Evgeny Zamyatin (Penguin).
Red Cavalry and Other Stories, by Isaac Babel.
Soviet Russian Literature: Writers and Problems and The Epic of Russian Literature, by Mare Slonim.

Alexander Solzhenitsyn (Collins Harvill, 1988).
The House by the Dvina, by Eugenie Fraser (Corgi, 1986).
In the Beginning, by Irina Ratushinskaya (Hodder & Stoughton, 1990).
Into the Whirlwind; Within the Whirlwind, by Eugenia Ginzburg (Collins Harvill, 1989).
The Making of Andrei Sakharov, by G. Bailey (Penguin, 1990).
On the Estate: Memoirs of Russia Before the Revolution, edited by Olga Davydoff Bax (Thames & Hudson, 1986).
Russia: Despatches from the Guardian Correspondent in Moscow, by Martin Walker (Abacus, 1989).
Ten Days that Shook the World, by John Reed (Penguin, first published 1919).

Art

Folk Art in the Soviet Union (Abrams/Aurora, 1990).
The Hermitage (Aurora, 1987).
History of Russian Painting, by A. Bird (Phaidon, 1987).
The Irony Tower, by Andrew Solomon (Knopf).
The Kremlin and its Treasures, by Rodimzeva, Rachmanov and Raimann (Phaidon, 1989).
Masterworks of Russian Painting in Soviet Museums (Aurora, 1989).
New Worlds: Russian Art and Society 1900–3, by D. Elliott (Thames & Hudson, 1986).
Russian Art of the Avant Garde, by J.E. Bowlt (Thames & Hudson, 1988).
Russian Art from Neoclassicism to the Avant Garde, by D. V. Sarabianov (Thames & Hudson, 1990).
Street Art of the Revolution, Tolstoy, V. I. Bibikova and C. Cooke (Thames & Hudson), 1990.
Travel and Natural History Among the Russians, by Colin Thubron (Penguin, first published 1983).
Atlas of Russia and the Soviet Union, by R. Millner–Gulland, with N. Dejevsky (Phaidon, 1989).
The Big Red Train Ride, by Eric Newby (Picador, 1989).

Caucasian Journey, by Negley Farson (Penguin, first published 1951).
Epics of Everyday Life, by Susan Richards (Penguin, 1991).
First Russia, Then Tibet, by Robert Byron (Penguin, first published 1933).
The Food and Cooking of Russia, by Lesley Chamberlain (Penguin, 1982).
Imperial Splendour, by George Galitzine (Viking, l991).
Journey into Russia, by Laurens van der Post (Penguin, first published 1964).
The Natural History of the USSR, by Algirdas Kynstautas (Century Hutchinson, 1987).
The Nature of the Russia, by John Massey Stewart (Boxtree, 1992).
The New Russians, by Hedrick Smith (Vintage, l990).
Portrait of the Soviet Union, by Fitzroy Maclean (Weidenfeld and Nicolson, 1988).
Russia (Bracken Books, 1989).
Russia, with Tehran, Port Arthur and Peking, by Karl Baedeker (l914).
Salling to Leningrad, by Roger Foxall (Grafton, 1990).
The Taming of the Eagles: Exploring the New Russia, by Imogen Edwards-Jones. Photographs by Joth Shakerley (Weidenfeld & Nicolson, 1993).
The Trans–Siberian Rail Guide, by Robert Strauss (Compass, 1993).
Ustinov in Russia, by Peter Ustinov. (Michael O Mara Books, 1987).

Other Insight Guides

Among the 190-title Insight Guide series are two companion volumes to the present book. **Insight Gulde:**

Moscow and **Insight Guide: St Petersburg** cover Russia's two major cities with insightful text and great photography.
In addition, two other Insight series have books on Russia:

Insight Pocket Guides

Insight Pocket Guides to **Moscow** and **St Petersburg** are designed for visitors keen to make the most of a short stay. In each case, a local "host" provides carefully timed itineraries and recommends places to see and things to do. Each book comes with a full-size fold-out map.

Insight Compact Guides

Insight Compact Guides to **Moscow** and **St Petersburg** are the perfect on-the-spot reference guides. This low-price series packs an astonishing amount of information into a portable format, with text, photographs and maps all carefully cross-referenced.

ART & PHOTO CREDITS

Picture Spreads

INSIGHT GUIDE
RUSSIA

Cartographic Editor **Zoë Goodwin**
Production **Stuart A. Everitt**
Design Consultants
Carlotta Junger, Graham Mitchener
Picture Research **Hilary Genin**

Index

Note: page numbers in italics refer to illustrations

Orlov, Grigory 43
Ostankino 117
  miniature theatre 117
Ostrovsky, Nikolai 252
overseas missions 340
Ovstug 227

P

palaces
  Bakhchysaray Tatar Palace
    (Ukraine) 324, 326
  Batashev (Moscow) 154
  Beloselskikh-Belozerskikh
    (St Petersburg) 201
  Bolshoi Kremlyovsky (Great
    Kremlin Palace, Moscow)
    145
  Bolshoi Yekaterinsky
    (Catherine Palace)
    (Pushkin) 203
  Dom Pashkov (Moscow)
    158-9
  Ekaterina Romanovna
    Vorontsova (Moscow) 161
  Emir of Bukhara's palace
    (Zheleznovodsk) 254
  Gatchino 204
  Granovitaya Palata (Palace of
    the Facets, Moscow)
    144-5
  Iosifa Zolotovo (Joseph the
    Golden, Vologda) 213
  Kikiny (St Petersburg) 202
  Letny (Summer Palace,
    St Petersburg) 192
  Livadyysky (Palace of Livadia,
    Yalta, Ukraine) 324
  Mariinsky (Kiev) 315
  Mariinsky (St Petersburg) 196
  Menshikov (Moscow) 161
  Menshikovsky (St Petersburg)
    197
  Mramorny (Marble Palace,
    St Petersburg) 194
  Oranienbaum 203
  Orlov (Moscow) 161
  Pavlovsk 204
  Petrodvorets 202, 202-3
  Sheremetyevykh
    (St Petersburg) 201
  Tavrichesky (St Petersburg)
    202
  Teremnoy Dvorets (Terem or
    Belvedere, Moscow) 145
  Yushkov (Moscow) 155
  Yusupovsky (St Petersburg)
    196
parks and gardens

Alexandrovsky Gardens
  (Moscow) 146
Botanical Garden (Tomsk) 264
Drendariy Park botanical
  garden (Sochi) 251
Gorky Park (Moscow) 158, 163
Letny Sad (Summer Garden,
  St Petersburg) 192
Mikhailo Kotsiubinsky park
  (Chernihiv, Ukraine) 317
Neskuchny Garden (Moscow)
  163
Nikitsky Botanical Gardens
  (Yalta, Ukraine) 327
Riviera Park (Sochi) 251
Pashkov, Peter 159
Pasternak, Boris 111, 112
Pavlovsk Palace 204
Pechory 222
  Pskovo-Pcherskaya Lavra
    (Monastery of the Caves)
    222
  Uspensky Sobor (Cathedral of
    the Assumption) 222
people 65-72, 75-7, 249, 286
  Buryat culture 269
  Magyars 29
  "New Russians" 72
  Slavs 27-9, 283, 297
  Tatars 33-5, 326
  Varangians 27, 283
  women of Russia 75-7
perestroika 57-8, 77, 93, 10-4
Pereyaslavl-Zalessky 175
  Goritsky Monastyr (Monastery)
    and museum 175
  Kremlin 175
  Muzei Botika ("Little Boat"
    Museum) 175
  Spasopreobrazhensky Sobor
    (Cathedral of the
    Transfiguration of the
    Saviour) 175
  Tserkov Petra Mitropolita
    (Church of Peter the
    Metropolitan) 175
Perm 245
  Etnografichsky Muzei
    (Ethnographic Architecture
    Museum) 245
  Gosudarstvennaya Kartinnaya
    Galereya (State Picture
    Gallery) 245
Perov, Vasily 100
Peter the Great 39, 41-3, 99,
  116, 185
  burial place 190
  Wooden Cabin Museum
    (St Petersburg) 191-2

Petrodvorets Palace 202, 202-3
Petrokrepost 219
  krepost (fortress) 219
Petrov 112
  Twelve Chairs 112
Petrov-Vodkin, Kuzma 103
  The Bathing of the Red Horse
    103
Petrozavodsk 217
  accommodation 349
  Geological Research Institute
    and Karelian Science
    Centre 217
  Kruglaya Ploshchad (Round
    Square) 217
photography 360
Polatsk (Belarus) 305
  Muzey Belkarushka
    Knihadrukavanni (Museum
    of Historical Books and
    Printing) 305
  Saphiyskyy Sabor (Cathedral
    of St Sophia) 305
politics 53-8, 291-3
  Bolsheviks 53, 185, 202,
    302, 311
  Communism 65, 185
  Communist Party 68
  corruption in government 69,
    78
  The Duma (Russian
    parliament) 68
  Muzei Molodyozhi museum of
    Soviet history
    (Yekaterinburg) 242
pollution 18, 20, 240, 244,
  245, 269
  acid rain 18
  atomic bomb testing
    (Orenburg) 245
  Chernobyl disaster 18, 287,
    294
  nuclear accidents 245, 287
  radiation poisoning 18, 245,
    287, 304
  in Siberia 261
  toxic waste 18, 20
Polzunov, Ivan 266
Port Baikal 267
postal services 338-9
Potanin, Vladimir 73
Potemkin, Grigory 43, 202
Povolzhye 229-35
Powers, Gary 240
  U2 spy plane incident 240
Prigozhin, Lucian 122
Prokofiev, Sergei 119, 121
Pskov 222
  accommodation 349

The Insight Approach

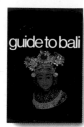

The book you are holding is part of the world's largest range of guidebooks. Its purpose is to help you have the most valuable travel experience possible, and we try to achieve this by providing not only information about countries, regions and cities but also genuine insight into their history, culture, institutions and people.

Since the first Insight Guide – to Bali – was published in 1970, the series has been dedicated to the proposition that, with insight into a country's people and culture, visitors can both enhance their own experience and be accepted more easily by their hosts. Now, in a world where ethnic hostilities and nationalist conflicts are all too common, such attempts to increase understanding between peoples are more important than ever.

Insight Guides:
Essentials for understanding

Because a nation's past holds the key to its present, each Insight Guide kicks off with lively history chapters. These are followed by magazine-style essays on culture and daily life. This essential background information gives readers the necessary context for using the main Places section, with its comprehensive run-down on things worth seeing and doing.

Finally, a listings section contains all the information you'll need on travel, hotels, restaurants and opening times.

As far as possible, we rely on local writers and specialists to ensure that information is authoritative. The pictures, for which Insight Guides have become so celebrated, are just as important. Our photojournalistic approach aims not only to illustrate a destination but also to communicate visually and directly to readers life as it is lived by the locals. The series has grown to almost 200 titles.

Compact Guides:
The "great little guides"

As invaluable as such background information is, it isn't always fun to carry an Insight Guide through a crowded souk or up a church tower. Could we, readers asked, distil the key reference material into a slim volume for on-the-spot use?

Our response was to design Compact Guides as an entirely new series, with original text carefully cross-referenced to detailed maps and more than 200 photographs. In essence, they're miniature encyclopedias, concise and comprehensive, displaying reliable and up-to-date information in an accessible way. There are almost 100 titles.

Pocket Guides:
A local host in book form

However wide-ranging the information in a book, human beings still value the personal touch. Our editors are often asked the same questions. Where do *you* go to eat? What do *you* think is the best beach? What would *you* recommend if I have only three days? We invited our local correspondents to act as "substitute hosts" by revealing their preferred walks and trips, listing the restaurants they go to and structuring a visit into a series of timed itineraries.

The result: our Pocket Guides, complete with full-size fold-out maps. These 100-plus titles help readers plan a trip precisely, particularly if their time is short.

Exploring with Insight:
A valuable travel experience

In conjunction with co-publishers all over the world, we print in up to 10 languages, from German to Chinese, from Danish to Russian. But our aim remains simple: to enhance your travel experience by combining our expertise in guidebook publishing with the on-the-spot knowledge of our correspondents.

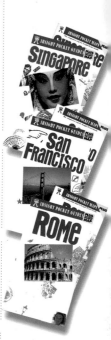